James Barr

CW00473482

THE SEMANTIC_ ᴕᵢ
BIBLICAL LANGUAGE

XPRESS REPRINTS

1 85931 052 4

First published 1961
by Oxford University Press
Reprinted six times

Reissued 1983 by SCM Press Ltd
by arrangement with Oxford University Press
Reprinted twice

Reissued 1996 by
XPRESS REPRINTS
SCM Press Ltd
9–17 St Albans Place, London N1 0NX

Printed in Great Britain by
Optichrome Ltd
Woking, Surrey

Preface

ONLY a little need be said about the occasion and purpose of this book. It is a main concern of both scholarship and theology that the Bible should be soundly and adequately interpreted. In recent years I have come to believe that one of the greatest dangers to such sound and adequate interpretation comes from the prevailing use of procedures which, while claiming to rest upon a knowledge of the Israelite and the Greek ways of thinking, constantly mishandle and distort the linguistic evidence of the Hebrew and Greek languages as they are used in the Bible. The increasing sense of dependence upon the Bible in the modern Church only makes this danger more serious. The fact that these procedures have never to my knowledge been collected, analysed and criticized in detail was the chief stimulus to my undertaking of this task myself.

The book is written mainly with the instructed theological public in view. Some small knowledge of Hebrew grammar and vocabulary is presupposed. Hebrew words are transliterated on a simple system, in which for example certain differences between vowels are not marked; Hebrew script is used only where special reasons require it. With Greek the opposite is done, and words are transliterated only in special circumstances. The few words of modern Hebrew which occur are transliterated by a system different from that used for the biblical language, as any speaker of the modern tongue must surely find most natural. I apologize to readers who may feel that I have used technical linguistic terms excessively or injudiciously. If I had used them less, the argument would have needed many tiresome circumlocutions. If I had used them more I might have made the argument more precise and satisfying at certain points; but I should have required a lengthy outline of linguistic method in order to define and locate my terms before approaching my special subject at all.

It remains to record my thanks to those who have helped me.

On the theological and philosophic side I have been greatly assisted by discussion with my colleague Rev. John McIntyre, Professor of Divinity in this university, and with Rev. Donald D. Evans, Assistant Professor of Philosophy of Religion in McGill University, Montreal. In linguistic questions the criticism and advice of Mr Trevor Hill of the Linguistic Survey of Scotland has been of the greatest value. My former colleague Rev. Arnold A. Anderson, now of the University of Manchester, has helped me especially from his thorough knowledge of the Qumran documents. Though all of these have read and discussed with me parts of the book in various draft states, none of them has seen the whole of it in its final form, and of course my opinions are not necessarily theirs. The greatest faults of my book are probably where I failed to take their advice.

The writing of the book has depended on the resources of the libraries where I have worked; and I am glad to acknowledge my debt to the Librarians and staff of Edinburgh University Library, of the National Library of Scotland, and of New College Library.

Finally I must express my gratitude to the Delegates of the Oxford University Press for accepting the book for publication, and to their officers and staff for their help.

J.B.

THE UNIVERSITY
EDINBURGH

Contents

1. THE IMPORTANCE OF THE PROBLEM   1

2. THE CURRENT CONTRAST OF GREEK AND HEBREW
    THOUGHT   8

3. PROBLEMS OF METHOD   21

4. VERBS, ACTION AND TIME
    (*a*) General   46
    (*b*) Verbs and the Dynamic   50
    (*c*) Stative Verbs in Particular   54
    (*d*) The Verb 'To Be'   58
    (*e*) Verbs and Time   72
    (*f*) Detached Note on Earlier Studies connecting
    Verbs with Action and Dynamism   85

5. OTHER ARGUMENTS FROM MORPHOLOGICAL AND
    SYNTACTIC PHENOMENA
    (*a*) The Construct State   89
    (*b*) The Numerals   96
    (*c*) Roots and Ideas   100

6. ETYMOLOGIES AND RELATED ARGUMENTS
    (*a*) Introductory   107
    (*b*) An English Example — 'Holy'   111
    (*c*) Some Typical General Statements   114
    (*d*) *Qahal* — ἐκκλησία   119
    (*e*) *Dabar* 'word, matter'   129
    (*f*) The Word 'Baptism'   140
    (*g*) 'Man' — the Adding of Significances   144
    (*h*) Some other examples   147
    (*j*) Concluding Remarks about Etymologies   158

7. 'Faith' and 'Truth' — An Examination of some
   Linguistic Arguments

   (a) The Argument for 'Faithfulness'   161
   (b) The Hebrew verb 'believe' — Grammar and
       Sense   176
   (c) Faith, Righteousness and Truth   187

8. Some Principles of Kittel's Theological
   Dictionary

   (a) General   206
   (b) Particular Examples   219
   (c) The lexicographical Tradition behind *TWNT*   238
   (d) Christianity and Language   246
   (e) Conclusion   257

9. Language and the Idea of 'Biblical Theology'   263
   Detached Note on the non-use of certain words in
   the Greek Bible   282

10. Languages and the Study of Theology   288

   Abbreviations   297

   Bibliography   299

   Index of Hebrew Words   304

   Index of Greek Words   305

   Index of Persons and Subjects   307

Chapter One

The Importance of the Problem

By 'semantics' I understand the study of signification in language. A distinction may be made between semantics as a branch of logic and semantics as a branch of linguistics.[1] The present study belongs to the latter. The field of study is the survey of the way in which the meaning of biblical language is understood, and for the present more particularly the criticism of certain methods, which I hold to be erroneous, of using linguistic evidence from the Bible.

Such matters as modern symbolic logic are therefore beyond the horizon of this book, and I am not competent to handle them. Moreover, this study takes a somewhat different field from the general problem of 'religious language'.[2] The problem here is not the relation of religious thought generally to religious language, but the question whether there is a relation between the religious structures found to exist within one particular linguistic group and the linguistic structure of the language of that group; and further, the question of whether and how the transference of religious structures and thoughts to another linguistic group is affected by the change of linguistic structure involved in the use of a new language. The material of the study is entirely historical; it does not enter into questions of possible or hypothetical ways of expressing religious thought, but confines itself to the problem of the accurate evaluation of the meaning of expressions which have actually been used. Nevertheless I am aware that important questions of logic and of general philosophy are involved in discussing

[1] See S. Ullmann, *The Principles of Semantics*, pp. 7–42, for a survey of the problems involved.

[2] As discussed for example by I. T. Ramsey, *Religious Language* (London, 1957).

the matter at all. But though at certain points I shall suggest that traditional philosophical (and of course theological) beliefs have been an obstacle to the accurate evaluation of linguistic phenomena, I shall make no attempt to suggest a better philosophy of language. I do not suppose that one can make linguistics a substitute for a philosophy of language, but I assume that by studying language linguistically one is making a genuine and valid contribution to the understanding of it, however much more remains to be done beyond linguistics in the area of philosophy.[1]

Another clarification is necessary in respect of the term 'biblical language' which appears in the title. This term does not coincide with 'religious language', which is larger since it must include extra-biblical religious terminology and smaller since it will presumably exclude a good deal of terminology which occurs in the Bible but which most people would not regard as specifically religious. In principle I include in the field of my subject all the linguistic usage of the Bible, because much that is *prima facie* sociological or anthropological is in fact of great importance in the cultural and therefore the mental shape of Israel and of the Church. In other words, the sacred tradition of the apostolic Church is never purely 'religious language', and still less so is the Old Testament as the sacred tradition of Israel. But the non-religious language of the Bible is of theological importance just as the religious language is.

There is no intention here to separate the biblical language from other language as belonging to a different kind — quite the reverse. I do however wish to concentrate on the Bible because the semantic problems connected with the transfer of a religious tradition from one linguistic environment to another can be studied very clearly in the Bible, where the phenomena are very noticeable. The examples occasionally given from later theological language or from modern popular usage are therefore primarily illustrative.

---

[1] Even the word 'linguistic' is perhaps not too clear, since it is used very much for certain procedures distinctively philosophical. In this book 'linguistic' always refers to the science of linguistics and the material it handles: the phonology, grammar and lexicography of various languages and the semantic value of the various forms observed and classified in these processes.

It would seem that, within the general field of linguistic sem-antics, the semantics of a theologically acknowledged tradition such as the Bible will take a special place for the following reasons:

(a) One would naturally expect the language of a religious tradition to have certain special semantic developments and problems over and above those which occur in every-day speech. This is true also of other specialized language-circles, such as that of philosophy or of law. It is worth while however to notice that the conscious definition of terms as an attempt to mark the semantic value of words is common in philosophy and fairly common in law but is quite uncommon in biblical language, although it reappears in some, if not all, kinds of later theology. In all these specialized language-circles an understanding of the general structure of that circle, its philosophical thought or its legal system or whatever it may be, is a necessity for the accurate discussion of the semantics of the words used, beyond the need to know the general cultural environment which is a necessity for any linguistic interpretation at all. We cannot assume in general, however, that biblical language is in itself 'specialized' to any great extent in its original setting. In Israel at any rate much of the biblical language is unspecialized, for the religious structure is roughly coincident with the linguistic group and the nation as a whole. With the translation of the Old Testament into Greek we have a considerable specialization, for this translation was something used in the synagogue of Egyptian Judaism and did not represent the way in which the Egyptian Jews spoke in their daily life, though of course their daily speech has left its marks upon it. In the New Testament certain kinds of specialization may be discernible, although the problem of defining their nature and extent is a difficult one. We merely note here that social groups in which specialized semantic developments occur may exist, and that varying degrees of such specialization may reasonably be expected to appear within the biblical literature.

(b) Compared with the semantics of everyday life, the semantics of a theological tradition have a much greater reference to a datum in the past: in the case of modern theology, to the Old and New Testaments; and of the New Testament itself, to the Old. And this interest in a past datum is not an interest for the theological scholar only, but for all members of the Christian community. The scholar, when he speaks about the 'atom', may have some thought in his mind of the usage of the word in Democritus or Lucretius, but the ordinary speaker has not. But in the theological realm, it makes a very considerable difference not only to the theologian but also to the simplest reader of the Bible that his use of the words 'God' or 'sin' or 'love' should have some recognizable relation to the usage of corresponding words in Greek or Hebrew by writers and speakers of two thousand years ago or more.

This datum in the past is also, and has been since large numbers of Jews first began to speak habitually in languages other than Hebrew, a datum in a foreign language and a different culture. Between us today and the men of the Bible, and between the men of the New Testament and those of the Old, there was a problem therefore not only of translation but of transculturation. We have to consider therefore a linguistic gap between a Semitic language, an Indo-European (Greek), and our own modern language (which might be Chinese or a Bantu language); and the corresponding cultural gaps between the Ancient Near East, the Roman Empire and the modern world. It is doubtful whether any other sphere of life than the theological has common people without special training so continually attempting a semantic transference across such gaps.[1]

The wide and complicated series of questions about how far and how accurately the theological thought of the Bible can be transmitted through different languages, cultures and periods is much more than can be attempted in this book. What I propose to do, rather, is to survey and to criticize certain lines on which modern theological thinking has been assessing and using the linguistic material of the Bible; I hope that such a survey and criticism may help to clear the way for a re-assessment of biblical language, of the use that may be made of it in theology, and of the possibility of understanding the language of the Bible to-day. The lines of modern theological thought that I intend to examine are those very

[1] The excellent value of the translations of the Bible for the observation of a certain kind of semantic change (significance-loan words, *Bedeutungslehnwörter*) is mentioned by H. Kronasser, *Handbuch der Semasiologie*, p. 140 f.

roughly associated with the movement for so-called 'biblical theology'. More will be said later about the idea of 'biblical theology'. At present we may note two points in particular. Firstly, the movement connected with biblical theology is very strongly conscious of the contrast between the Israelite mind and the Greek mind. It is not too much to say that for it the full appreciation of the Israelite mind is the essential key to the understanding of the New Testament. Since the latter is written in Greek, however, questions of linguistic contrast between Hebrew and Greek are very naturally raised. Secondly, the same movement is very much concerned to understand the Bible 'as a unity'. This does not mean the denying of modern insights into the variety of authorship and circumstance in the Bible. It does mean the belief that there is some general underlying point of view which informs the whole in its variety, and which is usually connected with the given and essential Hebraic background. The expression of this 'unity' is commonly seen in the existence of a number of terms of rich theological content which are well rooted in the Hebraic soil and which form a kind of framework for the theological structures of the New Testament. These terms are Greek words, however, and thus linguistic questions are raised once more. The assembly of these basic terms by an appropriate lexical procedure which will bring out their coherence with Hebraic thought is thought to be an important step in the advance of biblical theology. The following quotation expresses well the ethos of the movement:

'New Testament studies are passing from the stage of "divide and rule" into a stage of more positive theological exegesis. In the stage of "divide and rule" we subjected the Scriptural teaching to *our* analysis. This involved *our* control, for, so long as we employed merely critical methods, the element of individual judgement entered disproportionately into the reckoning, and it was only too easy for us to allow our own preconceived ideas to dictate what we got out of the Scriptures. In the stage of more positive theological exegesis we let the Scriptures speak to us in terms of themselves, and allow a synthetic approach to gather up the results of analysis. The resulting solidity and unity of the biblical teaching withdraws it from our control. In this situation the Word of God *controls us*, and presses upon us a deeper theological understanding of the Scriptures.

An outstanding characteristic of this advance in biblical studies is that we are gaining a fresh understanding of the unity of the Bible, particularly of the unity in grace of the Old Testament and the New Testament. This means that a reinterpretation of the New Testament in terms of its setting in the Hebraic mind, rather than in terms of its Hellenic affinities, becomes essential.'[1]

The purpose of this book is not to criticize biblical theology or any other kind of theology as such, but to criticize certain methods in the handling of linguistic evidence in theological discussion. The popularity of these methods is however particularly great in the biblical theology movement.

Two things may be added. Firstly, where linguistic evidence has been used in aid of a theological argument, and where I believe that evidence to have been misused, I do not necessarily believe the conclusion of the theological argument to be itself wrong in particular. Quite often I think that theological arguments which I have examined would have been better and more convincing without the linguistic evidence which has been used in their support. But while in some such cases I do not hold the particular point argued to have been disproved because of bad use of evidence, I commonly do think that such misuse of evidence argues a wrong understanding of biblical interpretation in general, and almost certainly implies a seriously faulty theological method.

Secondly, I regret to have to spend much space in pointing out what seem to me to be mistakes in the interpretation of language. I do this not for the sake of pointing out mistakes but because these mistakes in my opinion follow from, and illustrate the weaknesses of, certain fundamental procedures of interpretation. A case pointed out here and there may easily be shrugged off as a passing oversight; in such cases the pointing out of one mistake will not prevent another of the same kind. Also I feel it necessary to discuss

[1] Church of Scotland, Special Commission on Baptism, *Interim Report* (Edinburgh, 1955), p. 3. For a useful statement of the history of the term 'biblical theology' and the problems connected with it at present, see G. Ebeling, 'The Meaning of "Biblical Theology" ', *JTS NS* vi (1955) 210–25.

some of these cases in order to stimulate and guide the critical faculties of students and others, who may often feel certain interpretations of language to be repugnant to common sense, but find that common sense in itself is not a sufficient guide to correct method in, let us say, the understanding of some linguistic phenomenon in Hebrew. It is part of the thesis of this book that certain interpretative procedures now in use will almost certainly lead to the distortion and wrong assessment of linguistic evidence. Only by keeping this general thesis in mind can my purpose in criticizing so many mistakes in detail be understood rightly.

Chapter Two

The Current Contrast of Greek and Hebrew Thought

The habit of contrasting Greek and Hebrew modes of thought has become extremely commonplace in modern theology and has had very great influence upon it. A brief and quite unoriginal sketch of the way this contrast is generally made may be given here. We may begin by remarking that the interest in the contrast has been found not only among theologians. Professor John Macmurray, for example, lays great emphasis upon it in his book *The Clue to History*. For him as for much of the modern theological movement it can be laid down that 'Christianity is essentially Jewish'. The contrast of the Jewish and the Greek needs to be drawn out so that we may truly identify the Hebraic elements in our heritage of culture or religion. There is a danger otherwise that these elements may be obscured, whether because the European mind has an emotional barrier against Jewish culture, as Macmurray holds, or because we naturally tend to think in the Greek manner and tradition, and thus interpret away the Jewish element, as some of the theologians put it.

In the tendency to emphasize this contrast, different interests may be seen at work. With Macmurray it is a desire to delineate Jewish culture as the one truly religious culture, and to see in the reaction to its contribution the clue to cultural history. From the theological side, however, other interests may appear. In one way it is a means of asserting the uniqueness of Christianity. Christianity, as long as it is properly understood (and this means, to a large extent, adequately demarcated against the Greek-dominated European culture), belongs with Jewish thought as a roughly homogeneous entity clearly set apart from the other currents of European thought. In another respect the contrast of Greek and Hebrew thought, and the alignment of Christianity with the latter, go to emphasize what is now called 'the unity of the Bible'. This unity is said to lie not only in the rather formal old-fashioned way of prediction of the New Testament events in the Old, or in the foreshadowing of the New by certain patterns of life and worship in the Old, or in the discernment of a historical continuum through the Old Testament history and down into the New, but in a common way of thinking, a common cast of mind and mould of expression, which operates throughout the Bible and which is more noticeable and influential than the variations which it of course undergoes in the minds of individual authors and traditions.

Two particular circumstances have led to the emphasis on this in the present mid-century theological situation. The first is the reaction against the predominantly analytic and divisive techniques of literary criticism which were so dominant early in the century in biblical study. Against the tendency to fragmentation of the biblical traditions in literary criticism it could now be argued that even where sources were of different origin and interest something of the common biblical mind could be discerned among their variations. Indeed it could be argued that neglect to perceive this common mind and its characteristics was a methodological fault in much literary criticism, and that the divisiveness of these techniques was in part a symptom of the critics' own failure to escape from modern European categories and to perceive the unitary though paradoxical Hebraic mind.

The second circumstance is the reaction specifically in the New Testament sphere against the 'Hellenistic' interpretation of large parts of the New Testament, with its emphasis on the Greek environment, on the normal *koine* character of NT language, and on the influence on the Gentile church of mystery religions, of Hellenic philosophy, and of the more emphatically Hellenized forms of Judaism. This reaction tried to show that the NT did not necessarily share the typical forms of Greek thought just because it was written in Greek, and that a better and more natural sense could be made of its words by relating them to the heritage of Hebraic thought.[1]

Another important event is the rise after the first World War to leadership in Protestant theology of theological viewpoints which were willing to borrow very little from 'natural theology' or philosophy and which rejected more or less abruptly the idea that a philosophy not founded on the special 'revelation' of God and correspondingly unrelated to the Bible and its Hebraic thought might serve as part of the substructure of Christian theology. To those influenced by this point of view it became natural to think of the 'philosophy' or 'natural theology' which was rejected from the theological structure as something akin to the 'Greek outlook' which was so sharply contrasted with the Hebraic heritage; and conversely that the Hebrew way of thinking, so sharply identified and isolated by the contrast with the Greek, occupied a position of independence analogous to that of a theology conscious of its unwillingness to lean on the Western philosophic tradition. It should however be added that this correspondence is by no means a universal one, and that some of those who are most anxious to assert the independence and unity of the Hebrew mind and its contrast with the Greek belong to theological traditions much more sympathetic to a philosophic sub-structure independent of the Bible.

The main contrasts drawn between Greek and Hebrew thought are usually the following:[2]

1. The contrast between static and dynamic. The Greeks were ultimately interested in contemplation, the Hebrews in action. Movement could not be ultimate reality for the Greeks, to whom

[1] It should perhaps be added that these problems extended beyond the exegesis of the New Testament into the post-apostolic development of Christian thought. Here too there was, and still is, discussion about how far Hebraic thinking maintained a hold in the Greek-speaking Church and how far the great theological developments of the first four centuries are to be reckoned as a triumph for the Hellenic spirit within Christianity. For a very strong statement of the point of view that the Hellenic mind came to dominate the Biblical-Hebraic in this period, see G. A. F. Knight, *A Biblical Approach to the Doctrine of the Trinity*, pp. 1–10 and *passim*.

[2] For a recent brief statement, see G. Friedrich, 'Die Problematik eines theologischen Wörterbuchs zum neuen Testament', *Studia Evangelica* (ed. Aland, Berlin, 1959), p. 483 f.

being must be distinguished from becoming, and the ultimate must be changeless. For the Israelites the true reality was action and movement, and the inactive and motionless was no reality at all.

With this may be associated the Greek contrast of appearance and reality. The world was full of changing phenomena, but since reality must be static the change was unreal appearance. To the Israelites however the appearance of a thing was the manifestation of its being or reality, and a valid and adequate manifestation at that. What did not appear in action and movement would not be real, and what did appear was not a pale or secondary shadow of the reality but the reality itself. There is therefore no contrast of appearance and reality.

The dynamic approach of the Hebrews to reality is expressed in their interest in history. Their God is characteristically one who acts in history, and these actions in history are the core of the religious tradition of Israel. The interest in history corresponds to and presupposes a realistic view of time. Time is not an empty vanity but a scene of meaningful action. There is no distinction between time and eternity, not at any rate in any sense in which eternity would mean timelessness and be considered a higher reality than time. The Hebrew words sometimes translated as 'eternity' really mean a remote point in time. The fact that the Greeks also wrote history is not felt to be an obstacle to describing history as a distinctive interest of Hebrew thought. The highest philosophical developments of the Greeks were interested in an unchanging reality and paid no attention to action in history. Greek history was akin to anecdote or to tragedy; it did not see in historical process a higher power than fate or necessity. For ultimate reality the Greeks turned away from history into the unchanging. Typically, therefore, it is held, their view of time became cyclic in the philosophical refinements of thought.

2. The contrast between abstract and concrete. It is a characteristic procedure of Greek thought to work with abstractions. It is not good enough to know what is a good horse or a good table, you must find out what is 'the Good'. Abstract terms of the kind we call qualities and properties are central in discussion. This procedure can be connected with the static nature of Greek thought

mentioned above; to get at the reality you abstract the problem from the particular time and place, and the abstraction is a static term. Hebrew thought on the other hand does not work with abstractions; its terms are always related to the actual object or situation and not to an abstraction from it. Similarly the Israelite argues not by making one premise and then showing what must follow from it but by presenting a series of related situation-images. The greater use of abstraction by the Greeks can also be called an intellectualization of thought compared with the Hebrews.

It is rather vaguely felt that the distinction between abstract and concrete, and the supposed absence of such a distinction, are somehow related to different psychological modes of perception, to different kinds of aesthetics in general; but attempts to advance along this line have been very uncertain and are hardly common-places of modern theology in the way that the rest of the Greek-Hebrew contrast is.

The distinction of subject and object is felt to be a product of the static and abstract tendencies of Greek thought. It arises from the abstraction from action and movement in order to think. The contemplative approach means the dissociation of the mind from involvement in action. In Hebrew thought the thinking subject is the acting person, and there is no expression of a relationship between subject and object in thought which is other than that between subject and object in action.

3. The contrast in the conception of man. The Pythagorean-Platonic tradition is usually taken as the typically Greek tradition for this purpose. In Greek thought man is seen as a duality, with an immortal soul imprisoned or confined in a mortal body; the two are only temporarily or accidentally related. In Hebrew thought the 'soul' is the living person in his flesh; 'soul' and 'flesh' are not separable but one is the outward and visible manifestation of the other. There is no thought of the soul living apart from the body. In contrast with Hebrew thought, Greek thought at once makes man too near to the superhuman and divine in the idea of the soul and over-materializes and depersonalizes him through treating the body as matter. The importance of this particular difference for Christian theologians has been of course its connec-

tion with the different conceptions of the immortality of the soul and the resurrection of the body.

It is similarly felt however that Hebrew thought saw man as a person within a totality, while Greek thought tended to see him as an individual, i.e. in essence as one separated from others, and then to form collectivities by grouping individuals together. The conflict of individual and collectivity thus arises from the Greek tradition. But Hebrew life was lived in a social totality of religion and justice.

Finally, and to sum up, the contrast may be expressed as the contrast between the divisive, distinction-forming, analytic type of Greek thought and the totality type of Hebrew thought. Hence, and several examples have been given already, Greek thought is supposed to have been productive of splits and distinctions unknown to the Hebrews — being and becoming, reality and appearance, time and eternity, body and soul, spirit and matter, group and individual. The use of these distinctions is supposed to have remained common in European culture, and some at least of them have worked their way into Christian theology, where they have created problems which would never have arisen if the Jewish basis of Christian thinking had been kept in mind.

One can hardly say whether those theological circles who hold these views most strongly are convinced that the Hebraic way of thinking is a live option for the present day, a mental habit which Christians or others might be practicably urged to adopt, or whether they feel that the recognition of the essential contrast can be merely historically used so as to avoid misinterpreting the Christian faith and its historical documents (principally the Bible); so that we could use non-Hebraic terms if necessary in modern life, provided we recognized that the Hebraic terms were essential for the understanding of the biblical documents themselves. It would in any case, I think, be normally recognized that a great deal of modern culture and science could not exist or progress on the basis of the classical Hebraic mode of thought alone.

It is no part of the purpose of this study to criticize the current contrast of Hebrew and Greek thought, as it has been summarized above. One may perhaps remark in passing that in a contrast like this which is becoming increasingly popular property it is unwise to over-dramatize it, for example by quoting only one of several Greek traditions (usually the Pythagorean-Platonic) for the idea of the soul, or by comparing Hebrew historians not with Greek historians but with the more mythological parts of the Greek philosophers.

Our interest here however is in the connections made between the contrast outlined above, which was a contrast of ways of thinking, and the differences between the Greek and Hebrew languages. The validity of the thought contrast is no part of our subject; our subject is (a) the way in which the thought contrast has affected the examination of linguistic evidence, and (b) the way in which linguistic evidence has been used to support or illustrate the thought contrast.

Here it becomes more difficult to point to any agreed opinion, and for this there are several reasons. Firstly, it is quite possible to outline and accept the contrast of ways of thought without any reference at all to the differences of the Greek and Hebrew languages as such. Professor Macmurray, for example, seems to make none in his *The Clue to History*.[1] Secondly, it is just at this point that the theological approach begins to become quite un-systematic and haphazard, and what is noticed by one scholar may be neglected by another. Thirdly, statements which are originally probably meant to refer to the thought contrast may be taken by others to be applicable in realms of grammar or lexicology.

An example of this third case may be given. It is often said[2] that the characteristic expression of Hebrew thinking is the verb, while that of Greek thinking is the noun. At first sight this would appear to be connecting or correlating the dynamic-static contrast in thought with the verb-noun difference in grammar.[3] But it is

---

[1] Cf. also J. Hessen, *Platonismus und Prophetismus* (Munich, 1939).

[2] These ideas may be traced with some certainty to Herder; see below, p. 85. For a discussion of some of Herder's ideas about language, see E. Sapir in *Modern Philology* v (1907–8) 109–42. Sapir was presumably writing mainly for linguists and might, I think, have been more severe towards Herder's ideas if he had thought of the effect of their survival in fragmentary form in popular ideas about language among those who were not as Sapir was in the forefront of modern linguistics.

[3] Herder himself meant something like this; see below, p. 85.

possible that the statement does not always intend as much as this. It may possibly be taken to mean that the typical vehicle of Hebrew thinking is the historical narrative or the future prediction, both forms of literature in which the verb is likely to be of great significance; and that the typical vehicle of Greek thinking is the philosophical discussion in which nouns (or adjectives) are more prominent and in which verbs may be less important. Even the casual reader of the Old Testament is impressed with the frequency of certain verb phrases such as 'and it came to pass' or 'I will bring evil'. But, taken at this level, the statement is still not a statement about the structure of the grammar of either language; it is a statement about a favoured literary type, the frequency of which produces a frequency of verb forms or noun forms respectively, which frequency may lead one to regard the verb or noun forms as characteristic of the literature of this nation as a whole.

But the same statement, about the characteristic expression of Hebrew thinking being the verb, can be used in other ways than this. I recollect an occasion when I was explaining a Hebrew verb as denominative (it was in fact *kihen* 'act as priest') and a student declared himself quite surprised by this, because he had understood that 'Hebrew was founded on the verb'. I do not think there is much doubt that this impression had been created by the kind of statement about nouns and verbs which has been quoted above. But it brings the statement into the realm of strictly grammatical phenomena. There is now a correlation being contemplated between a characteristic of Hebrew thought, viz. its dynamic nature, and a grammatical phenomenon of verbal derivation. The dynamic nature of the thought can perhaps lead us to expect some priority of the verb in the grammatical system; conversely any such priority observed may be regarded as a support for our judgement about the essentially dynamic nature of the thinking. Further discussion of the problems involved here must wait till later. The essential point is to observe the attempt to establish a correlation between a dynamic way of thought and a grammatical phenomenon.

Some other examples may now be added. We have already seen the contrast of abstract and concrete in ways of thought. The same terms are however used in certain systems of grammar, for 'abstract' and 'concrete' nouns. Once again there is more than one way in which the correlation may be made. It may be said that the Greeks, because they used abstract methods of thought, therefore came to use very frequently the nouns of the 'abstract' type such as 'greenness', 'being', 'becoming'. To say this is really to make a statement about the frequency of this type of noun, and to connect this frequency with the type of thought. One may however go farther and assert that not only the frequency but the very existence of and facility in forming the 'abstract' type is to be correlated with the abstract thinking; and conversely that Hebrew, as the language of a people whose thought is not abstract, does not form 'abstract' nouns and that its words are characteristically 'concrete'. This latter statement goes beyond questions of style and frequency of usage and suggests a more fundamental correlation between the Hebrew thought and the basic grammatical structure and lexical stock. The following statement is characteristic: 'The Hebrew, almost invariably, thought in terms of the concrete. There are few abstract nouns in the Hebrew language. Even the adjective is at a rudimentary stage of development in classical Hebrew'.[1] The problems connected with the ideas of abstract and concrete here must be examined later.

Equally it seems natural, if we assert that the Hebrew mind holds a unitary or total picture of certain things which in Greek thinking are split in two by the familiar Greek distinctions, to quote examples of Hebrew words in support of this, for example that *nepeš* means the whole living being and not the 'soul' as separate and distinct from the body; or likewise to quote the absence of Hebrew words, for instance that the distinction of 'be' and 'become' could not be expressed in Hebrew since distinct terms do not exist. Similarly, one might cite the word *'adam* which is usually 'mankind' rather than 'individual man', or argue that there is no word in Hebrew for 'matter' or 'infinite', or no word for 'eternity' which is not 'remote time', no word therefore for 'timelessness'. There are in fact many ways in which linguistic facts might be and have been adduced along these lines in support

[1] Knight, op. cit., p. 8.

or illustration of the contrast in thought. In general they are observations of lexical overlap between one language and another, or of lexical oppositions existing in one language and not in another.

For the moment we shall not examine any of these methods of using linguistic evidence. We have simply illustrated the way in which it appears natural for the current contrast between Hebrew and Greek thinking to be supported by evidence from linguistic phenomena.

Meanwhile it is convenient to outline one or two problems about the use of the current contrast among theologians, which are connected with the correlation of the thought contrast with linguistic phenomena but which can be discussed before we enter into detailed linguistic problems.

The first of these is that we note some uncertainty whether one pole of the contrast is the thought (or language) of the Israelites in particular or of the Semitic peoples in general; and correspondingly whether the other pole is represented by the Greeks in particular or by the European peoples generally or at any rate those of Indo-European language. Many of those who make the contrasts do not seem to care whether Greek is contrasted with Hebrew or Semitic with Indo-European, whether in thought or in language. Dr Hebert,[1] in talking about 'faith', contrasts its meanings in Hebrew and Greek, but also in Hebrew and in 'all our European languages'. Taken literally, this would be going even farther than Indo-European to include Finno-Ugrian languages and others, but this is probably not meant. Boman[2] tells us that 'In particular, the thought of the other Semitic peoples is on the whole of the same formal structure as Israelite thought'.

This creates one or two problems. The characteristics of Greek thought as picked out in the thought contrast are by no means universally shared by the thought of other peoples using Indo-

---

[1] In *Theology* lviii (1955) 373–4. See below, p. 161 f.
[2] T. Boman, *Das hebräische Denken im Vergleich mit dem Griechischen* (2nd ed., Göttingen, 1954). English Translation, *Hebrew Thought compared with Greek* (London, 1960), with certain revisions by the author. Quotations by me are from the German edition, and translated by myself; but page references to the English edition are added. For the above, see p. 16; E.T., p. 25 f.

European languages. But those characteristics of the Greek language which are picked out as notably contrasting with Hebrew may in all probability be shared with other Indo-European languages. The ramifications of this problem are very considerable and cannot be dealt with here. Obviously the question can be put: is there an Indo-European cast of mind which somehow corresponds to the known common linguistic stock of Indo-European? Or: if the Greek language can be somehow correlated with certain abstract or static features of Greek thought, how is (say) the Albanian language, which is also Indo-European, related with these features? It would be possible of course to say that the extension from Greek to Indo-European as a whole applies only in so far as the language group as a whole has been affected by the cultural expansion of Greek influence. But to say this is to say that the Indo-European languages as such, apart from and before the Greek cultural influence, are not related to these features known in Greek thought, or that such relation as they potentially had was not in fact developed; and to say this is to invite questions about the location of the special characteristics found in Greek as distinct from Indo-European as a whole. But by now the main impression made is that argument of this kind is likely to be too general and hypothetical to be helpful. The uncertainty between Greek and Indo-European (or even 'all European languages') as the contrasting element to Hebrew indicates mainly the quite unsystematic and haphazard approach that has been used to linguistic realities.

Similar considerations apply on the other side, where it is likely that such characteristics as are absent from Greek but prominently present in Hebrew will be shared by the latter with the Semitic field as a whole. Perhaps it is true to say that more thought has been given by theologically-minded thinkers to this side of the contrast, and that many of them are willing to concede that the Hebrew linguistic pattern is not essentially different from the general Semitic.[1] But if it should be thought, as it certainly is

---

[1] Compare however such a rather different statement as this of D. N. Freedman, in *JBL* lxxviii (1959) 331: 'The thought-pattern of biblical religion was firmly fixed in the Hebrew language by long centuries of usage; and Aramaic, not less than Greek, is essentially a translation tongue for theological communica-

thought, that the uniqueness of New Testament thought and its distinctness from its Greek environment is emphasized by relating it to Hebrew thought and language, then the same argument damages the uniqueness of Old Testament thought and its distinctiveness from its Semitic environment. 'God chose Israel to be the vehicle of his Revelation. . . . Now, if God chose Israel, then he chose to use the Hebrew language'.[1] This argument may be theologically reasonable. But if it is to be extended to mean that God chose the Semitic languages, and the Semitic culture group, and that his chosen group was the Children of Shem as much as the Children of Israel, one wonders if theologians are really willing to go so far; and it is hardly to be reconciled with the constant and obvious struggle of the Israelite religion, which was not against Hellenism at all until the latest period, but against neighbouring religious forms expressed in closely allied Semitic language and culture.

This brings us to the second main point I have in mind. The contrast of Greek and Hebrew cultures and languages has its value because of the relation of the two in the New Testament; and also for its importance for us in disentangling the different threads in our culture since the beginning of the Christian era. But it is not really helpful for the study of the Old Testament, except perhaps in so far as the modern scholar has to learn to recognize in himself his own heritage of Greek thought before he can appreciate a tradition untouched by its influence. As for theological ideas of divine communication, the same arguments which emphasize the special place of the New Testament by pointing out its Hebraic heritage in language are in danger of obscuring any special place the Old Testament may have — unless it is possible that the Old Testament, while sharing the grammatical forms of Semitic language to the full (to a much greater extent than the NT, for example, shares those of the OT), is able to express through them an outlook considerably different from that of the surrounding

tion even if it was the native language of the speaker or writer. The language of biblical religion is Hebrew, as the Dead Sea scrolls have shown, not only for sectarian Judaism of the 1st century B.C., but also for NT Christianity of the 1st century A.D.'
[1] Knight, op. cit., p. 6.

culture. But to say that this is possible is to break the close correlation of thought and language which is presupposed by so many theological arguments about the New Testament.

Here is a rather extreme statement of the contrast we have been discussing: 'The distinctive ideas of Old Testament religion . . . are different from the ideas of any other religion whatsoever. In particular they are quite distinct from the ideas of the Greek thinkers.'[1] Leaving aside the question whether the ideas referred to are different from those of any other religion whatsoever, we would point out only how unjustified this 'in particular' is for the understanding of the Old Testament. For the question of its distinctiveness, its differences from Greek philosophy are of little account. The whole discussion of the subject, as Dr Snaith makes plain in his preface, is animated by the belief that most of traditional Christianity has been synthesizing Zion and Greece, and that the cure for its troubles is to get these separated. But for the understanding of the Old Testament what we need to know is how its ideas differ from those of 'in particular' not the Greeks but the Canaanites, the Arabs and the Babylonians.

These last points have been put in to suggest that for theologians interested in the relation between the uniqueness of Christianity and the influence of its Hebrew background there are difficulties and snags in the use of the Hebrew-Greek contrast, independent of the validity of the use of linguistic evidence in support of it; it is this last, however, which is our subject.

[1] N. H. Snaith, *Distinctive Ideas of the Old Testament*, p. 9.

Chapter Three

Problems of Method

In this modern theological attempt to relate theological thought to biblical language I shall argue that the most characteristic feature is its unsystematic and haphazard nature. For this lack of system I think there are two reasons — firstly the failure to examine the relevant languages, Greek and Hebrew, as a whole; and secondly the failure to relate what is said about either to a general semantic method related to general linguistics.

The first of these points I hope to substantiate in the course of discussion later. Certain general reasons, however, why the languages concerned have not been systematically examined in the course of this movement may be mentioned here. The most obvious is that it has been biblical theologians rather than linguists who have developed this movement. Linguists describing Hebrew have not always found themselves compelled to speak about the extraordinary 'concreteness' of this language or about its relatedness to a Semitic consciousness of time and history, any more than the writer of a Greek grammar will necessarily feel called upon to expatiate on the aesthetic subtleties and philosophical depths attainable by writers in this language. In fact the modern linguists who have worked on the grammar of Hebrew have said comparatively little that fits in with the modern theological assessment of the Hebrew language in its supposed relation to Hebrew thought; and Boman[1] scolds certain modern linguists, such as Brockelmann, Bauer and Leander, and Bergsträsser, for failing to allow scope in their treatments of the verb system to the special Hebrew psychology relating to time and the dynamic. Just here we discern an argument which, however innocently intended, can be very dangerous: the argument that a linguist who does not make proper

[1] Boman, op. cit., p. 15, 17; E.T., p. 23 f., 26.

use of the supposed special 'Hebrew mind' in his presentation of linguistic facts betrays himself as working from modern, European, Greek-dominated presuppositions. Thus Bergsträsser works, according to Boman's opinion, from *our* idea of time; and thus 'probably unconsciously proceeds from the assumption that this idea of time possesses universal validity'. Bergsträsser 'makes no attempt to uncover the psychological backgrounds of the Hebrew linguistic forms in order to understand them from the inside outwards'.[1] I regard this argument as a dangerous one (*a*) because it assumes the priority of the ethno-psychological[2] connections, which are so dear to Boman, over other methods of linguistic description; (*b*) because of its suggestion that a linguist like Bergsträsser can give only a purely 'external' description of Hebrew; (*c*) because in the present mood of theology any argument against a scholar on the grounds of using European presuppositions and failing to see the Hebrew way of thinking is likely to be accepted blindly and uncritically by people who know exactly nothing of Bergsträsser's work. I should add that I do not think Bergsträsser in fact 'works from our idea of time', and that it is a typical misconstruction of linguistic method by Boman which suggests that he does.

We see here how much the theological viewpoint is dominated by theory.[3] You *know* how distinctive the Hebrew mind is, and surely all this distinctiveness in concepts and in thought *must somehow* be manifested in the linguistic phenomena. If you *know* the unusual understanding of time which the Hebrews had, surely it is most natural that the peculiarities of their verb tense system should be explained as a reflection of that understanding. The idea of a linguistic treatment of this tense phenomenon which does not work from an ethno-psychology thus seems strange, and the most

---

[1] Boman, op. cit., p. 17; E.T., p. 26.

[2] I use 'ethno-psychology' to correspond, of course, to the German *Völkerpsychologie*. A great deal of the material I shall be criticizing is in many ways an attempt to make the supposed ethno-psychology of the Hebrews the key to the linguistic phenomena of Hebrew and at the same time the key to the theological understanding of the Bible.

[3] I think that most of the theologians engaged in the movement we are criticizing would be disposed to sympathize with Boman's attitude here, although as we shall see Boman occupies a strongly individual position in some other ways and is rather separate from the 'biblical theology' movement as a whole.

obvious explanation is that a linguist working in such a way cares nothing for the 'Hebrew mind'.

It is this starting from the theoretical end, from the assurance of understanding the Hebrew mind, and working from there to its linguistic form, that causes the haphazardness of modern theological treatments of linguistic evidence. A person deeply conscious of the features of the Hebrew mind will notice some linguistic feature which illustrates it. He does not search about to see if there are other features which point in the opposite direction; and if there are still others which do not openly bear the stamp of the Hebrew mind, they are presumably 'neutral' facts which have nothing to say one way or the other. Thus, since a systematic examination or description of the language is not being done, a few phenomena which illustrate the theory seem to be striking confirmation of it, and what were occasional and possible illustrative examples come to appear as a total system corresponding to the realities of Hebrew thought. The theory thus becomes presumptive evidence for the interpretation of facts that are doubtful.[1] Some kind of accord with the patterns of the Hebrew mind as indicated in the contrast with the Greek may be presupposed in a Hebrew linguistic phenomenon unless there is a special reason against it.

Even if such accord with the patterns of the Hebrew mind were simply put forward as a working hypothesis for the understanding of Hebrew linguistic phenomena, this hypothesis would require proper testing. To test it we should have to ask such questions as not only 'Are there linguistic phenomena which can be correlated with such patterns?' but also 'Are there phenomena which cannot at all be so correlated?' and 'Are these phenomena which can perhaps in some way be so correlated adequately explained by such correlation, so that no other and better explanation can be given?' And in addition it should be asked: 'Is the establishment of such a

---

[1] Thus for example according to Knight, op. cit., pp. 16–20, a 'diversity in unity in regard to the nature of God' is characteristic of Hebrew thought; they think of the 'oneness' of their God not as a mathematical oneness, or a 'mere monad of being'. It is therefore natural to use these characteristics of Israelite thinking to explain the peculiar phenomenon of the apparently plural form of the well-known word *ᵉlohim* 'God'.

hypothesis, even only as a working hypothesis, in line with established and normal linguistic practice or strikingly out of line with it?' Our discussion of a few examples as treated in modern biblical theology will indicate how far such examination has been from taking place.

It may be mentioned here in a preliminary way that the field of ethno-psychology in its connection with linguistic phenomena is widely recognized to be a difficult and slippery area, even when entered by linguists and psychologists, of which most biblical theologians are neither. Thus Kronasser,[1] reviewing an earlier stage of research, judges that the conclusions for ethno-psychology drawn from linguistic phenomena were the most precarious of its achievements. He mentions in particular the attempt of Oertel to draw conclusions for the mentality of the early Indo-European-speaking peoples from the development of *woida from 'I have seen' to 'I know' (Greek οἶδα) and the related but much more exaggerated attempt of Mandel to describe the nordic races as 'men of the eye', while other groups, including those of the Near East, are 'men of hearing and of the word'. Kronasser shows that such conclusions have often been reached only by overestimating certain linguistic phenomena and underestimating others. But in general the similarity of these arguments to many now current in the area of biblical theology, some of them to be discussed in this study, is evident.

This brings us to our second point, namely, the failure to relate what is said about either Hebrew or Greek to a general semantic method related to general linguistics. I do not mean here merely the failure to accept guidance from the whole progress of modern semantic studies. I mean also certain things which should be obvious even without special guidance from general linguistics. The following points would seem essential to the kind of use of linguistic evidence which is intended: firstly, a strict and systematic method of discussing the relation between grammatical structures and lexical phenomena on the one hand and the Hebrew or Greek mind or any other national or cultural mind on the other. Secondly, a systematic examination of the relevant language as a whole,

[1] Op. cit., p. 75 f.

not purely motivated by the interest in correlating the Hebrew mind with the Greek, so as to display the structure of the language as such and not to emphasize unduly those elements which can be specially fitted into the contrast between the Hebrew and the Greek minds. Thirdly, a semantic method which is used for Greek or Hebrew must be integrated with general linguistics as a whole, and must therefore be open to relevant data for semantics of any language, since otherwise the languages specially relevant in this case, namely Hebrew and Greek, receive a distorted image from their isolation.

I do not suggest that these requisites can be readily supplied in a form applicable to the needs of theological study. I do suggest however that to embark on the correlation of the difference of the Hebrew and Greek languages with the difference of Hebrew and Greek thought, or on demonstrating how the features of Hebrew thought are built into Hebrew language, without giving full thought to these requisites, indicates a serious over-confidence and an ignoring of basic problems.

As soon as evidence from linguistic phenomena is used in the contrast of Hebrew and Greek ways of thinking, a relation is being established between mental pattern and linguistic structure. What has not been apparent when such evidence has been used in theological discussion in recent years has been the consciousness of how difficult a problem such a relation constitutes and how impossible it is to by-pass the discussion of it in philosophy, psychology and linguistics. Even on the most general theoretical level, if a relation is assumed to exist between the mental pattern of a certain linguistic group and the structure of their language, one would have the choice of at least the following simple relations: (a) that the mental pattern is determined by the linguistic structure; (b) that the linguistic structure is determined by the mental pattern; (c) that they are in some way reciprocally interactive. Under (c) can perhaps be added the further alternative (d) that the interaction is not constant and uniform, but occurs only haphazardly and at certain points, and therefore for reasons and circumstances which have to be separately determined for each case. These alternatives are put here only in a general way so as to indicate the problems; I do not suggest that one must in fact accept one of these in the end. With the inclusion of an historical perspective other possibilities could be discussed, for example that at certain points a linguistic structure reflects a mental pattern operative at a historically earlier stage.

The modern users of linguistic evidence in biblical theology can hardly be said to have thought much about these questions, and may with good reason feel it beyond their ability to answer them. It may be also that not only theologians but also philosophers and linguists are far from any final decision about this. But this means not that the theologians can leave the matter alone; either they can offer a tentative statement about their conception of the relation of mental patterns and linguistic structures, a statement which can then be tested and judged;[1] or else they should be much more reserved in their use of linguistic evidence where it is allegedly related to such mental patterns.

An interesting article called 'Language and Philosophy — some suggestions for an empirical approach' was published in 1947 by A. H. Basson and D. J. O'Connor.[2] They began with a mention of the opinion that the structure and perhaps the vocabulary of a language determines the lines of thought of those using it, and accordingly that insoluble philosophical problems may arise from inadequacies in a language, or, in a more extreme form, that all such problems do so arise. The writers thought that if this were in any way true some empirical evidence should be forthcoming, and they sent out a questionnaire to a number of philologists asking for information about certain structural relations in many languages which might be expected to find some reflection in logic or philosophy. Among the linguistic phenomena about which they sought information were: the verb 'to be' as copula or existential; quantifiers like 'all' or the definite article. Tense in verbs was also noted as an important problem.

From the answers to the questionnaire the authors were, how-

---

[1] Boman here as so often forms a partial exception, since he quotes and appears to accept as adequate a sentence about the modern philosophy of language, based on Humboldt and Max Müller, op. cit., p. 15; E.T., p. 24; see below, pp. 47–49, 85–88.

[2] *Philosophy* xxii (1947) 49–65. Cf. Ullmann, op. cit., p. 20 ff.

ever, unable to give any ready answer to the general problem. They were able however to suggest one or two further lines of approach, e.g. the comparison of philosophic works existing in the same tradition but in different languages, and of works belonging to different cultures and expressed in very different languages.

They did not give any special attention to theological words or problems. It is noticeable however that theological writings could be compared in the suggested further investigation just as readily as philosophical ones could; and that, as we have already seen, biblical theologians have already been working to some extent with a correlation between Greek and Greek philosophy and Hebrew and Hebrew religious thought. Finally, some of the particular aspects mentioned in the enquiry are specially relevant in the theological discussion, and in particular we must mention the place of verbs 'to be' as copula or existential, the definite article, and tense or aspect systems in verbs.

I mention the discussion of Basson and O'Connor here only to emphasize how the modern use of linguistic evidence in theology suggests that the problems raised and discussed by them either are not real or can be ignored for practical purposes. Some of the detailed points which they mention will reappear in our discussion later. Meanwhile we may proceed to indicate one or two serious difficulties.

First of all, the picking out of classical Greek and classical Hebrew for comparison may, as I have already suggested, produce a distortion. From a purely linguistic point of view the idea of selecting these languages must seem an arbitrary one. If one attempts to apply to either of these languages the terms 'abstract' or 'concrete' and 'static' or 'dynamic', one can hardly produce any clear result unless these terms are placed against some scale which is related to all languages and not to these only. This means also that the terms used would have to be fixed and defined in their relation to a general linguistic comparison and not *ad hoc* for the special comparison of Greek and Hebrew. In other words, (a) the isolation of Greek and Hebrew tends to accentuate differences between them, and (b) the use of terms like 'abstract', 'concrete', 'static' and 'dynamic' in much biblical theology has been formed and fixed in the realm of comparative theology and philosophy, and has never been measured for its adequacy for linguistic comparison at all; in fact the use in linguistic discussion quickly evaporates into cloudy unreality and has to be eked out by repeated appeals back into the comparison of philosophies and religious attitudes. There is a deceptiveness here in the fact that some of these words, such as 'abstract', are in fact used in grammatical description.

Some questions about 'abstract' and 'concrete' in this regard may be briefly discussed here. We have seen that it is customary to describe Hebrew thought as concrete and free from abstraction, and that this has been connected by Knight with the supposed fact that "There are few abstract nouns in the Hebrew language. Even the adjective is at a rudimentary stage of development in classical Hebrew'.[1] What is said here seems to be widely accepted in theological circles.

This opinion may be criticized as follows. (a) We may ask if this opinion rests either on any attempt to reach a workable use of the term 'abstract', or on any count of the actual number of abstract nouns as so defined; it may be said almost certainly that neither of these procedures has been used. The reason why care must be taken in reaching a definition is that 'abstract' is far from clear or suitable as a term in linguistic description, although it is hallowed by its use in school grammar. Presumably it is not intended to include the action noun type such as 'arrival' or 'ascent'; this leaves in question mainly the type like 'redness' or 'beauty', i.e. what Jespersen calls predicative nexus-words.[2] Now the data for nouns of this type have been collected by Gulkowitsch,[3] and it may be asked whether his material, classified for the biblical, the talmudic and the post-talmudic periods, suggests that this type of word is so lacking in Hebrew. Thus there are in physical relations such words as 'length', 'height', 'thickness'; and in moral and religious relations such words as 'holiness', 'guilt', 'innocence', 'untruth', and so on. It will no doubt be answered that nevertheless the Israelites 'did not think abstractly' about such things. Perhaps not, but our

---

[1] See above, p. 16.

[2] Jespersen, *Philosophy of Grammar*, p. 136, and see generally pp. 133–44.

[3] L. Gulkowitsch, *Die Bildung von Abstraktbegriffen in der hebräischen Sprachgeschichte* (Leipzig, 1931).

point under discussion is not whether they thought abstractly or not but whether this alleged absence of abstract thought is connected with or supported by the presence or absence of certain linguistic types. And even if we admit that the Israelites used certain nouns of 'abstract' type without thinking 'abstractly' about the matters concerned, it would be necessary to ask whether this is not the case in other languages too; which brings us back to our first point, failure to think about what is implied by 'abstract' when used of linguistic types. After all, we 'go out in the darkness' in English without necessarily being abstract thinkers about night and day.

(b) We may now continue by asking what evidence there is for the statement that the adjective is 'at a rudimentary stage of development in classical Hebrew'; and even supposing it to be true in some sense, what contribution it makes to the argument. And when we see that Knight points to the place taken by the construct mechanism[1] where an adjective with a noun might otherwise be used, we must ask how this demonstrates the non-abstract character of either Hebrew language or Israelite thinking. For it is hard to see how such characteristic Hebrew phrases as 'the mountain of my holiness' or 'a man of strength' or 'words of truth' are signally less abstract than 'my holy mountain' or 'a powerful man' or 'true words'.

(c) Since we thus see the failure of the attempt to relate the concreteness of Hebrew thought to an absence of abstract nouns, we may now consider the judgement of a competent linguist like Bloomfield, who points out that the formation of abstracts depends on and arises from the existence of a 'part of speech' distinction in the language system. 'It is an error to suppose that abstract forms like these occur only in the languages of literate peoples; they occur in all languages that limit different form-classes to different syntactic positions.'[2]

---

[1] Knight, op. cit., p. 8; cf. below, p. 89.

[2] Bloomfield, *Language*, p. 271. With regard to the position of adjectives, two points may be added. (a) A difference of classical Hebrew from some other languages is that it is not easy to form an adjective from a noun and then another noun on that adjective, as in English *hope — hopeful — hopefulness*. (b) The adjective class in Hebrew has a similar position to that of Latin or Greek, belonging morphologically largely with the nouns, having no independent declension system, and showing concord with the noun in syntax.

This may bring us to a related but slightly different point, the question of concreteness and generalization in vocabulary. It has been common to point to an extreme degree of 'concreteness' or absence of generalization in certain languages of 'primitive' peoples, for example when there is a word for 'red cow' or 'white cow' but no word for 'cow', or for 'younger brother' and 'older brother' but none for 'brother'.[1] I do not see that there is much in Hebrew like 'concreteness' of this kind, and if 'abstraction' or 'generalization' is so understood as to include such things as the ability to express 'cow' as distinct from 'red cow', it is difficult to know how far Hebrew would differ from Greek or from modern European languages.

We must point out however that the idea of the extreme concreteness of the languages of 'primitive' peoples has been much criticized. We have already seen that Bloomfield relates the presence of 'abstracts' to the existence of a 'part of speech' system. And many of the examples of 'concreteness' in vocabulary are related to particular sectors of the culture, such as marriage and family relationships. Moreover, the existence of this 'concreteness' at all has been questioned. A. A. Hill maintains that this impression arose in some cases (among American Indians) through the inadequate procedures of missionaries and other early contacts with the peoples involved, who had no means of eliciting terms other than the most concrete; which they did by pointing at an object in order to elicit its name.[2]

This is of importance for two points which Pedersen makes. He notes that in Hebrew, where there are no verb compounds, we have quite different and unrelated words for 'go up', 'go down', 'go in', 'go out'. In English we have the one word 'go' with the various adverbs; which fact is for Pedersen 'because we have an abstract idea, i.e. "to go", which may be supplemented now in one, now in another direction'.[3] The fact Pedersen works from here is an important point of Hebrew structure, but is quite misinterpreted

---

[1] For examples see Jespersen, *Language*, pp. 429 ff.; Kronasser, op. cit., pp. 114 ff.

[2] In *Language* xxviii (1952) 259 f. Cf. the interesting 'Note on Primitive Languages' of the same writer, *IJAL* xviii (1952) 172–7.

[3] Pedersen, *Israel* i–ii. 111.

by him. (*a*) The utmost one could do would be to speak of 'generalization' here, and not of 'abstraction'. (*b*) The interpretation of 'to go' as being an 'abstraction' simply because it may be supplemented with direction markers is quite artificial and unnatural, and arises from the obsession in this school with 'abstract' and 'concrete' as the matrix for all contrasts between Greece and Israel in thought or in language. (*c*) The same difference which Pedersen so emphasizes for the contrast between English and Hebrew would also be found between English and French to a considerable extent.

Secondly, it is through calling attention to this sort of phenomenon that Pedersen argues the 'primitive' character of Hebrew, upon which his method of exposition depends in many ways. He says: 'Hebrew, like other Semitic languages, has preserved its primitive character and gives an immediate expression of the processes of thought.'[1] Of course the use of the word 'primitive' is notoriously difficult to define adequately, and need not concern us here. What is important is that for Pedersen Hebrew by being 'primitive' is understood to express the thought-processes directly and to reflect the mental structure, clearly in a way contrasted with other less 'primitive' languages where this is not so. Such arguments about abstractness and generalization as we have reviewed have not proved any 'primitiveness' for Hebrew which justifies the conclusion made and used by Pedersen.[2]

Some attention should also be given to another matter which is relevant to problems of abstraction and generalization, namely the existence of the definite article. I mention this principally because the question of the definite article was one of the points noticed as relevant to philosophical problems by Basson and O'Connor. The possession of a form which can be recognizably termed 'definite article' is something that Hebrew (unlike some other Semitic languages, e.g. Accadian) has in common with Greek (unlike some other Indo-European languages, e.g. Latin). They are incidentally

[1] Op. cit., p. 112.
[2] Naturally certain social situations in a culture may be reflected by certain aspects of vocabulary stocks, e.g. marriage and family systems; see Kronasser, op. cit., p. 115; but this is different from a language as a whole being an immediate expression of the processes of thought.

also alike in that they do not have a form distinct from the numeral 'one' which can be called an 'indefinite article'. If it were true that the definite article arose in response to a need to distinguish between 'dog' and 'the dog', ar.d hence displays a certain sense of contrast between the general and the particular, and that within Indo-European the article was a cultural gift from classical Greece,[1] it would be worth pointing out that Hebrew had the definite article well established as distinct from a demonstrative as early as the time of David and Solomon, although in poetry of course it was still frequently not used. I find Bonfante's account of the matter difficult to believe, however.[2]

Although I would much doubt the idea, therefore, that increasing use of abstraction and generalization in thought occasioned the rise of the Greek article, it may well be true that the existence of this article was a great convenience for the expression of abstract thought.

Greek phrases like τὸ ἀγαθόν or τὸ ψυχρόν were of course very convenient, and this use of the definite article is carried very far by cases like Aristotle's τὸ τί ἦν εἶναι. The use of the article with adjectives in Hebrew is also established, in phrases of the type which we would probably translate with 'what is good' or 'what is right'; e.g. Jud. 17: 6, ʾiš hay-yašar bᵉ-ʿenaw yaᶜᵃśeh, 'each man used to do what was right (hay-yašar, lit. the right) in his own eyes'. In precisely what way does this differ from τὸ ἀγαθόν or τὸ ψυχρόν? It may be answered that there is some different kind of mental process involved, but the linguistic forms are quite closely similar. I do not see any linguistic reason why the Hebrew form should not have been used as much and extended as much as the Greek form was. I also quote this matter of the definite article not because I myself think it throws very much light on the problems we have been discussing but because, if the facts had been other than they are and if Hebrew had not had a definite article in prose, as in poetry in fact it often does not have, I have no doubt that this

---

[1] As is argued by G. Bonfante, 'Semantics', *Encyclopaedia Britannica* (1958 ed.), xx. 313 G.

[2] For a careful study of these problems in Indo-European see E. Schwyzer, 'Die nominale Determination in den indogermanischen Sprachen', *KZ* lxiii (1936) 145–67.

absence of an article in Hebrew would have been held up to us as a clear example of how the Israelites were so removed from abstraction that they had no linguistic means of distinguishing between 'dog' and 'the dog'.[1]

The other main point of importance to us which arises from the article of Basson and O'Connor is that in certain currents of biblical theology according to my observation the way in which Hebrew linguistic phenomena are being correlated with the patterns of the Hebrew mind means in effect that linguistic structure reflects or corresponds to the thought structure. In this view, however, there are very great difficulties, and though it may be possible to maintain it in some greatly modified sense, the way in which it is at present used in theology may well be regarded as wholly outmoded and a survival from the time before the scientific study of language began.

A good statement of the correspondence idea, and that from one who was hardly a theologian although his work has had a deep influence on theological study, is this from Pedersen:[2] 'The Semitic languages are as perfect expressions of Semitic thinking as the European languages of European thinking'. Likewise Boman holds that: 'The unique character (*Eigenart*) of a people or of a family of peoples, a race, finds its expression in its own language'.[3]

Gerleman[4] begins by making a number of interesting remarks about Hebrew style, and then goes on to correlate its characteristics explicitly with the linguistic structure itself. The stylistic character, he says, would no doubt still be visible even if the same literary and psychological phenomenon were to be expressed in another language. But for the Old Testament it is in his opinion clear:

'That its conception of reality and its manner of narration have their correlate and their reflection in the structure of the Hebrew language, in the construction of sentences and in the lexical stock.'

Thus Gerleman can go on to speak of 'this affinity of narrative art with syntax, of Old Testament experience of reality with

---

[1] Cf. also such remarks as those of H. Seidler, *Allgemeine Stilistik* (Göttingen, 1953), p. 112; K. Bühler, *Sprachtheorie* (Jena, 1934), pp. 303–15.
[2] Op. cit., p. 513.
[3] Op. cit., p. 18; E.T., p. 27.
[4] G. Gerleman, 'Struktur und Eigenart der hebräischen Sprache', *SEA* xxii–xxiii (1957–8) 252–64.

Hebrew grammar'. This affinity can be seen most clearly when we consider the orientation of the Old Testament towards events and action; the natural correlate with this is of course the emphasis on the verb in Hebrew (p. 256). At this point Gerleman brings some detailed evidence. He argues for example that the emphasis on action through the verb is shown by the use of verbal rection by the Hebrew infinitive (i.e. its being followed by the 'accusative' particle ʾet) in contrast with the nominal rection (i.e. being followed by the genitive case) of the Arabic verbal noun. Such points as this would seem to me to form an extremely slender basis for his argument. Even in this case one could point to the cases where Arabic will not use a verbal noun or infinitive at all but an actual verb form such as a subjunctive, where Hebrew uses the infinitive; an observation which could be used in the exact opposite direction to Gerleman's argument, if in fact one had any confidence in getting anywhere by this sort of comparison. Gerleman's observations may be valuable when kept on the stylistic level but are spoiled by the insistence that details in the morphological-syntactical structure can be found to agree exactly with the stylistic features.

Gerleman carries his correlation on into the New Testament. Here also events and action dominated the scene. The emphasis on dynamic movement recalls the Old Testament and forms a contrast with Rabbinic literature. Here again the linguistic correlation is made:

'This regained understanding of history, in which the spirit of the Old Testament narrators and prophets came alive again, has its correlate and vehicle in the language of the New Testament' (p. 264).

There is more than one way in which the supposed correspondence of thought structure and linguistic structure has been exploited in recent theological work. One way is to work on the lexical side, from vocabulary stocks. We shall for example later notice and discuss an argument in which the various aspects of man according to the Hebrew understanding of him, his earthiness, his power, his weakness, are related to different Hebrew words for 'man'. The distance between the various lexical terms, the words, is taken to correspond with the distance between the different aspects of man in the thought structure.

The effect of this method is to produce those arguments of the 'the Greeks had a word for it' type which so proliferate in biblical theology; except that in that movement it is usually the Jews who have the word for it rather than the Greeks. Consider this argument from a work of highest repute in the biblical theology movement[1] (the writer has just remarked that Greek has two words, σάρξ 'flesh' and σῶμα 'body', where Hebrew has only one, baśar 'flesh'):

'If we ask why it was that the Jews here made do with one word (baśar) where the Greeks required two (σάρξ and σῶμα), we come up against some of the most fundamental assumptions of Hebraic thinking about man. Our contention will be that the Pauline use of σάρξ and σῶμα is to be understood only in the light of these assumptions, and, consequently, that the Greek presuppositions, which necessarily demanded two words instead of one, are simply misleading if made the starting point in interpreting Paul's meaning. . . . It is possible to account for the difference in vocabulary we have noted only on the presupposition that the Hebrews never posed, like the Greeks, certain questions, the answer to which would have forced them to differentiate the "body" from the "flesh".'

This statement could not have been written except in a total neglect of linguistic semantics. (a) Where one language has one word for an object and another language has two, the writer assumes that the only possible explanation is the asking of questions or making of distinctions by the speakers of the latter, a kind of simple philosophy in fact. (b) Where such questions or distinctions are formed, he assumes that they will necessarily demand (and apparently receive) the availability of two words to represent the distinction accurately and conveniently.

These assumptions are self-evidently absurd. What are the questions asked which produced the disparity in vocabulary stocks in the following cases (I take examples of some theological interest): Latin vir and homo, German Mann and Mensch, Greek ἀνήρ and

[1] J. A. T. Robinson, The Body (London, 1952), p. 12 f.

ἄνθρωπος, Hebrew *ʾiš* and *ʾadam*, but English only *man*, French only *homme*? Or again, what distinctions of popular philosophy produced French *savoir* and *connaître*, German *wissen* and *kennen*, Greek ἐπίσταμαι, γιγνώσκω and οἶδα, but English only *know*, Hebrew only *yada*^c? Conversely, since we all in English-speaking literate circles (and especially in theology) are very aware of the great difference between knowing facts and knowing people (a difference much emphasized in recent theology), why do we not 'necessarily demand' and arrange for the provision of two verbs between which the meaning of our present 'know' will be divided? Why did the Hebrews, for whom the distinction between death and life was a fairly important one, not necessarily demand two words corresponding to our 'meat' and 'flesh', and rest content with *baśar* itself for both? The attempt to explain vocabulary stocks in this way is wholly perverse, and indeed quite comical as soon as it is taken beyond the isolated example. It is true of course that specialized coinages can be made, for example by philosophers, for distinctions of this kind; but (*a*) words so produced are of a particular type which can usually be identified, and the words under discussion are certainly not of this type (*b*) it is by no means true that such coinages can be produced always when the need for them is felt, and we often in fact find ourselves embarrassed by difficulties of expression just because this cannot be done (*c*) such new formations depend normally on the availability of linguistic analogy, or on the existence of forms in foreign languages which are sufficiently present in the consciousness of the group concerned, or similar circumstances.

It remains therefore to register briefly Robinson's failure to think at all of historical or diachronic semantics; and of such things as the inheritance of a vocabulary stock from the past. His Greek words after all were well established in the time of Homer. But the questions which he believes were asked are those formulated in such contrasts as that of form and matter, which he believes to be 'basic to Greek thought'. But the formulation in this way is usually taken to have been unknown to the earliest Greek philosophers, or so Aristotle understood it,[1] much more to the average

---

[1] Arist. *Metaph.* 983 b.

Greek speaker. It is impossible to understand the distinction of form and matter as having been active in influencing the vocabulary stock at a time hundreds of years before those first philosophers who themselves did not use the distinction.

But from the side of synchronic semantics the important question must also be asked, whether the Greeks ever in fact correlated the difference between their two words σῶμα and σάρξ with the opposition of form and matter.[1] Robinson merely assumes as obvious that the one difference is related to the other. And this raises the greater question of principle, whether a procedure that isolates a group of one or two words, on the grounds that they form a cohesive group within NT and LXX usage, but does not examine the Greek non-biblical system to see with what groups the words belong there and in what ways, and which then relates the contrasts thus formed to a developed system of thought contrasts, is not simply arranging the material in a way which is certain to produce the predicted result. But enough has been said to demonstrate the precariousness of much work done with comparisons of vocabulary stocks in biblical theology.[2]

We may set in contrast with Robinson's position the following considerations by a professional linguist.[3] He is discussing the

---

[1] Thus one might suppose that it would be possible for Aristotle to say that the σάρξ of an animal is related to its σῶμα as matter to form; but I find no example of his saying it in fact (see Bonitz, *Index Aristotelicus*, s. vv.). In *de Part. Anim.* 651 a 14 he says that *blood* is the matter of the body. In *de Gen. et Corr.* 321 b 22 he says that σάρξ may be the name of either form or matter. In *de Part. Anim.* 653 b 21 he says that σάρξ is the ἀρχὴ καὶ σῶμα καθ' αὐτό of animals. Nor does Plato appear to have related the two words in the ways suggested by Robinson.

[2] It is beyond my purpose to discuss what difference these criticisms may make to the general thesis of Robinson's book. In detail I should add that it is a false argument when he maintains that since both his Greek words translate *baśar* in the LXX 'this means that both the most decisive words in Pauline anthropology, "flesh" and "body", represent a common Hebrew original'. The cases of the translation of *baśar* by σῶμα within the Hebrew canon are in an extremely restricted section of the text and nearly all refer to bodily hygiene, washing, etc. What Paul is doing is quite different from what the LXX were doing; he is not 'representing' a Hebrew traditional text by translating it into Greek. Thus the word 'represent' is quite misleading here, and this argument from LXX usage is of very limited value for Pauline usage. In any case no one supposes that the two words are completely synonymous in Paul; what then is the value of the 'common Hebrew original'?

[3] R. E. Longacre, *Language* xxxii (1956) 302.

linguistic theories of Whorf, which suggest that a vocabulary stock represents a way of organizing the world.

'To put the question baldly: does the fact that in English we use three words *key*, *wrench* and *faucet* for objects called *llave* in Mexican Spanish indicate anything significantly different in the ways an American and a Mexican regard these objects? May it not be — inasmuch as the meaning of a vocabulary item is a function both of the item itself and of the item as occurrent in various contexts — that there is for all practical purposes as good a distinction of the various sorts of objects in Mexican Spanish as in English (aside from possible ambiguity of *llave* in rare ambiguous contexts and the added capacity for punning in Spanish)?

The fineness and adequacy of the items-in-particular-contexts as a descriptive calculus is such that there is probably a sense in which divergencies in the vocabulary grids themselves are ultimately irrelevant. The abstraction and hypostatizing of the "vocabulary grids" may be the fundamental fallacy.'

It seems to me probable that theological linguistic interpretation has not only not overcome, but has not faced or recognized the existence of, such an argument as this.

To show the variety of arguments from differing vocabulary stocks in biblical theology, I may quote two from *TWNT*. In the article κρύπτω, Oepke mentions the number of Hebrew words for 'hide', and goes on: 'The number of synonyms leads us to infer the richness of the relations in which the concepts "hide", "be hidden" and "hidden" stand within the OT religion; a fullness which in the LXX pours itself almost exclusively into the much too narrow bed of a single word-stem.'[1] In the article μάταιος Bauernfeind argues from a similar premise that: 'It is as if a quite considerable number of Hebrew words had been just waiting to pour their negating content into the Greek concept μάταιος.'[2] Arguments of this sort are very common in biblical theology; but no attempt seems to have been made to consider systematically whether they are well founded.

It is also possible to work rather from the morphological or

[1] *TWNT* iii. 967.
[2] *TWNT* iv. 526. Cf. also the cases discussed below, pp. 144–8.

syntactical structure than from the lexical stock. Thus Boman,[1] noting that the Israelites have no word quite corresponding to our 'time', tries to reach their conception of time by an examination of the tense system. Knight[2] argues to a picture of the way in which the Israelite mind related two objects from the grammatical phenomenon called the 'construct state'. In many cases the two kinds of argument, from the morphological-syntactical structure and from the lexical stock, are mingled; but they are isolated here for the sake of clarity. We now turn chiefly to problems of argument from morphological and syntactic structure.

The idea that the grammatical structure of a language reflects the thought structure of those speaking it, and that it correspondingly reflects the differences from the thought of those speaking a language with different grammatical structure, has very great difficulties. Of these difficulties we may first of all point out the existence of numerous grammatical structures (or absences of such) which clearly do not correspond to thought structure. The clearest example is grammatical gender, a very noticeable and pervasive structure in many languages. No one would suppose that the Turks, because they nowhere distinguish gender in their language, not even in the personal pronouns as we do in English, are deficient in the concept of sexual difference; nor would we seriously argue that the French have extended their legendary erotic interests into the linguistic realm by forcing every noun to be either masculine or feminine. The absence of correlation between the linguistic types of masculine, feminine and neuter and the real or conceptual distinctions of male, female and inanimate is very obvious in German and other languages. In Hebrew itself he would be a bold man who would draw conclusions for the 'Hebrew mind' from the feminine gender of *yad* 'hand' or of *ruaḥ* 'spirit', or from the contrast of the latter with the neuter Greek πνεῦμα.

On the other hand it is not true in many languages that the distinction of gender is entirely unrelated to the differences of sex; if it were there would be no problem for us here. There are

---

[1] Boman, op. cit., p. 121 ff.; E.T., p. 141 ff., but the statement that the Hebrews have no word corresponding to our 'time' appears to have been removed in the E.T.

[2] Knight, op. cit., p. 8; see below, p. 89 ff.

enough cases, let us say, where the difference between masculine
and feminine gender corresponds to the difference between real
male and female, to create some sense that the grammatical gender
classes can be named 'masculine' and 'feminine' with some degree
of propriety. Nevertheless in many systems of grammatical gender
it is only at certain points that the correspondence of gender and
sex is preserved, and at other points it is not. The determination of
the points at which the former and the latter occur is not however
made by distinctions in thought or by distinctions in the actual
objects named but by matters of linguistic form and type, along
with the force of linguistic analogy, a force which is not directed by
relations existing really in the objects spoken about. Thus the
phenomenon of grammatical gender is logically haphazard in
relation to the real distinctions between objects or to the distinctions thought to exist between them. Grammatical gender, then,
is a prime example of a linguistic structure which cannot be taken
to reflect a thought pattern. In this I think it is true to add,
however, that the characteristics of grammatical gender form a
good indication of the nature of language as a whole and of the
relation of its structures to mental or real structures.[1]

Equally it is possible to see great difficulties in the idea which we
have already met, that the 'unique character' of a people finds its
expression in its language. One has here to avoid the vague and
unscientific generalizations often made about nations and their
languages. When people observe the behaviour and character of a
nation they also observe their ways of speech, and naturally they
associate these closely with one another. It is another thing to

---

[1] That the origin of the masculine-feminine distinction in Indo-European lay
in linguistic form and not in sexual difference or in mythopoeic 'personification'
was shown as early as 1889 by Brugmann in *IZAS* iv (1889) 100–9; cf. *PBB* xv
(1891) 523–31. That the feminine is a late development in Indo-European is
now well known, especially through Hittite which has no feminine. According to
Burrow, 'the major distinction in Indo-European was between neuter action
nouns accented on the root and masculine, originally common gender, agent
nouns accented on the suffix' (*The Sanskrit Language*, p. 132); but even this
distinction is not a clear-cut one, and for the development of the system see his
entire treatment, op. cit., pp. 117–218 and especially pp. 200–7. For a simple
treatment of the more general questions, see Jespersen, *Philosophy of Grammar*,
pp. 45–57, 226–43, 338–9. For Semitic see Brockelmann, *Hebräische Syntax*,
§ 16, and literature cited there; id., *Grundriss*, i. 404, and literature cited there
from an earlier period; BL § 62.

suppose that for features of character observed it will be possible
to see corresponding patterns in the linguistic structure when
analysed in itself. And even if it may be possible to see such
relations occasionally in particulars, this does not entitle us to
begin by taking as an obviously valid instrument of investigation
the idea that a language is a full expression of the national
character.

Thus we may again ask what exactly Pedersen means when he
says[1] that 'The Semitic languages are as perfect expressions of
Semitic thinking as the European languages of European thinking'.
If he means that Semitic thought was in fact expressed in Semitic
languages, that we cannot imagine it expressed as well in any other,
and that no one can think Semitic thought as well as a Semite
speaking a Semitic language, then we may perhaps agree, but we
are not saying very much. Pedersen in fact seems to mean much
more than this. He appears to mean that the Semitic languages are
so perfect a reflection of Semitic thought that from their grammatical structure one can read off the contours of Semitic thought,
and that if a statement can be identified in some way with 'European ideas' it can be rejected out of hand from any application to
Semitic phenomena.

The connection in which Pedersen made this remark forms a
good illustration of the problems. He is discussing Bauer's description of the function of a Hebrew verb tense (at an earlier stage
when, according to the theory, it was the only existing verb tense)
as 'timeless, i.e. omnitemporal'. In Pedersen's judgement Bauer
was forced to such a formulation because he ignored in the first
place the Semitic use of tense forms to mark the character rather
than the time of an action, and therefore took for granted the
Latin and modern European conception of marking the time.
But even if Bauer did take this for granted, he used it in the form
not of making the Semitic phenomenon agree with the Latin and
European, but apparently of making it mean the opposite, in the
earlier stage at any rate.

Though Bauer's essay is now considerably out of date,[2] and it is

---

[1] Pedersen, op. cit., p. 513; cf. above, p. 33.
[2] *BAss* viii (1910–12) 1–53.

not to our purpose to argue here how far he was right or wrong, certain things about his method are still worth pointing out. The suggestion that Bauer took for granted the temporal conception of the Latin and modern European languages and presupposed it for Semitic is, I think, entirely confuted by a glance at his essay and the careful thought he gave to problems of method. He states quite clearly on p. 3 the danger of importing Indo-European distinctions into the study; the Semitic languages 'wollen zunächst einmal ganz aus sich selbst verstanden und nach ihrer Eigenart gewürdigt sein'. What more could an enthusiast for the uniqueness of Hebrew ask for? Bauer thus tries carefully not to assume a theory of time; but he does consider that his examination of the phenomena has 'removed the chief supports from the point of view that a different way of considering time was peculiar to the Semites' (p. 51).

For Pedersen on the other hand the first axiom is the orientation towards the peculiar Israelite psychology; and to this the idea of a time reference of the verb tenses is unwelcome because it obscures the supposed peculiarity of a verb system which marks the character rather than the time of actions. The idea of a timeless or an omnitemporal reference is also unwelcome because it is 'known how important time and history are for the Hebrew mind. The belief in a perfect reflection of thought by language makes it logically impossible for Pedersen to accept Bauer's theory. But his arguments against Bauer do not depend on faults in linguistic description committed by the latter, but upon his failure to begin from the psychological orientation which is foremost for Pedersen. But however much Bauer's theories have been modified and dated, one cannot but feel that he stood for linguistic method against a half-baked psychology. One of his sentences sums up the matter: 'you can't deduce from the boundaries of the kingdom of Bavaria a geometrical formula according to which it was designed' (p. 25).

But in general the idea that differences of thought structure will correspond to differences of language structure seems to be contradicted by facts. No doubt the Finns think somewhat differently from the Swedes, but is it probable that the difference is as great in extent as the very great difference between their linguistic structures? Or to take an example from nearer the biblical sphere, did the Semitic-speaking Accadians find it so difficult to understand the Sumerians and take over a great deal of mythology, law and religion from them, because their linguistic structures had very little in common, as they well knew from their extensive work in translation and lexicography? Or, working the other way, did Jewish thought in (say) the fourth century B.C. differ as little from that of the Phoenicians as would be suggested from the slight and merely dialectal difference of their languages?

All this can be summarized by saying that where linguistic evidence has been used in the Greek-Hebrew contrast it has not been adequately protected against, or indeed has positively pre-supposed, the idea of a logico-grammatical parallelism, a doctrine which can be traced from Aristotle through scholasticism, and which gained some of its plausibility from the predominant position of Latin and the corresponding attempt to force the forms of other languages into the moulds of Latin grammar. It will be sufficient here to give only a brief quotation from a survey of this parallelism: 'It had been wrongly believed that in the morphology and syntax of a language there were registered the fundamental sentiments and the logical categories of the thinking being. To expect a correspondence between grammar and thought-forms is, since the development of scientific methodology, an illusion . . .'[1]

We have mentioned the relation of Latin to the traditional doctrine of logico-grammatical parallelism. It is not unreasonable to suggest that the way in which the Hebrew language is built upon and emphasized in some modern theology, being linked with the structure of the Hebrew mind and, still more, with the theological realities of God and his action, is something like an attempt to re-establish the traditional parallelism, with Hebrew instead of Latin taking the central place as the language which really fits the ultimate realities. This is so even if it is objected that the Hebrews did not think 'logically'; the idea is of a parallelism between a

[1] C. Serrus, *Le Parallélisme logico-grammatical* (Paris, 1933), p. 385; cf. Ullmann, op. cit., p. 16; W. Brandenstein, 'Ueber die Annahme einer Parallelität zwischen Denken und Sprechen', *GRM* xii (1924) 321–7; M. Sandmann, *Subject and Predicate* (Edinburgh, 1954), *passim*, and including some criticism of Serrus, p. 81 f., also literature cited by him on p. 69 n. For an example of the problems created by the use of categories from Latin grammar, see Jespersen, *Philosophy of Grammar*, pp. 173–87.

language and 'processes of thought', as Pedersen calls them, whether we call these processes 'logical' or not. On the other hand some of the conclusions about Hebrew thought processes of which we shall see examples have themselves been produced not from accurate linguistic description but from the importation of an apparent logic to supplement such description, in a way not wholly unlike the use of logical arguments to support the interpretation of English grammar through Latin categories.

For a statement of the kind of view which implies that Hebrew is the language which fits the ultimate theological realities we may quote the claim of Torrance[1] that 'there is no language that expresses so profoundly and so tenderly the unaccountable love of God as the Hebrew of the Old Testament', and that the holding together of righteousness and love, grace and justice, within a single unity is 'so difficult for us to grasp and to express in any other language than Hebrew'. But apart from some slight examination of the LXX renderings, his article makes no attempt to give evidence that 'no language' has the same range as Hebrew in this respect. It is typical of this approach that it does not rest upon actual examination of languages.

I may perhaps refer also to the somewhat parallel conception of the Greek language as one of quite incomparable elaboration, richness and subtlety, and accordingly as the linguistic summary and correlate of all the riches, splendours and potentialities of man in his natural or unregenerate state.[2] Like Torrance in respect of Hebrew, Hermann Cremer clearly took this assessment of Greek to be something so obvious as to require no argument or demonstration.

I cannot resist ending with the quotation of a passage which seems to me to carry linguistic fantasy to its most extreme and which carries the parallelism of language and thought one further stage to a parallelism with action also. The writers have been expounding the absence of abstract terms from the Hebrew language, and maintaining that:

'This linguistic quality corresponds to a thorough and insistent concreteness in the Hebrew mind.'

[1] In *SJT* i (1948) 55, 63.   [2] Cf. the passage quoted from Cremer below, p. 238.

They now go on to a further point:

'Does the relationship which undoubtedly obtains between a people's language and its way of thinking carry over into a relationship between language and action? Chinese, which is monosyllabic and uninflected, belongs to a people who have always been practical, "down to earth", and ill disposed towards external imperialism. Similarly, it was usually not the Hebrew people who started the many wars which overran them. In contrast, the inflected and involved tongues of Greece, Germany, Rome and Japan have belonged to peoples who were at once mystical in their religious or patriotic devotion and aggressive in their relations with their neighbours. Of course there are exceptions, but on the whole there does seem to be a difference of behaviour between peoples whose mode of expression is concrete and agglutinative, and those who use a more abstract and inflected tongue.'[1]

[1] H. H. Shires and P. Parker, in *The Interpreter's Bible* ii. 481 (exposition of Deuteronomy). The appearance of this passage in the exposition, i.e. the more popular portion of this work, shows how influential is the Greek-Hebrew thought contrast and its correlation with a linguistic difference in quite wide areas in the churches. Cf. in general also A. R. McAllaster, 'Hebrew Language and Israelite Faith', *Interpretation* xiv (1960) 421–32. He maintains that the retention of a reduced vowel in Hebrew is 'parallel' to the shadowy continuance of the soul after death and to the maintenance of a dead man's name through the levirate marriage (p. 431). Again, he says that 'There is no neuter gender in Hebrew, because they recognized no neuter objects' (p. 426). By the same logic, presumably, the Hittites had a neuter but no feminine because they saw no essential difference between man and woman.

Chapter Four

Verbs, Action and Time

GENERAL

It is not possible to make a complete separation for our purpose between lexical phenomena and grammatical phenomena in the narrower sense, namely morphological and syntactic phenomena. For the present however we shall pursue mainly the latter, some examples of which have been mentioned in the latter part of the last chapter, and we shall leave until later questions of the range of meaning of specific Hebrew words except for very general connecting-words like those meaning 'to be'. We take up first of all such questions as: the place of nouns and verbs and modes of connecting them; ways of expressing 'to be' in Hebrew; whether the 'tense' system of the Hebrew verb reveals anything of a mode of thought about time, or of a specially 'dynamic' conception of events.

Some remarks should be made here about the work of Thorleif Boman.[1] He has gone farther in the investigation of this matter, and in drawing conclusions from it, than any of the writers with whom I am acquainted from the biblical theology standpoint. That Boman's general cultural-philosophical opinions are greatly at variance with those of the biblical theology school is at once plain, for while he contrasts Greek and Hebrew thought quite emphatically he believes that they have a kind of inner unity and sympathy, to the discussion of which he devotes his last section. 'I claim that Platonism and Christianity are related in essence[2]' is the opposite of what most of the biblical theology school are maintaining. It is none the less plain that in his analysis of Hebrew and in his

[1] For substantial reviews of Boman's work see J. Hempel, *ZDMG* civ (1954) 194 ff.; L. Knothe, 'Zur Frage des hebräischen Denkens', *ZATW* lxx (1958) 175–81; R. Bultmann in *Gnomon* xxvii (1955) 551–8. Cf. also Boman's early essay, 'Den semitiske tenknings egenart', *NTT* xxxiv (1933) 1–34.

[2] Op. cit., p. 12; E.T., p. 19.

methods of using linguistic evidence Boman follows the same lines
as those biblical theologians who have used linguistic evidence
from Hebrew. The same watchwords which they use continually,
the 'dynamic' nature of Hebrew, the verb as the centre of expression, the concentration on history and time, appear repeatedly
in Boman's work. The lines of his judgement about Hebrew
linguistic structure would be found agreeable to many biblical
theologians, although few of them will have taken such pains over
the linguistic structure and few will agree with his general opinion
about the essential 'complementarity' of Greek and Hebrew
thought and the possibility of making a synthesis between them.[1]
It should however not pass without comment that it appears
possible, by using these methods of linguistic investigation and
by bringing out the strong thought contrast between Greece and
Israel, still to come to the opposite result from that of most
biblical theology.

I have already quoted passages which show how fully Boman
believes in the reflection of mental structure by linguistic structure,
and shown how in this he follows very much the tradition of
Pedersen's *Israel*. It need only be added that Boman never seems
to consider that he might be on uncertain ground in this, and
therefore never stops to justify the close parallelism which he sees
and which is the presupposition of his method. He does in his
introduction tell us that modern philosophy of language, as
founded by Humboldt, is 'completely clear that languages are
expressions of the peculiar (*eigenartig*) thought of peoples'.[2] Now
Boman is not telling us this because he feels there could be any
doubt about this conception of language, which he shares and
presupposes throughout.[3] The main thing he is saying at this
point is that he is dismayed to find the modern philosophy and
psychology of language, for all the validity of this method, failing
to discern what is his own other great presupposition,[4] namely the

---

[1] Op. cit., p. 166–8; E.T., p. 205–8.   [2] Boman, op. cit., p. 15; E.T., p. 24.
[3] Boman, op. cit., p. 18; E.T., p. 27 f., says again that 'The peculiarity of a
people or of a family of peoples, a race, finds its expression in their own language'.
[4] E.g., Boman, op. cit., p. 18; E.T., p. 27, 'Hebrew, a language exceptionally
unusual to our feeling and our way of thinking'; cf. also pp. 11, 15; E.T., pp.
17, 23.

extraordinary peculiarity of the Hebrew language (and of course of Hebrew thought); former investigators have mentioned, in his opinion, only externals and unimportant details in their few remarks about Hebrew.

I cannot help feeling that here Boman has accepted the worse part and rejected the better part in the thinking of a man like Humboldt, with whom there is certainly a common mental outlook in Boman. Even at the most positive and willing acceptance of Humboldt's conception of language as expressing the peculiar thought of peoples, one would have expected some of the difficulties in maintaining such a conception to be mentioned. Humboldt's conception of language has certain strong characteristics of the idealism of his time. The moving force in language was the spiritual force or *Geisteskraft* active in human life and culture. The difference of languages can be considered as the striving of this force, favoured or hampered by the indwelling spiritual force of the peoples, to break forth. In these circumstances to see language 'genetically' is to see it teleologically, as a spiritual work directed to a specific aim but accomplishing this aim only in varying degrees.[1] The idea of a 'people' or 'nation' is also a characteristically romantic-nationalistic one. The genius of the individual is effective and permanent only in so far as it is also uplifted by the spirit dwelling in the nation.[2] Languages always have a national form, and are, unlike some other activities, fields in which nations as such (and not individuals) are properly and directly creative.[3]

Now perhaps not many people understand language in just this way now, and I do not suggest that Boman himself wants to agree with all of Humboldt's philosophy of language. But there are all sorts of survivals from such philosophies of language which continue to have much influence unless newer insights are used to

---

[1] W. von Humboldt, *Sprachphilosophische Werke* (ed. Steinthal, Berlin, 1884), p. 193. 'Ihre Verschiedenheit lässt sich als das Streben betrachten, mit welchem die in den Menschen allgemein gelegte Kraft der Rede, begünstigt oder gehemmt durch die den Völkern beiwohnende Geisteskraft, mehr oder weniger glücklich hervorbricht.'

[2] Ibid., p. 244.

[3] Ibid., p. 245: 'In den Sprachen also sind, da dieselben immer eine nationelle Form haben, Nationen, als solche, eigentlich und unmittelbar schöpferisch.'

correct them. It seems to me therefore very dangerous to adopt, as something given and established by a movement from Humboldt's days on, that 'languages are expressions of the peculiar thought of peoples'. For, to take one point only, once we understand the 'genetic' study of language as historical description of changes, only a fairly small part of which can be traced directly with any confidence to the peculiar thought of any people, and no longer understand it as a teleology of Spirit seeking to express itself but favoured or hampered by national spirit, we must adopt a quite different idea of the degree in which linguistic phenomena and changes can be seen as 'expressions' of thought, whether peculiar or not. I shall later argue that the idea sometimes cherished in biblical theology that the biblical language corresponds to or coheres with the inner thought of the Bible is a reproduction on another level of the idealist picture of reality or spiritual power bringing forth its own expression in language.

In this sense I think Boman has identified himself with an aspect of what he calls 'modern philosophy of language' which he might have done well to criticize rather more. But on the other hand his chief complaint against this philosophy, just as against numerous psychologists and grammarians, namely the failure to attend to the extraordinary peculiarity of Hebrew language and thought,[1] may after all be just one point where this philosophy knew very well what it was doing. For whatever one may think of the philosophical principles of Humboldt, he certainly had experience of enough languages not to be too easily astonished by the peculiarity of Hebrew; and this is true of others of those named by Boman as well. It is no part of the purpose of this book to argue that Hebrew has no peculiarities, an undertaking which I would regard as purposeless in any case; but I do hope to show that

---

[1] Boman (op. cit., p. 15, 17; E.T., p. 23 f., 26) mentions among philosophers Cassirer, among psychologists Kainz, Bühler and Wundt, and among grammarians Brockelmann, Bauer and Leander and Bergsträsser. Though one does not suppose that modernity is a guarantee of correctness, one cannot help being taken aback to see so many prominent modern Hebraists and specialists in language described as 'unusable'; and it is not by chance that Boman has to appeal frequently to a classical but old-fashioned grammar, and not by chance that for his discussion of Gk. λόγος he has to appeal to a dictionary over a hundred years old (see p. 53 ff., notes 100, 101 and 103; E.T., p. 67, notes 2, 3 and 5; cf. below, p. 236 f.).

Boman's arguments frequently fail in fact to demonstrate a peculiarity such as he has in mind.[1]

VERBS AND THE DYNAMIC

Boman starts by accepting the term 'dynamic' as characteristic for Hebrew thought. For Greek thought however he would rather use 'harmonic', since 'static' is too negative, indicating only what is not dynamic. For a linguistic indication of the 'dynamic' in Hebrew Boman like other investigators looks into the verb system. The dynamic nature of the thought is shown most of all by the verbs, 'the basic meaning of which always expresses a movement or activity'. This is so (and here we come to the peculiarity of Hebrew) even in verbs denoting immobile states like standing, sitting or lying. You do this with a verb which can also indicate a movement. This is possible only because the Hebrews see the relation between movement and rest differently from us. 'Our analysis of the Hebrew verbs which express standing, sitting, lying etc., teaches us that for the Hebrews rigid unmoving being is nothing (*ein Nichts*); it does not exist for them. Only a being which stands in inner connection with something active, something moving, is a reality to them.'[2]

To this argument there are certain obvious objections.

It may well be true that the two senses of 'to lie' (to take only one example), i.e. 'to be lying' and 'to lie down', are expressed by the same verb in Hebrew. But to claim any distinctive value for this he would have to show that this is not so, or is less so, in other languages, and this he quite neglects to do. Is the state of affairs here in Hebrew really so much different from that in our modern English? We also use 'stand' for 'be standing' and 'stand up'. It is true that the two uses are often placed syntactically in different contexts. In 'be standing' the state is meant, in 'stand up' the movement. But this is not always so; the verb 'stand' alone can be used for either. Thus we can say 'you should stand when a lady

---

[1] For a review of the continuing influence of Humboldt in linguistics and in particular the revived or 'neo-Humboldtian' school, see the short and valuable article of H. Basilius, 'Neo-Humboldtian Ethnolinguistics', *Word* viii (1952) 95–105, and literature there cited; also see below, p. 294 f.

[2] Boman, op. cit., pp. 18–21, E.T., pp. 27–31.

comes into the room' (movement), but 'I stand while lecturing' (state). The fact that in English we can quote the verb 'lie' or 'stand', and then within its usage differentiate between the senses of state or movement, is itself a disproof of Boman's case for a peculiarity of Hebrew here. In fact Boman's distinction is not between Hebrew and some other language at all, for in fact he does not examine at this point the verb system of any other language. His contrast is between the linguistic fact of the Hebrew verb which means state and/or movement and the logical or psychological fact that we make a mental distinction between the two types of state and movement. This demonstrates the completely one-sided and unsystematic nature of the contrast.[1]

Also it must be remembered that if the context and the verbal form count in English (for example, the difference between 'be sitting' and 'sit down'), this is so in Hebrew also. We use 'sit' or 'stand' for both types, state and movement, but certain verb forms and connections go normally with one or the other. The same may be true of Hebrew. Boman quotes *yašab* as '1. sit down, 2. sit, 3. dwell (almost always with personal subject)', and seems to think that because various forms occur with meanings as indicated this unites the meanings into one unitary concept with the 'dynamic' element of a sitting movement infecting them all. From this he thinks it is clear that even thought about unchanging states was deeply impregnated with thought about a dynamic action. When God is described as *yošeb hak-kᵉrubim* 'sitting upon the cherubim' it is most unlikely that the Hebrew mind thought of him as 'taking his seat' or 'sitting down' or 'performing a dynamic action in being seated' any more than we do. In 1 Kings 1: 13 the emphasis is hardly either the purely momentary one of the action of sitting down, as if to say 'he shall take his seat (at a certain moment) upon my throne', nor the continuous idea 'he shall be sitting (for a long time)'; it is rather 'he, and not some other, will do in due course what I now do, viz., sit on this throne'. The fact that forms of the

[1] Cf. Boman, op. cit., p. 170, n. 37; E.T., p. 29 n.: 'The Hebrew words for "stand", "sit", "lie" have thus two meanings which *to our way of thinking* are opposed to one another.' (My italics.) But the question whether 'our way of thinking' distinguishes these meanings is a different matter from the question whether we have separate verbs for these different senses.

same verb are used in the various senses Boman mentions is no
proof that these senses are in some way indistinguishable to the
Hebrew mind and that there is therefore some important clue in
the fact that the same verb is used for both state and movement.
But without this proof Boman's argument falls to pieces.[1]

Boman is supposed to be comparing Hebrew thought with
Greek, but he makes no reference here to the Greek language in
contrast with his discussion of the Hebrew verb. If we do make
such a reference, we would find that the distinction Boman intends,
that between 'stand up' and 'be standing', would correspond in
some respects to the *Aktionsart* distinction between aorist and
present (or perfect in some cases).[2] One might then want to say
that Greek like Hebrew usually uses the same verb for both cases
but tends to make a tense distinction between them. But one must
now object that (*a*) it cannot be argued that this tense distinction
in Greek corresponds to the Greek mental distinction between
state and movement, for it is a distinction running through the
whole Greek verb system and including for example verbs where
only movement is denoted and never an immobile state (e.g. βάλλω
'throw'); (*b*) one would have to consider the relation of the tense
distinctions in Hebrew also; the participle type in Hebrew, like
many perfects in Greek, will be used very largely for the indication
of state in words like 'stand' or 'lie'.

Similar criticisms apply to the other aspect of the argument
from these verbs. Because they can indicate either the state or the

[1] In fact, as I have already suggested in another connection, much of this kind
of argument starts from a certainty of understanding some kind of 'unitary
perception' or 'totality perception' in the Hebrew mind, and then picks up
anything in the language that looks in some way 'unitary'. The consequent
incoherence of the argument can well be seen in the note just referred to, which
mentions as related totality patterns (*a*) the double use of verbs like 'stand' for
state and movement (*b*) the idea that ' "life" and "death" form a unitary pair of
concepts, since death is the weakest form of life'. We thus have the two propositions:

    (*a*) State and movement form a unitary concept, because the same word is
        used for both, and

    (*b*) Death and life form a unitary concept, although the words have nothing to
        do with each other.

I do not say that these are contradictory; but it is clear that they belong to two
different kinds of argument.

[2] Those unaccustomed to this term will find a simple introduction in C. F. D.
Moule's *Idiom Book of New Testament Greek*, p. 5 ff.

movement, some kind of dynamic action is implied in both; and so Boman thinks we can see that rigid unmoving being is a nothing for the Hebrews. This is an argument constructed by bringing in a totally foreign consideration. It is quite artificial, and typical of the domination of this argument by philosophical interests rather than linguistic method, to expect the notion of 'rigid unmoving being' to find any expression or reflection in a series of verbs for 'stand', 'lie' or 'sit'. Is Boman really asking us to suppose that a language might reasonably be expected to have a series of verbs meaning 'stand (in a form of rigid unmoving being)' or 'lie (as an aspect of rigid unmoving being)', and to be surprised and interested to find that Hebrew has not?

It is rather interesting to find that classical Egyptian, the language of a people whose way of thinking notoriously laid great emphasis on what might be called 'rigid unmoving being', uses *ḥmsi* in much the same range as Hebrew *yašab*, i.e. 'sit down, sit, dwell'; cf. *sḏr* 'lie down, lie, spend the night'.[1]

To sum up, then, in this section Boman (*a*) fails to give any real contrast between Hebrew and other languages (*b*) fails to make allowance for the conditioning by context, tense, and so on, of the alternation between 'state' and 'movement' senses in Hebrew as in other languages (*c*) assumes quite unjustifiably from the use of one verb for both 'state' and 'movement' that there is a unitary concept in which movement is dominant (*d*) introduces the philosophical category of 'rigid unmoving being' which is no part of the normal semantic content of words of the type under discussion.

The final argument of this section,[2] which tries to show that 'it lies in the very nature of the verbs of motion and of immobile state that the subject should be a man, an animal or a living being', is full of contradictions both factual and logical. In fact these verbs *are* used with non-living beings as subject, as Boman himself has to admit: waters can 'stand' (*ʿamad*) and so can the pillar of cloud (Jos. 3: 13, 16; Deut. 31: 15); a city can 'stand' (*ʿamad*) (Jos. 11: 13), and it can be subject to the verb *yašab* 'sit'; no doubt this may mean 'be inhabited' here, but it is this verb nevertheless.

---

[1] Erman-Grapow, iii: 96 ff.; iv. 390 ff.
[2] Boman, op. cit., pp. 20–21; E.T., pp. 30–31.

There is no real reason to suppose that when such words are used of an immobile state it is 'either the end or the result of a movement, or contains a latent movement'. And it is just nonsense to say that 'For the Hebrews dwelling is connected with the dwelling person, for the Greeks and ourselves with the dwelling place and the household goods'. The first half of this seems to be meant as a linguistic statement, namely that the subject of the verb 'dwell' is a person; the second is an incommensurable, since it is apparently intended to state some mental association and not a linguistic one, since neither we nor the Greeks say or said 'My house dwells' or 'My furniture dwells' in normal speech.

It may well be however that there is some difference in the extent to which verbs like 'stand' are used of inanimate objects like mountains in Hebrew literature compared with other literature. If this is so, I think it has to be evaluated on a stylistic level, and may be important there. Boman has misinterpreted the verbs in question by taking them as a lexical class which 'by its nature' must go with animate subjects. Even if cases with inanimate subjects did not occur (which, as we have seen, is not the case), this would not be evidence that living subjects alone were used because they alone were capable of the 'dynamic' motion inherent, according to Boman, in sitting still or standing still or lying asleep, as the Hebrew mind sees them. It would be evidence only that verbs originally used of movements or states of living beings had never in fact been extended to include mountains or stones or houses. For the absence of such extension, however, other reasons might be suggested.

STATIVE VERBS IN PARTICULAR

Boman next gives a survey of that verbal class usually known as 'stative' in Hebrew, which may broadly be taken to represent states and conditions rather than actions. Strictly, however, 'stative' is used not as a semantic but as a morphological category; that is to say, it comprises verbs which have *e* or *o* (from earlier *i* or *u* respectively) as the vowel of their second syllable, e.g. *zaqen* 'be old', *qaton* 'be small'. There are verbs which are 'intransitive' in the usual English sense and which designate states, which are not 'stative' morphologically in classical Hebrew; and there are verbs of the 'stative' morphological type which indicate actions and are followed by objects, e.g. 'fill'.

Now no one probably will want to argue that Hebrew thought is 'static' because there are 'stative' verbs in Hebrew. It might however occur to someone's mind that the existence of 'stative' verbs as well as of 'active' verbs forms some kind of argument against the conception that Hebrew verbs always express 'dynamic' action. Boman[1] tries to reverse this argument by saying that stative verbs are not static; the state they describe is not a rigid one but a condition in flux, becoming constantly operative, a becoming as much as a being. It is an 'activity of the subject, emerging from within', neither a being nor a becoming. Therefore neither 'to be' nor 'to become' will translate it. If for *zaqen* we say 'he is old', with our copula and adjective, we make it into mere being; if we say 'he grows old', we make it into mere becoming. Thus Boman uses the stative verbs, which might have been used as an objection against the 'dynamism' he sees in the Hebrew verb, as a confirmation of his thesis. The true verbal character, he maintains (and this means of course a dynamic character), is to be felt in the statives, though we cannot translate it without difficulty. It is significant that 'we and the Greeks have relatively few stative verbs in our languages' (one would like to know how this was reckoned) 'while the Hebrews on the contrary have very many'.[2]

It is doubtful if Boman has any real linguistic evidence to offer for this. The argument *looks* like a linguistic one but is really a general logical one:

Verbs are dynamic.

Stative verbs are verbs.

Therefore stative verbs are somehow dynamic and indicate an
    action or activity of the subject.

What is needed, however, and is positively lacking in Boman's presentation, is some real evidence that the contexts demand the kind of sense he suggests. If the verb *zaqen* is to mean an 'interior activity', something like 'act old', 'show oneself old in action', is

---

[1] The section is Boman, op. cit., pp. 21–25; E.T., pp. 31–35.
[2] Boman, op. cit., p. 24; E.T., p. 34.

there any place in the Bible where such an interpretation makes better sense or makes sense at all? Is it really any better than to take it at some places to be 'be old' and at others 'become old', as the context demands? Surely in Gen. 18: 13 Sarah laughed at the idea of bearing a child 'when I am old' (*zaqanti*). In 2 Chr. 24:15 at the end of the life of Jehoiada we hear 'and he became old (*way-yizqan*) and became sated with days'. There is no reason to suppose that the translations 'be old' and 'become old' can be improved on here by something that is 'neither being nor becoming'. That Boman will not have the alternatives 'be old' and 'grow old' according to form and context, and must replace them by an overarching sense containing both, is in line with his whole argument, synthetic and logical, working not from an assessment of detailed semantic values in contexts but from a categorizing of the idea of 'verb' and the rigid application of 'dynamic' to any occurrence of a verb.

Boman dislikes the idea of translating the statives with an adjective plus auxiliary verb or copula, for example by saying 'be old', since this destroys the verbal character. It is worth mentioning, however, that with this kind of verb the kinship with adjectives is philologically very strongly marked, so much so that with verbs like 'be old' or 'be small' in the 3rd sing. masc. perf. it is often impossible to tell whether the form is verb or adjective; and strictly speaking the question may be an improper one, for it is possible in such forms to speak of an adjective with verbal inflexion.[1] Thus *zaqen* or *qaton* are from one point of view the same word, verb, participle or adjective, and can be provided with the verbal inflexions or with the nominal as adjectives.

We may add that the derivation of the perfect formation in Hebrew from nominal-adjectival types is a further justification of translations like 'be old' or 'be small'. In general the stative perfect retains much more of the semantic effect of the origin from nouns than does the active perfect; hence the well-known fact that its equivalent is the English present tense much more commonly than in the active perfects.

In conclusion we need not say much of Boman's final argument

---

[1] Brockelmann, *Grundriss* ii. § 76, p. 149; *Hebräische Syntax*, § 41 b.

that the relation of an action to its object (the transitive-intransitive contrast) is not of the same significance in the Hebrew mind as in ours, and that the nature and degree of the activity counts for more. This argument is merely a result of his having concluded that stative verbs (roughly similar to our 'intransitive') are designations for dynamic activity just as active verbs are. I must reiterate that this whole construction of argument does not rest on the examination of sentences as semantic units in detail, but on the theoretical premise that verbs represent dynamism and that stative verbs by involving in many cases only the subject and by suggesting 'neither being nor becoming' reveal the nature of this dynamism specially clearly. Hence the more stative verbs you have, the more it shows your spirit to be directed towards the active and dynamic.

Boman argues that the use of the *niphᶜal* as passive to the *piᶜel* or *hiphᶜil* is another indication of the peculiar Hebrew experience of the relation between an action and its object. But in all probability such phenomena as can be cited here (he does not give precise examples) are products of linguistic analogy and form no foundation for such an explanation. Boman at least recognizes that the *niphᶜal* can have either passive or reflexive function. We may contrast with this the procedure of Barth[1] in his exegesis of the creation story. Anxious to avoid the suggestion that the elements of the world took any active part in their own creating or ordering, he brings into service the *yiqqawu* of Gen. 1: 9. It is 'a passive form', and so not 'let the waters gather themselves' but 'let the waters be gathered'. This cannot be proved, however, from the use of the *niphᶜal*. The 'basic' function of this theme is reflexive rather than passive, and whether the value is reflexive or passive has to be determined individually for each case. In this particular case it is perhaps difficult to make a hard and fast distinction between them. This is all the greater reason against a dogmatic laying down that the form is 'passive' in such a way as explicitly to exclude the reflexive. It is doubtful in any case whether any theological point is at issue here; Barth simply uses the supposed passive value of the verb as additional support for his general exegesis. The case is

---

[1] *KD* iii/1. 162; E.T., p. 145.

mentioned here to illustrate an unfortunate schematism in using Hebrew linguistic phenomena in exegesis.

THE VERB 'TO BE'

In modern biblical theology it is commonly held that the Israelites were not interested in 'existence' as distinct from active existence, action or life; and correspondingly that the language has no means of expressing mere existence. The same seems to be the opinion of Boman, who several times says that a static being is a nothing to the Israelites.

It was mentioned earlier that 'the verb "to be" as copula or existential' was one of the subjects of the questionnaire circulated by Basson and O'Connor and reported on in their article. On this question they got an answer, and they report as follows: 'Semitic languages have in general no copula, but Hebrew and Assyrian both have a special word for "exists"'.[1] Does this contradict the opinion I have just described?

There are at least three linguistic phenomena which are relevant to the discussion of 'to be' in Hebrew:

(a) The ordinary type of sentence where the copula 'is' is used in English, such as 'David is the king', 'he is the man', has no verb as copula in Hebrew. Hebrew uses the nominal sentence, which is a mere juxtaposition of the two elements 'David' and 'the king'. The nominal sentence is a very well-established feature of Semitic syntax. A common addition is the pronoun 'he' or 'she' introduced after the subject, giving the sentence 'David-he-the-king'. Since this pronoun is not indispensable and is indeed very frequently not so inserted, I think it can be neglected in a discussion of the copula.[2]

---

[1] *Philosophy*, xxii (1947) 59.

[2] See the discussion in Brockelmann, *Hebräische Syntax*, § 30 a; for him the presence of the pronoun constitutes a separate type of nominal sentence, the 'Dreigliedrige Nominalsätze'. See also M. Cohen, *Le Système verbal sémitique*, p. 41. Brockelmann maintains that the pronoun is a true copula. This seems to me rather confusing because 'copula' is really a designation of a logical function rather than a linguistic description. For my purpose the main thing is that the pronoun can be omitted, and is not therefore a *necessary* linguistic reflection of the logical copula function. In my opinion, however, for what it is worth, much of the Hebrew usage could be explained as reference back to the subject. This interpretation is supported by those cases where several words intervene between

(b) The verb *hayah* 'to be'. This is discussed at length by Boman, and I shall later make some remarks about his treatment of it. For the present we have to make clear only the most important fact for the co-ordination of *hayah* with other terms corresponding to English 'to be': it is only at certain points that this verb coincides in function with ' "to be" as copula or existential'. In a very large number of its occurrences it will be well translated by 'come to be' or 'come to pass'. Or, conversely, English sentences using 'is' in the present tense either as copula or as existential will seldom be rendered into Hebrew with *hayah*; they will much more normally use the nominal sentence, or the particle *yeš* 'there is'. We are not on the other hand justified in removing *hayah* altogether from the sphere of what is relevant to English 'is' and making it equivalent (say) to English 'become'. For example, a statement like 'the earth is waste' will have the nominal sentence, and no verb; but if we put it in the past and say 'the earth was waste (and is no longer so)', then the verb *hayah* is used, as in Gen. 1: 2. It would be quite perverse to insist on the meaning 'became' here, and so a certain overlap with 'be' has to be observed. In fact the sense of 'come to be' or 'come to pass' is not to be explained by going over to 'become' as the basic sense, but by noticing that very frequent uses have an ingressive element which with a verb meaning 'be' will lead to a sense roughly of 'come to be' or 'come to pass'.[1]

(c) The word *yeš* 'there is' and the opposite *'ayin* or *'en* 'there is not'. This is of course the 'special word for "exists" ' mentioned in the report above. Boman in his discussion of 'being' does not mention this frequent and important word at all. Moreover, a considerable complication is introduced into the discussion by this word. Basson and O'Connor are right in saying that it is a 'special

the main word of the subject and the predicate, so that the pronoun constitutes a resumption, e.g. 1 Kings 18: 24, *wᵉhayah ha-'elohim 'ašer-ya'aneh ba-'eš hu' ha-'elohim* 'and the God who answers by the fire, be he the God'.

[1] In past situations the LXX had no form of εἰμί for this ingressive sense, and very frequently used the aorist ἐγένετο; but where the sense was descriptive of a past continuing situation they often used ἦν, as in Gen. 1: 2. For the future however they could express the ingressive sense without going outside of the verb εἰμί, and ἔσται is in fact very frequent, especially of course in prophetic passages.

word for "exists" ', in the sense that it is not normally used as a
copula in sentences like 'David is the king'.[1] You use it in sentences
like 'There is a dish on the table' or 'There is a God in heaven'.
The complication to which I refer is that this word, which we
might best describe rather vaguely as a particle, is certainly not a
verb, has some of the characteristics of the noun and may be
translated 'being, existence' in a rather over-literal rendering.[2]
As an absolute noun form it is commonly taken to occur at Prov.
8: 21: 'to make those who love me inherit substance (*yeš*)'.
Although *yeš* may have its origin in a demonstrative[3] and *'ayin* in
the interrogative 'where?',[4] in use their syntax has a similarity in
large degree to that of the noun, and the commonest forms are like
noun constructs approximately meaning 'existence of' and 'absence
of' respectively.

BDB (s.v. *yeš*) are of the opinion that this word 'tends to pass
into a verb'.[5] This is no doubt very natural, although one may
doubt if there is really adequate evidence of it within Hebrew.
There is here a difference between Hebrew and Accadian (the
'Assyrian' of Basson and O'Connor), for in the latter language we
have *išū* related to Hebr. *yeš*, but it is a verb in the sense 'have',
while the word *bašū*, also related and having the sense 'exist, be
present', is also, unlike Hebr. *yeš*, a verb. If there then was a
tendency to move words of the type *yeš* into the verb class, Hebrew
did not follow it very far.

Now the fact that there is a common Hebrew word for 'there is',
and that it, if hardly fully a noun, is certainly no 'dynamic' verb,

[1] Brockelmann, *Hebräische Syntax*, § 30 b, uses 'copula' for the use of *yeš*
with pronoun suffixes, especially after *'im* 'if' and before a participle. Again I feel
the term 'copula' misleading. For some remarks on the use of this traditional
logical term as a linguistic designation, see Jespersen, *Philosophy of Grammar*,
pp. 131 f., 305 f., and the section on 'There is', ibid., p. 154 ff. In any case this
particular use in Hebrew does not affect my main argument.
[2] E.g. '*Vorhandensein, es gibt*', Rundgren, *Bildungen*, p. 125; translation of
Gen. 28: 16 as '*Jahwes Dasein an diesem Orte*' by Brockelmann, ibid., § 12;
'en is '*eigentlich "Nichtsein*" ', Bergsträsser, *Einführung*, p. 45.
[3] Brockelmann, ibid., § 12; Rundgren, ibid., p. 125.
[4] Brockelmann, ibid., § 32 d; BL § 80 t.
[5] BDB suggests that in *yešno* 'he is' we have the use of the verbal pronoun
suffix, but I would prefer to regard it as an analogical formation on **'eno* (not
biblical) with BL § 80 w, and hence as hardly evidence for a verbalizing tendency
in Hebrew.

might well be a difficulty for those who have argued for a dynamic sense of 'being' among the Israelites based on the primacy and the dynamism of their verbs; and those who do so argue are bound to take due note of its existence. I do not propose to use it as an argument in the other direction, that is, towards some 'static' sense of being among the Hebrews. What it really indicates is that the presence or absence of 'static' or 'dynamic' thinking cannot be correlated with the characteristics of the verb system or the characteristics of such Hebrew expressions as translate the English 'is'.

Now another point of some importance can be illustrated from this word. The point I wish to make is that the question whether the Israelites laid any emphasis on 'mere' existence as distinct from active existence of some kind is a different one from the question whether their language had words that could express 'mere' existence.

The word *yeš* can be well translated by 'there is', and as in English 'there is' we press *yeš* too far if we try to find in it the expression of 'mere' existence. In fact many cases which use it have also some locality indicated: 'There is bread in my house', 'There is Yahweh in this place'. This is no doubt the 'existential' sense of 'is' as against the 'copula' type. Nevertheless 'exists' would not be a good translation in these sentences, since we would not normally say 'Bread exists in my house' or 'There exists a dish on the table'. In other words, the 'existential' use of the word 'is' does not coincide semantically with 'exists' and does not raise the problem of 'mere' existence, especially when a locality is indicated.

But we must beware of doing the sort of thing that is so often done in biblical theology and concluding that because the sense is not that of 'mere' existence we would render the semantic function of the word better by saying 'is present'. The sense of 'is present' (as opposed to 'is absent') is not built into *yeš* as its own semantic contribution, but is received from the locality indication which is added. There is no reason inherent in *yeš* which makes it impossible for it to mean 'mere existence'. This is why I say that the discussion of *yeš* and its semantic value has to be separated from the question of whether the Israelites thought about 'mere' existence. One cannot argue that mere existence was an unknown concept to the

Israelites and connect this with the suggestion that they had no words for it anyway.

There is, as far as I can see, no inherent barrier to the development of *yeš* and *ʾayin* to a use in sentences referring to what we would call 'existence' as such. You cannot, as I have said, deduce from the sense 'is present' which appears by the addition of a locality designation that the sense must always be 'is present' and not 'exists'. You cannot, I think, for example, translate the *ʾen* *ʾelohim* of Ps. 14: 1 as 'there is no God present'. I think it is true that the fool who makes this statement is no absolute and theoretical atheist; but I derive this knowledge not from a sense that *ʾen* cannot mean absolute non-existence, but from the relating of the passage to what is known generally about the thought of the period. As a matter of fact, I rather wonder whether theologians have not gone too far in this case in playing down the 'atheism' of the fool referred to; for certain parts of the wisdom traditions go rather farther than to suggest that the gods do not require to be reckoned with practically.

However that may be, there is another point to be made of a kind which is liable to be missed in theoretical discussions but which is important for the evaluation of linguistic evidence of this kind. There is probably an element of deixis in the history of *yeš*, which makes its connection with local indications very natural. This deictic element in the semantic history is a certain obstacle to the development of a sense 'exists' absolutely, i.e. independently of any localization. But with the negative *ʾayin* 'there is not' the element of deixis is much weaker, and there is a much slighter gap between 'there is not (here)' and 'there is not (at all)'. This strengthens the point I have already made, that the word *ʾen* at Ps. 14: 1 could perfectly well mean 'absolute non-existence', and that if the thought of the foolish man means something other than absolute atheism our knowledge of this depends on other considerations. The same phenomenon, the greater absolutizing of the question of existence, appears also when *yeš* is used in questions, especially of the rhetorical question kind; both types are found in Deutero-Isaiah.[1]

---

[1] E.g. Is. 44: 6, 8. Cf. BDB s.v. *yeš*: 'In questions, or protestations, *yeš* often implies a doubt whether what is asked about is to be found or exists.'

Our study of *yeš* and *'ayin* thus brings forward the following points: (a) any attempt to emphasize the verb as the basis of Hebrew speech and therefore to assert its peculiar 'dynamism' is not only theoretically dubious but must reckon with these important words which are distinctly not verbs of any kind, and (b) there seems to be no linguistic reason why they should not come near the significance of absolute existence and non-existence in certain contexts, and if these concepts were unknown to the Hebrew mind it is hardly because they had no linguistic means of expressing them.

We may now return to the nominal sentence, which serves in Hebrew where we use the so-called copula 'is'. One might have supposed that the very great frequency of the nominal sentence, which has no verb in it, not even the verb 'is', would give pause to those who feel Hebrew thought to be essentially dynamic and its dynamism to appear especially in the centrality of the verb.

What Boman does here is to switch over from the 'dynamic', the aspect of Hebrew thought which he has associated with the verb, to another aspect commonly mentioned in contrasts of Greek and Hebrew thought, namely the way in which Hebrew thought sees 'identities' or, as other writers say, 'totalities'. We Europeans say 'The altar is wood', and we use the copula 'is' because we are joining two different things, in this case the form and the matter. We are predicating one thing of the other, because we see them in the first place as different and then bring them together. The Israelites said 'The altar wood' without copula, for there is no predicating of one thing of another and for them 'the material *is* the thing'. So also with 'All the ways of the Lord are loyalty and truth' (Ps. 25: 10). The ways of the Lord are identical with loyalty and truth; indeed the latter inhere in the subject, so that the sentence is a tautology.[1]

Boman's discussion of this whole matter is very confused, and he gives no real evidence that the omission or presence of the copula either makes any difference to the way of thinking or is a valid clue to a difference in the way of thinking. First of all, it may or may not be true that for the Israelites 'the material *is* the thing' and that

[1] Boman, op. cit., pp. 25–27; E.T., pp. 35–38.

they did not distinguish form and matter; but it is absurd to suppose that this explanation, which may have some faint plausibility for 'The altar (is) wood', is of any use for vast numbers of other nominal sentences such as 'The land is good' or 'Her name is Shiphra' or 'The children of Israel are great and powerful'.[1] It is quite absurd to suppose that all such sentences can be explained by the 'thing and material' type, which is not specially prominent, and of which there is no reason to suppose that it has any historical priority over other nominal sentence types.

Secondly, Boman confuses the issue by introducing in contrast to the type of 'The altar — wood' that of 'And the earth was waste and void' (Gen. 1:2). This is different, according to Boman, because 'waste and void' does not inhere in 'the earth' as 'wood' does in 'the altar', but rather contradicts it, since 'earth' always means the civilized, inhabited earth. Therefore the predicate could not be directly fixed to the subject, but the verb *hay^etah* 'was' must intervene. Now for one thing 'earth' (*'ereṣ*) does not necessarily mean 'civilized, inhabited earth' at all. For another, the verb 'was' is here to indicate a situation which was so and is no more so and which therefore cannot be fully indicated as such by the nominal sentence. For this function the verb must be expressed, even if the 'predicate' 'inheres in' the subject. If you want to say 'the altar was wood (and is so no longer)' you have to use the verb. In fact the verb thus employed because the situation is no more as it was is not really relevant to a discussion of the value of the Hebrew omission of the 'copula'.

Thirdly, the use of the term 'predicate' in this connection by Boman is very confusing. When we say 'the altar is wood', it may be good traditional logic to say that we are taking 'altar' and predicating 'wood' of it, but it is not linguistic science, either for English or for Greek or for Hebrew. This is no more an explanation of the presence of 'is' in English than of its absence in Hebrew. It is quite absurd linguistic explanation to say that the English

---

[1] Boman appears here to be following GK § 141 b: 'Specially characteristic of the Semitic mode of expression are the cases in which both subject and predicate are substantives, thus emphasizing their identity ("the thing is its measure, material, or equivalent")'. See my further discussion of GK's treatment of this, below, p. 65 ff.

speaker uses 'is' because he holds form and matter apart and is predicating 'wood' of 'the altar'. Even Aristotle himself, as a little observation shows, frequently uses grammatically nominal sentences without the verb 'is', in this respect resembling the Hebrew. The holding of form and matter apart and the 'predicating' one of the other is no more an explanation of the presence of 'is' in English than of its absence in Hebrew. In other words, the idea that the Englishman is 'predicating' one thing of the other in this way does not come from an examination of the English language linguistically at all, but from the application to it of a logical system which is highly traditional and which does not fit all possible types of linguistic expression. Here as elsewhere the linguistic illustration of the contrast of Greek and Hebrew thought is obtained not through the ostensible thorough examination of the Hebrew language but through the misuse of inadequate logical categories upon the Greek (or other European) language. Boman's discussion of 'predicate' and 'predication' is a good example of this.

I do not suggest that the term 'predicate' cannot be properly and usefully used in linguistic description and explanation, if it is adequately defined and understood. But anyone talking about language should be aware of the difficulties it makes for grammar and the distortions which have been forced upon grammar through its influence.[1]

A good illustration of this distortion may be found in the discussion of the nominal sentence by GK, which provides Boman with the basis of his argument. Let us agree, with GK § 141 a, that the 'subject' of a nominal sentence is a noun or pronoun. Very well. But a difficulty is felt by GK in a sentence of the common type of Gen. 10: 12: 'it (i.e. Resen) is the great city', *hiʾ ha-ʿir hag-gᵉdolah*. The pronoun 'it' is in spite of appearance not the subject here but the predicate (§ 141 b (d) note). For the reason we are referred to § 126 k. The difficulty arises from the definite article with 'city'. Generally speaking, the Hebrew definite article goes only with nouns which are 'determined'. It is

---

[1] On this see Jespersen, *Philosophy of Grammar*, pp. 145–56; Serrus, op. cit., pp. ix–xvi and *passim*; Sandmann, *Subject and Predicate.*

omitted when a person or thing is indefinite or unknown; 'consequently also before the predicate, since this is from its nature always a general term, under which the subject is included' (§ 126 i). Therefore 'it' becomes the predicate. But the idea that the grammatical predicate of a noun or pronoun subject of a nominal sentence is 'always a general term, under which the subject is included' is not at all derived from the examination of Hebrew or of any other language, but from the traditional logic, 'from nature' as GK rightly put it. We may add in passing that when such adjustments of grammatical phenomena to a logical framework are made, they usually still do not work. Thus if our subject is now 'the great city' and the predicate is 'it', one is still far from seeing that 'it' is 'a general term, under which the subject is included', and GK have in fact to make an exception here to their own rule: 'the only peculiarity of these cases is that the subject is not included under a general idea, but is equated with the predicate' (§ 126 k).

Now this idea of 'predicate' has further effects in GK, and consequently in Boman also. It seems to have been because of it that they singled out the type where both subject and predicate are substantives ('the altar is wood') as specially characteristic. It conforms quite well to the traditional S-P type, but is somehow specially Semitic (why?) in emphasizing their identity. The idea here may be that expressed by Davidson:[1]'With a certain simplicity and concreteness of thought the Hebrew said: The altar is brass, the table is wood, instead of: The altar is brazen, the table is of wood.' One may question whether this really indicates simplicity or concreteness. One may also ask whether an English speaker will not sometimes say 'That house is stone' or 'That table is wood', and therefore whether there is really anything specially Semitic in this way of speaking. It is perhaps likely that Davidson felt 'brazen' and 'of wood' to be more 'proper' in English. But this kind of propriety does not derive from descriptive grammar at all, but from a preference for a locution which appears better to fit the common understanding of the logical form of the sentence. There may also be some influence from such a remark as Aristotle's that

[1] A. B. Davidson, *Hebrew Syntax* (2nd ed., Edinburgh, 1896), § 29, p. 39.

in this kind of context one says not λίθος but λίθινος in Greek.[1] It is doubtful if the sentence type here singled out as specially Semitic has any such peculiarity in linguistic comparison; it differs only from certain types esteemed as proper.

Another example: when the predicate is an adverb or adverbial phrase, as in 'Riches are in his house', GK state (§ 141 b) that the predicate may be an adverb or 'any specification of time, place, quality, possessor, etc., which may be regarded as the equivalent of a noun-idea'. Now there is no linguistic evidence that the Hebrews had to think of an adverb as a noun-idea before they could admit it in a nominal sentence, and the statement depends on the general theory of the priority of the sentence with noun predicate. Likewise there is no linguistic reason to suppose that the type of 'riches are in his house' is somehow secondary or subsidiary to that of 'the altar is wood'. Fragments of traditional logic are here confusing grammatical description, and it is from grammatical description thus confused and distorted that pictures are so often given of the 'characteristic' mental processes of the Israelites.

In view of this it is striking that Boman feels he must rely on an older grammar like GK, and that more modern grammars like Bergsträsser or BL are unusable because they see things from the modern Western point of view.[2] The truth is rather the opposite; Boman's kind of interpretation of language (and with it much that is written in biblical theology) depends to a great extent on the logico-grammatical unclarities of the older grammars and evaporates with the stricter method of modern linguistics.[3]

We may summarize then by saying that Boman has not succeeded in his attempt to relate the nominal sentence in Hebrew to the Hebrew mode of thinking in totalities and not making distinctions.

It is worth adding that the nominal sentence, though very prominent in Semitic, is by no means uncommon in Indo-European, and according to Meillet is ancient in this family of

---

[1] *Metaphysics* 1033 a 7.   [2] Boman, op. cit., p. 17; E.T., p. 26.
[3] Boman sometimes makes the same criticisms of GK, however, as of the more modern grammars; cf. ibid., p. 27; E.T., p. 37 f.

languages.[1] It is frequent in Greek, more so than in Latin, and is used especially where predicatives come first, as in the English 'Happy the man who . . .'; so Soph. *Ant.* 332 πολλὰ τὰ δεινά 'wonders are many', and Mt. 5: 3 μακάριοι οἱ πτωχοί 'blessed are the poor'.[2] In Russian it is extremely frequent. As Jespersen says,[3] the nominal sentence construction is not to be explained by ellipsis of 'is' or by saying that 'is' is 'understood'; but this is just how Boman explains away some German examples in order to show that the real nominal sentence is peculiar to Hebrew.[4] Once again his defence of the uniqueness of a Hebrew usage depends on a semi-logical and linguistically doubtful interpretation of a modern idiom.

Another point that should be mentioned is not related to Boman's treatment itself but is relevant to the whole mode of arguing from Hebrew thought in reference to the New Testament. If the nominal sentence can be related in some special way to the Hebrew mind, and if the Hebrew mind is strongly alive and dominant in the New Testament, we may ask how far the nominal sentence is found there. Nominal sentences occur in the NT as in Greek generally. But the very numerous uses of the verb ἐστί in the present indicate that the NT does very little to carry on the Hebrew heritage of the nominal sentence. The LXX, very naturally, seems to have kept much closer to Hebrew usage here. In the Greek Psalms, for instance, I find ἐστί appearing in certain contexts, such as in οὐκ ἔστι for Hebrew 'ayin 'there is not', and also usually where the copula-like Hebrew pronoun is used; but in other conditions its use is greatly outnumbered by cases where the nominal sentence is used. In a majority of such cases the subject does not come first, but sometimes it does, e.g. Ps. 7: 12 ὁ θεὸς κριτὴς δίκαιος.

Some attention should still be given to the common verb *hayah* usually translated 'to be'. I have already said something of

---

[1] A. Meillet, 'La Phrase nominale en indo-européen', *MSL* xiv (1906) 1 ff. Cf. the criticisms of Sandmann, op. cit., pp. 218–25, who believes the type with copula to be genetically earlier. This would certainly not be true for Semitic.

[2] A. Meillet and J. Vendryes, *Traité de grammaire comparée des langues classiques* (Paris, 1924), § 835–9.

[3] *Philosophy of Grammar*, pp. 120–2.

[4] Boman, op. cit., p. 171, n. 50; E.T., p. 35 n.

Boman's treatment of this word.[1] I do not wish to criticize his treatment of it in detail but to take up from it a particular point which will be of importance throughout this study. This point is the danger of taking a case of a word along with its context and suggesting that the significance which is given through associations of the context is in fact the indicator value of that word. For example among the survey of meanings of *hayah* we find the following:

(a) '*Hayah* as "to effect" (*wirken*): "Thus saith the Lord: I make this water healthy; no more shall death and miscarriage come from it," i.e. henceforth it is supposed to cause (*verursachen*) neither death nor miscarriage. (2 Kings 2: 21).'[2]

(b) Under *hayah l^e* 'to become something, act as something' we read: 'To become = "work or act as", 2 Sam. 13: 28; 1 Kings 2: 2; Jer. 20: 8 (the Word of Yahweh brought upon Jeremiah mockery and abuse). If *hayah* is connected with *l^e*, the meaning "to work" presses more into the foreground.'[3]

(c) Under 'being beautiful' we read:
' "Being beautiful" can be construed with *hayah* (Gen. 29: 17; 39: 6 b; cf. 2 Sam. 14: 27). Leah's eyes (were) without sparkle, but Rachel was (*hay^etah*) fair of face and beautiful of appearance (Gen. 29: 17); the same construction 39: 6 b. *Hay^etah* indicates that the whole person had a charming effect (*wirkte anmutig*) in qualities and demeanour. The same is said of Absalom's daughter; she, Tamar, was (*hay^etah*) a woman of fair appearance (2 Sam. 14: 27).'[4]

Let us take these cases one by one. In the first it is true that the water is no longer to cause death or miscarriage. This does not mean that 'cause' or 'work an effect' or anything like it can be taken as a reasonable equivalent of *hayah* 'be'. The sense is 'there shall no longer be death from this water'.

In the second case three passages are cited. The first two are

---

[1] See above, p. 64. Boman's treatment leans considerably on that of C. H. Ratschow, *Werden und Wirken, Eine Untersuchung des Wortes hajah als Beitrag zur Wirklichkeitserfassung des AT, BZATW* lxx (1941).
[2] Boman, op. cit., p. 29; E.T., p. 39.
[3] Boman, op. cit., p. 29; E.T., p. 40.   [4] Boman, op. cit., p. 32; E.T., p. 43.

both cases of expressions like 'be a man', using the verb *hayah* 'be'. It is true that 'be a man' or 'be a man of valour' means as a phrase roughly the same as 'act like a man of valour'. This does not mean that any element of 'act' within the phrase as a whole is provided specifically by the verb 'be'. The phrases are quite intelligible with the indicator value of the verb kept at 'be'. The same is true of the Jeremiah passage, where the Word of Yahweh 'was' or 'became' to him 'for a mockery and abuse'. The word became this, turned into this. To suggest 'to work, effect, bring upon' is thus to bring the general picture of the context into the word *hayah*; unjustifiably, for the sense can be found quite adequately with the translation 'became', which may be taken here as pretty well the ingressive past form of 'be'.

The third case could not, I think, be taken seriously by anyone. That 'be' can be used in the combination 'be beautiful' does not say anything about 'be'. That the whole person of Rachel had a charming effect is what is said by the whole sentence; the verb 'was' is an element in it, but contributes precisely nothing to the beauty of the lady. It is interesting that Leah, who was not so good-looking, did not get the verb *hayah*, but this is hardly because this verb did not go so easily with less attractive people.[1] The whole thing is a grotesque attempt to overload *hayah* with the associations of the incidents and situations in which it is used, with the intention of maximizing the sense of 'effect' rather than that of 'be', since the former is supposed to fit the presupposed picture of the Hebrew mind and its dynamism.

It is obvious that such a method naturally tends to maximize the meaning of any word so studied; we shall see later that this treatment has been given to a good many words by some studies in biblical theology. The method does not do so much harm if you stick to one passage at a time, for instance, if you say 'act as a man of valour' instead of 'be a man of valour' in one particular case.

[1] This passage is a case of *hayah* used in plain description (cf. M. Cohen, *Le Système verbal sémitique*, p. 111). In the first part, the treatment of Leah's eyes, the nominal sentence is used, but with the change of syntax in the next part where Rachel herself becomes subject the verb, which is here surely unemphatic, resumes the time of the action and links Rachel with the qualities mentioned. It is quite impossible to get out of the verb here the sense of 'effect' which Boman seems to be wanting.

The reality signified by the sentence as a whole is pretty well the same. It is still inaccurate, however, for you are giving a translation 'act' where you could perfectly naturally give 'be', which would be infinitely closer to the normal semantic range of *hayah*. The inaccuracy becomes deadly, however, when you begin to add up the usages of *hayah*, for now you are adding up the semantic effects of various contexts and not the specific contributions which the word made to these contexts; and from this you get a general picture which can purport to be the total 'concept' of *hayah*, or, working another way, all this apparently overwhelming evidence can be used to interpret the sense of *hayah* in an uncertain case.

Thus Boman[1] comes to review the 'supposedly static' cases of *hayah*; such are apparently the cases where Ratschow accepted the sense 'to be'. An example is Is. 51: 6, *wišuʿati lᵉ-ʿolam tihyeh*. It would be natural to translate 'My help will last (*bestehen*) for ever'. But we must beware of a static idea, and 'help' (or 'salvation') must mean something dynamic. Therefore Boman thinks we should translate 'My help will be actively present for ever'. The two fallacies involved are: (*a*) Boman is so obsessed with the contrast of static and dynamic that he does not see that to use 'be' is not necessarily to say anything 'static' (*b*) it is argued that since 'help' or 'salvation' is not a static thing in itself the verb used with it cannot mean 'be' or 'last'. Comparison with the other hemistich in fact makes the sense of the permanence of help or salvation most probable.

It is not surprising that *hayah* thus comes to be almost hypostatized; it ceases to be a word we are studying and becomes an aspect of ultimate reality. It is the summary of the verbal thinking of the Hebrews, and especially of the 'inner activity' expressed chiefly in the stative or 'internal-active' verbs. In this kind of Being we have no distinction of subjective and objective. It is in the first place Personal Being. We can then go on to speak of 'the *hayah* of God'. 'It is God's *hayah* to come forward and act as God, to execute his will as God (*sich als Gott durchzusetzen*).' 'It is characteristic of the *hayah* of God that it appears in direct

[1] Op. cit., p. 30 f.; E.T., p. 42.

connection with the *hayah* of the people.'[1] With this sort of sentence we have departed entirely from the realm of actual usage of the word *hayah*, even though one may quote sentences in which this verb does occur twice with God and with the people as the two subjects. *Hayah* has now become an airy concept with a life of its own in the world of thought, and though there is intended to be a correlation between the shape of that life and the shape of the linguistic use of the word *hayah*, the details of the linguistic use have come to be remote from the place of 'God's *hayah*' or any other *hayah* in the world of thought.

VERBS AND TIME

I have already mentioned that Boman tries to use the Hebrew verbal system and its organization as an indication of the Hebrew conception of time. I have also mentioned that in the common theological contrast of Greek and Hebrew thinking it is often maintained that the view of time was one aspect in which these two peoples differed fundamentally. For Boman, following Pedersen,[2] we can quote this general statement:

'For *us* time is an abstraction, in as much as we make a distinction between time and the incidents which take place in time. The old Semites do not do this; for them time is identical with its content. Time is the concept of what takes place (*der Begriff des Geschehens*); it is the stream of incidents.'

One difficulty about demonstrating and elaborating this, and especially in contrasting it adequately with Greek thought, is that the Hebrews in Boman's opinion hardly have a word quite corresponding to our 'time' in some of its uses, and that they possibly hardly gave much conscious thought to 'time' at all, in contrast, say, to the Greek philosophers who gave careful and deliberate thought to the matter; Boman quotes a definition of time from Aristotle. To make a comparison with this one has to work out for the Hebrew side a view of time which is implied unconsciously or less deliberately in other things. Boman tries to

---

[1] These sentences, with others of the same kind, are in Boman, op. cit., p. 35; E.T., p. 46-47.

[2] Boman, op. cit., p. 120; E.T., p. 139. Pp. 109-33 (E.T., pp. 123-54) are devoted to the Israelite idea of time in general.

work from: (a) mentions of the heavenly bodies and recurring
periods and seasons (b) the idea of life as a rhythm, which he
believes he can discern in certain ways of speaking (c) the
etymology and associations of certain words, roughly corresponding to 'moment', 'suddenly', 'now', 'endless time' and so on
(d) the consciousness of historical time, and the possibility that,
allied with the idea of the 'time of the soul', this may disclose some
notion of seeing all time as a unity (e) the verbal system, its 'tenses'
and their relation to time. The last of these is the most important,
probably, for Boman, and fits in with his emphasis elsewhere on
the verbal system, and I shall concentrate on it for the most part.

Boman first connects conceptions of time with verbal systems by
saying[1] that '*Our* idea of time has given itself a plastic expression
in our verbs'. We (Europeans) think of time as a line; we stand at
one point, the present, and the future lies before us and the past
behind. Our verbal tense system can be marked off unambiguously
by points on this line. There are two main points combined here:
(a) time as a line, with future and past lying before and after us
(b) the tense system of verbs as a marker of points on the line.

In contrast with (a) Boman argues that in Hebrew future events
are not thought of as lying before us but 'always' as coming after us.
Neither straight lines nor circles, nor indeed any spatially-related
concept, counts for the Hebrew understanding of time. As for (b),
in contrast with the European system with its schema of Past,
Present and Future, Boman places the Hebrew, which according
to him distinguishes two kinds of actions, the complete and the
incomplete, because this and not the abstract time reference is what
counts when the actions are related to the living rhythm of the
person speaking. In other words, the Indo-European verb has a
'time' system, and Semitic an 'aspect' system, and these are
basically different and strange to one another.

Boman now must argue against any who should suppose the
Hebrew verbal system, being an aspect system, to be 'timeless'.
This is of course very important for Boman, who has all along
regarded the verbal system as the key to Israelite thought and has
also held time (rather than space, for example) to be the basic

[1] Boman, op. cit., p. 105, reaffirmed, pp. 107 and 124; E.T., pp. 124, 126, 144.

category of Israelite experience. How is it possible for a people whose language had no word for 'time' and whose verbs were timeless to become the people of *history*, while the Greeks, who had the linguistic apparatus for 'time', had a much less powerful apprehension of history? This problem Boman solves with the magnificent sweeping style of one cutting a Gordian knot. It solves itself indeed very simply, he maintains (though somewhat paradoxically for us), if we admit that the Semitic and not the Greek-European idea of time is the right one.[1]

What Boman means, if I understand him rightly, is tha⁺ that indication which the Hebrew aspect system gives of events, i.e. whether they are complete or not in relation to the speaking person and his interest and participation, comes close to the realities of temporal events. By concentrating on this and paying no attention to past, present or future, the Hebrew verb is not 'timeless' but is showing itself heavily charged with the real understanding of what time is. Its concentration on 'aspect' can thus be correlated directly with the depth and richness of the Hebrew understanding of time. Along with this on the negative side goes a certain depreciation of the 'Greek-European' system, the preoccupation of which with past, present and future is a transference of *spatial* categories into matters of time, a feature which according to Boman can be generally traced in language but not in Hebrew, and not a token of any real appreciation of time.

Now in all this there are some serious difficulties. The first is one which will have occurred to any reader with experience of philological research, namely that an 'aspect' system for verbs is very strongly represented in Indo-European, for example in Greek, which is after all the language supposedly being contrasted with Hebrew here. It is therefore quite wrong to contrast a rigid time system as Indo-European with a rigid aspect system as Semitic (to say nothing of mixtures of the two, as in Russian where there is a twin aspect system with several tenses related to time within each aspect).

The astonishing thing is that Boman acknowledges this to be so. 'We must not overstress the contrast and represent the Hebrew

---

[1] Boman, op. cit., p. 124; E.T., p. 144.

tense idea as something unique.'[1] But he has already stated that the two systems and their related conceptions of time are basically different and strange to one another.[2] To admit on second thoughts that this is not so cannot be taken as a warning that a good argument should not be pressed too far, which is what Boman seems to mean; it is a judgement that it was a bad argument in the first place. In fact it is clear that the contrast in the verbal systems was in fact pressed as far as it could go by Boman, and was made to serve as the instrument of a very violent contrast in the conceptions of time. Boman's identification of the Greek system with a 'time' marking system on a linear basis is quite unambiguous,[3] and his contrast with the Hebrew mind depends on this identification.

The contradiction here has come really from Boman's habit of contrasting Hebrew language and its alleged implications with Greek thought and not in the first place with the Greek linguistic structure at all. The actual observation of the Greek verbal system comes in as an afterthought, and immediately indicates how aprioristic the idea was that Indo-European verbal systems give precise indications of time on a lineal scale.

A second difficulty comes from Boman's attempt to show that the Hebrew expressions relating to time were not derived from spatial terms; he has in mind words such as adverbs and pre-positions. He has to do this as part of his argument that the use of a 'time' indicator system in verbs is not a sign of a 'real' appreciation of time but rather of a spatialization of time; and that conversely the Hebrews, whose language was free from this 'time' indicator system, understood real time and had not drawn on spatial terms at all. In Indo-European it is clear that a number of time expressions are derived from space expressions, and Orelli in a classical study claims the same for Arabic;[4] but Boman will not accept this for Hebrew, and says[5] that what psychologists

[1] Boman, op. cit., p. 127; E.T., p. 147.   [2] Boman, op. cit., p. 124; E.T., p. 144.
[3] Boman, op. cit., p. 105 ff.; E.T., p. 124 f.
[4] C. von Orelli, *Die hebräischen Synonyma der Zeit und Ewigkeit.* Cf. Boman, op. cit., p. 110 f.; E.T., p. 129 f. I have simplified this matter by stating what seems to be Boman's main point, without entering the more complicated question whether Boman has interpreted Orelli correctly and whether Orelli's views are themselves acceptable.
[5] Boman, op. cit., p. 130; E.T., p. 150.

of language say of the priority of spatial terms to temporal may be all right for what passes as 'time' nowadays, but not for real time as the Hebrews knew it. In Hebrew, the linguistic expressions for real time áre as original as those for space. And not only are they original, but they depend on a verbal basis of *activity*, so that we come back to the verb and its activity-content as the centre of Hebrew thinking.

In order to do this Boman has to venture into a dubious etymological swamp. As an example we may quote his treatment of the preposition *min*, in which the temporal meaning 'since' might naturally be taken as secondary in comparison with the spatial meaning 'from'. But Boman says that the 'basic meaning' of the preposition *min* is 'dividing, separating', and that from it are derived equally the spatial sense 'from' and the temporal 'since'. What lies behind the temporal use is not the spatial use but a verbal activity ('dividing'). 'At the basis of both ideas (the spatial and the temporal) there usually lies an action.'

This is a very precarious argument. Boman seems to think that if a verb from the same root exists, this shows a word to be dominated by the verbal sense of action, even if itself it is not a verb at all. It is far more natural to regard this preposition type as derived from nouns, and many examples are indeed stereotyped nouns in the construct form. Even where verbs with the same root occur, it is not likely that nouns such as are the basis of these prepositions are action nouns denoting the verbal activity (in this case Boman's interpretation of *min* as 'dividing') and much more likely that they are nouns of the result of the verbal action or something related to it (thus *min* = 'part' or 'partition').

Even less likely is Boman's attempt to do the same for *'aḥar* 'after' by deriving it from the verb *'eḥar* 'delay, fall behind'. The attempt to assert the priority of the verb in this way in such a case, and from it to deny the dependence of the temporal sense of the preposition upon the spatial, is an impossible one. Boman is aware of the existence of denominative verbs, but thinks them so small a minority that their paucity is a proof of the truly verbal character of Hebrew thought. He never seems to think of the possibility of a denominative in particular cases discussed. That there are certain cases where an action word has become a temporal expression with no spatial connection, e.g. *haškem* 'loading up the beasts' and hence 'early', does not conceal the failure of Boman's argument for the commoner temporal expressions. I must add again that Boman's analysis here is not really comparative, since he does not adduce the material of other languages to compare with Hebrew in this regard.

This failure is very clear in another argument.[1] According to Boman, we Indo-European speakers think of the future as lying before us, while the past extends behind us. Hebrew also, he says, uses *qedem* 'before' and *ʾaḥar* 'behind' of temporal relations, but, according to Boman, 'in the contrary sense': *qedem* means 'the time before', 'the first time', the past, and *ʾaḥᵃrit* 'the latter part', 'the end of a time', the future. It is very naive here not to notice that the same is the case in Indo-European, e.g. πρό or *pro* of what happened in the past, Eng. 'before', Germ. *vor*, etc.; Latin *post* 'behind', *postea* 'afterwards'. Not only does the Hebrew language contradict 'the Indo-European idea of time', but the Indo-European languages do so too. It is typical of Boman's method not to notice this as a fatal objection to the thesis of a Hebrew peculiarity here, and then immediately afterwards to cite words like 'progenitors' and 'posterity', the very words which contradict his statements about Hebrew, and say that we use them when we think in a special way of time as the transcendental design of history and the like.

It is Whorf's opinion[2] that Hebrew takes an intermediate position between Hopi, which does not use spatial terms for non-spatial realities at all, and Latin, through which in his judgement the development of spatial terms for the non-spatial has become normal, or at any rate very common and impressive. This if true suggests some difference between Hebrew and Latin, but would hardly suggest the great difference in kind which Boman professes to find between Hebrew and Greek. I do not suggest that these considerations are final, but I think they have been quite neglected

[1] Boman, op. cit., p. 128 f.; E.T., p. 149. The argument may have its origin in a misapprehension of some remarks by Orelli.

[2] Whorf, *Four Articles on Metalinguistics*, p. 43. Cf. Hoijer, *Language in Culture*, p. 51.

by Boman, in whose work the linguistic description is always dominated by the Hebrew-Greek thought contrast.

Another point is Boman's interest in 'simultaneity' or the unitary perception of historical movement. I shall not discuss how far his solutions are acceptable in general, but only criticize the use of linguistic evidence, which is supposed to be decisive at one point. For the Israelite conception of the meaning of history Boman cites the idea of 'contraction of times' proposed by Galling and that of 'timelessness' put forward by Hempel. Boman is not quite satisfied with either, and turns to his analysis of the Hebrew verb system. After this he has a section on 'simultaneity' in which he seems to feel that the problem has been cleared up. This is apparently because the Hebrew verb system works not from the time of the action in relation to the time of the speaker (and thus past, present or future) but from the kind of action which it is in relation to the speaker as living and acting person, and thus complete or incomplete but all in a sense present. 'One lives oneself so into another series of events that one becomes contemporary with it and joins in experiencing it.'[1] The perception of simultaneity as central to Christianity is the great achievement of Kierkegaard. But 'That concept of simultaneity, which we like Kierkegaard can form only with great difficulty because we are hindered by our way of thinking of the three time-spheres, was given without any trouble to the Semites and especially the Hebrews in their languages'.[2] Thus the structure of the Hebrew verb system leads straight to the solution of the problem of 'simultaneity' in our relation to history and events.

Is there really any evidence in the Hebrew verb system for this idea of simultaneity? I do not think so. The key to Boman's case is his emphasis upon the 'speaking person', which he takes from quotations of GK: you use the perfect for what *the speaking person* wants to represent as complete, and imperfect for what he wants to

---

[1] Boman, op. cit., p. 126; E.T., p. 146.
[2] Boman, op. cit., p. 128; E.T., p. 148. For the other material on 'simultaneity' see pp. 118–19, 121–3; E.T., pp. 137–9, 141–3. Cf. the similarly startling claim by Boman that the doctrine of forms, which Plato had a good deal of trouble to develop, is presented free to the Hebrews in the 'roots' of their language; see below p. 105 f.

represent as incomplete. The speaking person is the kernel of the matter. 'While we with our three tenses place actions in space and fix them on a line, the fixed point for the Semites is the consciousness of the speaking person.'[1]

Once again Boman has picked out a point that is not really unique. Even in a pure 'time' system of tenses the tenses used will be related to the position of the speaking person and his consciousness of the action signified. The contrast made by Boman depends on the entirely artificial explanation of the 'time' system as placing actions spatially on an imaginary line. This once again is a piece of theory which may fit some theories of time, or may be what we *think* we are doing when we use tenses, but is quite unreal as a piece of linguistic explanation. As so often, what is alleged to be the structure of the Hebrew language is contrasted not with the structure of another language but with some hoary piece of traditional pseudo-logic. And what GK says about the *relation* of the speaking person to the action as complete and incomplete is grossly inflated to make the consciousness of this person central to the expression of all experience, so that he becomes contemporary with it all. The whole series of connections which Boman makes between 'simultaneity' and the verb system of Hebrew have not arisen from data discovered by linguists which required explanation by such connections; they have been brought into being because certain mental points of view such as this 'simultaneity' perception of history are believed to have existed, and because it is assumed to be obvious that peculiarities in the linguistic structure will naturally be related to such points of view.[2]

There remain some further points about the Hebrew verb which should be made. I would not presume to give any kind of full treatment of the Hebrew verb here, or even a sketch of the principal points about it. All I shall say is certain things which have a bearing upon the discussion we have been carrying on.

First of all, a little more about the Hebrew verb and time.

[1] Boman, op. cit., p. 125; E.T., p. 145.
[2] On problems of time and aspect in verbs, apart from the specific work on Hebrew grammar, see especially G. Koschmieder, *Zeitbezug und Sprache*; G. Guillaume, *Temps et verbe*. For Hebrew I would add H. B. Rosen, 'Aspektim u-zmanim ba-ivrit ha-mikrait'.

Assuming with most modern grammarians that the opposition of the two tenses in Hebrew is not an opposition of time (such as past and future or past and present) but some kind of aspect difference (commonly stated as that between completed and incompleted action), there is a certain reason which should be urged against the drawing of exaggerated conclusions from this fact. I refer to the fact, which seems to me to be clear, that what is signified by the opposition structure of the two tenses and the choice between them is only a part of, or an abstraction from, the complete signification of an action done or to be done which is conveyed by the use of the verb. Conversely, what is not marked by the opposition structure of the tenses is not necessarily something of which the Hebrew speakers and hearers were unaware. Surely in the vast majority of cases the Hebrews were perfectly aware whether events referred to, whether as completed or as incompleted action, had already taken place (begun to take place) or would later take place; and were able to communicate accordingly.

The main point here is that tense distinctions are abstractions which from among the many characteristics of a complex action pick out a certain one or two only which will correspond to a morphological differential structure running throughout the verbal system. In the description of an action such different questions may be relevant for information as: orientation in past, present or future time; continuous or repeated action; commencement of action, or attempted action; action momentary or durative; action complete or incomplete. This list is by no means exhaustive. Only certain of these differences are systematized as a differential organization running throughout the verb system, i.e. as tenses and the like. Others may be expressed where specially necessary by other means, e.g. with particles[1] or lexically through particular word-formations.[2] The main point is that systematic morphological distinctions such as tense are abstractions from the totality of an action referred to; but a reference to such an action signifies the

---

[1] E.g., in modern Hebrew, where the tense called 'perfect' in classical Hebrew is a past tense, the sense of the English perfect (*he has finished* as distinct from *he finished*) is very commonly expressed when specially needed by the particle *kvar* 'already'.

[2] Cf. for example the 'inchoative' use of verbs in -*sco* in Latin.

action and may include in the mental picture of the hearer of such
a reference elements which are not referred to in the tense system.
We come here to a fact about language which is well expressed in
Kronasser's phrase, used in another connection: 'Das Unver-
mögen der Sprache, komplexive Gebilde ganzheitlich zu erfassen.'[1]
Much of what is written about Hebrew in the literature we are
surveying seems to want to exempt Hebrew from pronouncements
of this kind about the nature of language.

It would therefore seem dangerous to use the existence of an
aspect system in Hebrew too confidently as a guide to a peculiar
understanding of actions and events and their relation to time.

This point is important in another connection. If what I have
said is approximately true, it means that there is a possibility of
translating Hebrew into a language which does not have a tense
differentiation based on aspect, without giving a seriously misleading impression. As I shall argue later, some forms of theological
interpretation so emphasize the peculiarity of Hebrew and the
reflection of the thought structure by the language that they lead in
principle to the untranslatability of the Bible.

Naturally there may be a loss in any translation, and this is not
at issue. For tenses in particular, it is difficult or impossible to
indicate in English that a form translated in one place with an
English future (let us say) is the same form as in another place is
translated by an English past continuous. In this however there is
nothing peculiar to biblical translation, for the same situation
might arise, for example, in translating a Greek 'gnomic' aorist; or,
conversely, one might wish to translate both of the Greek infinitives βάλλειν and βαλεῖν as 'throw', since the circumlocutions
which can express the difference are cumbrous unless circumstances specially demand them. Secondly, it must be asked
whether an inability to represent these relations is at all a failure
in a translation. I would add that those Semitic linguists who
emphasize the 'aspect' nature of the tense system do not seem too
embarrassed by the need to provide translations of the forms they
are discussing.

---

[1] Kronasser, op. cit., p. 86 (title of chapter 9). In English: 'The incapability of
language to comprehend complex formations as totalities'.

Another point which is relevant for an assessment of the Hebrew verbal system is the nominal origin of certain elements of it. This is especially noticeable in the perfect, so much so that Bauer and Leander wanted to rename it as the 'nominal'. Thus Driver writes: 'The later tense-form *qata/i/ula* arose out of the affixing of the pronominal elements to the nominal forms *qata/i/ul*'.[1] Thus the origin of *qaṭal* 'he killed' is in a type of agent noun 'killer', and we can explain *qaṭal-ta* as from 'killer — you' and hence 'you killed'. As Driver points out, the same process repeats itself later in the individual languages, e.g. in the type of the Accadian permansive with pronoun suffix, as *šarrāku* 'I am king' and *ṣabtāku* 'I am an acquirer', and hence 'I have acquired', and the Syriac participial formation as *qāṭel-(')nā* 'I am a killer', hence 'I kill'. From this nominal origin we can explain why with the active verbs the sense of completed action is normal, and this often in the past but possibly also in the future, while in verbs referring to mental conditions and the like the reference is commonly to present time.

I do not wish to over-emphasize this, and no doubt what I have said is a historical statement about the origin of the Hebrew perfect rather than a descriptive statement about its classical function. Nevertheless these facts must be given their true value as a corrective of exaggerated views of the wholly verb-based character of Hebrew thinking. Those who feel that the traditional logic with its reduction of 'I killed' to an expression with substantive and copula, 'I am a killer', or of ἄνθρωπος βαδίζει to ἄνθρωπος βαδίζων ἐστί, is destructive of the dynamism of action, and that a logic expressing the dynamic action of verbs might find some inspiration in Hebrew thought, must give due weight to this nominal derivation of important parts of the Hebrew verb system. Some peculiarity in the pattern of differentiation between nouns and verbs has too often been assumed and used (*a*) without taking into account certain important and recognized facts about the Hebrew linguistic

---

[1] *Hebrew Verbal System*, p. 10 f.; cf. Bauer, 'Die Tempora im Semitischen'; BL § 42 f.; Brockelmann, *Hebräische Syntax*, § 40, and *ZfPh* v (1951) 133–54, with literature there cited; T. W. Thacker, *The Relationship of the Semitic and Egyptian Verbal Systems* (Oxford, 1954); recently also P. Wernberg-Møller, 'Observations on the Hebrew Participle', *ZATW* lxxi (1959) 54–67.

structure, such as the one just discussed[1] (*b*) without any general survey of noun and verb functions within language generally.

Under this latter head, one would have to examine in general how far the existence of a separate morphological category of verbs is necessary for the linguistic representation of action. I mention this because most of those theologians who are most emphatic about the verb as being the basis for dynamic Hebrew thought, and this thought as being the basis for Christianity, are constantly using action nouns and not verbs to describe those events which are supremely important to them, e.g. 'the Incarnation', 'the Resurrection'. By 'the Incarnation' they mean just the same degree of activity and dynamism as 'Jesus was born' or 'the Word became flesh'. It is of course *possible* that the use of the action noun may be accompanied by a shifting of the thought away into less 'event-ful' realms, for example by the use of 'Incarnation' for a principle rather than an event. But it is absurd to suggest that this follows necessarily from the use of the action noun. The action noun is used because it is more convenient for use within a certain kind of context than the verbal expression of the same event; for example, a wide range of connections, such as 'the unique significance of the Incarnation', are made much less awkwardly than with the verbal expression of the same event.

[1] Boman, for example, must surely have known of the theory that the Hebrew perfect is of nominal origin, for it is discussed in a note by Pedersen (*Israel* i–ii. 512, n. to p. 114). The existence of this theory gives no pause to Boman in his eagerness to derive everything possible from the verb.

Another illustration of Boman's method may be added, since it concerns the matters which we have been discussing. In a footnote (op. cit., p. 180, n. 299; E.T., p. 144 n.) he mentions Birkeland's opinion that the 'consecutive' imperfect in Hebrew (like *way-yomer* 'and he said') represents the past time (and not the aspect of completed action). Now Boman has just said that the 'Indo-European' interest in past, present and future is quite foreign to the Semitic idea of time, and disposes of Birkeland's suggestion by saying that, if he is right in it, then 'the consecutive forms contribute nothing to the illumination of the peculiar Israelite-Semitic conception of time'. This seems to me to be a blatant choosing of the linguistic material which you will allow to be relevant for the delineation of the Hebrew mind; it means that you know already what is the outline of that mind, that you illustrate it from linguistic evidence, and that when linguistic material does not fit in you can just rule it irrelevant. Similarly, after committing himself to a close correspondence of Hebrew thought and language, can he say that the placing of the verb first in the sentence is 'psychologically indifferent' (op. cit., p. 108; E.T., p. 127)? Cf. also on p. 27; E.T., p. 37, the assertion that a grammatical difference has no conceptual relevance, but is only grammatical-stylistic.

In the Synoptic Gospels the word κήρυγμα is found only once, while the verb is much more frequent. To Friedrich[1] the absence of the noun is not accidental, and shows that stress is not laid on the proclamation itself as if it were some new thing in its own content and meaning, like a new doctrine or a new vision of God. 'Rather the decisive thing is the action, the event of the preaching itself', and so on. It must be clear that this argument is quite without foundation, and whatever truth there may be in Friedrich's assessment of the nature of the Gospel as event, it has precisely nothing to do with the choice between noun and verb as markers of action. The idea that the use of a noun means the avoidance of expression of action, though typical of this theological school, is a quite wrong assumption and demonstrates a serious failure to think about linguistic structure.[2]

We may here conclude our study of arguments based on the Hebrew verb system, and it must be concluded with a negative judgement on those attempts which have been made to see that system as a correlate or reflection of certain features of Hebrew thinking as a whole. In particular we have seen that certain arguments which correlate the place of the verb in the linguistic structure with the 'dynamism' of Hebrew thought have no good foundation. I do not say that no such connection is possible at all. What is clear is that to approach it one would have to abandon the haphazard methods we have described; to relate the question to a general linguistic study of the function of verbs within various systems; and above all abandon the prejudice, sharpened in this particular case at the present time by the interests of biblical theology, that some such kind of correlation *must* be there somewhere to be found — in other words accept as a possibility of research that there may in the end be no such special correlation of

---

[1] *TWNT* iii. 702; cf. H. Diem, *Dogmatics*, p. 113.

[2] Cf. Snaith, *Distinctive Ideas of the Old Testament*, p. 174: 'Hebrew has very few abstract nouns . . . The Hebrews did not think of love as an idea or as an abstraction, they thought of it as an activity. Here, as always, their emphasis was on what happens. *This is why* the Hebrew verb ᵓaheb occurs in overwhelming proportions as against the noun.' (My italics.) This assertion has the same faults in general as that of Friedrich above; its accuracy in point of fact is also questionable, for in the Song of Songs, where one might expect to find a typical Hebrew feeling for the subject of love, the noun is more frequent than the verb.

Hebrew thought and Hebrew language as a whole school of interpreters has tried to demonstrate.

DETACHED NOTE

Earlier Studies connecting verbs with Action and Dynamism

The supposed special prominence of the verb in Hebrew was
very strongly emphasized by Herder. The chief passage[1] is as
follows:

'E. Let us proceed first to consider the structure of the language.
Did you not say, that action and vivid imagery was the essence of
poetry? and what part of speech paints or sets forth action itself to
view, the noun, or the verb?
A. The verb.
E. So the language, that abounds in verbs, which present a vivid
expression and picture of their objects, is a poetical language. The
more too it has the power of forming its nouns into verbs, the more
poetical it is. The noun always exhibits objects only as lifeless
things, the verb gives them action, and this awakens feeling, for it
is itself as it were animated with a living spirit. . . . Now with the
Hebrew the verb is almost the whole of the language. In other
words every thing lives and acts. The nouns are derived from
verbs, and in a certain sense are still verbs. They are as it were
living beings, extracted and moulded, while their radical source
itself was in a state of living energy. . . . The language, of which we
are speaking, is an abyss of verbs, a sea of billows, where motion,
action, rolls on without end.'

A. now reasonably objects:

'It seems to me however, that this abundance must always maintain a certain proportion to the other parts of speech; for if all be
action, there is nothing, that acts. There must be the *subject*,
predicate and *copula* — so says logick.'

Hence E. is able to answer that poetry is one thing and logic
another. A.'s objection was a good one, but he rather spoiled it by
making his appeal to logic. In fact, as A. saw, there have to be some

---

[1] J. G. Herder, *The Spirit of Hebrew Poetry* (translated by J. Marsh, Burlington, 1833, 2 vols.) i. 29–30.

things to act and be acted on, and the idea that the Hebrew nouns 'in a certain sense are still verbs' must have put some strain on his common sense. In general, for what it is worth, one may doubt whether a count of the proportion of verbs and nouns in a Hebrew passage and in a Greek passage of comparable literary type would produce a disparity such as Herder's statements would lead one to expect.

Herder was also impressed by 'the roots of the Hebrew verbs' which, he believed, 'combine form and feeling' in a quite remarkable way (ibid., p. 33, cf. p. 36), and with the absence of time distinctions in the verb system (ibid., p. 37).

In view of this emphasis on the verb as the centre of Hebrew speech in contrast with the Greek, it is amusing to note that according to Stenzel[1] Goethe regarded expression through verbs, especially through participles and infinitives, as typical of Greek in contrast with Latin, which uses substantives in a sense we might now call static. Stenzel himself, though he regards Goethe's opinion as one-sided, goes on to speak of a dominance (*Vorherrschaft*) of the verb in Greek. In his opinion we should not be deceived by the grammatical form of phrases like 'the good' or 'the right'. 'All the so-called ethical concepts have according to their structure much more relatedness to the verbal' (p. 161). Stenzel believes that a drive towards substantival expression sets in after Socrates; the use predominantly of nominal expressions, hastily attributed to Latin by Goethe, is well established by Aristotle's time. He concludes (p. 163) that a certain agreement has been demonstrated between the verbal structure of Greek and the Greek formation of concepts.

I may perhaps add that there are interesting similarities in method generally between Stenzel's essay and some of the treatments of biblical language which I have discussed. He too is sympathetic to Humboldt and begins from the work of the latter (p. 153; cf. pp. 155, 159 and 161 n.); he notices Humboldt's interest in the national, and mentions how for a man like Fichte the

---

[1] J. Stenzel, 'Ueber den Einfluss der griechischen Sprache auf die philosophische Begriffsbildung', in *Neue Jahrbücher für das klassische Altertum* xlvii (1921) 152–64 and in his *Kleine Schriften*.

living unity of thought and language is a matter of deepest national pathos. Within the linguistic detail, he finds the existence of a Middle in Greek of great significance, in contrast of course to Latin which has none. In the Middle the form does not clearly state whether I act or am the object of another's activity; its reference is to an inner experience or to inner participation in the activity. 'Alle die verschiedenen Bedeutungen des Mediums weisen auch im Griechischen auf ein "Erfahren im Innern" hin, wie Humboldt es bezeichnet, auf die für das Subjekt lust- oder unlustvolle innere Stellungnahme zu der im Verbum ausgedrückten Tätigkeit.' The similarity of this to Boman's treatment of the Hebrew stative verb ('an activity of the subject, emerging from within'; see above, p. 55) is very noticeable.

Stenzel also very naturally uses for Greek the same argument which Boman uses for Hebrew, namely the absence of a time reference in the verb; it refers to a *kind* of action, and the temporal fixation, important to other languages, is left to the context to determine (p. 157).

I do not quote these passages to suggest that Stenzel's assessment of Greek is more correct than Boman's of Hebrew, but for the sake of the parallels in method. They sympathize with the same philosophy of language, and they find very similar linguistic characteristics to be in close correlation with certain ways of thinking. Yet in one case the language is Greek and in the other it is Hebrew.

It is interesting also to see that L. Weisgerber, whose approach to language in general has something in common with Boman's, considers the contrast pairs intuitive (*anschaulich*) — abstract and dynamic — static to be suitable for the characterizing of yet another language, the German. In contrast with the Romance languages it is both intuitive and dynamic. In developing this thesis Weisgerber maintains for German just what Boman does for Hebrew, namely, that it has a much greater emphasis on the verb than is found in the contrasting languages. See his *Vom Weltbild der deutschen Sprache*, pp. 195–212 and generally; also his *Muttersprache und Geistesbildung*. Weisgerber's statements about the dynamism of the German language and its relation to a fundamental dynamism of the German relation to the external world (*Weltbild*, p. 211) need only to have the word 'Hebrew' substituted and they represent exactly Boman's assessment of the latter language.

When one finds such diverse languages being alike associated with 'the dynamic' and with its expression through the dominance of the verb, one wonders whether the impulse towards such an association does not come from some uncriticized philosophical heritage.[1]

---

[1] For the dependence of Stenzel in his understanding of language on German idealism, and on von Humboldt, cf. his *Philosophie der Sprache* (*Handbuch der Philosophie*, Abteilung iv., Munich and Berlin, 1934); e.g. the statement that 'the philosophical world-outlook of German idealism, whose new concept of reality was surprisingly well adapted to the spiritual-sensual nature of language' was of the greatest advantage to von Humboldt (p. 5). Cf. also his 'Die Bedeutung der Sprachphilosophie W. von Humboldts für die Probleme des Humanismus', *Logos* x (1922) 261-74.

Chapter Five

Other Arguments from Morphological and Syntactic Phenomena

THE CONSTRUCT STATE

In a passage expounding the concrete character of Hebrew thought we read:

'Instead of an adjective qualifying a noun the Hebrew language prefers to place two concrete nouns in the close relation of the construct state; there *must* be a connection between this grammatical peculiarity and the evident desire of the Hebrew to *see* the object of which the noun was a name'. . . .[1]

Similarly Pedersen writes:[2]

'If I say "oxen brass" (2 Kings 16: 17), then I call forth an image combining oxen and brass: brass oxen. This combination may be so intimate that two nouns also formally coalesce into one conception, through that which is called the *status constructus*. It is formed by putting first the word in which the chief interest centres, but it is designated as a link of the immediately following, this being specially emphasized, and so the form of the former word is modified. "House — mán" means that the two pictures form a unity, but the house belongs to the totality of the man. Thus three boys can be designated either as "triad boys" or "boys triad" or "triad — bóys". The nominal phrase is formed by modifying the image presented, thus enriching it by assimilating new nominal images. . . .'

How far can the construct state really be taken as evidence of a mental tendency to see things or combinations of things as totalities, to let them coalesce into one conception, to form connections

---

[1] Knight, op. cit., p. 8; my italics at '*must*'. Cf. above, p. 29.
[2] Op. cit., i–ii. 113 f.

not by adding things to each other but by giving first the image of one thing and then allowing it to be modified by another with which it forms a new totality-image, and so on, in any way different from associative processes used by speakers of other languages than Hebrew? In particular, to take an example, how far does *bet ham-melek* 'the king's house' differ in these respects from (say) *domus regis* with the same meaning? I repeat that my purpose here is not to make any full structural comparison but to examine how far the Hebrew phenomenon provides a case for any special way of thinking.[1]

Apart from the presence of the article, which has of course nothing corresponding in the Latin phrase, the main structural difference apparent between *bet ham-melek* and *domus regis* is that in the former the word *bet* 'house' has been 'modified' as Pedersen puts it (from absolute *bayit*) to form the construct, while in the latter *regis* is in the genitive and *domus* unchanged. It is to this difference that all the attention is usually drawn when the peculiarity of the Hebrew construct relation is discussed. In each case the combination once formed can be kept intact as a unit, e.g. as subject or object or in an adverbial relation, with only change of case in *domus* and no change at all in Hebrew which has no 'case' inflexions.

The peculiarity of the Hebrew construct relation then can be found only in two points: (*a*) that it is the first word, 'house', that is 'modified'; (*b*) that the order within the unit cannot be changed and the parts of it cannot be separated.

(*a*) The modification of the first word is not essential to the

---

[1] Since it is my purpose only to discuss the construct state as such, I shall only mention certain criticisms of Pedersen's statement in other respects, namely: (*a*) the appositional type of 'oxen brass' is a different thing from the construct state connection, and it is rather doubtful if Pedersen is not confusing us here by including under 'nominal combinations' all of which display a 'continued totality-formation' three types, firstly the nominal sentence *ʾiš ṭob* 'a man is good', secondly the appositional type of 'oxen brass', and thirdly the construct type; (*b*) it seems to me tendentious and unjustified to suggest that the construct connection arises when the combination is specially 'intimate' and produces a formal coalescence of the words 'into one conception'; (*c*) the use of 'triad' for the number 'three' presupposes the theory of the Hebrew numerals as abstracts, a theory which was certainly widely accepted but which has, I think, been replaced by a more likely explanation which will be mentioned later in this chapter.

construct relation. The word was not modified in order to put it into the combination, but became modified under certain circumstances because it was in the combination, by vowel reduction through loss of accent. Generally speaking only short vowels in open syllables were reduced, and in words where such vowels did not occur no modification took place.[1] In Arabic the construct is as well established as in Hebrew, and there is no normal modification of the word apart from the absence of nunation, which is used (like the article) only on the last noun of a series if at all.[2] If we construct a form earlier than that of classical Hebrew, we find (with case endings) *baytu malki, which is quite close to domus regis.

The modification of the first word of a construct group is not, then, essential to the structure, and it thus becomes very difficult to maintain Pedersen's conception of a psychological process in which 'house' is presented in a modified form in order to enrich it by associating it to other images. It becomes indeed difficult to argue from the construct state to any peculiar mental attitudes at all. All modifications which are found in the construct forms are normal vowel shifts under the accent conditions obtaining. It is true of course that the accent change which led to these vowel shifts was itself caused by the juxtaposition of the words with a reduction of stress on the first element. It is difficult however to make much of this for the outlines of the Hebrew mind.

(b) It is true and quite noticeable that in Latin domus regis the order can be reversed and the words separated by a good deal of intervening matter; this cannot be done in Hebrew, where the elements of a construct-state group must be kept together and in a certain order.[3] It must be regarded as precarious however to argue

---

[1] This statement is of course a simplification of the process which produced the construct forms extant; for example the change bayt > bet is not by reduction of a short vowel but by monophthongization of ay when unaccented or when with secondary stress only, BL § 17 v.

[2] The familiar plural endings in the absolute, i.e. -m in Hebrew and -na, -ni in Arabic, which appear to drop off in the construct, are themselves an addition, and their absence in the construct is the preservation of an earlier state, cf. BL § 63 g; Bergsträsser, Einführung, p. 14, etc.

[3] There are certain exceptions about keeping the words together; e.g. adverbial phrases of locality sometimes come between the two elements of the combination, especially where the first is a participle, cf. Brockelmann, Hebräische Syntax, § 70 f.

that the group represents a specially 'total' perception of the combination of the units, just because the words must be kept together in this order. In English too the order is more or less mandatory in ordinary usage, e.g. we can say 'the king's house' but not 'house the king's'.

One may also perhaps relevantly mention the productive class of compounds in Indo-European. In οἰκοδεσπότης, οἶκος 'house' and δεσπότης 'master' are united just as 'intimately' as the 'formal coalescence' of the Hebrew construct; and in certain types of compound, such as this example, there is a 'modification' of one element in that it appears without the case ending and in a form in which it cannot appear independently. For our example 'king's house' compare the Gothic *piudangardi* (Lk. 7: 25, etc.).

In all this I have no intention of suggesting that there is nothing in the Hebrew construct mechanism different from common Indo-European structures. I do suggest however that the claims for the peculiarity of the construct relation made in the quotations at the beginning of this chapter must be greatly relativized, and that the likelihood of deriving any radically different psychology of the association of objects from the construct relation is a very much thinner one than has been claimed.

It is however, I believe, worth while to notice at this example how the procedures of a standard learner's grammar can have a powerful effect upon the interpretation of a structure like the construct. The familiar, and long standard, *Hebrew Grammar* of A. B. Davidson begins its treatment of the construct forms by insisting that in cases like 'the palace of the king' 'the point is that the two words together make up one idea'. Now the first element 'son of — ' or 'palace of — ' is 'no complete idea in itself'; therefore the emphasis lies on the second part. The first half is hurried, and 'the construct is uttered as shortly as is possible in consistency with the laws of pronunciation in the language'.

Thus the whole explanation here begins from the notion of a 'complete idea', and is thus in a way akin to the kind of evaluation of the construct which we have just been discussing; it is clear that those who have learned their Hebrew from a grammar like Davidson's will be prone to believe those conclusions from the construct phenomenon which I have been criticizing. The reason for Davidson's procedure which begins from the 'complete idea' lies partly in the lack of a historical perspective and partly in the giving of a mental-logical perspective to replace it. The previous history of the absolute and construct forms is neglected, and so the explanations given are as if the construct were formed from the present form of the absolute. It is of course possible, given an extant absolute form, to form the construct from it by rules like Davidson's, with of course some exceptions or special cases. But the process of forming the construct from the classical absolute form is not the process through which the classical construct was in fact formed. Therefore the explanation of the construct form cannot be a historical one. Now it would not matter if no historical explanation were given, for a purely descriptive account of the construct with no historical suggestions could quite validly be given; it would simply register the extant construct forms tabulated against the extant absolute forms. But Davidson does not want to leave it at that, and wants to give a reason. But because he does not trace the historical process of formation he has to produce as his reason a special mental process the effect of which is to lead by the 'rules of pronunciation' to the construct forms actually found. The mental process has thus done for the form what a historical study should have done, i.e. has tried to explain why the form is what it is. This kind of procedure in grammar I shall call 'logicism', since I do not know a better word. My use of it differs from that of Serrus,[1] who means by it 'a scholastic attitude which consists in explaining a grammatical form always by a logical form which one makes to correspond with it', only in that the general mental attitudes invoked in the material I am criticizing might hardly be called 'logical forms'.

Some further remarks may be added. Firstly, Davidson is not consistent in avoiding a historical approach, e.g. when he mentions the lost case endings (§ 17. 1) or the previous form *malk of the 'segholate' type melek. Generally it seems that he put in historical matter if he felt that it would help in the immediate task of learning, as *malk certainly does.

[1] Op. cit., p. 142.

Secondly, Davidson has to use a normative conception of grammatical 'rules'. The rules are principles which have power to dictate the forms possible. The 'one idea' notion of groups like 'the house of the king' requires the first element of the group to be hurried over and therefore made as short as possible; but it can only be as short as is consistent with the laws of pronunciation. But these 'laws', even where they indeed fit the facts, are not norms which had power to delimit the forms permissible; at most they are only constatations of the patterns actually found.

But Davidson does not set them down as a mere constatation of the phenomena as they are; the 'rules' include a good deal purporting to be accounts of changes occurring under certain influences. The processes described are not a historical account of Hebrew sound-shifts but are in some cases invented processes which lead logically from one extant form to another, e.g. from the extant absolute of a noun to the extant construct. Thus from abs. בְּרָכָה we would get by fullest shortening *בְּרְכַת, and 'בְּרְ must by rule (the rule that two vocal shewas cannot come together) become 'בְּרְ giving us the extant form בִּרְכַת. Historically, however, the vowel i is not one raised from shewa because two shewas cannot come together, but is the a of the original *barakatu (with short vowels), which became i by a normal shift in closed unaccented syllables, just as it became shewa by a normal shift in certain other conditions. Davidson does mention this former shift (p. 28). In general then it would be more accurate to say that 'the rules' are a kind of short-circuiting of actual linguistic processes; thus they are occasionally accidentally accurate but often widely divergent from the changes which in fact occurred.

Thus (a) the normative use of the rules obscures any lines which might lead to a historical explanation of the forms as they are, and (b) since norms of this kind are not explanations at all, but merely requirements laid down, no one knows by whom (perhaps the genius of the Hebrew language), all the more weight is thrown upon the logicistic approach through the 'one idea', which is the only element in the presentation which appears to be truly explanatory. Thus grammars of this kind which are not truly descriptive either synchronously or diachronously tend to produce a prejudice in favour of the connection of a peculiar grammatical phenomenon with the special features of the Hebrew mind.

Thirdly, it is well-known that Davidson's explanation of the construct as being essentially a modification of the word by shortening does not always work. In the type of מַחֲנֶה 'camp' the final vowel of the construct מַחֲנֵה was a long vowel according to Davidson's own principles, while that of the absolute מַחֲנֶה by the same principles was normally a short one. Even if it is wrong to distinguish these vowels as long and short, no one can maintain that the construct here involved a shortening of the word. In fact these vowels have to be explained as effects of different accent relations on the diphthong *ay*, effects which are normal throughout the language and have nothing to do with the construct state and its meaning (cf. BL § 17 o, v).

Fourthly, it would seem that a large element in Davidson's method was a kind of apologetic, a strong effort to show to students that Hebrew, bewildering as it seemed to them, was very regular and 'methodical almost to the point of being mechanical' (p. 3). This is why historical material which must have been known to Davidson is not used as a rule unless it seems to have some paedagogic value; this is why what I call 'logicism' is prominent. The most extreme example of it, and one which Davidson himself can hardly have meant seriously, is this:

'If he (the learner) goes forward to the study of the language with a faith in its regularity, he will find its very phonetic and grammatical principles to be instinct with something of that sweet reasonableness, that sense of fair play, we might almost say that passion for justice, for which the Old Testament in the sphere of human life so persistently and eloquently pleads.' A footnote quotes Deut. 16: 20: 'Justice, justice shalt thou pursue', and promises that grammatical 'illustrations of the principle of compensation' will appear in the course of the grammar.[1]

I do not say these things about this grammar in order to discredit a work which has seen long and honoured service. It remains true that this grammar itself, and perhaps others using similar arguments, are only slowly going out of use; and will

[1] Davidson, op. cit., p. 3.

certainly have been the main introduction to Hebrew of many of those theologically interested people who may wish to judge the truth of what I have said about the construct state or other phenomena of Hebrew. My main point is that where a grammar does not strictly follow linguistic method, historical or descriptive, it is not unlikely to produce powerfully logicistic and linguistically unscientific attitudes to linguistic phenomena. What may be an adequate guide to a reading knowledge of Hebrew is not necessarily a guide to the assessment of linguistic structures in their relation to thought.

THE NUMERALS

Boman[1] follows the fairly widespread theory that the Hebrew numerals are abstract nouns in origin. This theory was mainly supported from the fact that the numeral with a masculine noun has the form of the feminine type (e.g. *šelošah* 'three'; contrast the simpler form *šaloš* with a feminine noun); and since the feminine is often used to form abstracts, the numbers can be taken in the same way. But Boman like the whole school of thought which we are examining holds the Israelites to have been opposed mentally to all abstraction, and so does not take the abstract form of the numerals as a token of abstract thought. Rather they are collectives. 'The smallest and fundamental numerals were felt to be qualitatively different totalities.'[2] In other words, number is not a counting up of the units but a quality of the given group. To think of arithmetical quantity is to hinder understanding of the Hebrew conception.

One or two comments may be made on this explanation. The theory that the abstract form is the original form for Semitic numerals, and that the 'masculine-type' form (as used with feminine nouns) is a later analogical extension, has been well

---

[1] Boman, op. cit., pp. 142–6; E.T., pp. 163–8. Pedersen's use of 'triad' and 'septiad' (*Israel* i–ii. 113 f., cf. above, p. 89), implies the same theory; cf. his *Hebraeisk Grammatik*, § 102 c.

[2] Ibid., p. 144; E.T., p. 166. Note the form of Boman's argument here: (*a*) the numerals are in origin abstract nouns (*b*) we can disregard the possibility that the Israelites had a special capability for abstract thought (*c*) therefore the numbers must have been thought of as qualitatively different totalities. The assumed ethno-psychology is decisive in the interpretation of language.

criticized by Driver, in an article in which he offers another explanation.[1] He suggests that the termination -*t* arose here as a collective indicator. It was not used with the feminine nouns because they already had the -*t*, but with the masculine nouns, which mostly did not have this termination, it was added to the numeral. The importance of this for our investigation is that we can omit any idea of an abstract or a quality of 'fourness' or a term like 'triad' or 'septiad' in the interpretation of the numerals. The peculiar form of the Semitic numerals has to be traced like many other, or all, linguistic phenomena to a formal linguistic basis and is not a clue to an extraordinary way of conceiving quantities.

A second point in Boman's treatment of the numerals is his attempt to find 'dynamism' in them as elsewhere in the language. Number is for the Hebrews 'not spatial-quantitative, but dynamic-qualitative'. His proof of this is by interpreting words of size and number as deverbative. They come from verbs and therefore 'originally' or 'properly' indicate an activity. Thus *šᵉnayim* 'two' comes from the verb *šanah* 'double, repeat, do again', *qaṭon* 'small' from the verb *qaṭan* 'be or become small', *rab* 'many, great' from the verb *rabab* with the 'fundamental' meaning of 'become thick or dense'. The word *min* 'from', used in comparisons like English 'than', means first of all 'from'. Saul was taller by a head than the people, that is, away from the people; he stuck up away above all the others, clearly a dynamic action. The emptiness of this kind of argument, and its dependence on a prejudice in favour of some kind of verbal origin for everything possible, should be clear from what I have said in connection with the verb.

A third point which is mentioned by Boman is interesting as an illustration, if in itself unprofitable. Following a passage in Cassirer,[2] he thinks that the act of counting may perhaps be

---

[1] 'Gender in Hebrew Numerals', *JJS* i (1948–9) 90–104. Cf. also Brockelmann, *Hebräische Syntax*, § 84 a, and literature cited there. Some other theories, such as that of Bauer *ZDMG* lxvi (1912) 267–70, while differing from that of Driver, would have similar repercussions on arguments such as that of Boman.

[2] Boman, op. cit., p. 143; E.T., p. 165; E. Cassirer, *The Philosophy of Symbolic Forms* (New Haven, 1953), i. 244. This relating of the roots for 'thou' and 'two' appears only in very old-fashioned works and appears to have left no trace in modern works like Pokorny. Cf. already Brugmann and Delbrück, *Grundriss* (2nd ed.) ii/2. § 1, 5.

related originally to the perception of 'I', 'you' and 'he'. He goes on: 'In particular in Indo-European a common etymological root seems to have been proved for the expression "thou" and the expression "two"·'. He then notes that the Hebrew word for 'two', in contrast with this Indo-European phenomenon, has nothing to do with 'thou' or with any other person, or indeed with any visible or spatial phenomenon at all; then he derives it from the supposedly dynamic verbal origin in 'to repeat'. In itself, as I say, this argument is of little value, for the linguistic suggestions on both the Hebrew and the Indo-European sides are of extreme pre-cariousness. What is to be noted is that if the facts had been true but had been the other way round, that is, if the Hebrew word for 'two' had in fact some common origin with 'thou', one can hardly doubt that it would have been pointed out to us repeatedly as a supreme example of the personalism of Hebrew thought. The Hebrews, we would have been told, could not even count up to two without bringing in the 'I — Thou' relationship. But if a piece of such built-in personalism appears on the Indo-European side, as Boman in fact supposes it to appear here, it is not evaluated as such — because it is known in advance that it is on the Hebraic side that the personalism and dynamism will be found.

Thus a case where a semantic reference to the three 'persons' might more plausibly be found in Indo-European would be in the provision of three demonstratives in some languages, roughly corresponding to the deixis of what is 'beside me', 'beside you' and 'beside him': Latin *hic, iste, ille*; Armenian *-s, -d, -n*.[1] I do not attach special importance to these cases, and do not myself wish to prove anything from them. I quote the matter as an object lesson to show how an accepted contrast of Hebrew and European thought is applied as a presupposition in the selection and evaluation of linguistic data. The possibility that Hebrew data will exist which do not fit an interpretation as reflections of the Hebrew viewpoint, or that Indo-European data will exist which would equally well fit with the arguments used to relate linguistic data to the Hebrew viewpoint, is simply not considered.

[1] For the latter see H. Jensen, *Altarmenische Grammatik* (Heidelberg, 1959), ¡213, 441 ff.

I do not dispute the possibility that there are different psychological ways of perceiving number, such as are discussed by Cassirer in the passage quoted by Boman. For my present study I am not entering the question whether the Israelites may or may not have had a different way of perceiving number from that which we have. I only maintain that the arguments I have discussed, with their attempt to interpret words of number and quantity in accordance with the assumed pervasive dynamism of the Hebrew mind, fail dismally in this attempt and demonstrate a strong irresponsibility towards linguistic evidence.

By now one is expecting an argument about *kol* 'all', and Boman gives us it. This word is a substantive and means 'totality'; it is never in the plural like German *alle*. This 'totality' is not a multiplication of the individuals, such as we would take a totality to be; rather the totality is the given, the individual the derivative. We recollect that quantifiers like 'all' were among the subjects of the investigation of Basson and O'Connor. Suffice it to say at this point that the nominal nature of *kol* is a grammatical fact which does not necessarily lead to the idea of a special mental totality perception. The word is syntactically connected in much the same way with collectives (*kol haṣ-ṣo'n* 'all the sheep and goats'), with plurals (*kol ha-'anašim* 'all the men') and with singulars either determined (*kol hab-bayit* 'all the house') or undetermined (*kol 'iš* 'every man').

Boman's attempt to distinguish the Greek from the Hebrew understanding of number, on the ground that the former was spatial, visual and geometrical, and the latter none of these things, thus contains some very strained arguments; one more, which seems to me very fanciful, may now be mentioned. Hebrew has, Boman tells us, no expression for even the simplest geometrical figures such as 'triangle' or 'rectangle' — unlike the Greeks, to whom geometrical, spatial thinking was fundamental. 'The passive participles *rabua'* and *m'rubba'*, formed from the verbal stem *rb'*, are certainly translated "quadrangular", but have nothing to do with angles and visual notions. They mean simply: what has been made into a fourness.'[1] This seems to me a typically perverse piece

[1] Boman, op. cit., p. 142; E.T., p. 164.

of logicizing and etymologizing, of which we shall see other examples later, at the fatal cost of ignoring the obvious semantic value of the word in the contexts where it occurs. The sense 'made into a fourness' is a purely theoretical product, worked out from the theoretical sense of the 'verb stem *rbᶜ*' (which does not occur except in the participle-type forms we are discussing) as 'make into a fourness'. In the contexts where it is found it is quite impossible to apply 'made into a fourness' as the sense actually meant. In Exod. 27:1 for example we read: 'And you shall make the altar of shittim wood, five cubits in length and five cubits in breadth; *rabuaᶜ* shall the altar be, and its height three cubits.' It is hardly to be doubted that in this and similar cases the word means that the altar was square, and not for example made with four sides of all different lengths (which would still be 'made into a fourness') or as a parallelogram with four equal sides but angles of other than 90°. The neglect of the semantics of actual usage, and its replacement by theoretical argument, by logicistic grammar, or by etymologizing, is a sure sign of linguistic irresponsibility in this type of discussion.

ROOTS AND IDEAS

One of the types of argument which I shall criticize in this study is that which places excessive emphasis on the meaning of the 'root' of Hebrew words. It seems to be commonly believed that in Hebrew there is a 'root meaning' which is effective throughout all the variations given to the root by affixes and formative elements, and that therefore the 'root meaning' can confidently be taken to be part of the actual semantic value of any word or form which can be assigned to an identifiable root; and likewise that any word may be taken to give some kind of suggestion of other words formed from the same root. This belief I shall for the sake of brevity call 'the root fallacy'.

It is of course true that in Hebrew words, especially those of the common triconsonantal pattern, there is a fairly characteristic stability of the consonant series along with variation of the vocalism for different forms, so that it becomes possible for practical purposes to speak of the consonant sequence as the 'root'. Thus we may say that *q-ṭ-l* is the 'root' with the general sense of 'kill', and from it we have such forms as *qaṭal* 'he killed', *qoṭel* 'killing' (participle), *qeṭel* 'slaughter', *hiqṭil* 'he caused to kill' and so on. Not only is there a somewhat notable permanence in the consonant sequence, but the existence of it is ceaselessly pointed out to students learning the language[1] — it becomes easy therefore to place too great a reliance on it.

Such an excessive reliance may be seen in a statement like this: 'Stems in Hebrew are considered to contain three consonantal letters. The noun may be regarded as expressing the stem idea in *rest*, and the verb the idea in *motion*. Hence the vowels of the verb are lighter than those of the noun.'[2]

A still stronger statement is this: 'There is no sharp distinction between the various classes of words; this is one of the fundamental characteristics of the Semitic languages. To the root *mlk* the signification of "kinghood" attaches itself, and according to the modification of the word it may mean the king, the kingdom and the fact of acting as a king.'[3]

This is simply not true. The great word-classes known as 'parts of speech' are very distinct in Semitic, though there may be fewer than in many Indo-European languages, depending on how the classification is made; thus Bloomfield[4] speaks of six for English and three for Semitic. 'The root *mlk*' is an abstraction, and all extant forms are readily distinguishable as 'king' or 'kingdom' or 'ruling' in the various classes.[5]

An example of an excessive reliance on the root of Hebrew words, along with an attempt to justify this from the nature of Semitic thought, may be quoted here: 'One must remember that Semitic thought is different from Greek-European thought; it is not analytic but synthetic, not causal but interested in the inner interrelatedness . . . The radicals of a root often have many "meanings" simultaneously which in our

[1] It may well be that the nature of the writing system, in which the main signs are for consonants, adds to this impression.
[2] Davidson, *Hebrew Grammar*, § 16.
[3] Pedersen, *Israel* i–ii. 110 f.   [4] *Language*, p. 198.
[5] For a criticism of the idea that the bearing of the 'root meaning' by the consonant sequence is a characteristically Semitic phenomenon, see E. Ullendorff, 'What is a Semitic language?', *Orientalia* xxvii (1958) 66–75.

eyes seem to have little or nothing to do with one another . . . In the root of a word the *thing* is there; the root is used in different applications, and these very applications belong together.'[1]

A moment's thought, however, should indicate that the 'meaning' of a 'root' is not necessarily part of the meaning of a derived form. Still less can it be assumed that two words having the same root suggest or evoke one another. A good case in point is the pair *leḥem* 'bread' and *milḥamah* 'war'. It must be regarded as doubtful whether the influence of their common root is of any importance semantically in classical Hebrew in the normal usage of the words. And it would be utterly fanciful to connect the two as mutually suggestive or evocative, as if battles were normally for the sake of bread or bread a necessary provision for battles. Words containing similar sound sequences may of course be deliberately juxtaposed for assonance, but this is a special case and separately recognizable.

In other words we have to distinguish between the more narrowly grammatical variation, e.g. the variation of different 'persons' in a verb, and what is word-formation. For example, *qaṭal* 'he killed', *qaṭalta* 'you killed' and *qaṭalti* 'I killed' are variations within a paradigm, i.e. a functional structure, observable throughout the verb system. But *leḥem* and *milḥamah* are both new word-formations from their 'root'; that is to say, for them the significance of the root is historical and is not a guide in itself to the sense of the words. For our purpose it is not necessary to define precisely where the boundary between the two types lies. I would think it safer, for example, to take the formation of the *hiphʿil* in a Hebrew verb as a new formation semantically rather than as a variation within a paradigm. This means that it may have its own semantic history; and hence its semantic value has to be determined for itself and not by a process of schematic reasoning from the *qal*, a process which may involve what I call 'logicism'. We shall see a case in which such an interpretation of the *hiphʿil* can be misleading.

A further cause for caution is the fact that the 'root' may not be

---

[1] W. C. van Unnik, 'Reisepläne und Amen-sagen', *Studia Paulina* (de Zwaan Festschrift), p. 220. I am grateful to Professor C. F. D. Moule for bringing this essay to my attention. For some remarks on the details involved in van Unnik's thesis, see below, p. 167 f.

extant at all, or extant not in Hebrew but in cognate languages, or not extant in the 'simple form' (more or less the verb *qal* perf. 3 sing. masc.) in which many dictionaries find it convenient to register the words. We shall see in a later chapter what harm can be done by giving over-emphasis to 'the root *ʾaman*', a form which can hardly be said to exist in Hebrew, by assuming the 'root meaning' to be dominant in derived forms like *ʾᵉmunah* and *ʾᵉmet*, and by neglecting correspondingly the particular semantic values of these nouns and of the derived form *heʾᵉmin*.

Thus we must regard as without foundation an argument such as the following, in a discussion of worship:[1]

'Λατρεύειν, which came in later theology to be the normal technical word for worship, means to serve, with the service of a hired labourer or slave. Significantly, there lies behind it the Hebrew word ᶜᵃ*bodah*, which is the same root as the noun ᶜ*ebed*: the Suffering Servant of the Lord, whose part Jesus assumed, is called in Hebrew the ᶜ*Ebed Yahweh*. The obedience of the Son of God, as the Suffering Servant of the Lord, is thus precisely the offering of λατρεία, or worship.'

Valuable as the general thought here is for the understanding of Christian worship, it must be evident that precisely nothing of value is contributed by the fact that the word for 'worship' and that for 'slave, servant' are from the same root in Hebrew. Though the Suffering Servant no doubt worshipped God, he was not so named because of this; his name does not mean 'worshipper' but 'servant', just as 'the servants of David' were not worshippers of that monarch but his officials and slaves. The connection made in the passage is a quite general association based neither on a semantic relation of the words, nor on any passage where conscious association takes place, nor on historical derivation of one word from the other, but purely on the possession of a common root.

In many cases the 'root fallacy' comes to much the same thing as 'etymologizing', i.e., giving excessive weight to the origin of a word as against its actual semantic value, a fault to which the next chapter will be devoted; and it will there be treated under the

---

[1] W. Nicholls, *Jacob's Ladder* (London, 1958), p. 15.

aspect mainly of lexicography rather than of morphology and syntax. It must however be mentioned here also, because the root fallacy is apparent in two of Boman's arguments which are general rather than applied to any particular words:

(a) His tendency to reduce everything he can to verbs is encouraged to some extent by the root fallacy. Thus the preposition *min* 'from' is interpreted by him as having a 'basic meaning' of 'dividing, separating'.[1] Hence an action of verbal type lies behind it. The suggestion is that the mere equivalence 'from' gives no adequate impression of the significance of the word. Observation however will suggest otherwise, and in fact the usual equivalences 'from', 'since' and 'than' give a perfectly good impression of the semantic value in most cases. In this case Boman makes a double use of the root fallacy; for he not only tries to give *min* the 'root meaning' but, since the root is taken to be a verb, he tries to impart to *min* something of the verbal character of action.

While talking about *min* we may before passing on mention another interpretation of it, this time by Pedersen, and in the interests of the idea of 'totality'.

'When we say that a man goes *from* one town to another, then the prepositions are meant to designate a starting point and a point of arrival, and for us the two towns play no other part in the sentence. To the Hebrew conception it is as if the man passes from making a *part* of the totality of one town to making a part of the totality of another town. The word *min*, which we translate by "from", characterizes something as a component of a totality.'[2]

I leave it to readers to consider whether the logic of this statement is not wholly fantastic, whether it is not a misuse of the 'root' of *min*, and whether if the thought was as Pedersen suggests we would not find in Hebrew two cases of *min*, one for the totality of the place you are coming from and another for the totality of the next place you are going to. It is surely rather peculiar to find that only the town you are leaving has its *min* or totality component mentioned. I admit that I have not quoted the whole of Pedersen's

---

[1] Boman, op. cit., p. 130; E.T., p. 150; see above, p. 76.
[2] *Israel* i–ii. 111; cf. the brief treatment also in his *Hebraeisk Grammatik*, § 109 d.

paragraph. In the latter part of it he goes on to assert that sometimes *min* should be translated 'in', 'at' or 'towards'; so when a
traveller is journeying towards the east he is in the east, forming a
part of the totality of these regions. Pedersen does not however
cite particular passages for this. In any case it seems a rather
different point, since he began quite explicitly from the case of
going from one town to another, which is not the same as travelling
in the east and towards the east. But I doubt whether the case as
put in the latter part of the paragraph is sound either.

(*b*) Only through liberal use of the 'root fallacy', I think, is it
possible for Boman to work out his surprising argument about the
similarity of the root of a Hebrew word to the Platonic Idea.

Boman begins from the notion of Hebrew terms as collectives.
They are not abstractions from a multiplicity of individual
phenomena, but real totalities which include individual things.
The general always dominates Hebrew thought. The word *moʾab*
suggests a type or sum (*Inbegriff*) of what is Moabite. The individual is named by the derivative form (*nisbeh* adjective) *moʾabi*.[1]
When the king of Moab acts, it is Moab that acts, for what is
Moabitic is involved in his actions. '*Moʾab* is thus strongly related
to a Platonic Idea of the Moabitic.'

Similarly there is no divorce between abstract and concrete.
ʿEṣ is not the concept of wood, but, like the Platonic idea of wood,
it is all the real stuff which has the qualities of wood. *ʾAdam* means
'man' and 'mankind', *rekeb* means 'a chariot' and 'chariotry'. *Tob* is
goodness, being good, and goods, that is, all that is good in various
forms. Thus there is no sharp distinction between the various
word-classes; the root *mlk* is 'royalty', and according to its
modification it can mean 'king', 'kingdom' and 'kingly action'.
Hence Boman says: 'If it is true that Hebrew roots express the
concept or idea, this means that the Semites are freely given in their
language something to which Plato attained only by a painful work

---

[1] Boman's discussion of the whole matter is op. cit., pp. 56–9; E.T., pp. 69–73.
The illustration from the Moabite is taken from Pedersen, *Israel* i–ii. 109 f.
Pedersen however does not mention any Platonic affinity here, nor in the passage
on p. 112 f., quoted by Boman, op. cit., p. 57 f.; E.T., p. 71, where Pedersen
says that Hebrew nouns designate 'the souls, the things, the ideas, that which is
and acts' — a passage which Boman takes to be a recognition of affinity with
Plato's theory of Ideas.

of thought.'[1] And so we conclude that, since in comparing Platonism and Yahwism one must be careful to compare like with like, the Platonic Idea of a thing must be compared with *the root of the Hebrew word*.[2]

I shall leave it to readers to judge for themselves whether there is any plausibility in the notion that the Hebrew root has some affinity with the Platonic Idea, and make only a few remarks.

Firstly, the evidence Boman uses to support his thesis is by no means drawn from the whole field of the Hebrew language. Many of the words cited are collectives of some kind, which by their nature may be expected to be something like 'real totalities which include individual things'; examples like *rekeb* 'chariot' and 'chariotry' do not seem much different from an English word like 'sheep'. If Boman wants to prove that the Hebrew root had some special notion of collectivity inherent in it, he really cannot draw his evidence from that special group of words which everyone knows to be collective in some special way. I must add also a criticism which I have used in other connections: Boman makes no effort to compare this supposedly special value of the Hebrew 'root' with the value of 'roots' in Indo-European or any other language.[3]

Secondly, while the idea that the root of a Hebrew word is something akin to the Platonic Idea will be painful to the anti-Hellenic spirit of many biblical theologians, it may be that it is in a way the prosecution to its rather improbable end of a treatment of the Hebrew language which some of them also have used and of an idealist approach to linguistic realities in which they also have shared.[4]

---

[1] Boman, op. cit., p. 57; E.T., p. 71. Cf. the remarks about Kierkegaard and 'simultaneity', p. 78 above.

[2] Boman, op. cit., p. 59; E.T., p. 73.

[3] Thus similarly when we read such remarks as 'The astonishing thing about these great Hebrew words is the facility they have of merging into one another or overlapping one another' (Torrance, *SJT* i (1948) 63) we probably have nothing more astonishing than a failure to make a real comparison with other vocabulary stocks than the Hebrew.

[4] In general, the danger of undue reliance on 'root meanings' was pointed out also by A. M. Honeyman in *The Old Testament and Modern Study* (ed. H. H. Rowley, Oxford, 1951), p. 276.

Chapter Six

Etymologies and Related Arguments

INTRODUCTORY

We now turn from the study of general grammatical structures to that of the meaning of particular words, that is, to the general area of lexicography. Etymology is a part of this area, and is concerned with the derivation of words from previous forms. It must be emphasized that this is a historical study. It studies the past of a word, but understands that the past of a word is no infallible guide to its present meaning. Etymology is not, and does not profess to be, a guide to the semantic value of words in their current usage, and such value has to be determined from the current usage and not from the derivation.[1]

Hundreds of examples could be adduced where words have come to be used in a sense widely divergent from, or even opposed to, the sense of the forms from which they were derived. A good example is English 'nice', derived from Latin *nescius* 'ignorant'. The meaning of the Latin word from which the derivation has taken place is no guide at all to the sense of this common word in modern usage.[2]

Nevertheless there is a normative strain in the thought of many people about language, and they feel that in some sense the 'original', the 'etymological meaning', should be a guide to the usage of words, that the words are used 'properly' when they coincide in sense with the sense of the earliest known form from which their derivation can be traced; and that when a word becomes in some way difficult or ambiguous an appeal to the etymology will lead to a 'proper meaning' from which at any rate to begin. Everyone must have experienced cases (like that of 'nice')

---

[1] For a simple statement on this, see Jespersen, *Language*, p. 316 f.
[2] For the shifts in significance, see *OED* s.v.

where this obviously does not work, but often people will still try it where there is no obvious obstacle; and so we hear from time to time that 'history' 'properly' means 'investigation' (Gk. ἱστορία) or that 'person' 'basically' means 'mask' (Lat. *persona*). The damaging thing about such pieces of etymologizing is not that they attempt to make historical statements about the words but that they are worked into arguments in which something seems to depend on these words, and commonly give a spurious twist to the meaning of a word at some crucial point in an argument. Casares[1] warns of the danger of an etymological obsession in lexicography itself. Ample examples of this obsession in theological study will be shown below. But how much greater is the harm of such an obsession when it appears not in lexicography but in theological argument!

There are of course reasons why it is valuable to know the etymology of a word you are using. The use of words is often deeply influenced by their past history of use, and the etymology may give helpful indications of how the word has developed and shifted in sense. But it must be remembered that a knowledge of the past history of usage of a word is rather different from an emphasis on its ultimate etymological origin. Thus one would suppose that for understanding 'nice' in present usage it is more important to know its history since the 17th century, during which time it has never meant 'ignorant', than to know that it came ultimately from a Latin word of this sense. Thus Jacob[2] surely exaggerates the importance of etymology when he writes that 'the first task of the Hebraist in the presence of a word is to recover the original meaning from which others were derived'. Important as this must be, one must doubt whether it is 'the first task'. Similarly, for the use of 'person' in modern theological discussion it is more important to know the use of πρόσωπον in the Greek Fathers or of *persona* in the Latin than to know the ultimate etymology.

Often (certainly in Semitic languages) an etymology may be fairly probably stated without any recorded knowledge of the actual usage of a word during a long period. In such cases the

---

[1] J. Casares, *Introducción a la lexicografía moderna* (Madrid, 1950), pp. 33–41.
[2] *Theology of the Old Testament*, p. 159.

etymology is commonly a deduction from, or a hypothesis to explain, a number of words in one language or in several cognate languages which by their extant form and known sense in the historical period offer a *prima facie* case for a common etymological origin. In other words the etymology of a word depends upon known usage, but may often be useful as an introduction to the history of known usage. But this history itself will often demonstrate that the word has moved far from the sense which belonged to its etymological source. The main point is that the etymology of a word is not a statement about its meaning but about its history; it is only as a historical statement that it can be responsibly asserted, and it is quite wrong to suppose that the etymology of a word is necessarily a guide either to its 'proper' meaning in a later period or to its actual meaning in that period.

We must also note that etymological interest plays a notable part in the minds of many religious people, so much so that it may be said to have a fascination for them. The reasons for this are probably numerous and diverse. In the biblical period we find a centre of popular etymologizing in personal names. Many Hebrew names were intelligible sentences, like Ezekiel ('May God strengthen') or Jonathan ('The Lord has given'). In the story of the birth of a child who was to become important an etymologizing interpretation of his name was a common literary feature; but the etymologies were often not correct ones, especially where the names were no longer in current use or where they represented fixations from an earlier or a foreign stage.[1] Place names were also etymologized, but less often in the OT period; in the NT we find a case like the etymologizing of Salem as 'peace' (along with that of Melchizedek as 'king of righteousness') in Hebr. 7:2.[2] A more systematic etymologization of the biblical place-names was carried out by Philo, Origen, Jerome and others.

Along with this treatment of names of persons and places goes

---

[1] On Israelite personal names the standard work is M. Noth, *Die israelitischen Personennamen*. For cases where erratic popular etymologies appear, cf. Gen. 4:1 (Cain), Gen. 29:31–30:24, 35:16–18 (the sons of Jacob), Exod. 2:10 (Moses).

[2] Cf. the beautiful early medieval line which uses the same idea, finding the Hebr. *r-ʾ-h* 'see' in the first part of the name:
urbs beata Jerusalem dicta pacis visio . . .

an etymologizing interpretation of specially important religious terms. This may be done on the quite naive level of the popular etymologizing of personal names in the OT, but often there is something more. than that in it. The etymologizing of personal names in saga or legend is part of the story about the people concerned, and is partly used because it is linked with the literary devices of assonance and rhythm which mark this kind of literature.[1] But the etymologizing of religious terms appears not so much as a literary feature of folk-legend but as an interpretative device of the authoritative expositors of a tradition. It is not part of the more naive creation of a tradition but part of the apparatus of authority in the exposition of an existing tradition, and as such it tends to assert a certain normative interest, a claim to a kind of scientific validity; the etymological interpretation demonstrates that such and such an exegesis is the right one, or at least supports it. Now in the. ea lie⸱ period such etymologizings for the sake of religious interpretation were very largely guesses from random similarities of words,[2] and in this they were not very different from much of the general investigation of language in the time before the normal sound-shifts and correspondences between languages were known. In a more modern period however they tend to assume a more scientific appearance and may even make appeal to the *Oxford English Dictionary* or other authorities which give etymologies generally recognized by linguists.[3]

The dangers involved in etymologizing interpretation may be illustrated with the following example, which is, I fear, all. too common.

[1] For a more sophisticated example cf. Aesch. *Ag*. 687–9; Helen is
πρεπόντως ἑλένας, ἕλανδρος, ἑλέπτολις
'For, true to her name, a Hell she proved to ships, Hell to men, Hell to city. . . .' (tr. of H. Weir Smyth, Loeb Classics edition).

[2] E.g. the well-known interpretation of the Hebrew divine name *šadday* as 'the Sufficient One', from the relative *ša-* or *še-* 'who' and *day* 'enough'; so Aquila ἱκανός at Ex. 6: 3, as also a few cases in LXX.

[3] I have for example heard Dr G. F. Macleod (in a radio broadcast) use the etymology of English 'lord' (from OE *hlaford*, once *hlafweard* 'keeper of the loaf') as part of a demonstration that the Christian message is concerned with economic matters as symbolized by bread. This is hardly 'popular etymology', since this understanding of 'lord' would hardly come naturally into the mind of the man in the street; it depends on the learned philological work put into a modern dictionary.

AN ENGLISH EXAMPLE — 'HOLY'

A regular church-goer is likely sooner or later to hear an interpretation of the word 'holy', which is of course frequent in the English Bible, as 'basically' or 'originally' or 'properly' meaning 'healthy, sound'. Those alarmed by the suggestion of superhuman religious effort in the exhortation to 'be holy' may thus be comforted, because what is being asked of them is simply the basic 'healthiness' or 'soundness' which no one would want to be without. All this is based on one fact or alleged fact: the words 'holy' and 'whole' or 'healthy' are etymologically connected; they 'come from the same root'.[1]

The fact that 'holy' and 'healthy' are etymologically 'connected' does not mean, however, that they now mean the same thing, or indeed that they ever did mean the same thing. To suppose that it does mean this is (a) to ignore the semantic history of the two words and (b) to ignore the force of the suffixes and other elements of word-formation which are added to the original etymological 'root'.

In fact 'holy' never meant 'healthy'. Even Ulfilas, whose translation of the Bible into Gothic is the first monument of Christian expression in a Germanic language (fourth century), knew perfectly well that those words which in later English can 'be rendered as 'holy' are nothing to do with 'healthy', and translated them by *weihs* 'sacred, holy' (cf. modern Germ. *weihen* 'consecrate') — this for Greek ὅσιος, ἱερός, ἡγιασμένος, but above all for the common ἅγιος. He also had the word *hails* 'whole, healthy', which he used for Greek words for health like ὑγιής, ὑγιαίνειν, etc. He did not have, or did not use, a word from the stem *hail-* in a sense 'holy'. I quote Ulfilas merely to indicate that even at his early date no one was treating words meaning 'holy' as if they were something to do with health, or using the words meaning 'health', which are ancestors of our words with that meaning, to translate Greek words which we now usually represent by 'holy'.

The word 'holy' (OE *halig*, from the adjective **hail-* 'whole,

[1] I have indeed heard this supposed etymological sense buttressed by the fiction that it was the sense actually used and intended by the Elizabethan-Jacobean translators of the Bible into English.

hale', OE *hal*, with the suffix *-ig-*) appears to have as its first sense 'to be kept whole, not to be touched, inviolable', and from this sense to have become almost entirely specialized in the religious sense as 'inviolable because belonging to the gods' and thus 'holy'.[1] The main point for our purpose is that, while the element from which our word 'whole' or 'healthy' is derived is used to form the word for 'inviolable', the sense of the latter word is not 'healthy' or 'whole' but 'inviolable' or 'holy'. The word 'holy' does not have and never did have the same meaning as the word from which it is formed, and from which the later 'whole' in our senses of 'complete' and 'healthy' is descended.

In any case all this argument should be unnecessary, since it is beyond dispute that the Greek and Hebrew words which are translated by 'holy' do not have anything to do with 'wholeness' and 'health'. The whole absurd construction of 'holy' as really meaning 'whole' could only arise on the basis of English and by ignoring the Greek and Hebrew represented by that English. It seemed to me worth while however to follow the subject out in some detail, partly because this treatment of 'holy' is common and persistent, and partly because it is true that there is an etymological connection of a kind between the English words 'holy' and 'whole', and it seemed a good opportunity to show that this did not mean a connection of significance.

We may add one or two other object lessons from the explanation of 'holy' as 'whole'. Firstly, those who use it must surely recognize however dimly that they are flying in the face of normal usage; for no ordinary speaker of English, surely, uses 'holy' with any idea that it means 'healthy'; and most such speakers, however great their unfamiliarity with the Bible and the Church, must have some picture of the significance of 'holy'; and it is hardly to be doubted that their picture of it is rather nearer to that intended by the English or Greek or Hebrew Bible than the picture suggested by the preacher who will have it mean 'whole, healthy'.

[1] I follow *OED* and R. Cleasby and G. Vigfusson, *An Icelandic-English Dictionary* (2nd ed., revised by W. A. Craigie, Oxford, 1957), s.v. *heilagr.* For further discussion and other views see A. Johannesson, *Isländisches Etymologisches Wörterbuch* (Bern, from 1951), s.v.; R. Meissner in *ZfDA* lxvii (1930) 54; W. Baetke, *Das Heilige im Germanischen* (Tübingen, 1942), and *PBB* lxvi (1942) 1–54; Bloomfield, op. cit., p. 433.

Secondly, the test of explanations of words is by their contexts. Supposing anyone to become convinced that 'holy' in the English Bible really means something like 'healthy, whole', he will find in his reading of the Bible many contexts where this sense produces sore difficulty. He may find it possible to understand the Third Person of the Trinity as 'the Healthy Spirit', but he will have difficulty with those inanimate objects such as valuables gained by capture which are specially devoted to the divine possession and are thus apparently 'healthy to the Lord'; and he will surely find it impossible to suppose that that rear chamber of the Temple usually called 'the Holy of Holies' is in fact a place specially healthy or specially whole in any other way. In other words, even if by some mischance the words now usually taken as 'holy' had come to be translated as 'whole' or 'healthy', the contexts would have become near-unintelligible in at least some places, and would almost certainly have forced the reader to the conclusion that even if 'healthy' or 'whole' was the word used it must have been meant in some unusually transferred or specialized sense.

In fact few people can suppose that this treatment of 'holy' is more than a kind of opportunistic homiletic trick, which can be used at a certain point but is not intended to work as a regular explanation at every point. Those who use it are not intending it as a regular interpretation, and are quite likely to come back at a later stage to the more usual understanding of 'holy'. They simply think that the uncomfortable suggestions of the word 'holy' need to be mitigated, and that the suggestion of some kinship with 'whole, healthy' will help in this. The use of such devices at all, however, is hard to reconcile with any claim to be a responsible interpreter of biblical language. In principle also such methods mean a disregard of the social nature of language as a means of communication; but this is not wholly disregarded, only at certain points. The etymologization departs from current usage and current understanding and at the same time makes some kind of suggestion that its interpretation is somehow 'proper'. It belongs to the nature of this kind of argument that it can only be done sporadically and haphazardly. If we agreed that all the words we use should be interpreted from their etymological background and remote historical connections we should reduce language to an unintelligible chaos.

The case of 'holy' is especially bad because its wrongness is so obvious and because it depends on a blatant ignoring of the original languages; but the basic etymological fallacies which appear in this case may also appear in interpretations of more learned appearance based on Greek and Hebrew words.[1]

SOME TYPICAL GENERAL STATEMENTS

A general statement which seems to me to involve a misapprehension of the nature of etymological study is that of K. J. Cremer.[2] In a series of studies in the area of Old Testament semantics he finds it necessary to distinguish semasiology from etymology. He does this by saying that the former investigates the nuance of meaning, the exact meaning in a particular case, while etymology is directed only towards 'the general, the original, the root-meaning'. Thus 'etymology seeks τὸ ἔτυμον, the essential of a word'. Thus its concern is with the formal aspect rather than the content of words. Etymology, if it gives any indication of the meaning of words, goes no farther than the 'proper' meaning of the word, while semasiology goes on farther and investigates the syntactic or factual sense.[3]

In another passage he avoids the terms 'proper' and 'general' but retains the suggestion that etymology is concerned with the 'form' of words and semasiology with their 'content meaning and possible alteration or *nuanciering*.'[4] He returns more than once to the position that etymology deals with the form and the fundamental or proper meaning of words.[5] The place of semasiology is

---

[1] K. L. Schmidt, in *TWNT* iii. 533–4, *BKW The Church*, p. 57–8, warns against this kind of etymological interpretation, and quotes the German habit of explaining *Sünde* ('sin') as *Sonderung*, separation. He rightly says that 'These considerations are all more or less pseudo-philological, and in them ideas which may often in themselves be right are turned upside down'. Unfortunately, not all the admirers of *TWNT* or the contributors to it have attended to this wise advice, as we shall see.

[2] *GThT* xlviii (1948) 193–209; xlix (1949) 1–15, 79–99; *Vox Theologica* xx (1949–50) 100–10.

[3] *Vox Theologica*, ibid., p. 104.   [4] *GThT* xlviii (1948) 203 f.

[5] E.g. ibid., p. 83: 'De etymologische is de formele of *eigenlijke* betekenis van een woord; de semasiologische is de syntactische of *feitelijke*.' Cf. ibid., p. 99,

in the study of variations and nuances occurring within this fundamental meaning.

This seems to me to enshrine some of the commonest faults in the theological practice of linguistic interpretation. It is true that etymology seeks the 'original', but this just because it is the (historically) original is necessarily not the 'general' or the 'proper'. The fact that Cremer appeals to the etymology of the word 'etymology', i.e. to the Greek τὸ ἔτυμον, and hence derives a suggestion that etymology deals with 'the essential' in a word, shows a failure to understand the historical nature of etymological research; in fact it means an acceptance of something like the Stoic theory expressed in the term τὸ ἔτυμον.

These faults are however checked in Cremer's treatment by his realization of the limits of etymological study, and by the fact that his real concern in his articles is not with what he calls etymology but with what he calls semasiology. He is wisely aware, for example, of the hypothetical nature of 'roots'.[1] But his conception of the 'basic meaning' as something always present but appearing always under variations and nuances in its factual syntactic relations seems to me to be a pseudo-philosophic conception and untrue to the facts of either etymology or semantics.[2] Nevertheless as I say Cremer shows a wise restraint towards etymological interpretation which has not been evident in some other theological interpreters.

The tendency towards etymologizing interpretation of words which seems to be so common in religious circles cannot, I think, fail to be encouraged by such a statement as this by N. H. Snaith:

'While it must be recognized that words can change their meaning in strange and unexpected ways through the centuries, yet in all languages there is a fundamental motif in a word which tends to endure, whatever other changes the years may bring.

where the distinction of semasiology and etymology is said to be that the latter 'is directed towards the word-*form* and the proper (basic) sense of the words, while the former is concerned with the factual (syntactic) *content* and possible (*eventuele*) changes'.

[1] *GThT* xlix (1949) 87.

[2] Ibid., p. 87 n., where the figure of a series of triangles on the same base is given; the base represents the 'basic meaning'. The apex of each triangle is a different *nuanciering* or variation of this basic meaning.

This fundamental "theme" of a word is often curiously determinative of later meanings.'[1]

From this general introduction Snaith goes on to give detailed illustrations. Two examples may be given.

The first word of the first Psalm is Hebr. 'ašre 'blessed is . . .', literally 'happinesses of . . .'. This is related to words in various Semitic languages meaning 'footstep', 'go straight ahead, advance' and also to the Hebrew relative pronoun. Snaith concludes:

'All this shows how apt is the use of the first word. The psalm tells of the true way as distinct from the false. The happy man is the man who goes straight ahead, because, as the last verse says, "the Lord knoweth the way of the righteous", while "the way of the wicked shall perish".'

Thus a word is deemed to be unusually apt because other words from the same root existing in other languages, or existing in the same language but no longer having the etymological sense (e.g. the Hebrew relative pronoun), have or may be supposed to have had in the past a sense of 'place' or 'way', and the theme of the psalm as a whole is about ways, the right way and the wrong way. There is not the slightest evidence that these associations were in the mind of the poet, and indeed some of them were almost certainly unknown and unknowable to him and his contemporaries. The etymological associations are used without any inquiry whether they existed in the minds of those who used the poem.

The second example is the Hebrew niham, which in various forms means 'comfort' (pi'el) and 'repent' (niph'al). According to Snaith,[2] 'actually' the word means 'take a breath of relief', and this 'implies' the sense 'to breathe hard (as of a horse)' as in Arabic. The word 'therefore' has to do with 'change of attitude', 'change of mind', any other association being accidental. Therefore we may conclude that when the niph'al means 'repent' the sense is 'change of mind or intention' and the word 'has no necessary connection with sorrow or regret'.

---

[1] N. H. Snaith, 'The Language of the Old Testament', *The Interpreter's Bible* i. 224.

[2] Op. cit., pp. 225–6.

It is of course a theological commonplace to point out that 'repentance' is something other than remorse or sorrow. Whether sorrow or regret is part of the meaning in usage need not be discussed here; all I wish to point out is that this piece of argument from the etymology cannot settle such a matter. It is patently absurd to suppose that a use in Arabic for the breathing of a horse is decisive for discovering the sense in a religious Hebrew text. Moreover, the idea that if a sense is not given or implied in the ultimate etymology that sense is 'accidental', and therefore need not be taken into account in understanding the meaning of the word, is surely an impossible one. The whole argument is directed towards the importation of some general religious reflections into the supposed sense of the word, as we see in the concluding sentences:

'The idea of sorrow for past sin, though necessary enough from the religious point of view, is not conveyed in the word itself. The emphasis is that, with whatever accompaniment, the man should change his attitude, turn right around, and go back along the road into which he ought never to have gone away from God.' This may well be a fair statement of the Old Testament's understanding of repentance in general, but cannot be legitimately connected with the etymological study of the verb 'repent'.[1]

Another way of thinking, which I have never seen formulated precisely but which may well be a powerful influence towards etymologizing procedures, may be as follows. For a very large number of objects or actions we can quote a Greek word and a Hebrew word, which are the usual names for these objects or actions in the respective languages. One might therefore think of saying that the Greek word 'means' the Hebrew word. In biblical theology however it may be felt that such semantic identifications are 'surface' or 'external'. Such a surface identification may be thought to conceal deep-lying differences of thought. It may therefore be thought that when we take the etymology, or when we look at the cognates of the Hebrew word, we shall find that the Hebrew word is 'related' to a quite different series of things from

---

[1] Snaith's article contains a study of the contrast of Greek and Hebrew thought, op. cit., pp. 229–32.

those to which the Greek word is related. Thus it is supposed we see a different 'inner life' or 'depth meaning' in the Hebrew word. Or, to put it another way, the fact that Hebrew words are derived from different origins, have a different past history behind them, from the Greek words, demonstrates a different mental approach to reality. That this argument is in general a dubious one is clear when we take seriously the historical nature of etymological study. But in particular it is not the case that past semantic changes which can be traced for Hebrew words are in any overwhelming number without analogy in the Indo-European or other groups, and a fairly large number of cases can be shown where a Hebrew semantic development has been fairly closely parallel to cases in Greek and Latin or other Indo-European languages. Consider for example such cases as:

Hebr. ʾamar 'say'; Accad. amāru 'see'; Eth. ʾammara 'show'; Lat. dicere 'say'; Gk. δείκνυμι 'show'; Germ. zeigen 'show'; Eng. teach.[1]

Hebr. ḥaṭaʾ '1. miss (a mark) 2. sin'; Greek ἁμαρτάνω '1. miss (a mark) 2. sin'.

Consider also the words meaning 'soul, spirit, mind' and their relation to words meaning 'breath, wind, smoke':

Thus Hebr. ruaḥ and Gk. πνεῦμα alike are '1. wind 2. spirit'; roughly so also Hebrew nepeš and Gk. ψυχή 'breath, soul'; cf. also Gk. ἄνεμος 'wind', Lat. animus 'mind', anima 'soul'; Hebr. ʾap '1. nostril 2. anger', Gk. θυμός 'life, soul, mind, courage, anger', Lat. fumus 'smoke'.[2]

I have no intention of suggesting that semantic changes in Hebrew have never taken peculiar or unique directions. The cases quoted however should be sufficient to show that the idea of bringing out the uniqueness of Hebrew psychology through emphasizing the etymological relations of words is not only wrong in principle but certain to fail in practice.

[1] The Semitic examples are commonly derived from an ultimate sense of 'be bright, make visible, make known' (KB); the Indo-European words may all with some fair probability be derived from a root *dei- 'shine brightly, glance, see', expanded in a sense of 'cause to see, make clear'; cf. Pokorny, Indogermanisches Etymologisches Wörterbuch, pp. 188-9.

[2] Numerous further examples are suggested in Palache, 'Beteekenisverandering'; Kronasser, op. cit.; for Latin and Greek, Struck, Bedeutungslehre.

QAHAL — ἐκκλησία

'It is the special use of ἐκκλησία in the Septuagint that gives the New Testament its technical term for the Church. In the LXX ἐκκλησία refers to the congregation regarded collectively as a people and as a whole, rather than to the actual assembly or meeting of the people. Behind the Greek ἐκκλησία there lies the Hebrew *qahal* or some cognate word from the same root. The Old Testament as a rule employs two terms to describe Israel as the congregation of God, ʿedah and *qahal*, and both are translated at different times by two Greek words, συναγωγή and ἐκκλησία. More and more the Old Testament writers, in its later books, prefer the term *qahal*, usually rendered by ἐκκλησία, but Judaism came more and more to prefer the term συναγωγή. Thus when the Christian Church came to refer to itself as the ἐκκλησία rather than συναγωγή (with one or two exceptions), it was clearly claiming to be "the Israel of God" in distinction from the Synagogue.

'Two further elements in the concept of *qahal*-ἐκκλησία should be noted here. (*a*) The fact that *qahal* comes from the same root as *qol*, the word for "voice", suggests that the OT *qahal* was the community summoned by the Divine Voice, by the Word of God. Of that ἐκκλησία is a very apt translation, indicating as it does the community as "the called" (κλητοί) of God. Ἐκκλησία is Church not in any sociological or political sense of assembly, and not therefore in any sociological or political continuity with Israel. It is Church as act of God, as the community called into being and created by God's Word. (*b*) In line with that is the fact that the OT *qahal* was first established at Sinai when God came and spoke, when his voice was heard by all Israel, and his Word founded the Covenant-Community. That was known as "the day of the *qahal*", and so *qahal* came to have a special significance as the community brought into covenant-relation with God for sacrifice and worship, and for the special end of revelation. *Qahal* denotes the OT Church actively engaged in God's purposes of revelation and salvation, that is, caught up in the mighty events whereby God intervenes redemptively in history, and involved in the forward thrust of the

Covenant towards final and universal fulfilment. *Qahal* is the community expecting eschatological redemption. . . .'[1]

The main point of interest here is the conclusion drawn from 'the fact that *qahal* comes from the same root as *qol*'.

Let us for the present admit that *qahal* is in some way connected etymologically with *qol*. This is a purely historical statement and has no value whatever as a proof that the semantic value of *qol* in classical Hebrew is in any way influential in the meaning of *qahal* in the same period. The statement quoted has been made without the slightest attempt to determine the semantics of *qahal* in actual usage. The fact that none of the standard dictionaries notes an element of 'voice' in the semantics of *qahal*, even when they consider some etymological connection with *qol* to be possible,[2] is merely ignored. All cases of *qahal* fit perfectly well with the sense of 'assembly', 'group'. It may be, let us say, that some such semantic history as 'speak>call>summon>assemble' has led to this sense, but there is no reason to suppose that the earlier elements in that historical sequence are still alive in the semantic value of the word. The verb forms *niqhal* and *hiqhil* are clearly denominative, meaning 'be made into a *qahal*, be assembled' and 'make a *qahal*, assemble'. The LXX themselves understood this latter verb as denominative, translating it by ἐκκλησιάζω 'form into an ἐκκλησία'.

Secondly, even if *qahal* is to be connected with speaking, calling, voices and the like, it is quite unrelated to the linguistic realities to go on to identify this with the 'Divine Voice'. If 'calling' is to be taken as part of the semantic development, it is clearly the calling of the person who summons the assembly. This could of course be anyone, since there is no reason to suppose that the development from 'call' to 'assembly' had any special connection with any deity. This does not need to be substantiated from the Old Testament, but for what it is worth I may point out that God is nowhere the śubject of a verb meaning 'to summon' a *qahal* in the OT, nor as far as I see is there ever any special conjunction of the

---

[1] T. F. Torrance, 'Israel and the Incarnation', *Judaica* xiii (1957) 1–2; also in his *Conflict and Agreement* i. 285 ff. and in *Interpretation* x (1956) 305–20.

[2] So GB, KB, but not BDB.

qol of Yahweh and the summoning of the *qahal*. Sometimes God speaks to the *qahal* or assembly; e.g. in Deut. 5: 22, where the people hear his voice. I would consider it unlikely that at Deut. 5: 22 there is any play on the two words *qol* and *qahal* either for assonance or for common meaning. Quite apart from any weaknesses in the etymology of *qahal* through connection with the root of *qol*, therefore, there is no reason to suppose that the use of *qahal* is in any special way derived from or determined by the speaking of God, though of course God does impart his word to Moses to communicate to the *qahal* or assembly.

It might of course be possible in theory that the word *qahal* was etymologized in popular understanding as meaning something to do with 'voice'. I have already indicated however that the LXX gives no hint of this. Indeed the LXX evidence goes in quite the opposite direction, for *qahal* is frequently translated by terms meaning 'group, assembly, lot of people', all of which have even less to do with 'voice' than ἐκκλησία has. The rendering συναγωγή is universal in the Tetrateuch, and preponderant in the Prophets (13 cases against 4 of ἐκκλησία); other similar translations are λαός (2?), ὄχλος (6, of which 5 in Ezekiel), πλῆθος (2), συνέδριον and σύστασις (one each). It is therefore probable that the rendering ἐκκλησία was used purely for its general surface meaning of 'assembly' and corresponded simply to an understanding of *qahal* as 'assembly'; and that the derivation from καλέω 'call' or any associations with ἔκκλητος 'called out' or κλῆσις 'calling' (in the theological sense) had no importance. There is in fact little or no basis in the Semitic word for such a series of connections. It is possible in theory however that such connections were made in the Greek-speaking church, working from the Greek terms alone. K. L. Schmidt however[1] considers such connections unlikely for the New Testament period. The other Semitic terms which can also be considered as background for the NT ἐκκλησία have, of course, no such connection at all.

Whatever truth there may be then in the considerations about the NT ἐκκλησία advanced in the passage we are discussing, the attempt to support them from the Hebrew *qahal* is entirely

[1] *TWNT* iii. 533–4; *BKW The Church*, p. 57.

unsuccessful. There are still some further reasons to add to those I have given.

Firstly, *qahal* is used for groups and assemblies of nations, mainly where their numerousness and their power is in view,[1] and for groups of the wicked and the enemies of God.[2] This usage is very much alive in the Qumran documents.[3] This is an additional reason for affirming that, even if there is some truth in some historical connection with the root *qwl* 'speak', this has nothing to do with the Divine Voice or Word of God.

The second point has a greater theoretical and methodological interest. The fault which I believe we can detect may be called that of 'unjustified determination', and two examples can be seen in the passage we are criticizing. The first is when, a trace of the sense 'voice' having been detected behind *qahal*, this quite indeterminate voice is at once given the definite article and becomes '*the* Voice' or '*the* Word'. By means of this determination a sense 'voice', which may at the most be something quite particular related only to a particular stage in the history of the word *qahal*, is integrated into a coherent and overarching theological image.

The second and more important instance is in the treatment of *qahal* itself. We may illustrate this through the two English phrases 'the Church' and 'the meeting'. In spite of many different conceptions of the Church's nature, the phrase 'the Church' is recognized as indicating an entity of which people have some reasonably clear impression; it is a continuing entity of which — and this is the main point — the phrase 'the Church' is itself recognized to be an adequate, normal, and indeed the best, linguistic indicator. With 'the meeting' it is quite different. If we say 'the meeting believes so and so', then the natural answer is

---

[1] E.g. Gen. 35: 11.

[2] Ps. 26: 5; Ezek. 38: 7.

[3] Thus *qahal* is used of groups of evil-doers or evil nations in 1QM 11: 16, 14: 5, 15: 10; 1QH 2: 12 (*qhlt*). In 1QS it does not occur, but it appears in 1QSa, but means 'assembly', and the word for the 'congregation' or the sect as a whole is *ᶜedah*, with a very great numerical preponderance. Where the word occurs in the legend of a battle standard, 1QM 4: 10, it is the sixth in a series which uses up most of the terms available for a group of this kind; *ᶜedah* is the first. Some other cases are practically quotations from the OT, e.g. 1QSa 2: 4. On CD 7: 17 see Rabin's note.

'What meeting?'.[1] 'The meeting' is just as clear and accepted a linguistic indicator as 'the Church', but it is normally referred to a particular occasion. 'The Church' can quite rightly be taken to indicate a wide area of history and experience for which it, and no other phrase, is a proper indicator; 'the meeting' has a much narrower area of indication, and is usually supplemented by information about particular occasions. Or to restate the matter in the terms of the use of the definite article: 'a Church' and 'the Church' mean different senses of the word 'Church', while 'a meeting' and 'the meeting' do not mean different senses of the word 'meeting'.

Now the passage we are criticizing seems to draw *qahal* into the type of 'the Church' rather than the type of 'the meeting'. We meet an entity called ' "the" *qahal*' which carries a wide periphery of indication such as 'the Church' has in modern speech; one can say that 'the *qahal*' was established at Sinai; it is the community brought into covenant-relationship for sacrifice and worship; and so on. Thus the impression given is not that *qahal* is a word used for the church of the Old Testament, a group which (as we know from the biblical narrative, including sentences which at points use the word *qahal*) was actively engaged in God's purpose of revelation and salvation. Rather the impression is that *qahal* is a word specifically meaning the-OT-church-actively-engaged-in-God's-purpose-of-revelation-and-salvation. Or, again, it is the-community-expecting-eschatological-redemption. All these impressions arise from the device of using determination by the definite article for *qahal* in a way that assimilates it to the entity of the type 'the Church'. The ignoring of the semantic importance of determination and its absence is a serious fault in the treatment of linguistic evidence.[2]

A number of minor questions may be passed over lightly. We may for example leave aside exaggerations in detail, for example the statement that '*qahal* is the community expecting eschatological

---

[1] It is true that any statement using 'the Church' may be met by the question 'What Church?'; but the asking of such a question will probably mean a move on to different ground, a misunderstanding of the first statement — something that does not happen with 'meeting'.

[2] Thus in theological discussion 'a covenant' can be tacitly transformed into '*the* covenant'.

redemption', a general theological reflection quite unrelated to any actual basis in the usage of *qahal*. We may also leave aside the question which has had some discussion elsewhere,[1] whether *qahal* is a technical term or not, which is a rather different one from our purpose. A term may be technical and still like 'the meeting' require definition in respect of particular occasions.

The more important criticisms are two. Firstly, it may be suggested that the content of word-groups which include *qahal*, such as *qᵉhal yahweh* or *qᵉhal yiśraᵓel*, has been offered us as the content or sense of *qahal* itself.[2] This may be condoned on the grounds that *qahal* is here used as a kind of shorthand for these phrases. It is none the less seriously misleading, for it conceals the possibility that *qahal* itself may be theologically empty or neutral (as witness the possibility of using it with evil-doers or nations), and correspondingly risks inflating the heritage received through the correspondence in the LXX of ἐκκλησία to *qahal*.

Secondly, we have to make the criticism that the word *qahal* is given a sense like that of 'Israel' itself, the word which in the OT comes nearest to our phrase 'the Church'; *qahal* is treated rather like a proper name, a designation specific to Israel and implying all the theological characteristics of Israel, and those ways in which *qahal* is similar to our 'the meeting' are obscured. 'The *qahal*' becomes something which was founded or established; it is 'the community' seen under a specially significant aspect. Israel is 'the' *qahal*. But it is doubtful if there are any cases where the sense of 'the assembly' is impossible, and there are many cases where the *qahal* referred to is clearly a particular assembly for a particular purpose, e.g. Jud. 21: 5, 8, where the *qahal* is a particular assembly of the armed men to make war on a troublesome group.

It is in fact clear that both these faults go back to the emphasis on the etymological connection with 'voice'; and that the force of this connection seems convincing because:

(a) The Church or People of God is indeed summoned or called into existence by the Word or Voice of God.

---

[1] *TWNT* iii. 531–2; *BKW The Church*, p. 52 f.; Rost, *Vorstufen*, p. 14; Kritzinger, *Qᵉhal Jahwe*, p. 14 ff., 149.

[2] Cf. the treatment of λαός and ἔθνος mentioned below, p. 234 f.

(b) The word *qahal*, corresponding to ἐκκλησία 'church', is related to the word for 'speech', 'voice'.

How can there fail to be a correlation between these two things? It is because of the unfounded belief in this correlation, and the accompanying necessary emphasis on the etymology, that *qahal* is isolated from the phrases in which it occurs, that its neutral senses are disregarded, and that the sense 'meeting, assembly' in a particular reference is left aside.

Thus we may ask whether it is justified to say of the Sinai events that 'that was known as "the day of the *qahal*" '. Within the context of the passage quoted the impression given is that this meant 'the day of foundation or establishment of the *qahal* or Covenant-community'. But such an interpretation is surely impossible. A far more natural sense is given by 'the day of the assembly (i.e. the particularly memorable assembly at Mount Sinai)'. It is really misleading to say even that 'that was known as "the day of the *qahal*" '. It is a reference to a known event rather than the setting up of a standard designation for such an event. The phrase is Deuteronomic, and Moses is reminding his hearers that what he is now telling them was previously told by God to 'the whole of your assembly' (Deut. 5: 22); and thereafter he can refer back several times to 'the time (*yom*, day) of the (aforesaid) assembly' (so Deut. 9: 10; 10: 4; 18: 16). It follows also that it does not agree with OT usage to use such a phrase as 'the *qahal* was established' for the events of Sinai or any other events.

It is clear that the distortion was introduced as early as the second sentence in our quotation, where the reference of ἐκκλησία in the LXX is said to be 'to the congregation regarded collectively as a people and as a whole, rather than to the actual assembly or meeting of the people'. It is difficult to know what reason can be given in support of this statement. One cannot escape the impression that the emphasis on *qahal* as the community itself rather than its assembly has been overstressed in order to bring out a similarity to the Christian ἐκκλησία.

Torrance's statement here is closely parallel to one of Hoskyns and Davey,[1] who in their turn refer to Hort's *The Christian Ecclesia*.

---

[1] *The Riddle of the New Testament*, p. 22 f.

Hort indeed (p. 7) says that for Greek-speaking Jews ἐκκλησία 'would mean the congregation of Israel quite as much as an assembly of the congregation'. For the Hebrew words, however, he states explicitly on p. 4 f. that unlike ʿedah, which means the society of Israel 'whether assembled or not assembled', qahal is 'properly their actual meeting together'. Is there good evidence that the LXX was understood otherwise than the Hebrew in this regard? In Philo and Josephus every case is unquestionably 'assembly' and there is no hint of the use of ἐκκλησία for 'the people'.[1] An assembly after all is what an ἐκκλησία in Greek was.

We should now perhaps say something about the etymology of qahal from which we started. All our arguments so far have supposed that the connection with qol 'voice' is a real connection, and have merely tried to show how unjustified are the conclusions which have been drawn from this supposition. According to Bauer, whose authority has been a powerful force towards the popularity of this suggestion,[2] our form qahal 'assembly' goes back to the participle *qâl 'speaking' or 'calling'; from this Bauer traced our form qahal through the influence of the circumflex or double (zweigipflig) accent.[3] Qahal thus begins as 'caller, speaker', and develops from there to 'assembly', on the semantic parallel of Arabic nādī 'caller' and hence 'assembly'.

It must be pointed out that on such a suggestion the separation of the form qahal must have taken place very early. The word is found in several languages and all with the sense 'assembly'; thus:

South Arabian qhl 'congregatio hominum, multitudo congregata'[4]

Syriac qhal 'come together, assemble'[5].

In such circumstances the semantic connection with 'voice' might well have been entirely lost. In fact the equal sense of 'assemble'

[1] For Josephus, see the Lexicon of Thackeray and Marcus; for Philo, Leisegang's index to the edition of Cohn and Wendland. For the matter as a whole see TWNT iii. 530 ff.; BKW The Church, pp. 51–6; Rost, Vorstufen, pp. 4–32; Kritzinger, Qᵉhal Jahwe. Q-h-l means 'people' (regularly translating Greek λαός) in Christian Palestinian Syriac; cf. Schulthess, Lexicon Syropalaestinum, s.v. But (a) this hardly proves anything for our subject here, and (b) other words are used for 'church' or 'assembly' in this dialect.

[2] But cf. also for instance Palache, Sinai en Paran, p. 113.

[3] ZATW xlviii (1930) 75.

[4] Rossini, Chrestomathia, p. 230.   [5] Brockelmann, Lexicon Syriacum, s.v.

over such a wide area suggests that the derivation from *qwl* 'speak' is not a good one. More recently Cohen has suggested that the word should be taken along with Cushitic words meaning 'crowd, clan', and this fits the Hebrew semantics much better.[1]

One or two points remain for comment. Firstly, in general, within the general purpose of the article quoted from, which is to discuss the 'Israel of God' as a preliminary to a discussion of the relations between Church and Israel, many of the same conclusions which are in fact reached could be reached from actual *statements* made explicitly in OT and NT and without the attempt to draw evidence from the significance of particular *words*. In other words, what may be a good theological case is spoiled by bad linguistic argument; and is not supported by actual exegetical argument from texts which *say* things from which the general thesis could be supported. It is not the presence of theological method, but the belief in the necessary reflection of theological structures in the linguistic structures, which causes the distortion of linguistic evidence.

Finally, I must dispute the judgement that 'Thus when the Christian Church came to refer to itself as the ἐκκλησία rather than the συναγωγή (with one or two exceptions), it was clearly claiming to be "the Israel of God" in distinction from the Synagogue'. That the Church may have thought itself to be the 'Israel of God' in distinction from the Synagogue may or may not be true, and does not concern me here; but I do not think that the existence of such a belief can be traced from the use of ἐκκλησία rather than συναγωγή, and there is no reason to think that the use of ἐκκλησία rather than συναγωγή constituted such a claim.

The suggestion that the use of ἐκκλησία constitutes a claim to be the true 'Israel of God' seems to presuppose that *qahal* is *the* term *par excellence* in which the nature of Israel as the people of God is expressed. Now even if this were the case it is far from clear

---

[1] M. Cohen, *Essai comparatif*, p. 124, no. 223 bis. It is also perhaps worth remarking that if Botterweck is at all right, a large number of Hebrew and Semitic roots including the sequences *k-l*, *g-l* and *q-l* may share something in common; *Der Triliterismus im Semitischen*, pp. 40–44; 53. But it must be said that such relationships would be too remote to be relevant for the kind of semantic connections we are discussing.

that the use of the Greek ἐκκλησία would be understood by anyone
to point unambiguously to this term *par excellence*, for this latter is
translated by συναγωγή and not by ἐκκλησία in about one case in
three in the LXX, and ἐκκλησία predominates only in the
historical books and Psalms and not in the important sections of
the Pentateuch and Prophets.[1] But in any case it is not at all true
that *qahal* is a term *par excellence* of this kind, in which the aspects
of the true nature of the people of God are summed up and made
clear; this has already been made clear, I think, in my arguments
above, and especially in the demonstration of the etymological
fallacies employed. It is only because of the etymological attrac-
tions, as far as I see, that *qahal* is so preferred, and the other main
OT word for the assembly of the people, *ʿedah*, is neglected. That
this latter word is not translated by ἐκκλησία does not seem to me
an adequate reason; in the area where *ʿedah* is most used, the P
sections of the Tetrateuch, ἐκκλησία is not used for *qahal* either.
And there are just as many suggestions of 'covenant-relation for
sacrifice and worship' and of 'expecting eschatological redemption'
connected with *ʿedah*, especially in Qumran usage; not that I think
it right to try to draw these wide and complex suggestions and
relations *out of ʿedah* any more than out of *qahal*.

Nor is it correct to suggest a rising use of *qahal* by the later books
of the OT; and even if it was, this would be no reason to justify
the idea that by using ἐκκλησία the Church was asserting itself to
be the true 'Israel of God'. The phrase 'more and more' suggests a
gradual increase in *qahal* over *ʿedah*, but *qahal* predominates in
Deut., *ʿedah* in P, and *qahal* in the Chronicler. At Qumran the
community calls itself more frequently the *ʿedah*, and *qahal* is often
used in the bad sense of groups of evil doers.

Moreover, several matters are confused in the discussion here:
(*a*) which Hebrew word was used by Hebrew writers at different
times (*b*) which Greek translation was used for these words in
rendering the Bible into Greek (*c*) which words (whether Hebrew,
Aramaic or Greek) were used for a place of worship by the Jews at
various times. These are completely different questions, but are
confusedly mingled in the sentence beginning 'more and more'.

[1] See the table setting out the translation statistics below, p. 253.

In general, it must be said that the argument we are examining follows much modern biblical theology in reading the maximum possible theological content into a linguistic choice. There are great difficulties in maintaining that the use of ἐκκλησία would naturally convey to anyone the idea of a claim to be the true 'Israel of God' in distinction to the Synagogue, even if such a claim were in fact also made. It is at least equally possible (a) that the use of ἐκκλησία arose from that of 'particular meeting', which was after all a well-established sense in the OT, or of 'group of persons assembled';[1] (b) that the choice of ἐκκλησία by the Christians was a purely linguistic specialization as opposition to the established Jewish use of συναγωγή; both words after all have about equal roots in the Hebrew and the Greek OT. In any case the actual use of συναγωγή in Jewish Greek must have corresponded very largely to words from the root *kns*, such as *k^eneset* 'assembly', rather than to *qahal*. Many NT scholars have held the same to be true of the words of Jesus in Matthew about the ἐκκλησία.[2] This word has of course none of the possible etymological associations with 'voice' and so on which have been described; and the words from this root have only a very slight footing in the OT itself at all.[3]

Dabar 'WORD, MATTER'

T. F. Torrance writes:[4]

'This (word) appears to derive from a Semitic root *dbr* meaning "backside" or "hinterground", which is apparent in the expression

---

[1] Cf. J. Y. Campbell, *JTS* xlix (1948) 130–42.

[2] E.g. K. L. Schmidt, *TWNT* iii. 529, *BKW The Church*, p. 48.

[3] One must also remember that the use of a word like ἐκκλησία or συναγωγή in Jewish Greek may well not have been derived from the LXX rendering of *qahal* or of *^cedah* at all. The fact that the LXX is often our earliest evidence for Jewish Greek must not make us think that the usage of Jewish Greek arose from this translation. Probably συναγωγή would early be used for words like *k^eneset* which were rare in the Bible or non-existent but current in late Judaism. It was used of course of a religious 'gathering' or 'assembly', but was not at first specialized in this sense; in the LXX a συναγωγή may be not of people at all, but is occasionally of waters (Gen. 1: 9), of crops (Exodus, twice), of stones (Job 8: 17). In Daniel LXX it translates *hamon* 'crowd'. It is clear that such questions as the nature and identity of the 'people of God' or the 'Israel of God' are not necessarily raised by the use of such a word at all.

[4] *Royal Priesthood*, p. 1 f.

for the Holy of Holies just mentioned, the *d^ebir*, which was lodged at the very back of the Tabernacle or Temple. This term *dabar* has a dual significance. On the one hand it refers to the hinterground of meaning, the inner reality of the word, but on the other hand, it refers to the dynamic event in which that inner reality becomes manifest. Thus every event has its *dabar* or word, so that he who understands the *dabar* of an event understands its real meaning.

'The Septuagint (with some exceptions) regularly translates the Hebrew *dabar* either by λόγος or by ῥῆμα, while the plural *d^ebarim* like the plural ῥήματα may mean "history", like the Latin *res gestae*. It is especially in regard to the Word of God that this dual significance is apparent, particularly as the Word of God comes to the prophet and enters history as dynamic event (ὁ λόγος τοῦ κυρίου ἐγένετο). In this connection it is also instructive to find that where word and event coincide there is truth (ἀλήθεια *^emet*). Thus God's Word is Truth where his Action corresponds to his Word. That is characteristic of man's word too, for his word is true where there is a relation of faithfulness (*^emunah* = πίστις = *^emet*) between the speaker and the speaking of the word, and also between the speaking of the word and the hearing of it. . . .

'This is one of the dominant conceptions behind the Old Testament understanding of the cult, and indeed it looks as if the whole Tabernacle or Temple were constructed around the significance of *dabar*. In the very back of the Tabernacle or the Holy of Holies, the *d^ebir*, there were lodged the ten Words or *d^ebarim*. Those Ten Words form the innermost secret of Israel's history. It is therefore highly significant that in the Old Testament's interpretation of its own history and its ancient cult, they were lodged in the hinterground of a movable tent which formed the centre of Israel's historical pilgrimage. . . . All through Israel's history the Word enshrined in the form of *d^ebarim* was hidden in the *d^ebir*, but was again and again made manifest when God made bare his mighty arm and showed his glory.'

Let us grant for the moment the etymology of *dabar* from a root like *d-b-r* 'behind'. What is noticeable about the statement quoted is the way in which this etymology is theorized and generalized, one might almost say hypostatized; and correspondingly how remote the locutions and meanings suggested are from actual usage of the word *dabar* in Hebrew. The whole statement is built not upon Hebrew usage but upon the etymology. But I have already indicated that an etymology need not be a good indication, or indeed an indication at all, of the actual semantics of the word in contexts.

Firstly, it should be said that 'hinterground of meaning' is a semantic indication which is quite unreconcilable with any use of the Hebrew *dabar*. No lexicon recognizes a sense even remotely approaching this. I am not clear what is meant to be the relation between 'hinterground of meaning' and 'the inner reality of the word'. The inner reality of what word? Perhaps what is meant is a case like Ezek. 12: 23, *dᵉbar kol ḥazon*, 'the *dabar* of every vision', where however an adequate translation would be 'the matter, the substance', avoiding the semantic suggestion of 'hinterground' and 'inner reality' and following the well-established one of 'matter, thing'.

Not only however is the 'hinterground' suggestion impossible, but that of 'the dynamic event in which that inner reality becomes manifest' is also exaggerated and far-fetched. Let us for the moment take the chief senses of *dabar* as any standard dictionary will give them, i.e. (*a*) 'speech, word' (*b*) 'thing, matter'. Our attention is at present for the latter. Consider now this English sentence:

'The thing happened at Waterloo in 1815.'

The reference is to a historical and presumably 'dynamic' event. We can not therefore conclude from this case (and numerous other similar) that 'dynamic historic event' is one of the basic meanings of 'thing'. Quite clearly it is nothing of the sort. 'Thing' may be used in reference to a dynamic historical event without itself having the significative value of 'dynamic historical event'. That meaning is given not by 'thing' but by the context in which it is used. Now this is in fact quite closely parallel to the use of *dabar* in Hebrew. Consider:

Gen. 24: 66. 'And the slave told Isaac all the things he had done.'

Jud. 6: 29.   'It was Gideon who did this thing.'
Amos 3: 7.   'The Lord does not do anything without revealing
              his counsel to his servants the prophets.'

In all these cases actions or events are meant; but there is no reason
to suppose the essential signifying of 'dynamic historical event' to
lie in *dabar*; in fact the much more neutral sense of 'thing' can be
given it; it is the context that shows that these 'things' are in fact
events. Indeed if you say 'all the *d⁽e⁾barim*, things, that he did', you
can say the same just as well without the *d⁽e⁾barim*, e.g. Ex. 18: 1,
'Jethro heard all that Yahweh had done'. What Yahweh had done
were the mighty acts or salvation events so often referred to in
biblical theology; but they are referred to without the word *dabar*.
Thus the conception that the Word of Yahweh enters history as
dynamic event may or may not be a true representation of an
aspect of the theological thinking of the Israelites, but has nothing
to do with the meaning of the word *dabar*, except in so far as *dabar*
is or may be used for 'word'.

If it is misleading to give 'event' as a guide to the meaning of
dabar, it is equally misleading to give 'history' as the meaning of its
plural *d⁽e⁾barim*. It may reasonably be said that certain senses of
'history' are approached by certain collocations of words which
include *d⁽e⁾barim*, for example *dibre hay-yamim* 'matters of the days,
i.e. chronicles'. With a personal genitive the 'matters' of such and
such a king are certainly more or less his acts or *res gestae*, in the
common phrase in the summary at the end of a reign. This does
not give 'history' to the meaning of *d⁽e⁾barim* itself.

Even where the 'matter' indicated by *dabar* is in fact a 'dynamic'
or historical event, it is misleading to speak of 'the dynamic event
in which that inner reality becomes manifest'. This appears to
suggest that the reference to 'event' (or more correctly, as I would
hold, 'matter') arises from and depends on the sense of 'inner
reality'; in such a case one would have to explain linguistically how
a word meaning 'inner reality' came to mean or simultaneously did
mean 'external manifestation of inner reality'. There is however no
reason to investigate the question, since there is no foundation for
all this talk of 'inner reality' or of external manifestation of inner
reality in the usage of *dabar*. Its source is in the supposed etymo-

logical sense 'hinterground'. It may or may not be a reasonable description of the psychological way in which the Israelites thought about events and their significance to use these phrases about 'inner reality' and its external manifestation. It is only the etymologizing use of 'hinterground' that makes plausible the application of this theological-psychological judgement to the semantics of *dabar*. Like some others of these pieces of theological ethno-psychology, their use in relation to linguistic phenomena has its origin not in an observation of Hebraic psychology but in a misuse of fragments of Western and modern linguistic knowledge.

Even assuming the origin of *dabar* in *d-b-r* 'behind', it is scarcely to be doubted that the sense 'matter' is derived from the sense 'word'. For the semantic development of words meaning 'thing, matter' from other meanings cf. Germanic *thing* 'assembly > case > thing', *Sache* from *saka* 'lawsuit > matter', Latin *causa* 'case' > Fr. *chose* 'thing', Aramaic and late Hebrew *ḥepeṣ* 'pleasure > thing', Arabic *šayʾ* 'wish > thing', Polish *rzecz* 'word > thing'.

A characteristic procedure of the type of argument we are criticizing is its attempt to synthesize two senses of a word where they exist, and this tendency finds full play with *dabar*. The senses of this word are 'word' and 'matter'; the alternation of these will depend on the context. Torrance gives no hint of this and his terminology ('a dual significance') suggests not so much that *dabar* may mean either but that it means both ('on the one hand' and 'on the other'), or at any rate that when it primarily means one it suggests the other; when it is the event it suggests its own inner meaning, when it is the word it suggests the manifestation of this word as dynamic event. But this reasoning is far in the air above actual usage. We have indicated that the senses 'word' and 'matter' are alternative. This does not mean that we can always distinguish them clearly. We cannot therefore argue that the ancient speaker meant both. There are cases where the senses coincide, for the obvious reason that they are related to a verb of speaking (a common case), and 'to speak words' and 'to speak matters' are not really distinguishable; in fact we have here the area of usage in which the transition from 'word' to 'matter' was very naturally made. But in most cases the sense is clear:

Gen. 22: 1 'And it happened after these dᵉbarim, i.e. after these things.'

Gen. 47: 30 'I will do like your dabar, i.e. as you have spoken.'

Thus dᵉbar yahweh means 'word of the Lord' and not 'event of the Lord' or 'act of the Lord'. Hence it is wrong to say that the 'dual significance' is specially apparent in the case of the divine word. Ὁ λόγος τοῦ κυρίου ἐγένετο certainly is used of the divine word coming to the prophet. This word may have been, or may have accompanied, or may have predicted, a dynamic event entering history. But we cannot use the occurrence of dabar (λόγος) in the phrase to prove that such a dynamic event was intended, for dabar does not mean 'event' here. Further, the Greek sentence has been wrongly divided in the quotation of the phrase in this form, thus giving a certain impression that ἐγένετο means 'took place', a sense that might suggest 'event' for dabar. But the complete sentence is Ὁ λόγος τοῦ κυρίου ἐγένετο πρός με λέγων and fixes the sense of the words in question as 'word' and 'was' or 'came'.[1] The same is the case in the Hebrew form of the same sentence.

The supposed 'double meaning' of dabar is also expounded by Pedersen:[2]

'No distinction is made between the word and the matter described, and consequently the Hebrew denominations of a word may just as well apply to the matter. This holds good of both d-b-r and ʾ-m-r. The most ordinary term for word, dabar, also implies an action, that which happens, the event with all it implies (Gen. 15: 1; 22: 20). . . . For the Israelites there is upon the whole no difference whatsoever between the idea, the name and the matter itself. . . .'

Here we may question first of all the 'consequently'. This word implies that the use of the same word in Hebrew for 'word' and 'matter' is a consequence of the psychological non-distinguishing of 'the word and the matter described'. Such a psychological phenomenon by no means needs necessarily to be invoked to explain the semantic development here, any more than the

---

[1] Cf. the faulty segmentation ὁ λόγος ἐγένετο, Torrance, Royal Priesthood, p. 9, as if ἐγένετο meant 'entered history'.
[2] Israel i–ii. 167–8.

semantic histories of Germanic *thing* or *Sache* require the invoking of a Teutonic psychological inability to see the difference between argument and what you are arguing about. It must also be asked conversely whether a delineation of Hebrew psychology is soundly based when it is using as evidence for a psychological peculiarity a phenomenon of semantic change which is very widespread in many languages.[1]

There is a logical fault in Pedersen's argument where he quotes OT passages. His quotations are evidence, not that 'the most ordinary term for "word", *dabar*, also implies an action', but that *dabar* frequently in certain contexts means 'matter' and is not correctly indicated by 'word' at all since 'word' suggests some kind of linguistic communication.

We must also call attention to Pedersen's statement that there was no distinction between the word 'and the matter described'. This may well be true if we are talking about a 'matter described', i.e. about the relation between words and what they say, between a speech of Yahweh, shall we say, and the things which he says in it he will do. If the Hebrews made no distinction here they were not so exceptional; we too use 'message' or 'story' both for the words of a communication and the matter referred to in it. This is a long way from the idea that *dabar* in itself means 'event' or 'action'. There can be imaginary or false or vain *d*ᵉ*barim* in Hebrew. I think that Pedersen has been influenced by those mentions of 'the word of the Lord' which will certainly be accompanied by action, and has generalized this as the meaning of *dabar* in any context. When he goes on to speak of the close relation, or the absence of difference, between 'the idea, the name and the matter itself', this may well be a true psychological observation; but the relation believed to exist between the name of something and the thing named is quite a different matter from the relating of two senses in one word, even where the word is *dabar*.

All this criticism so far has been of methods of using linguistic evidence; the evidence itself we have not questioned. But it remains to point out that the connection of *dibber* 'speak' with the root *d-b-r* 'behind' is not certain; and that even if there is some

---

[1] See for example the survey by Kronasser, op. cit., p. 125.

such connection it certainly need not imply the semantic associations suggested by Torrance. The strangeness of the 'hinterground' association already discussed may be not so much a glimpse into a different mental world from our own as a good reason for looking for a different etymology. Two such may be mentioned: firstly that of Koehler,[1] who derives the group from a stem meaning 'to buzz, to hum' and hence 'to speak', which would fit in with $d^e borah$ 'bee'. In this case there is of course no connection at all with words of the group d-b-r 'behind'. Secondly Leslau[2] connects our group with Sidamo $dabar$ 'answer', related to the Cushitic root d-b-r 'turn, return' and hence 'answer'; in such a case there might be some connection also with Semitic d-b-r 'back'. The full semantic development of $dabar$ 'matter' in this case would be 'return > answer > word > matter'.

It is possible of course to suggest that, even though $d^e bir$ 'back room' has no semantic relation (and possibly no etymological relation at all) with $dibber$ 'speak' or $dabar$, such a relation was created by popular etymologizing. I know of no evidence in the Hebrew Bible, however, that such etymologizing did in fact take place in this case. The LXX simply transliterate.' the word as δαβειρ, hardly a sign that they attached a significance to it beyond its function as the name of this place. The earliest evidence of etymologization is with Aquila and Symmachus, who translated the word $d^e bir$ by χρηματιστήριον; cf. the use of χρηματίζω for $dibber$ 'speak' in some cases in Jeremiah and one or two other places. The original LXX text at 3 Bas. 8: 6 was certainly δαβειρ and the reading from a late hand in B, registered in Hatch and Redpath, namely χρηματιστηρί, must certainly be an echo of the Hexapla. The etymologizing of the word was followed by Jerome (*oraculum*) and so by the 'oracle' of AV. But there is no early evidence to justify a play on words between $dabar$ and $d^e bir$, or between the $d^e barim$ or decalogue and the $d^e bir$. In any case it must be clear that when the etymologizing interpretation does appear it is an interpretation of the obscure word $d^e bir$ from the well-known word $dibber$ 'speak', and is not in the slightest evidence that the

[1] KB, s.v.
[2] *Language* xxv (1949) 316, in a review of Cohen's *Essai comparatif*.

nature or the associations of the dᵉbir itself were felt to be any clue to the meaning or associations of the words for 'word' or 'to speak'.

In conclusion, something may be said of another argument which uses Hebrew *dabar* as part of a very strong contrast between the relation of word and deed in the Old Testament and their relation in Greek thought.[1] The argument is that this Hebrew word for 'word' can be used for something as solid and actual as 'a head of cattle'.

'The word means an affair, a matter and all the circumstances attached to it. It is used in a perfectly concrete manner about that which is. When Yahweh killed the cattle of the Egyptians, no *dabar* of that of the Israelites was killed (Exod. 9: 4). (The LXX renders here by ῥητόν, by the way, quite properly, but also, for the classical Hellenist, quite impossibly. How could an ox possibly be described as a "statement"?). . . .'

The following points must be made against Macnicol's treatment of this passage. (*a*) *Dabar* with a negative has more or less the same semantic range as our 'nothing, not a thing', and is not a bit more 'concrete' than our 'nothing'. Any question of concreteness depends on the other things you are talking about in the sentence and not on the *lo . . . dabar*. (*b*) It is not only the classical Greeks, but probably the Hebrews and perhaps anyone else as well, who would find 'statement' a peculiar designation for an ox. You do not express 'put these oxen out in the field' by some locution which can be taken also to mean 'put these *statements* out in the field' in Hebrew, or very likely in any language. The whole possibility of the diction of the Hebrew sentence of Exod. 9: 4 is given not by the considerations advanced by Macnicol but by the negativity of the sentence, which he leaves quite out of consideration. You use *dabar* this way because it is *lo . . . dabar* '*not* a thing'. (*c*) It is unlikely that the LXX either understood ῥητόν as a word meaning 'ox' or that they used this translation because they were aware of any values in using terms meaning 'statement', 'word' or 'speech'

[1] J. D. A. Macnicol, 'Word and Deed in the New Testament', *SJT* v (1952) 240. This article is an example of the application to biblical theology in general of the position about *dabar* we have been discussing. It contains numerous examples of those misstatements of linguistic fact and confusions of linguistic and philosophical comparison which have been studied in this book.

as a designation for a living being. Their translation is, firstly, an etymologizing translation which, regarding *dabar* as 'word' or 'speech' (often ῥῆμα), wants to use here also a translation from the same group of words as ῥῆμα. Secondly, the Greek translation depends in the same way as the Hebrew original does upon the negativity of the sentence; οὐ . . . ῥητόν thus means 'not a thing that can be expressed, spoken of', translating very literally. For the semantic development here compare numerous cases in negative particles and in particular late Hebrew *šum dabar* 'something', used negatively as 'not a thing, nothing'.[1] (d) Finally, it is doubtful if the LXX thought they had really translated 'quite properly' here, for there is only one other case of ῥητός in the whole LXX and it is not parallel. The phrase *lo . . . dabar* they much more frequently and, we may perhaps say, more 'properly', translated by οὐδέν 'nothing' (e.g. Exod. 5: 11, Deut. 22: 26).

This argument may stand as a paradigm of the danger of working from a generalized lexical method and ignoring the place of syntax. To determine the sense of *dabar* here independently of the syntactic relations in the sentence is to misinterpret it altogether. Yet the use of *dabar* in this passage is one quite straightforwardly set out in BDB.

A few general remarks may be added in conclusion to the study of the arguments from *qahal* and *dabar*. If these arguments have any validity in them at all, you can make the scripture mean anything you like at all. For this there are two main reasons. Firstly, the grossly misused etymologizing method. Let us suppose that from a given Semitic root three different words can be recognized, and that for each of these three different senses can be seen in different dialects or languages or in different historical stages of the same language. If one may argue arbitrarily from the 'connection'

---

[1] For Hebr. *šum dabar* see Rundgren, op. cit., p. 155. The etymologizing literalism of this type of rendering appears also with λόγος in the historical books, e.g. 4 Bas. 20: 13, οὐκ ἦν λόγος 'there was not anything' (which Hezekiah did not show). In some such cases of course the phrase *lo . . . dabar* is fixed in the sense of 'not a word' because it is with a verb of speaking, e.g. 1 Kings 8: 56, 'not a *dabar* from all the good *dabar* which he spoke'; in others the sense 'word' is the natural one, e.g. 1 Sam. 3: 19, where God did not allow any of the *debarim* of Samuel to fall to the ground. The same style appears in the New Testament, Lk. 1: 37, 'nothing will be impossible with God' (οὐ . . . πᾶν ῥῆμα), cf. LXX Gen. 18: 14 (μή . . . ῥῆμα).

of two or three out of the nine possibilities thus present, one has great freedom in the selection of associations which are supposed to be relevant; especially when the interpreter, if he finds no attractive etymologizing associations or connections to work from, can simply ignore etymology for this root and use it on another word where it appears to 'work'. The interpreter thus twists the material in any way he likes.

Secondly, the nature of the synthesis of biblical thought with which the words thus interpreted are supposed to fit. This biblical thought is itself no clear and simple system, but a complex and often paradoxical fabric of historical and theological traditions from different times and sources. Therefore the interpreter enjoys a great power of selection not only over the etymological 'connection' which he cares to notice for the words but also over the strand or aspect of biblical thought which he makes them fit. Thus if we suppose that *qahal* was somehow connected not with a Semitic root meaning 'speak' but with a Semitic root meaning 'silence', then the *qahal* could have been made to 'mean' the assembly of the people where man must keep silence but only God may speak. Or if *d^ebir* were 'connected' by the interpreter primarily with *midbar* 'wilderness' then no doubt its function in the temple would be to remind the people that God never resided permanently in his house but was always on the march with his pilgrim people, as in the time in the wilderness.

As soon, therefore, as the semantics of the words, within the period of the texts and the language of the texts, are neglected, the interpreter has arrogated to himself a very large power of selectivity over the material. In this regard it is interesting to remember that in biblical interpretation in general the insistence of historical criticism on discovering what the text meant at the time of its writing has more recently undergone some criticism in theological study; such a demand has been labelled 'historicism', and it has been held that the discovery of the 'meaning for to-day' is also a legitimate object of research. This question I shall not discuss here. Whatever be the answer to it, however, it is clear that there is no such question about the meaning of *words*, as distinct from texts. Words can only be intelligibly interpreted by what they meant at the time of their use, within the language system used by the speaker or writer.

It must also be pointed out that this kind of interpretation does very much more damage than a simple misstatement of the sense of a word in a particular place. The interpretation is given precisely and intentionally because it is supposed to be much more than the meaning of a word here or there, to be in fact a guide to a pervasive and recurrent element in biblical thought. Even therefore if only a few words are interpreted in this way, they will in the nature of the case be common words which will appear in many connections; and in each of these connections the mind will be infected by the spurious associations attached to *dabar* or *qahal* or whatever it may be, even if these words are only of marginal importance at the particular point being studied.

On the other hand, it is surely because the themes of biblical thought, with which words are associated in such interpretations, are genuine biblical themes, that the inadequacy and often complete absurdity of the word-interpretations so easily escapes notice. The reader may be puzzled or doubtful about the procedures used in the interpretation, but he feels that after all what comes out of it seems genuinely to represent something in which the Bible is interested. This is surely the reason why interpretations which make ludicrous departures from well-known and recorded word-meanings can nevertheless escape question so easily.

THE WORD 'BAPTISM'

How important is it that the word used for Christian baptism is not βαπτισμός but βάπτισμα? Consider this statement:

'The word used . . . is βάπτισμα, a word found only in the New Testament and Christian usage, referring to Christian baptism. This word described not simply a rite of washing (βαπτισμός) but the event, or the act of God, behind the rite. It is rather like the word κήρυγμα which describes not simply preaching, but the great events of the Gospel that are proclaimed and which are mightily operative through proclamation. The fact that βάπτισμα is applied to John's baptism indicates that John's baptism is drawn into the great salvation-events wrought by Christ on our behalf.'[1] We may compare the treatment of βαπτισμός and βάπτισμα by Oepke.[2] For these words he gives 'Immersion (das Untertauchen) or Baptism; in this βαπτισμός designates the act in itself, but βάπτισμα the act including the result, and so the institution'. Later he adds: 'The NT, by forming or reserving for Christian baptism (including its forerunner) an expression not elsewhere used and not loaded in any way with previous cultic associations, and by using it always in the singular, never in the plural, and by never substituting for it the word otherwise in use, indicates that it feels the Christian action to be something new and unique in spite of all apparent relative analogies.'

Oepke does not make clear how he knows that βαπτισμός is 'the act in itself' and that βάπτισμα includes the result of the act and thus represents the institution. It would seem probable, in the absence of any other indication, that he bases himself entirely on the difference of the suffixes -μός and -μα. We may compare a standard grammar, which in treating of the suffixes used in forma-tion of verbal nouns says in general that formations in -μα 'mostly indicate the result of the action' and later of our pair of words in particular says that 'βαπτισμός is the action of dipping, while with βάπτισμα the result is included', but without further precision about what 'result' in particular is meant.[3]

Now it is true that nouns in -μός and -μα often mean the 'doing' of the action of the verb, while those in -μα often indicate the 'thing done'; e.g. τείχισις and τειχισμός are both 'wall-building' (both Thuc.) while τείχισμα is 'fortification', i.e. what has been so constructed. Βασανισμός is 'torturing', ῥαντισμός is 'sprinkling'.

---

[1] Church of Scotland, Special Commission on Baptism, Interim Report, p. 7 f. Cf. the very similar statement by T. F. Torrance, 'The Meaning of Baptism', CJT ii (1956) 130; also The Biblical Doctrine of Baptism, a Study Document, issued by the above commission (Edinburgh, 1958), pp. 17–18. I was myself associated with the production of this document (see the Introductory Note) but would now disagree with much in its approach, which in my opinion does not sufficiently depart from the methods of the Interim Report. This latter report contains numerous examples of the kind of misinterpretation of language which is criticized in this book. Cf. also ThZ xiv (1958) 245–7.

[2] TWNT i. 543.

[3] Blass-Debrunner, Grammatik des neutestamentlichen Griechisch, § 109.

There is a danger however that the sense of 'the result of the verbal action' may be misleading when given for the suffix -μα. It might be better expressed as 'the thing done', as distinct from 'the thing being done'. Now in verbs of 'making something' the 'thing done' is pretty well the same as 'the result of the verbal action', e.g. γένημα 'produce', φύραμα 'mixture', ὀχύρωμα 'stronghold'. There are however also many verbs in which the verbal noun in -μα designates 'the thing done' not in the sense of something produced by that action but of the fact of that action itself. New Testament examples would include such as ἀγνόημα, ἀδίκημα, ἁμάρτημα, αἴνιγμα. So ἀδίκημα is not 'an unjust act with its consequences' — it is the 'unjust act' itself which is 'the thing done' or 'the result of the verbal action'.[1]

There is therefore no general ground for pronouncing nouns in -μα to refer to 'the act including the result' as if this result were an object brought about by the action and other than the doing of the action itself. There is therefore no reason to suppose that just because of its different nominal formation-element βάπτισμα differs from βαπτισμός in indicating more than 'the act in itself'. There is not indeed very much evidence to show just what βαπτισμός meant in its NT occurrences, but it may more probably be suggested that βαπτισμός indicates the act being done, seen as in progress, and βάπτισμα the act done, seen as completed. The preference for βάπτισμα in the NT would be explained fairly naturally in this way, since it was the act as something done and not as something in progress that is important in many NT contexts. This may indeed be all that Oepke meant, for his statement is very brief, and the logical sequence in 'the act including the result, and so the institution' is far from clear.

Whatever Oepke means, it is clear that the other statements quoted go farther. Βάπτισμα has now become not only 'the act including the result, and so the institution', but the 'event, or the act of God, behind the rite' — and thus different from βαπτισμός which is 'simply a rite of washing'. The linguistic difference

---

[1] Thus one must surely interpret the statement of Blass-Debrunner (see last note) in the sense that the 'result included' is simply the fact that the baptism has been performed, and not any consequence or further effect of its performance.

between βαπτισμός and βάπτισμα is now being used as evidence for the colossal theological difference between a mere rite and an event or act of God. It is at once evident that the evidence is being exaggerated, and at the same time there is a clear departure from the semantics of actual usage in the NT. Even if 'rite of washing' fits in pretty well as translation of any case of βαπτισμός in the NT, the sense of 'event, act of God, behind a rite of washing' will hardly fit such cases as Matt. 21:25, 'The baptism of John — whence was it?' It is clear that 'event, act of God' is a theologumenon about baptism, the acceptance of which is being imposed upon us by the attempt to interpret the force of the word-formation in -μα. That some of the NT writers, or all of them, may have thought of baptism as the operation of an act of God, makes no difference to this. 'Act of God' is not part of the semantic value of the word.

It may be added that if the very strongly supported reading βαπτισμῷ is correct at Col. 2:12,[1] the semantics of βαπτισμός also in the passages quoted are probably erroneously determined, since it is hardly likely that the writer of Colossians intended 'simply a rite of washing' and all the depreciatory association which has been supposed by the writers on baptism above to have attached to this word.

Though it is not expressly stated, the attempt to adduce κήρυγμα as a parallel is presumably based on the use of the same word-formation in this noun. We are told that κήρυγμα describes not simply preaching but the reality or event which is proclaimed. This is true but is no analogy for βάπτισμα. That κήρυγμα includes not only the act of proclaiming but the reality or event which is proclaimed is nothing to do with the ending -μα, or with any other similarity to βάπτισμα, but is because this is a word of saying, and it is a common semantic development for nouns from words of saying to indicate the content of what is said — e.g. Norse saga, Hebrew haggadah. This is a quite simple and natural result of the semantic value of the 'saying' verbs, and it is equally simple and natural that a verb like βαπτίζω has no such indication in its

---

[1] This reading was already preferred by Lightfoot, long before the discovery of p46, on the good grounds that it was the less normal word in NT usage.

verbal noun. There is therefore no linguistic ground for associating βάπτισμα and κήρυγμα in the way suggested, and the linguistic fact that βάπτισμα is used is no ground for the assertion, however true, that 'John's baptism is drawn into the great salvation-events wrought by Christ'.

The argument we have examined here has been not from the etymological 'root' of the words, but from the word-formation elements used in them. The neglect of actual semantics appears in both cases alike.

'MAN' — THE ADDING OF SIGNIFICANCES

In a treatment of 'man' in the Old Testament Jacob begins with 'some semantic considerations'.[1] The section goes on to list four words which may be roughly translated 'man' — Hebrew *ʾadam*, *ʾiš*, *ʾᵉnoš* and *geber* respectively. For each of these he gives an etymology. Although there are certain details in these etymologies of which one might be critical,[2] my purpose is rather to examine the general method followed and the structure of the result. Here the following criticisms may be offered:

Firstly, it must be asked if a statement of the ultimate etymology is what is needed here. The first need is a statement of what the words are used to signify in classical Hebrew. Jacob does try to give this to some extent, but it is very tangled up with etymological material. Thus in treating the word *geber* he seems to be describing usage when he states its use for a man in distinction from a woman

---

[1] E. Jacob, *Theology of the Old Testament*, pp. 156–7. Cf. my review, *JSS* v (1960) 166 ff.

[2] Jacob makes it clear, for example, that *ʾadam* has a common origin with *ʾadom* 'red' and *ʾᵃdamah* 'earth', but I find his remarks confusing if we ask what comes from what and in what sense. Thus *ʾadam* 'means he who has been brought forth from the *ʾᵃdamah*, that is, the earth'. But later we hear that 'the basic meaning of the root *ʾadam* is probably that of the colour red which man has in common with the earth, an association which facilitated the myth of man brought forth out of the earth'. Surely *ʾadam* cannot be derived *both* from the word for 'red' and the word for 'earth'. Later again we hear that this word 'stresses his origin and his external appearance'. This seems to me rather like an attempt to combine (a) an etymology of the words 'man' and 'earth' from 'red' (b) the biblical legend that man came from the earth, a legend whose growth may indeed (though I rather doubt it) have been fostered by the obvious similarity of the words, and (c) the fact that there was a popular etymology of the word *ʾadam* in just this sense, Gen. 2: 7. But is all of this alike essential to the etymology of the word, and how far is all of it decisive for its normal usage?

or child; but when he says that 'the term *geber* lays stress on power'
I suspect this to be an etymological statement, but one intended to
be a guide to usage. That it is not a statement about actual extant
cases of *geber* but about its 'basic' sense I judge probable, because
the passages quoted from Ps. 12: 5 and Job 15: 25 do not actually
use the noun *geber* 'man' but use verb forms from the same root.
In the treatment of *'iš* all that Jacob says even about usage seems
to be concentrated around the etymology, forming an attempt to
explain the usage in terms of that etymology.[1] One has a feeling
that the treatment here presupposes that the most remote accessible
etymology must be taken as the 'basic meaning' for discussion of
the words in their sense as 'man'. That such dependence on
etymology can be dangerous has already been sufficiently indicated. We have here to note another effect of it: namely that by
spacing the four terms not according to the spread of their actual
usage but according to the spread of their etymological 'basic
meanings' we run the risk of separating them more widely in sense
than usage warrants; in another case the same method might have
the opposite effect and bring words too close together because their
etymological senses are more closely related than their actual ones.

   Secondly, and perhaps more important, one must question the
method here employed of taking the four terms (and this means
virtually the four etymologies) and adding them up. Thus:

   'From these terms some conclusions can be extracted about the
nature of man and his vocation. If it is true that *'adam* insists on
the human kind, *'ᵉnoš* on his feebleness, *'iš* on his power, *geber* on
his strength, then we can say that added together they indicate
that man according to the Old Testament is a perishable creature,

---

[1] Assuming Jacob's etymology, I find the semantic development which he
suggests unlikely. The root means in his opinion 'be powerful', and so *'iš*
expresses man's power of will and choice. Then 'choice is particularly present
in the case of marriage; so a man is the *'iš* in the presence of the one he chooses'.
Certainly *'iš* is the word for 'man' which also means 'husband', cf. Lat. *vir* etc.
I would regard it as probable that if the original sense is of power, the development would be simply through 'the powerful one', i.e. in the case of marriage
the man; the bringing in of the power of *choice* and its particular presence in the
case of marriage seems without any special evidence, and may perhaps be
influenced by the importance of the power of choice and the place of marriage
in the theological doctrine of man, various aspects of which can in Jacob's
procedure be related to the etymology of the words for 'man'.

who lives only as the member of a group, but that he is also a powerful being capable of choice and dominion. So the semantic survey confirms the general teaching of the Bible on the insignificance and the greatness of man.'

It must be seriously doubted whether this method is valid. Notice again that the method is not to work from statements about man made in the Old Testament and using one or other of these words as a term in the statement; the work is done from the words themselves; and since the words are taken for themselves there has to be an excessive reliance on etymology as a guide. And then the etymologies can be added and you find that each of the several aspects of the general Hebrew idea of man has found its expression. All this surely implies an extremely close correlation between the lexical stock (i.e. the relation of words meaning 'man') and the thought structure (i.e. the perception of various aspects of man). Where you find two words related to something, you will find two aspects of that thing to which these words can be correlated.

In particular there is one point in which facts are evidently obscured by this kind of analysis. *Geber* certainly 'comes from' the well-known 'root' meaning 'be powerful'; but there are a good number of cases where there is no reason to believe that 'strong, powerful' is any part of the semantics, of the significative value of the word, and where there is every reason therefore to take it as having come to mean simply 'man'; so that it can be used in cases where man as an earthly and mortal creature is being contrasted with God or where the weakness and mortality of man is otherwise being involved. Examples are: Ps. 88: 5 (4 EV); 89: 49 (48); Job 3: 23, 10: 5, 33: 29; Lam. 3: 1. In such cases the semantic contribution of *geber* to the sentence is not 'man as strong' or 'man as proud' or 'man as other than God' but simply 'man'. But to admit this is to say that the etymological 'basic meaning' of 'strong' is not necessarily a contribution made by this word to the general picture of man, and therefore conversely that an aspect of man as *strong* in the thought of the Hebrews is not *necessarily* (though it may be in fact, but only on the basis of further evidence from usage) to be correlated with the word which has 'strong' somewhere in its etymological history.

While I do not say therefore that Jacob has led us far astray in his treatment of the Hebrew idea of man, I do think he has used a very dubious method of working from linguistic realities and has failed to protect it against a misuse which he could very harmful.

SOME OTHER EXAMPLES

Many other examples of this kind of interpretation can be cited. Here is one which I have already cited elsewhere;[1] the writer is discussing miracle in the Old Testament:

'This aspect of miracles, as wide as it is diffuse, is confirmed by the language. The fact that Hebrew has not *one* but several terms to signify miracle attests its frequency, but also its fluidity.'

This argument seems to me completely to lack foundation. By the same logic Germans must think more frequently and more variably about humanity because they have two words corresponding to English 'man'. Linguistically, the argument ignores the existence of synonyms, just as the theory implicit in it ignores the phenomenon of polysemy, i.e. the fact that one word can have more than one sense, although polysemy is one of the most important factors in linguistic change.[2] In connection with theology, it is clear how this type of argument tends to bring linguistic material under the domination of systematic theological method. Systematic theology will naturally handle such a theme as the different 'aspects' of miracle or indeed of any theological theme. The aligning of the different words with these aspects is a necessary preparatory step to the handling of linguistic material under the methods of dogmatics — precisely what is happening now so frequently under the name of biblical theology. It may be added that where synonymy appears in biblical language its presence is often concealed by the constant appeal to etymology, an example of which we shall see next.

Surveying the Hebrew terms for anger in preparation for a study of NT ὀργή, Grether and Fichtner[3] begin by saying that 'Hebrew

---

[1] Jacob, op. cit., p. 223. Cf. my review in *JSS* v (1960) 166 ff.

[2] Cf. for example Ullmann, op. cit., p. 117.

[3] *TWNT* v. 392. I cannot resist mentioning also a remark made in the study of the first Hebrew word, namely ʾap 'nostril, anger'. Of it we are told that 'The Old Testament values the nose less as an organ of smell than as an "organ

is rich in expressions for anger, each of which originally circum-
scribed a particular essential feature of anger'. There follows a list
of nine words, in most of which etymological data are emphasized.
In fact however no evidence is given that different features of anger
are or have been indicated by each of these terms.

This same article contains another common procedure of the
linguistic methods of biblical theology. Mentioning that common
terms for wrath like ʾap and ḥemah are frequently connected in a
construct combination with the divine name יהוה, and rarely with
other divine names, it argues: 'the consistent combining of nouns
for anger with Yahweh, the God of the covenant, is of considerable
theological significance; it shows that the idea of wrath is widely
connected closely with the covenant belief.'[1]

This is far from convincing. The argument is entirely by associations. The article does not quote a single case where any of the
texts used actually *says* the thing it is drawing from them, any
case which says that 'Yahweh is angry because he is a god of
covenant' or anything like that. The argument may be analysed:

(a) Common words for anger are with few exceptions connected
    in construct combinations with the name Yahweh.

(b) Yahweh is the God of the covenant.

(c) Therefore the idea of anger is closely connected with
    covenant.

The only stage in this series resting on the linguistic evidence
quoted is stage (a). The series does not form a convincing argument

of wrath" '. The absurdity of this argument is, I think, obvious. No doubt the
Old Testament made more reference to wrath than it did to smell, and therefore
quantitatively the word ʾap appears more frequently in the former sense; but
one can hardly judge from this how far the Old Testament valued the nose, an
organ to which it may indeed have given little thought. A statement about the
frequency of use of the word in its second sense 'anger' is taken to imply a
judgement of the value and function of the real object, the nostril or nose, for
which the word in its first sense is the usual name. This argument is on a
similar logical level to that of Boman (op. cit., p. 98; E.T., p. 115) that the
Greeks greatly admired the colour blue, but Hebrew 'had no word for the colour
"blue" ' — the Hebrew word meant the murex; and, presumably because the
murex had to be caught, a very dynamic matter, 'The origin of the term is thus
not a seeing but an action'.

[1] *TWNT* v. 396. In any case there is no valid reason for isolating the *construct*
combination as decisive; and the admission of other combinations admits exceptions such as Num. 16: 22, Jud. 6: 39.

from linguistic usage unless the other stages are in fact linked in the same complex of linguistic evidence as that from which (*a*) is drawn. The utmost that I think can legitimately be drawn from this evidence is that certain archaic phrases about 'the wrath of Yahweh' were current; the term *ᵉlohim* might perhaps not be used so much in this connection because it is less personal than Yahweh. It is a true judgement that Yahweh was the god of the covenant; but its truth goes nowhere to support the conclusion drawn in the *TWNT* article. A schematic importation of the covenant idea as a chief integrating concept of the OT is frequent in this kind of theological study.

Here is an etymological argument based not on Hebrew but on Greek:

'In profane Greek the words λειτουργεῖν and λειτουργία have a political and corporate sense. They refer to the work, ἔργον, of the λαός, i.e. they refer to the people's work or the people's service conceived in terms of corporate public duty. But that is gathered up to a head and is representatively undertaken by the chief of state or the king, who can therefore be spoken of as λειτουργός and as exercising λειτουργία, both in the cultic and civil sense. That corporate and kingly connotation fits in very well with the biblical notion of royal priesthood, though there is no Hebrew word or expression to correspond properly to the Greek significance of λειτουργεῖν and its cognates.'[1]

The following faults appear in this argument:

(*a*) The etymologizing method and failure to investigate the semantics of actual usage. The meaning was not what 'the people' did corporately, but certain public services rendered by individuals from their private means. But by Aristotle's time the sense of 'service' or 'function' of any kind was already current, that is to say, the word had been greatly generalized, and a bodily function or the public service of the gods could be referred to by this group of words.

(*b*) Even etymologically the construction quoted is quite wrong, for the word is not formed from λαός 'people' but from the

---

[1] Torrance, *Royal Priesthood*, p. 15.

adjective λήϊτος. The treatment ignores word-formation and merely takes the two 'basic' words in their simple forms 'people' and 'work' without bothering to ask in what forms and senses the new word-formation took place.

(c) Since there never was a reference to 'the people's work or the people's service conceived in terms of corporate public duty', any cases of such works being undertaken by a king or chief of state cannot legitimately be interpreted as the 'gathering up into a head' or as the 'representative undertaking' of a general work of the people. It must also be asked if any such cases existed and if the statements here about this function of a king or chief of state are not a pure invention. In any case it is clear that the words involve no 'corporate and kingly connotation' to relate to the biblical notion of royal priesthood. The facts which have been quite neglected here are set out clearly in *TWNT* iv. 222–5 (Strathmann).[1]

(d) It is highly unlikely that the etymology of λειτουργία, whether the right one or a wrong one, was in the minds of either the LXX translators or of the NT writers at any point. The associations suggested are thus the result not of an ancient but of a modern piece of etymologization.

In this interpretation therefore we have a case where a pattern resembling in some respects 'the biblical notion of royal priesthood' has been simply imposed on the Greek words, with no other basis than the (incorrect) etymology of 'the people's work or the people's service'. The reason why a (supposed) Greek semantic development is received with such unusual favour is its apparent suggestion of a corporate work summed up in the service of a leader or representative, a suggestion apparently helpful for the Christology, but one which cannot be obtained from the Hebrew words. In fact the Greek words were already being used in the quite general sense of 'service' or 'function' as early as Aristotle; the use for a religious service or ministry is surely a particular case of this; as Strathmann rightly says, the cultic sense did not arise

---

[1] For more general information see PW xii. 2, col. 1871 ff. For Hellenistic times see Rostovtzeff, *Social and Economic History of the Hellenistic World*, index s.v.

through the idea that a 'public service' was done through the cultus, but through the use of the general sense of 'service' in the cultic relation to the gods. The general sense of 'serve' with the frequent application in the cult fitted very closely the Hebrew terms which were translated by this group in the LXX.

I must add however that Strathmann's section on the interests which led the LXX to use these words seems to me perverse (*TWNT* iv. 228 f.). He holds that the current religious use of the words could not have influenced the LXX towards their adoption; for 'if these words had been current with the translators as technical terms of heathen cults and if they had so thought of them, they would have avoided them'. Hence he has to make a very strained argument back to the older sense of public service, suggesting that this was in some way coupled with the idea of priestly mediation. But it is far more natural to take the process as I have suggested above. If the LXX had thought about words used in heathen cults as Strathmann believes, they could never have used ὁ θεός 'God' or countless other words. It is mistaken, I think, to regard words of this kind as technical to heathenism or to any particular religion. The adoption of our words in the natural and normal sense of 'service, ministry' did not carry any necessary involvement in the theology or the practice of such service in the cults of the environment.

Another example of fascination by etymology is as follows:

Stating that 'In Hebrew the terms for ascension and oblation are the same: ʿolah',[1] Torrance tries to use this to interpret the Ascension of Christ, linking ascension and self-oblation, and linking also perhaps such other goings-up as Paul's visit to Jerusalem with the offering of the Gentile church.[2] Even if we grant that ʿolah 'burnt-offering' comes from the verb ʿalah 'go up', it is a complete ignoring of word-formation to suggest that the same word means 'ascent'. 'Ascent' in Hebrew is maʿaleh; the one case where ʿolah might have this sense, at Ezek. 40: 26, is probably textually unsound and in any case no foundation to build upon. Nor is it true that the meaning of ʿolah is 'oblation', since this

---

[1] *Royal Priesthood*, p. 39 n.   [2] Ibid., p. 17 n.

word is specialized to mean a *burnt* offering as distinct from other sacrificial offerings, and a different word would have to be used to render 'oblation' into Hebrew. Nor is there evidence that ʿolah was etymologized as 'ascent' in the biblical period. Though the LXX render it with as many as seven different Greek words in different places, they nowhere etymologize it as ἀνάβασις or the like;[1] nor, apparently, was it so treated by Aquila or by the Aramaic and Syriac versions, which would surely have used a word of the root *s-l-q* 'go up' to express such an association. Moreover, the passage in Hebrews thinks of the ascension as similar to the entry of the High Priest to the holiest place, an entry which was not connected with the ʿolah but with the blood of a totally different type of sacrifice. The attempt therefore to relate to Hebr. ʿolah the connection certainly made in Hebrews between Christ's ascension and sacrificial expiation is most probably gratuitous and worthless.

Some further errors in the interpretation of linguistic evidence may be illustrated from this argument:

'The word for pattern in the Old Testament, *tabnit*, is translated in the Septuagint either by παράδειγμα or by εἶδος, two important terms used in the Platonic philosophy to express the eternal forms or the exemplars of the eternal forms. It is highly significant that the Epistle to the Hebrews will not use those terms, and takes the liberty of correcting the Septuagint by using instead an obscure word, ὑπόδειγμα (found in Ezek. 42: 15). By that is meant that the worship on earth is not a transcription of the heavenly reality, but a pointer in observable form to a higher reality. And in order to make very sure that the ὑπόδειγμα is not to be regarded in any eternal or Platonic sense, he points out that it requires the cleansing blood of atonement (Heb. 9: 22 ff.).'[2]

Compare further:

'The Epistle to the Hebrews, in its employment of this term (i.e. ὑπόδειγμα) instead of the terms παράδειγμα and εἶδος, expressly rejects a Platonic interpretation of the relation between the

---

[1] The words used by LXX are: ὁλοκαύτωμα, ὁλοκαύτωσις, ὁλοκάρπωμα, ὁλοκάρπωσις, κάρπωμα, κάρπωσις, θυσία.
[2] Torrance, *Royal Priesthood*, p. 20 f.

heavenly Priesthood of Christ and the priesthood of the Church in terms of μίμησις.'[1]

The following criticisms may be made of this argument:

(a) The assertions about LXX usage are quite incorrect. In fact εἶδος is not used to translate *tabnit*; but several other words as well as παράδειγμα (e.g. ὁμοίωμα actually more frequently than the latter) are so used. It is also wholly unjustified to describe ὑπόδειγμα as 'an obscure word', since it can be seen from a glance at the dictionaries that it was well established in Hellenistic usage. It is used in the LXX in a sense close to some of the occurrences in the letter to the Hebrews. It was rejected by the Atticists in favour of παράδειγμα.

These inaccuracies may, however, be left aside, since the argument as a whole would probably be about equally valid or invalid even if the facts had been stated correctly.

(b) More important therefore is the question whether the Septuagint is really being 'corrected' by the writer to the Hebrews. It is typical of the argument we are examining that no evidence is offered to show that the LXX by using παράδειγμα intended a reference to Platonic philosophy; or that Hebrews by not using this word intended a repudiation of that philosophy; or that the readers of this letter could possibly have been so clairvoyant as to infer from the non-use of a word used in Plato (whom they had very likely not read) that the writer of the letter was thus rejecting a Platonic interpretation of his ideas; or that Hebrews intended to correct the Septuagint; or that any reader could have understood his usage to constitute a correction of the Septuagint. The semantics of the words in the actual usages are not investigated, and the question what the writers meant is not asked. To use a word which is common and important in Plato is to become involved in the Platonic philosophy, and to use another word is obviously to repudiate that involvement. The interpretation is in fact done straight from the dictionary and not from the texts at all.

(c) We may thus point out that where LXX used παράδειγμα for *tabnit* the sense was that of the 'plan' or 'design' of a building, a sense well established in Greek from Herodotus (v. 62) and still

[1] Ibid., p. 94 f.

used much later, and a sense which corresponded exactly to that of the Hebrew. It seems therefore unlikely that either the LXX intended, or was unconsciously influenced by, or was taken by its readers to intend, any suggestion of Platonism, merely on the ground that this word, which was used in the LXX in its straight-forward sense in these cases, was also used by Plato in a rather transferred sense to describe the nature of the forms. It is very much *more* unlikely that Hebrews was correcting this translation, because (*a*) it makes no actual reference to it, and the mere use of one word where another might conceivably have been used hardly constitutes a 'correction' of the latter (*b*) the word which it uses is quite a common and well-established one in the senses it intends (*c*) in the one place where it quotes an actual sentence from the LXX which in Hebrew included *tabnit*, namely Hebr. 8: 5 = Exod. 25: 39 (40), it quotes the LXX almost verbatim and in particular retains the word τύπος used by the translators, a word frequently used by Plato in reference to his forms.

(*d*) Thus when he tells us that Hebrews is 'expressly' rejecting a Platonic interpretation, Torrance is using 'expressly' in a sense the exact opposite of that which it is usually taken to have.

(*e*) It is perhaps worth adding that both the παράδειγμα of the LXX and the ὑπόδειγμα of the NT bear in a number of cases a sense of roughly 'example' which probably cannot be connected with Hebrew *tabnit* at all and certainly not with its use in the Bible. It is unlikely therefore that this Hebrew word and its various Greek translations can properly be made the basis for discussion of ὑπόδειγμα in the NT.

(*f*) You can in fact prove anything by the methods which have been used here. Working from a similar set of data in similar ways one could demonstrate the following:

'A word much beloved by Plato and used by him explicitly in his doctrine of forms was τύπος "type". Aware of the danger of Platonism, the translators of the LXX avoided this word, using it only four times in all, and of these only twice in the books of the Hebrew canon. One of these cases however was in the important passage of Ex. 25: 39 (40), translating Hebrew *tabnit*. The famous Christian Platonist Paul, on the other hand, was naturally fond of this word, and used it about eight times in his letters. The letter to the Hebrews, however, adhering to the anti-Hellenic strain of Christianity (perhaps because it was written for a destination in Palestine?) never uses the word at all except in a quotation from the Septuagint. By a strange mischance the quotation is of that one passage where the word is used to translate Hebr. *tabnit* "design". Uneasy as the writer to the Hebrews must have been to find this favourite Platonic word entrenched in an important passage (the only one he quotes which contained *tabnit* in the Hebrew), it seems clear that he felt it unjustified to "correct" the Septuagint text which he so deeply revered.'

(*g*) More seriously we must point out the overloading of argument at one point. Even if Torrance's exposition of the 'correction' were acceptable, how could such a thing demonstrate ('By that is meant') that earthly worship is not a transcription of a heavenly reality but a pointer in observable form to such a reality? We here have an example of a common fault in this sort of interpretation, namely, failure to see any difference between what is indicated by a word and other things which may in fact exist in or in association with the object referred to by the word. It is by this kind of argument by association that biblical theology often forces its general and synthetic picture of the Bible upon a particular word or text. To take another example from the same work, the discussion of θυσία[1] states that 'In the Greek Bible this word is used regularly for the Hebrew *zebah* and *minhah, referring to substitutionary sacrifice which is to be realized in life*' (my italics). The italicized passage makes a typically confused statement of what is 'referred to'. It is true that the Greek word translates these two Hebrew words, and these are names of types of sacrifice. For such sacrifices this Greek word may thus be called a designation. It is not clear however that its use necessarily also designates other characteristics which in fact belong to these sacrifices. To determine whether these are intended one must consult the contexts individually. The mere appearance of the word may not necessarily prove them to be intended. It must further be questioned whether in this case the 'substitutionary' nature of the sacrifice is implied by the

[1] *Royal Priesthood*, p. 17.

use of its name. The sacrifices involved in this case are those of which a 'substitutionary' interpretation is much more difficult than in others. And when we go on to read of how this 'substitutionary' sacrifice 'is to be realized in life' we are adding something that goes quite beyond the semantics of the words from which we began and which has practically no meaning in the discussion of their semantics; it is in fact a part of the developed theological thinking about sacrifice and its relation to the Church. If this is something 'referred to' it is something 'referred to' in a quite different sense than the semantic reference of the word θυσία as a lexical unit in the Greek Bible. There is a confusion in much of this kind of discussion between two things: firstly, the use of biblical words as a reminder of the sense of biblical texts in which they occur; secondly, the use of biblical words as counters which can be moved in modern theological thinking. The latter may be legitimate in some way, but tends to pretend to be the former. Thus we should be clear that when one speaks of how 'the liturgical forms (εἴδη) are turned into idols (εἴδωλα)'[1] we are not saying anything about biblical language at all; for εἶδος is not used either in the LXX or the NT with the semantic value of 'liturgical form', nor are εἴδωλα so called because they are distortions or degenerations of εἴδη, nor is it likely that any writer of the biblical literature formulated the thought that εἴδωλα arise by degeneration of εἴδη. The words are thus mere counters in a piece of modern thinking, and can only be used in it in neglect of their semantics in the Bible. Whether the use of such counters is of value I leave to readers to consider.

A rather similar case, and with some etymologizing effect, may be found in the treatment of NT σπλαγχνίζομαι by Barth.[2] He introduces this 'remarkable' word while discussing the solidarity of Jesus with his fellow-men. Jesus has no hidden place which belongs to himself and to which he can take refuge from the claims of his fellows; his relation to his neighbour reaches to *his most inward part*. Since this Greek word is formed from σπλάγχνα 'in-

---

[1] *Royal Priesthood*, p. 5.
[2] Barth, *KD* iii/2. 252. I owe this case to the observation of Mr. J. M. Kellet, M.A. Cf. G. S. Hendry, *The Gospel of the Incarnation* (London, 1959), p. 103.

ward parts of the body', Barth explains it to mean that Jesus not only took human misery to heart but took it into his heart, absorbed it into himself and made it his own. Hence the usual translations 'he took pity on him' or 'he was moved with compassion' are inadequate and only approximate; the word is really untranslatable. It is used, says Barth, significantly only of Jesus and 'of three figures very close to him in the parables'. It must not be taken to mean a passive feeling of sympathy.

What Barth here says about Jesus may well be true. He not only felt the misery of man but took it upon himself. But this is no evidence that this is the meaning of σπλαγχνίζομαι, and the use of this word is no evidence of the truth of what is here said about Jesus, or at least no more specially evidence than any other story of his healing, his weeping, his fatigue or his dereliction. Barth hankers after giving the word the actual *meaning* of 'absorb into the σπλάγχνα' but is restrained by its evident impossibility. This interpretation is etymologizing in a way, but not the way in which the verb was in fact derived or understood. The insistence on the untranslatability of the word is a consequence of insisting on reading into it an impossible sense. In fact the translation 'he was moved with compassion' is a very good one and much closer than can be achieved for many words. If Barth thinks this gives a suggestion of a cool passive observer, he has neglected to think of what people mean when they say 'compassion'. It is true that the verb is used only of Jesus in the NT, but this is natural in a body of literature in which the pity of Jesus will certainly be emphasized; it does not mean that a word meaning pity means a unique absorption of misery, simply because in fact Jesus does absorb misery in a unique way. But the final decision in the whole matter lies in the impossibility of fitting the suggested meaning, 'a drawing of their need into his inmost being'[1], with the syntactical context in cases like Matt. 9: 36, 14: 14 (with prepositional phrases περὶ αὐτῶν and ἐπ᾽ αὐτοῖς) and 20: 34 (participle absolutely).

[1] The formulation of Hendry, loc. cit.

CONCLUDING REMARKS ABOUT ETYMOLOGIES

There are of course good reasons why etymological research has been of greatest importance in modern research in Hebrew. In particular, there are many obscure words in classical Hebrew. The classical literature was of small compass, and many such words were of rare occurrence; of such there was sometimes little reliable information in later tradition, or contradictory information, and the only way of reaching their meaning was by comparative etymological research. A great deal has been accomplished by such methods for the elucidation of the Bible.[1] Words that are rare in the Bible can be identified as cognates of a known Arabic or Accadian word. Such identifications do not of course mean that the Hebrew word means the same as its cognate; very frequently it does not. But the etymological recognition may be used in conjunction with the context of the Hebrew word to give a good semantic indication for its occurrence. Also etymological methods are essential for the recognition of homonyms, or cases where two different words have by sound-changes become alike in form. This occasionally means that the meaning of a word which occurs rarely is eclipsed in later memory by its more frequent homonym and can be resurrected by the etymological scholar to the much better understanding of the passage involved.[2] All this goes to show the importance which etymological study has had and still does have for the understanding of the Bible. It remains true that there are gaps which good etymological study does not try or profess to fill. In particular, where there is a long period of no recorded usage, the gap can be filled from etymological considerations only with the utmost reserve; and where there is recorded usage, etymology may be of help to supplement the study of that usage and to show how it has developed; but it cannot impose a sense authoritatively upon known usage.

[1] One thinks for example of the outstanding work of G. R. Driver in this connection.

[2] For example the recognition that the verb *daʿā* 'call', well known in Arabic, also occurred in Hebrew, but that the forms from it were mistakenly understood as from the familiar Hebrew *yadaʿ* 'know'. This is not homonymy, but homography of the two words in the unvocalized writing of certain (but not all) forms of them. Examples will be found at Prov. 24: 14, 10: 32 etc. See Winton Thomas, *JTS* xxxviii (1937) 401.

It is just this assumption of authority which is most damaging where etymological associations are allowed to do the work in interpretation that should be done by semantics on the basis of actual usage. There are different degrees in which this fault may be allowed to occur. One form is that where the etymological sense is regarded as 'fundamental' and extant senses regarded as contingent 'modifications' of it — the root fallacy as I have called it. In more serious cases etymological connections which appear to be theologically attractive are simply allowed to take charge of the whole interpretation and no real attention is given to the things being said and the particular semantic contribution of words used. I have pointed out that this procedure is necessarily arbitrary, since it would be impossible to explain all words as if the etymology was the guide to their semantics without making chaos of language; in fact the etymologizing is inconsistent and is used to give a twist to interpretation at certain strategic points; it is also arbitrary because etymological fact is historical and relative, and there is much selection possible in the choosing of the words to be explained through etymology, the remoteness of the etymological associations noticed and used, and so on. A crassly arbitrary method can be avoided only when it is accepted that etymological statements are historical and not authoritative and that semantic statements must be based on the social linguistic consciousness related to usage.[1]

In conclusion it should be added that the characteristics of the Hebrew mind, as delineated in the common thought-distinction, may well have a pre-disposing effect towards the etymologizing interpretation of words in biblical theology. Thus the idea that it is Hellenic to make distinctions may discourage the search for the real

---

[1] Anyone with some ingenuity can make up etymological suggestions of the same kind and value as the more striking cases mentioned in this chapter. One could hardly do better than to begin with the interesting connection of the Gospel (Hebr. $b^e\acute{s}orah$, translated $\epsilon\dot{v}a\gamma\gamma\dot{\epsilon}\lambda\iota o\nu$ by the LXX) with Flesh (Hebr. $ba\acute{s}ar$ = NT $\sigma\acute{a}\rho\xi$) or Incarnation — a connection which has all the appearance of being written into the heart of the Hebrew language itself. I have never actually seen this connection made before. The riches of the English language have also hardly been fully explored, and one may begin here from 'believe', which according to the OED is from the Indo-European root lubh- 'to hold dear, whence also LOVE, LIEF' — a connection the significance of which will escape no theologically-minded person.

oppositional semantic value of a Hebrew word; and the idea conversely that the Hebrew mind sees reality as a mesh of interrelated
life may encourage the belief that the etymological 'relations'
between words are a guide to these mental relations. Similarly the
supposition that the Hebrews saw things as a totality may encourage interpreters to look for some hint of the totality in which things
are seen in the etymological relations of words and the 'roots'
which lie 'behind' them. This does not however explain the
existence of etymologizing interpretations depending on a Greek
etymology; and probably we have to discern a general partiality
towards etymologizing, which in the case of Hebrew words
however receives some spurious encouragement from the custom-
a ry characterization of Hebrew thought.[1]

[1] The etymological obsession of some modern theology, and some of its general
attitudes to language, may be in part a heritage from the philosophical methods
of M. Heidegger; see his *An Introduction to Metaphysics* (London, 1959), and
the remarks of J. Macquarrie, *The Scope of Demythologizing* (London, 1960),
p. 193 ff.

Chapter Seven

'Faith' and 'Truth'—an Examination of some Linguistic Arguments

(a) THE ARGUMENT FOR 'FAITHFULNESS'

In recent years there has been some attempt to emphasize the Hebrew background of the term 'faith', and in particular on the basis of this Hebrew background to emphasize the moment of the faithfulness of God towards man as well as the faith or believing of man towards God.[1] The examination of this attempt in some detail will disclose some basic procedures in dealing with linguistic evidence which deserve full criticism. I do not seek to discuss how far in fact the faithfulness of God is related to the faith of man, or in what way; or how far it is good or bad theology to express their relatedness in any particular way, but merely to examine the linguistic arguments used in the discussion, and in particular the arguments from the Hebrew background. Although both Hebert and Torrance discuss the exegesis of Greek passages, it is quite explicitly to Hebrew usage and background that they appeal; and presumably it is by the correctness of their assessment of Hebrew usage that their arguments stand or fall. The question as Hebert's opening sentence puts it is: 'whether the word "faith", as St Paul uses it, carries a Hebrew rather than a Greek meaning.' Similarly Torrance thinks it impossible for anyone to be surprised by his exegesis of Paul unless he is 'tempted to forget that Paul was a Hebrew of the Hebrews'.[2]

---

[1] A. G. Hebert, ' "Faithfulness" and "Faith" ', *Theology* lviii (1955) 373–9; T. F. Torrance, 'One Aspect of the Biblical Conception of Faith', *ET* lxviii (1956–7) 111–14; with criticism by C. F. D. Moule, ibid. pp. 157 and 222, and rejoinder by Torrance p. 221; also Torrance, *Conflict and Agreement* ii. 74–82. For an earlier study cf. C. H. Dodd, *The Bible and the Greeks* (London, 1935), pp. 65–75.

[2] Torrance, ibid., p. 221.

We may begin by quoting the opening section of Hebert's appeal to the Hebrew terminology. He states that 'in all our European languages "faith" is seen as an act or activity of man'. Then he goes on:

'It is just at this point that the Hebrew meaning is sharply different; the verb ʾaman in its various forms, and ʾᵉmunah and the other derivative nouns, have the fundamental meaning of "firmness", "steadfastness", "sureness"; and this applies above all to God; so that ʾᵉmunah, faithfulness, becomes a divine attribute: (Ps. 36: 5–7 is here quoted). As the psalmist implies, the Hebrew word denoting steadfastness and firmness applies properly to God and not to man, who is repeatedly characterized as physically frail (Is. 40: 6–8 is here quoted) and morally unstable (Ps. 36: 1–4 is here appealed to).'[1]

This argument may be criticized as follows:

(a) 'The Hebrew word denoting steadfastness and firmness applies properly to God and not to man.' The Psalmist implies nothing of the sort, and it is a serious methodological error to suggest that he does. It may be argued quite reasonably that the psalmist is comparing God and man (or certain men) and expressing his thought that God, unlike these men, is steadfast and faithful. This is a theological judgement of the writer, and a quite understandable one. It is a wholly illegitimate extension of it to suppose that it implies the linguistic judgement that ʾᵉmunah does not 'properly' apply to man.

Even the word 'properly' cannot be used here without introducing a confusion between theological and linguistic method. If I may coin an example, a theologian might disapprove of the phrase 'The Devil is good', as being an 'improper' use of the word 'good', i.e. inconsistent with what the Devil in fact is; but linguistically there is nothing 'improper' unless the phrase is linguistically unusable in the usage of the time and group under discussion. If a Moslem calls God 'great', it is absurd to deduce that the word 'great' is not used 'properly' when applied to a bus or a camel. Such a statement about the word 'great' would not be true, even if the user of the word himself thought theologically that only God

[1] Hebert, op. cit., p. 374.

was really great and buses and camels were quite slight things in comparison with him. The word 'properly' here belongs in the theological sphere of judgements about the juxtaposition of the terms 'God', 'man' and 'faithfulness'. As a contribution to linguistic evidence it has no validity at all.

And we must remember that it is linguistic evidence that Dr Hebert is looking for. He wants to get a decision which will be valid, not when the theological judgement of Ps. 36 appears again, but when the linguistic unit *ʾemunah* appears again (and not only *ʾemunah*, but cognate words). So he continues as a consequence of this argument: 'Hence the words "faith" and "to believe" (*heʾemin*) do not *properly* describe a virtue or quality in man . . .' (my italics for 'properly').

Now for linguistic evidence that Dr Hebert is wrong we do not need to look far. In both 2 Kings 12: 16 and 22: 7 we hear of a group of men whose financial dealings could be left unsupervised 'because they acted in fidelity or trustworthiness' (*ʾemunah*). The judgement that this usage is not 'proper' has absolutely no linguistic validity, and there is not any reason to suppose that the writers of the text felt it in any way theologically inappropriate either; and if they did it would not matter.

The conception that the 'proper' meaning of this root is only with reference to God is both wrong in itself and supported by an illegitimate confusion of theological and linguistic methods.

(*b*) There is a confusion in the use of the term 'fundamental meaning' as applied to the group of Hebrew words formed with the consonant sequence ʾ-*m-n*. This 'fundamental meaning' is an etymology and not a statement about the semantic value of each of the words formed within this group. Dr Hebert treats the etymology as if it was an underlying meaning present in each of the words and determining the value of all of them. Thus having taken the etymological 'sense' of 'be firm', and having found a noun form which incorporates roughly this (*ʾemunah*) being used of the distinctive faithfulness of God, he is sure that 'faithfulness' will be found all through the series, and the faithfulness of God at that.

Thus excessive etymologizing is accompanied as so often by the 'root fallacy', and the essential linguistic procedure of independent

semantic checking for each form and occurrence is correspondingly
neglected. Hebert (followed in this by Torrance) has no difficulty
in regarding any semantic observations made for *ᵉmunah* as
equally well established for, say, *heʾᵉmin*. We have already quoted
how Hebert, having established (wrongly) that *ᵉmunah* is 'properly'
applied only to God, goes on to argue that 'hence' the words
'faith' and 'to believe' do not properly describe a virtue or quality
of man. Two points must be made here:

(a) We must notice that the terms 'virtue or quality' are
deliberately and tendentiously loaded terms, remote from the
Israelite way of speaking and suggesting the Greek way of
philosophic thought. In other words, the matter is so expressed as
to suggest that the choice is between a Hebraic theological picture
of the faithfulness of God and a Hellenized static and abstract
'virtue or quality'. But when the question was first put it was in
rather different terms — 'in all our European languages "faith" is
seen as an act or activity of man'. It is only fair to put the question
to the Hebrew language in the same way: is 'faith' or 'to believe'
(*heʾᵉmin*) in Hebrew an act or activity of man? Put in this way,
there is only one answer. The use of *heʾᵉmin* with a human subject
is quite normal, while with God as subject it only occurs in rather
unusual locutions like Job 15: 15: 'He does not trust in his holy
ones'. In fact the whole structure built upon the supposed 'fundamental meaning' of the root collapses as soon as real attention is
given to the verb *heʾᵉmin* 'believe' — but neither Hebert nor
Torrance give it any real attention, since they build up their whole
case on the 'fundamental meaning'. The subject of the verb
heʾᵉmin is frequently or normally a man. This is, I think, as far as
linguistic evidence can go to indicate that in Hebrew *heʾᵉmin*, like
the corresponding words in our European languages, refers usually
to an act or activity of men.

It is of course perfectly possible to say that the actual work in
the act of faith is done by God, and to make statements such as
'It is not I who believe but God working in me who believes' or
'the work that is done by my believing is not done by me but by the
infinitely greater strength of God'. It might be possible to make
such theological judgements about texts in which the verb *heʾᵉmin*

occurs. It is quite another thing to try to extract such judgements from the word *he²emin* itself, as if the mere use of this term necessarily implied the making of such judgements.[1]

(*b*) Thus both Hebert and Torrance make a gross misuse of their 'fundamental meaning' of 'firmness, steadfastness', firstly in the way in which they allow the discussion of its significance to slide back and forth without discrimination between the various cognate words,[2] and secondly in the way in which they press and overplay this etymological and allegedly fundamental meaning against the semantic evidence of actual usage.

On the first of these counts, we must repeat that to be guided by the 'fundamental meaning' of a 'root' in discussing the various extant forms is to neglect the force of word-formation, which creates or may create separate fields of significance for what are independent forms. Even supposing there to be a 'fundamental meaning' throughout the forms from the consonant sequence ²-*m-n*, it must be clear that the way in which the 'fundamental meaning' becomes integrated into the actual semantic function of any form of the sequence depends separately on the function of the different forms. In other words, to talk of the 'fundamental meaning' as if it appeared in the same sense in each word-formation is to make the same mistake as those who explain 'holy' as fundamentally equivalent to 'whole'. Only by a total disregard for the importance of word-formation could Hebert argue that because ²emunah was the faithfulness of God *he²emin* could not be an act or activity (or 'quality or virtue') of man. The lack of common sense

---

[1] Theologically, it is quite obvious that neither of the authors under discussion wants to go so far as to deny the idea of man believing or having faith. They so emphasize the supposed 'fundamental meaning' of 'faithfulness' and so neglect the Hebrew word for 'believe' that they convince themselves that 'the faithfulness of God' must be a major part in any kind of 'faith' which goes back to forms from the Hebrew group ²-*m-n*. Hence the Hebrew 'fundamental meaning' goes to form evidence for the idea of a 'polarized expression' involving the faithfulness of Christ but also the answering faithfulness or faith of man (Torrance, op. cit., p. 113).

[2] Dodd also, I think, pays rather too much attention to the 'basic idea' of 'firmness or fixity'; but he takes care to give a proper semantic value of 'be convinced, trust' to the *hiph²il*, and so for the other forms individually; op. cit., p. 66. Dodd's careful grasp of detail prevents his argument from being carried away by what is in the writer's submission a misstatement; with Hebert and Torrance the latter becomes the foundation of the argument, and facts which do not conform are not noticed.

here must be traced in part to the conviction of the immense uniqueness of the Hebrew language and its total difference from European tongues, which so clearly fascinates this school of thought, and to the belief that the great theological truths are latent in the structure of Hebrew. Moreover, we have already seen that it is quite wrong to suppose that *ᵉmunah* is used properly only when used of the faithfulness of God.

On the second count, it is clear that Hebert's argument from Ps. 36, already quoted, is dependent on his pressing the supposed fundamental meaning of 'firmness' far beyond what is legitimate. To make the distinction which he does make between God and man he has to set the terms as 'strength' and 'permanence'. The word *ᵉmunah* is not properly applicable to man '*because he is physically frail and morally unstable*'. Now the question of physical strength or frailty is quite irrelevant here, and this contrast appears only because Hebert has leant heavily upon the English term 'firmness' and allowed it to be extended into a sense of 'strength'. 'Moral stability' is also an extension of the sense in a moralistic direction. But that neither of these is the sense in the passage being discussed is clear from the translation which Hebert himself quotes, in which the word *ᵉmunah* is quite well rendered 'faithfulness', and this sense is confirmed by the *ḥesed* of the other hemistich, rendered by 'lovingkindness', which might also perhaps be put as 'loyalty'. Even on Hebert's own terms presumably the physically frail and even the morally unstable might be faithful or loyal. He has made *ᵉmunah* applicable only to God by applying a theological contrast, which is not related to actual uses of this word, through an illegitimate extension of the idea of 'firmness'.

A still further extension of the supposed fundamental meaning of 'firmness' appears when both Hebert and Torrance begin to connect with the root *ʾ-m-n* a number of cases of verbs meaning 'confirm' in the New Testament, Greek στηρίζειν or βεβαιοῦν, such as 2 Thess. 3: 3: 'Faithful (πιστός) is the Lord, who will strengthen (στηρίξει) you'; or Lk. 22: 31 f.: 'I have prayed for you that your faith (πίστις) fail not; and when you are converted, strengthen (στήρισον) your brethren.' Of this Torrance writes:

'The verb *ʾaman* has, it would appear, mainly a twofold usage.

Primarily, it is used to mean "to make firm", "to establish", "to ground in the truth", and as such is sometimes translated in the LXX by στηρίζειν.' The other use which Torrance mentions is the sense 'believe in' or 'rely on'.

Now the obvious test of suggestions like this is to put the sentences into Hebrew in the way suggested, and a fatal difficulty is at once apparent. Granting that 'the verb ʾaman' with a sense like 'make firm' has existed in the prehistory of Hebrew and left its legacy in a number of noun and participle forms, it remains clear that no finite verbal form of *ʾaman qal exists in OT or later Hebrew with this sense or with any sense. The piʿel ʾimmen in Middle Hebrew[1] is uncommon and seems clearly secondary and derivative. The most important case cited by Jastrow, at Tos. Ter. i. 4, may be said to mean 'confirm' but might be taken more exactly as 'make confirmation, approve' since it is intransitive; so also the cases from the Jerusalem Talmud cited by him, if they belong here at all. These circumstances alone make it unlikely that the piʿel is relevant to NT usages of 'to confirm someone'. 'The verb ʾaman' and the sense 'make firm' are deductions from the etymology and there is no good evidence that they were available to be in the mind of either St Paul or St Luke. That there is any relation between the βεβαιοῦν or στηρίζειν of these NT passages and the Hebrew root ʾ-m-n is extremely improbable; and there is an overwhelming likelihood that, if any Hebrew word was in the mental background of these Greek sayings, it was a normal Hebrew term frequently known in roughly this sense, such as ḥ-z-q or s-m-k. It remains to add that Torrance's sense 'to ground in the truth' is pure etymologizing and a wild departure from usage.[2]

The argument of van Unnik on the other hand depends on Aramaic rather than on Hebrew;[3] but as far as I can discover, the corresponding forms in Aramaic (pᵉʿal, paʿel) do not exist, and van Unnik does not cite evidence for the existence of an Aramaic

[1] M. Jastrow, Dictionary of the Targumim s.v.
[2] It also seems to involve using etymology in two opposite directions at once: 'truth' takes its sense from 'make firm', and 'make firm' depends on 'truth' in the sense 'ground in the truth'.
[3] Van Unnik, op. cit., pp. 215–34.

form from the root ʾ-*m-n* which could fit into the verbal contexts of 2 Cor. 1: 15–24. His suggestion therefore that the passage is held together by associations from the root ʾ-*m-n* and thus affords a proof that Paul thought in Aramaic is surely extremely precarious. The Christian Syriac versions do not seem to have perceived these associations, nor do they use a form from ʾ-*m-n* meaning 'confirm'. Van Unnik's article adopts the 'root fallacy' as a basic principle (see above, p. 101 f.). It also leans heavily on Schlier's articles on βέβαιος (on which see below) and on ἀμήν in *TWNT*. This latter article is heavily etymologizing in parts; to call a supposed original sense an 'inner' sense is to show a basic misunderstanding of semantic change.[1] What Schlier says about how the LXX translation of ʾ*amen* by γένοιτο 'causes the concealment of the original dialectic within the concept' is, I think, linguistically nonsense. Not surprisingly he has to call on the evidence of the inveterate etymologizer Aquila.[2]

Some more detail should perhaps be given about this. The line of usage actually found in the OT to which the 'primary meaning' of 'make firm' can be attached is a very narrow one, and consists of those nouns and participles like ʾ*omen* which occur in connection with nursing or guardianship of children, plus the single case of ʾ*om*ᵉ*not* 'doorposts' at 2 Kings 18: 16. Now in what I may call the 'guardian' series it is clear that the words have already been specialized, so that 'make firm' is no longer the meaning, even assuming that the series was derived from that sense in the first place. Only an etymologizing method can offer 'make firm' where the sense is clearly 'nurse, care for'. The line where a sense really something like 'make firm' appears in usage is thus extremely thin. That it did exist may perhaps be deduced from the LXX; but here again the evidence does not go beyond certain participles and derivative noun forms within a limited range.

The LXX evidence is as follows:

The cases where words of the root ʾ-*m-n* have been rendered by words of the στηρίζω group are only four:

(*a*) Exod. 17: 12 καὶ Ααρων καὶ Ωρ ἐστήριζον (=*tam*ᵉ*ku*) τὰς

---

[1] *TWNT* i. 341; van Unnik, ibid., p. 218.
[2] *TWNT* i. 340.

χεῖρας αὐτοῦ . . . καὶ ἐγένοντι αἱ χεῖρες Μωυσῆ ἐστηριγμέναι (²ᵉmunah) ἕως δυσμῶν ἡλίου.

(b) 2 Bas. 20: 19 ἐγώ εἰμι εἰρηνικὰ τῶν στηριγμάτων Ἰσραηλ (MT reads ²anoki šᵉlume ²ᵉmune yiśra²el).

(c) 4 Bas. 18: 16 συνέκοψεν . . . τὰ ἐστηριγμένα (ha-²omᵉnot).

(d) 4 Bas. 25: 11 τὸ λοιπὸν τοῦ στηρίγματος (probably reading Hebrew ha-²amon).¹

On these translations we may comment: in (a) very considerable influence in producing the translation ἐστηριγμέναι must be attributed to the previous ἐστήριζον (= tamᵉku); (b) is recognizably a mechanical and unintelligent one.

There are two other places where the other Greek translators are known to have used the στηρίζω group in rendering words with the consonant sequence ²-m-n:

(a) Prov. 8: 30, Hebr. ²amon ο΄ ἁρμόζουσα α΄ τιθηνουμένη σ΄ θ΄ ἐστηριγμένη.

(b) Jer. 52: 16 (15), Hebr. ²amon α΄ θ΄ τοῦ ὑποστηρίγματος (cf. 4 Bas. 25: 11).

It should be noted therefore that:

(a) All cases are noun or participle formations.

(b) These cases form quite a small proportion of the total cases in which LXX or other Greek versions use words of the στηρίζω group; and the uses of the verb στηρίζω itself are nearly all in translation of well-known Hebrew terms for 'strengthen' or 'support', or in the sense of 'setting' or 'fixing' the eyes in a direction.

As for the words of the βέβαιος group, these are seldom used in the LXX and the verbs of the ²-m-n group are never translated by them. Of the other Greek translators Symmachus uses βεβαιότης and βεβαίωσις three times altogether for Hebr. ²ᵉmunah (Ps. 35 (36): 6; 88 (89): 25; and 142 (143): 1; in this last I attribute to Symmachus the translation attributed to Aquila by the source, see Field's note ad loc.); but Symmachus also uses πίστις in several places for the same word. It is surely doubtful that Symmachus translated thus in these three cases because he thought it the

¹ Surely rather badly cited by LS, who give a rendering of the Massoretic text rather than of the Greek.

'proper' (i.e. the etymological) meaning, as Schlier suggests.[1] More likely it was because βεβαιότης or βεβαίωσις, roughly 'assurance' or 'surety' perhaps, seemed to him a variation pretty near the usual sense of 'faithfulness'; his fondness for variety and his avoidance of literalism were known already to Jerome.

Van Unnik seems to me therefore mistaken in assuming that the use of these nouns by Symmachus (he actually quotes the adjective βέβαιος, which does not occur in this case) entitles us to take the verb βεβαιόω in Paul to be a reference to the (supposedly existing) Hebrew or Aramaic verbs of the same root as the noun so rendered by Symmachus. In any case, two or three cases in Symmachus are very little to go on, especially when he does not use the verb βεβαιόω at all in the fragments we have. Since van Unnik wants to show an etymologizing association in Paul's mind, he could do as well by associating the ναί of the Pauline passage with words of the βέβαιος group, since about six cases occur where this group is used for expressions containing the Hebrew sequence *k-n*, which could give an association with Hebr. *ken* 'yes' — so Symmachus at Gen. 41: 32, 1 Bas. 23: 23, Ps. 88 (89): 22, Ezek. 33: 20; other translations at Exod. 6: 6, Hos. 6: 3. I would be doubtful however whether this association need be taken any more seriously. I do not doubt that Paul may have etymologized from time to time, but feel there is little substance in van Unnik's arguments that he does so in this case. A series of 'links between concepts which are not necessarily linked by Hebrew or Septuagintal usage, but only by associations in a theological mind' (the formulation suggested to me by a friend) seems to me more probable.

The suggestion that in 2 Thess. 3: 3 there is a 'play upon the original sense of '-*m-n*'[2] must therefore be deemed highly improbable. That Paul in a Greek letter should be making a play upon a Hebrew verb which to say the least must have been poorly known in the sense intended and which probably did not exist in the form required, by using a Greek verb which in the LXX commonly represents other Hebrew verbs in the sense and form here required, and which only in very scattered cases represents out-of-the-way derived forms of the verb supposedly alluded to, is in my opinion

[1] *TWNT* i. 601.   [2] Dodd, op. cit., p. 68.

incredible. The absolute naturalness of the Greek phrase tells in any case against an allusive word-play.

What I have said about the specialization of the semantics of the 'guardian' series seems to me to be decisive against the play which Torrance makes of this group. He writes:

'As in the case of so many Hebrew words, the fundamental significance of ʾ-m-n seems to be related closely to the intense family consciousness of Israel . . . Thus the vivid picture of the constancy and steadfastness of a parent to her child lurks behind the Old Testament concept of faithfulness.'

It is hardly necessary to point out that this is semantic confusion. A word means 'nurse' or 'guardian'; therefore it is related closely to the intense family consciousness of Israel. The same might be said about almost any Hebrew word. Word meanings have to be investigated by asking what is specific about the word. The intense family consciousness of Israel is a sociological (and perhaps theological) fact; it is not therefore a specific semantic function of any word denoting a person or action or thing occurring within that environment. My other main objection is that one cannot in this way assume without special reason the relevance of the 'guardian' series to the explanation of the sense 'faithfulness' simply because they 'come from the same root'.

The vagueness of method here is betrayed by the verbal phrases used: 'seems to be related closely to', 'lurks behind'. It is clear that this is because there is no attempt at a methodological separation between what is the function of a series of words in their particular contexts and what is generally true about the Israelite culture or way of thinking. We may suspect that behind this way of inter-pretation there lies (or lurks) a philosophy of language and of the nature of Hebraic thought which regards such separation as intrinsically wrong. The result in practice is the introduction into the linguistic investigation of any consideration which is culturally noticeable (and/or theologically attractive) just because it can be generally 'related to' a particular usage.

A further point must be added about the use made of the guardian' series in Torrance's article. He refers to Weiser's article on πίστις[1] and says on the basis of it that 'the *qal*, *ʾaman*, is applied to a mother, or a nurse, or the guardian of a child, with reference to the faithfulness and reliability of that relationship'. This is in itself quite a reasonable suggestion, making the sense of ʾ-*m*-*n* in the 'guardian' series to be derivative from the sense 'trust', and thus fairly closely parallel to English 'trustee'. But this if true would damage Torrance's argument in two other ways. Firstly, if the 'guardian' sense is secondary to and derivative from the 'faithfulness' or 'trust' sense, then it provides no evidence at all for the origin of the sense 'faithfulness' or 'trust'. Secondly, it removes a great deal of what strength there is in the 'primary' meaning of 'make firm, establish'. It is practically only from the 'guardian' series plus a few other isolated pieces of evidence that support can be brought for verb forms (and these only participles) with some sense like this. This in fact is the interpretation of BDB, who understand the semantic development of the 'guardian' series as 'confirm>support>nourish'. Koehler on the other hand, though he takes 'be steady, firm, trustworthy' as the original sense, recognizes the specialization of the 'guardian' series by taking them separately,[2] and consequently has no material left to give a sense of 'make firm, establish' or the like to any *qal* verbal form.

We may now turn to the rendering of our group of words by the LXX, concerning which Torrance writes as follows:

'We are faced with a problem when we have to translate the Hebrew into Greek, for the Greek πίστις and πιστεύειν are not very happy equivalents for the words denoting faithfulness in Hebrew; πιστός, however, is more applicable. Certainly the LXX is very uneasy about their use, and significant facts emerge which require far greater consideration than, I think, we have given to them. Πίστις, for example, is never used in the LXX to signify

---

[1] *TWNT* vi. 182–97. It is not clear however that Weiser in fact intends that the word is used because of the faithfulness of the guardian; on p. 183 he says it is not clear how the use for 'guardian' is related to the religious use, and on p. 187 n. he seems to suggest that 'reciprocal relationship' may be the original connection.

[2] KB, s.v. It is not clear how Koehler understands the semantic development of the 'guardian' series in relation to the other senses of the words from the root ʾ-*m*-*n*.

"faith" or "belief", and πιστοί is not used to describe the Old Testament "believers" — indeed it occurs but once in the canonical books in application to the members of the covenant-community, in Ps. 101: 6: "Mine eyes are upon the faithful (πιστούς) of the land", where clearly πιστοί is properly rendered "faithful". The term πιστεύειν is used frequently in the LXX and used also in a strict religious sense, but this usage is dominated by the Old Testament conception of faithfulness.'

This is a very misleading and confusing statement. There is no word in the OT in Hebrew meaning 'faith' or 'belief'; that is to say, there is no noun form representing nominally the act indicated by the verb *heʼᵉmin* 'believe' — a fact which is widely known and acknowledged.[1] And just as there is no *nomen actionis* corresponding to *heʼᵉmin*, there is also no *nomen agentis* meaning 'believer'. The nearest to this would be the participle of the verb *heʼᵉmin* itself (cf. the frequent Islamic use of the corresponding Arabic participle *muʼminūna* 'believers') — but this is of course semi-verbal in Hebrew usage and in the two places where it occurs in the OT is translated into Greek very naturally by a verbal form of πιστεύω (Deut. 1: 32) and by the corresponding Greek participle (ὁ πιστεύων Is. 28: 16). The Seventy were simply translating the text that lay before them, and there is absolutely no means of proving that they were 'very uneasy' about using certain Greek words when their Hebrew text gave them no occasion to use these words in the senses mentioned by Torrance.

Secondly, the case of 'the faithful of the land' (Ps. 101: 6). Πιστοί certainly means 'faithful' here, as Torrance remarks, and therein gives a normal and adequate rendering of *neʼemᵉne*, which means precisely this and not 'believers' and is not relevant to a discussion of how 'believers' may be put into Greek. The other

---

[1] E.g. Dodd, op. cit., p. 68. Some would wish to make an exception of *ʼᵉmunah* in the famous place Hab. 2: 4. J. C. C. van Dorssen, *De Derivata van de Stam ʼ-m-n in het Hebreeuwsch van het Oude Testament* (Amsterdam, 1951), believes that the immediate meaning of *ʼᵉmunah* there is 'faithfulness', but that within the general context its value is to all intents and purposes that of our 'faith', though not of course the special sense of Paul — a remark in which there may be much good sense; see his pp. 117–22, summary in English p. 129. Cf. also E. Perry, 'The Meaning of *ʼᵉmuna* in the Old Testament', *JBR* xxi (1953) 252–6. I have to thank the editor of *JBR* for helping me to obtain this article.

point made is that πιστοί is infrequent even for 'the members
of the covenant-community'. To test this statement we simply take
the cases of the form ne²ᵉman (i.e. 'faithful', πιστός) occurring in
the OT in the masculine plural, nine cases in all, and observe that
in only one case is the reference to what we may agree to call
roughly 'the members of the covenant-community'.[1] Far therefore
from πιστοί being exceptional with reference to this community,
it was used by the LXX in the only case where they were translating the corresponding Hebrew word in the reference stated. In this
they merely followed their usual practice, πιστός or (once) its
compound ἀξιόπιστος being used for example in all the nine
cases mentioned. There is therefore no reason to suggest any
difficulty about the use of πιστοί here. Moreover, while it is true
that only one case occurs with reference to 'the members of the
covenant-community', there seems to be no good reason why the
use for these members in the plural should be specially mentioned
when πιστός = ne²ᵉman is used of prominent individual members
of that community[2] and of the covenant itself.[3] But the whole
argument here has lost its relevance when we noted that there is no
word 'believers' in the OT for which we might usefully discuss
whether the LXX were or were not happy with the translation
πιστοί.

Thirdly, something must now be said of the last sentence of the
paragraph: 'The term πιστεύω is used frequently in the LXX and
used also in a strict religious sense, but this usage is dominated by
the Old Testament conception of faithfulness.'

It is not quite clear in what direction this sentence is intended to
lead, and in particular what is the force of the 'but'. From the
context it may reasonably be interpreted as follows: 'Unlike the
terms πιστός and πίστις, about which there was some uncertainty, especially in the latter, πιστεύω was in fact frequently
used and in a religious sense (but cf. the statement earlier that

---

[1] The cases are: Dtn. 28: 59 (sicknesses); Is. 8: 2 (witnesses), 33: 16 (water),
55: 3 (the Davidic covenant); Ps. 101: 6 (already quoted), 111: 7 (command-
ments); Prov. 27: 6 (wounds); Job 12: 20 (reliable men in general); Neh. 13: 13
(treasurers).

[2] Moses, Num. 12: 7; Samuel, 1 Sam. 3: 20; David, 1 Sam. 22: 14.

[3] Is. 55: 3.

πιστεύω was not a happy equivalent); but whatever difficulties there were in expressing a Hebrew concept with it have been overcome and its use is under the control or domination of that Hebrew concept.' The idea of a Greek word in the LXX or the NT being dominated by a Hebrew concept is an important one, which will be discussed further later. At this point we might only mention two questions: (a) what evidence there is in detail for this domination in the case of πιστεύω, and (b) why this domination could not or at any rate did not extend to the other words πίστις etc.

The basic error in this section is the constant harping on the sense 'faithfulness' for the words we are discussing. Πιστεύω, we are told, is not a very happy translation for a word 'denoting faithfulness in Hebrew'. But this Hebrew word, heʾᵉmin, does not mean and never did mean 'be faithful, show faithfulness'; it means 'trust, believe'. Hebert and Torrance have become so mesmerized by their supposed 'fundamental meaning' of 'faithfulness' that they do not notice that it does not fit heʾᵉmin, which is perhaps the most important word of the series for this subject.[1] And having become persuaded that the words from this root basically mean 'faithfulness', they naturally feel it must have been very hard for the LXX to translate one of them by a Greek word 'to believe'; but since the Seventy did so translate it, and with a great frequency which makes it doubtful if they were really 'uneasy' about the word, then we have to infer that they could do so because the usage was still dominated by the 'Old Testament concept of faithfulness'. The argument is dominated throughout by the emphasis on the 'original meaning' on the one hand and on the other by the theological sense that any human 'faith' must be subordinate to a fundamental 'faithfulness'. It is only from these that any support is offered for the domination by 'the Old Testament concept of faithfulness'. Neither of these however is directly relevant to the determination of the actual meaning of heʾᵉmin and πιστεύω.

[1] Torrance does of course notice the sense of 'believing in', 'relying on', see above, p. 167, but he goes on afterwards as if 'faithfulness' were the meaning all the same. In such matters, indeed, the LXX commonly understood the Hebrew text better than the would-be 'Hebraizing' interpreters of to-day.

(b) THE HEBREW VERB 'BELIEVE' — GRAMMAR AND SENSE

We must now turn to another point and one of great importance for the interpretation of he'*min* 'trust, believe'. The question is: what is the force of, or the reason for, the fact that the verb 'trust, believe' in Hebrew is in the form or theme known as *hiph'il*? It is surprising that Hebert and Torrance do not make much of this point, for by taking the *hiph'il* form as declarative-estimative in function they would have had an argument which is perhaps better for their case than some which they have in fact used. The sense of he'*min* would then be 'regard as firm or steadfast, declare to be firm or steadfast'; and from this it could have been argued that the 'firmness' supposedly inherent in the root was in this form clearly the firmness of the person in whom the trust is put and not of the person who trusts.[1] Hebert seems to follow this line when he argues that he'*min* describes 'man taking refuge from his own frailty and instability in God who is firm and steadfast'. But just below he interprets the 'if ye will not believe' of Is. 7: 9 as 'if you will not make-yourselves-firm (on God)', which may indicate a different understanding of the *hiph'il* here. It is probable however that neither of these statements should be understood as strictly philological statements about the way in which the 'root meaning' is related to the given form *ta'aminu*; they are more general statements about the ultimate source of the 'firmness' and the relationship in which it is attained; general statements which are made, however, with some vague hope of elucidating the philological basis of the form at the same time.

The confusion of method can be seen in the very significant addition of the 'understood' complement '(on God)'. This phrase is needed of course to clinch the suggestion 'make-yourselves-firm', for the reason clearly that only God is really 'firm'. Its insertion is of course no proof of anything. The phenomena could be equally well explained by adding '(on what I have just said)' or by rendering 'if you do not believe (what I say)'. But we might do justice to

[1] In this they would have had the support recently, for example, of E. Pfeiffer, 'Glaube im Alten Testament', *ZATW* lxxi (1959) 151 ff.; he holds to the declarative-estimative function with the sense 'für fest, sicher, zuverlässig, erklären oder halten'.

the absence of any such complements or additions in Hebrew by adding none in English either. The choice to add the 'understood' phrase '(on God)' as distinct from such other possibilities as '(on what I say)' is the result of the theological drive to see God as the one true example of steadfastness. The result of such an interest is commonly that other possibilities, such as exist here, are ignored.

It is of course true that even if the prophet was asking for belief in his words he would understand this to be because his prophetic message came from God. This theological judgement is perfectly easy to substantiate in the texts. It is characteristic of the method of Hebert and Torrance that they repeatedly try to make the theological judgements, which can be validated from what the texts say and mean, emerge inevitably from the inherent structure of the language, in this case the semantic relations of the group with the root $'$-m-n.[1]

We return to the question of the *hiph'il* and its function in *he'emin*. Here there are two possibilities to discuss: (*a*) a declarative-estimative function, such as 'regard as firm or reliable'; such an explanation may include the treating of *he'emin* as denominative; (*b*) a so-called 'internal-transitive' function, defined as used for 'the entering into a certain condition and, further, the being in the same' (GK § 53 e). I shall argue that the latter represents the true function of the *hiph'il* in *he'emin*; though this has been the judgement of great grammarians who need no confirmation from me, I wish to go over part of the ground again, partly because the declarative-estimative explanation has appeared in several recent works, and partly because of the illustrative value of the discussion for theological interpretation.

Among supporters of the declarative-estimative explanation we have already mentioned Pfeiffer. I mention his arguments especially because they have appeared so recently and not because they are well conceived. Of the opinion of GK that our word belongs to

---

[1] The unwillingness of much modern theology (in contrast with the 'fundamentalist' type of thinking) to admit that belief or faith can be properly given to a saying or words, or its tendency to insist that such belief in something said is totally different in kind from faith understood as a relationship with a person, may also affect the exegesis here.

the 'internal-transitive' type he says that it is 'scarcely to be held', but gives no reason. From BL he quotes a passage about the force of 'the causative', but unless I mistake his meaning fails to see that the passage quoted is about the causative function of the 'intensive' themes (*pi'el*, etc.) and that the actual verb under discussion, and the function of the *hiph'il* in general, is handled elsewhere.[1] And it seems extremely cavalier to say of Bergsträsser that his treatment of the *hiph'il* 'complicates the problem unnecessarily' and leave it at that.

The obvious objection to an explanation as declarative-estimative is that one would expect a verb derived in this function to be followed by a direct object, to be 'transitive'. It is presumably with this difficulty in mind that Pfeiffer goes on to assert that the word *he'emin* is transitive 'in the sense that, although the declarative judgement directs itself upon its object, it none the less as an act of the subject remains with the latter'.[2] This transitive character is, in his opinion, evident where the verb is followed by the prepositions *le* or *be*. Pfeiffer may of course redefine the term 'transitive' as he pleases. But in these remarks he seems to use it as a kind of philosophical category rather than as a term of linguistic description. The point I want to make is on the descriptive plane: verbs undoubtedly declarative-estimative like *hisdiq* 'pronounce just' will frequently and normally be followed by the word expressing the person pronounced just, with the object-particle *'et* where appropriate; but this is never so with *he'emin*.[3] That this verb is regularly followed by prepositions or used absolutely puts it at once descriptively in a different category from *hisdiq*.

In general Pfeiffer's methods of handling language are those used in biblical theology, although he has criticisms of certain other workers in this movement. He acknowledges Boman's influence, and it can be seen in a sentence like this: 'We translate *he'emin*, following the LXX, as "believe", and thus we draw it out of its history-bound peculiarity into our Western world of ideas'.[4] To

---

[1] Pfeiffer, op. cit., p. 152. The passage in BL referred to by him is § 38 r''; but for the handling of *he'emin* see § 38 b''', d'''.

[2] Ibid., p. 152 f.: 'in dem Sinne, dass sich das erklärende Urteil wohl auf seinem Gegenstand richtet, aber doch als Akt des Subjektes bei diesem bleibt.'

[3] I leave aside the special case of Jud. 11: 20.   [4] Pfeiffer, op. cit., p. 151.

say 'believe' at all is to obscure the Hebrew background. For Pfeiffer the decisive thing about faith in the OT is the reciprocal relation of activity and passivity, and this is related to two linguistic aspects: (a) the etymological sense of 'firmness' (i.e. the firmness of God; on this side man is passive) (b) the declarative-estimative function of the theme (man is active in 'taking God to be firm').[1]

The association of the declarative function with a denominative connection is made by Weiser. After dealing with the word *ʾamen* and on the basis of his discussion of it (*von da aus*), he says that *heʾᵉmin* can most simply be 'transcribed' (he uses *umschreiben*) by 'to say Amen to something with all consequences for object and subject'. So, he continues, in the relation of man to God, the word has not causative but rather declarative meaning: 'to declare God to be *neʾᵉman*' or ('transcribed') 'to say Amen to God'.[2]

Philologically this would mean that *heʾᵉmin* is a denominative either of *neʾᵉman* or of *ʾamen*. But, as often in this article, it is hard to see whether Weiser is making statements here about the detailed linguistic data or giving a wider theological paraphrase of the associations of the term 'believe'. Probably the latter is the case. Certainly no one is likely to believe that *heʾᵉmin* in fact developed from the practice of saying 'Amen', and probably Weiser does not mean this.

Weiser's interpretation includes other aspects which are of importance for our subject in general. From the variety of connections in which forms like *neʾᵉman* are found he believes that the usual rendering with 'firm, sure, reliable', far from being too purely etymological as I have rather suggested, does not reach down to the deepest and ultimate meaning, which can be seen in the connection of the word with objects like places, streams, and sicknesses. The deepest meaning is then that ʾ-*m-n* is a 'formal concept, the content of which is differently determined in each case by the particular subject'; it means roughly 'specific'. Here however we have to remember the totality-thought of Israel. 'The essence of the Hebrew spirit requires further to see this relation

[1] Ibid., p. 164.
[2] *TWNT* vi. 186–7. Footnote 110 on p. 187, by a curious slip as far as I can see, refers for the declarative function to GK § 53 d, although this word is actually put quite definitely in the 'internal-transitive' type by § 53 d–e.

between concept and reality not in the abstraction of logical thought, but always in the nearness to life of practical experience, so that in the formal concept the corresponding content is always also thought, felt and experienced; in this way the logical relation always means at the same time a relation in life.'[1]

Applied to *he'emin* 'believe', the formal character of the concept leads to 'the knowing and acknowledging of the relationship, into which God enters towards man, the placing oneself within this relationship, so that here too the reciprocal relation between God and man belongs to the essence of faith'. But also it involves the thought of all those characteristics through which God is God. 'Thus the religious usage of the OT points in the direction of "taking God as God seriously without reservation" and thus contains as an essential moment also the exclusiveness of the relation to God'; and again, 'to the external exclusiveness there corresponds an internal one in the sense that the '-*m-n* concept brings in the totality of human expressions of life into the relation with God'.[2]

We need not spend long on detailed criticism of this position; the following points may be noted: (*a*) the whole idea of the 'formal concept' seems to me to bear the marks of a philosophical-theological origin, and to go far beyond what can be documented as a linguistic fact from the uses of forms from this root; (*b*) the appeal to the totality-structure of Israelite thought may be justified in the discussion of ideas, but that structure may not be so formative in the linguistic area that we can assume it to have been reproduced in the spread of meanings of this or of any Hebrew root; (*c*) through the idea of the 'formal concept' almost everything about the structure of relations between God and man in the OT finds its linguistic reflection in the words from this root.

One other point should be mentioned here. As a result of his interpretation of '-*m-n* Weiser is able to make an important distinction between it and the other common verb *baṭaḥ* 'trust, feel safe'. The latter, even where the means or the origin of the security is named, expresses not a relationship but the condition of 'feeling oneself safe because of'. Hence the use of the word for a

---

[1] *TWNT* vi. 184.   [2] Ibid., p. 187 f.

sense of security encouraged by riches, by one's own power, by armaments; and for a false security as well as a genuine one.[1]

Now even for those unwilling to accept Weiser's idea of a 'formal concept' for ʾ-m-n, there may be an attraction in this kind of distinction; for *baṭaḥ* would then express a 'subjective' security[2], while in *heʾemin* the emphasis would be not on the inner sense of security but on the 'objective' reality of God as the source of security, because the 'basic meaning' of ʾ-m-n is the 'firmness' or 'steadfastness' of God, with no reference to the mental state of the man concerned. Such a distinction would undoubtedly fit in with theological distinctions commonly made about the nature of faith and its relation to an inward sense of security. I wish to point out here only that such an understanding of the matter, whether in Weiser's own terms or on the alternative which I have just described, would depend entirely on a declarative-estimative function of the *hiphʿil* form in *heʾemin*. If this function is not declarative-estimative, then as far as the grammatical form can indicate the 'firmness' is that of the person who 'believes' or 'is sure', and the sense no less 'subjective' than that of *baṭaḥ*.[3]

Along with the two arguments for a declarative-estimative function by Pfeiffer and Weiser we may say something of the treatment by Pedersen,[4] which is really an attempt to explain *heʾemin* as a real causative. Pedersen comes to this subject having just asserted that, in comparison with 'justice', 'truth' is specially centred in the inner soul and its firm construction. Then he goes on:

'To make a man true, *heʾemin*, means the same as to rely on him. . . . Faith, ʾemunah, is the mutual acknowledgement condi-

---

[1] *TWNT* vi. 191 ff. Weiser's survey includes of course many important observations in other connections. The domination of his idea of the 'formal concept' appears again however in his summing up, pp. 196–7.

[2] Weiser's words are (*TWNT* vi. 192) 'dass hier die Ichbezogenheit des subjektiven Sicherheitsgefühls von den durch ʾ-m-n bezeichneten Beziehungs-begriffen zu unterscheiden ist'.

[3] It is true of course that *baṭaḥ* is used quite often of false security and *heʾemin* is not so used. But this is a matter of the general habits of usage of the two words, and is an entirely different matter from the question of whether the 'firmness' supposedly inhering in the root ʾ-m-n is that of the person trusted or that of the person trusting.

[4] *Israel* i–ii. 347–8 and 530 n.

tioning the covenant. Without mutual confidence the covenant cannot exist. The weaker members of the covenant help to uphold the stronger by their confidence. They *make* him "true", i.e. firm and strong.'

Later he goes on to say that to 'justify' a man requires greater strength than to 'make him true' or 'believe in him'; in the latter case the person confirmed is already sure of his position and has only to be supported by his inferiors. 'Justification' however reinstates a man into the position he comes from. Then he continues:

'This expresses itself in the *usus loquendi*, justification denoting a more powerful and direct action upon another. One says "to justify a man", whereas not "to make a man true" but to create truth in or for a man.' The note on p. 530 accordingly points out the use of *hiṣdiq ʾet* (i.e. direct object) but *heʾᵉmin bᵉ* (*bᵉ* means 'in'). The phrase *heʾᵉmin bᵉhayyaw* is 'properly speaking to put truth, security into one's life, i.e. to be sure to live'.

It is hardly necessary to point out the precariousness of this interpretation of *heʾᵉmin*. Whether or not this has some sense as an example of Hebrew psychology, it can hardly stand a moment's examination as an account of linguistic fact. 'And Abraham created truth in Yahweh' would be too fantastic to be reasonably worth considering. We must not, moreover, let ourselves be deceived by the suggestion that we are here describing a psychology whole worlds different from our own. Whether or not the Hebrew psychology is as different as that, the line of interpretation given by Pedersen is dictated not by a psychological observation but by a 'logicistic' treatment of the *hiphʿil*; that is to say, a schematic treatment of *hiphʿil* forms as 'properly' causative in function because the causative is the 'original' function of this theme. The presupposition is that every *hiphʿil* is really a causative and that its causative function is a clue to the curious way of thinking which made the Israelites see the matter in this way.

For the linguistic evidence, one must say firstly that all competent grammars register a recognition that the *hiphʿil*, though the causative is one of its common and characteristic functions, is used in many words where no causative sense can be discerned and where the *hiphʿil* formation must be traced to analogy or other influences.[1] Bergsträsser gives a warning that categories such as 'reflexive' or 'causative' are very inadequate for the manifold modifications introduced by the verbal theme formations in Semitic languages generally.[2] GK on the other hand (§ 53 d) do make some attempt to suggest an ultimately causative notion: 'Among the ideas expressed by the *causative* and *transitive* are included, moreover, according to the *Hebrew* point of view, a series of actions and ideas, which *we* have to represent by periphrasis, in order to understand their being represented by the *hiphʿil* form.' The term 'inwardly transitive' is intended to express this conception. The point of view of GK here is a 'logicistic' one, and typically of this approach it has to make a connection with the 'Hebrew point of view'; but GK have a sense of proportion which prevents them from going too far with this, and it affects their treatment of words only a little. Pedersen goes much farther in appearing to maintain that the interpretation of *heʾᵉmin* as a real causative is quite obligatory.

Secondly, even where a causative function is obvious, it is doubtful whether we can produce parallels to the suggested sense 'create truth', as if, for example, *higbiah* were 'create height' or *hodiaʿ* 'create knowledge'. In other words, by using 'create' with a European abstract substantive like 'truth' Pedersen gives an impression which looks like a kind of 'causative' but which hardly fits the *hiphʿil* of causative function actually found in Hebrew. The same procedure can be seen in Levison's[3] treatment of *hipgiaʿ*, as used in Is. 53: 12. He says:

'It comes from the root *pagaʿ*, the primary meaning of which verb is "to meet, encounter, reach" . . . Would not a simple translation of the two words "and for the rebellious he makes a meeting place" (a place of reconciliation?) be more in keeping with the general intent of the passage?'

This treatment works on the simple assumption that if the *qal* means 'meet' then the *hiphʿil* means 'make a meeting' or 'make a

[1] BL § 38 b‴, c‴; Bergsträsser, *Hebräische Grammatik* ii. 19 d. Cf. Pedersen's own *Hebraeisk Grammatik*, § 28 h.
[2] Bergsträsser, *Einführung in die semitischen Sprachen*, p. 13.
[3] N. Levison, *SJT* xii (1959) 280

meeting-place'. For the semantic relation between *paga^c* 'meet' and *hipgia^c* 'intercede' compare Greek ἐντυγχάνω 1. 'meet' 2. 'petition, intercede'.

One may add briefly that Pedersen's suggestion 'create truth in' contradicts that of 'make a man true' which he has used earlier.

Thirdly, it is unlikely that any support could be found for the idea that the direct object after *hiṣdiq* indicates the more direct and powerful action while the use of prepositions after *he^ʾᵉmin* indicates a more oblique and less forceful support of the man. It would be an extreme form of linguistic 'realism' to suppose that an 'indirect' relation between words corresponds to an indirect relation between the persons acting in the situation described. It may be added that the explanation of *he^ʾᵉmin* thus through a contrast with *hiṣdiq* is a linguistically arbitrary procedure. The collocation of the two may have some justification from a degree of kinship within the psychological scheme Pedersen is following; but this does not mean that comparison of *these two* terms linguistically will produce the key to the understanding of the linguistic basis of either of them.

Although Pedersen hardly belongs to the movement of biblical theology, his work has a certain kinship with it in the synthetic approach to Israel's culture as a totality with a unitary psychological basis and in the attempt at certain points to show this as emerging from the linguistic structure.[1] His influence on Boman is very strong. In his discussion of 'believe' we see some of the same weaknesses as appear in the rather different treatment of Hebert and Torrance: the fastening on to a particular piece of data which appears to harmonize with the theologically or psychologically valuable thoughts, the failure to test the suggestions against the linguistic data as a whole, and the belief that the linguistic structure reveals the relations of ideas or objects as the Israelites understood them.

We may then regard the explanation of the function of the *hiph^cil* theme in *he^ʾᵉmin* as declarative-estimative as mistaken Any semantic development from a sense of 'firmness, sureness' was

---

[1] For the understanding of Pedersen's *Israel* in general one should not omit a comparison with V. Grønbech's *The Culture of the Teutons*.

made with reference not to the 'firmness', 'steadfastness' and 'sureness' of God, but to the sureness or certainty of the one who trusts or believes.[1] That one who believes in God does in fact regard the steadfastness of God as the only reality behind his faith may or may not be true, but is a different matter.

We may now proceed to another point. Up till now I have made some criticisms of the way in which the 'fundamental meaning' of 'firmness' has been used in the course of argument. It is now time to make a closer examination of this sense of 'firmness' itself.

The evidence to which I wish to point is the widespread existence in other Semitic languages of senses like 'feel safe, trust, believe', along with the sense 'truth', which may perhaps be explained from 'what is trustworthy, sure'; and negatively, the smaller extent of the evidence for a more general sense of 'firmness' existing independently of the sense 'feel safe, trust, believe' and remaining active.

For Arabic Lane gives the first sense of ʾamina as 'was, or became, or felt, secure or safe' and adds the opinion 'originally, "was or became quiet or tranquil, in heart or mind" '. The sense of 'be in a state of security or confidence' is frequently cited by him. Thus ʾaminahu means 'he became free from fear, thought himself secure or safe', and ʾamīn is 'trusted, relied on'. I have found no cases in the Arabic dictionaries which need to be explained from a sense 'firm', and all could be understood from the senses 'feel secure, trust'. The usual term for 'believe' in Arabic is the 4th theme, corresponding therefore exactly to Hebr. heʾᵉmin; the 1st theme (= Hebr. qal)'means generally, then, 'feel secure'.

In Ethiopic all usages recorded by Dillmann are readily explicable from the sense 'trust', with the slight exception of his citation from Lk. 1: 1 with the sense *verum esse vel inveniri, compleri, confirmari*, which can be connected perhaps with the sense 'true' — the translation here is of τὰ πεπληροφορημένα πράγματα. The same

---

[1] See in addition to the standard grammars van Dorssen, op. cit., p. 93 ff., 125, who takes the *hiphʿil* to be a 'subjective causative' meaning 'to make oneself firm, to exhibit firmness'. One may accept this broadly without laying any weight on such terms as 'subjective' or 'internal'.

is true of the modern Ethiopian Semitic languages so far as I have been able to check them (from Munzinger for Tigré, and from Guidi for Amharic). For modern South Arabian languages I may quote from Leslau:[1] Socotri *émon* '*dire la vérité*', cf. Mehri *īmôn bôṭel* '*incroyance*', Šḥauri *uñ* '*croire*'; Socotri causative-reflexive **šẹ̄ʾmon* '*croire*'; *ʾĭmehen* '*vérité*'.

In ancient South Arabian Rossini registers *ʾmn* IV '*fidei alicuius commisit*' and the corresponding substantive '*securitas*', with clearly derived senses of '*foederis securitas*' and hence '*protectio*'.[2]

The Accadian *temennu* 'foundation (stone, document)', which was earlier regarded as derivative from the root *ʾ-m-n*, is a loan-word from Sumerian.[3]

It is in Syriac that senses of 'persist, be steadfast, be constant or continual' are best established. The *pᵉ̔al* of the verb, the form corresponding to the Hebr. *qal*, as in Hebrew is not found in the finite forms; it appears in the participle-adjective type *ʾamīn*. The sense 'persist, persevere, frequent, remain' is found in the *ʾethpᵉ̔el*, and thus in circumstances comparable to the Hebrew *niphʿal*.[4]

On the basis of this it seems reasonable to suggest that, if there was a general sense of 'be firm' as distinct from the one of 'feel sure', it must probably have ceased to be productive and active except in certain forms at an early stage. With an early stage of the development could naturally be associated the Egyptian *mn* 'be firm, remain, be established',[5] Coptic *mun* 'remain', an association already suggested in the dictionaries.[6] That the association with Egyptian *mn* is a fairly distant one is indicated by the wide divergence in semantic development in Egyptian and in Semitic. From this early and fairly general sense later survivals would be the various 'permanence' senses in the Hebrew *niphʿal* and Syriac *ʾethpᵉ̔el*, and in some participial forms and substantives like Hebrew *ʾomᵉnot* 'doorposts' and also perhaps the 'guardian' series in Hebrew. It is possible however perhaps to explain some of these usages as derivative from the sense of 'trust'.

---

[1] *Lexique Soqoṭri*, p. 64.   [2] *Chrestomathia*, p. 106.
[3] Muss-Arnolt, i. 58; Deimel, part 3, ii. 470.
[4] Brockelmann, *Lexicon Syriacum*, s.v.
[5] Erman-Grapow, ii. 60 ff.   [6] KB, s.v.

In any case it is clear that a general sense of 'be firm' and 'firmness' continued active in Hebrew only in certain formations. It is the sense of 'feel secure', 'trust', that remains active in others and productive, and its verbal expression in Hebrew is *he³emin* 'trust, believe'.[1] Ultimately no doubt the senses can be united through a meaning like English 'be sure', which can be used for the external sureness of some object and also the internal certainty of the mind. But the specific form *he³emin* 'trust, believe' must with little doubt be traced to the latter. For other words like *³emet* 'truth' it is perhaps hard to separate the relation of the two senses in the background. But for *³emet* also it is excessively etymologizing to offer 'firmness' as the 'basic meaning'. 'Truth' is already the right translation as early as the only occurrence in Ugaritic literature.[2]

Even assuming, therefore, that the 'ultimate' etymology of words of the root *³-m-n* is 'firmness', we have here an illustration of the harm of paying excessive attention to the most ultimate etymology and failing to consider what forms were current at the relevant times and what senses they bore in actual usage. Extant forms are not derived directly from the ultimate etymology or from the 'root meaning'. There is a detailed and often complicated history for each form; the fact that for lack of knowledge we often cannot trace it does not mean that we can suppose it does not exist.

(c) FAITH, RIGHTEOUSNESS AND TRUTH

We must now return to the use of linguistic evidence in the articles of Hebert and Torrance; and we now quote another paragraph from the latter:

'The usual translation of *³emet* in the LXX is ἀλήθεια, but ἀλήθεια is not used to signify abstract or metaphysical truth, but what is grounded upon God's faithfulness, i.e. truth not as something static, but as active, efficacious reality, the reality of God in covenant-relationship. It is the steadfastness of God which is the ground of all truth. Primarily, truth is God's being true to himself,

---

[1] For my purpose it is not necessary to differentiate between 'trust' and 'believe', as is done by van Dorssen, op. cit., pp. 98, 126.

[2] G. R. Driver, *Canaanite Myths and Legends* (Edinburgh, 1956), p. 103 (*Baal* I* i. 18 f.).

his faithfulness or consistency. God's truth means, therefore, that he keeps truth or faith with his people and requires them to keep truth or faith with him. Thus the Hebrew *'emet* is translated not only by ἀλήθεια but also by πίστις and δικαιοσύνη. There is no doubt that again and again where we have the words πίστις and δικαιοσύνη in the New Testament we must see behind them the Hebrew words, *'emet* and *'emunah*, and where in the New Testament we have ἀλήθεια we must understand that not simply as a Greek word, but in the light of the biblical inclusion of πίστις and δικαιοσύνη in the concept of truth.'

From this paragraph the following points may be made:

(a) As soon as ἀλήθεια is mentioned an immediate qualifying 'but' is added: it does not signify abstract or metaphysical truth. Behind this we can easily detect the belief that Greek words, because they are sometimes or even frequently used to express abstract or metaphysical truth, are therefore deeply infected by that metaphysical sense. Just as biblical words are intrinsically related to the active and dynamic conceptions which are expressed through them, so Greek words are intrinsically related to metaphysical and 'static' thinking — unless, as in this case, they become 'controlled' by their Hebrew background or so 'dominated' by an Old Testament conception that their metaphysical sense is destroyed or subjugated.

The whole argument here presupposes that the sense of words is determined predominantly by their metaphysical or theological usages. One would expect ἀλήθεια to mean 'abstract, metaphysical truth'; but what it in fact means is 'the reality of God in covenant-relationship, God's being true to himself, truth as grounded upon God's faithfulness'. An (unwanted) metaphysical sense is corrected by a (true) theological one.

What is lacking from this discussion is any idea of a word as a semantic marker, indicating an essential difference from another word and having the ability to mark that differentia in any one of a number of contexts; not becoming intrinsically infected by any particular one of these contexts, and having its sense as a marker sustained and determined not by metaphysical or theological usage but by a general social milieu, in which the language has its life.

Compare the following random passages:

Homer Il. xxiv. 407.

ἄγε δή μοι πᾶσαν ἀληθείην κατάλεξον,
ἢ ἔτι πὰρ νήεσσιν ἐμὸς πάϊς, ἦέ μιν ἤδη
ᾖσι κυσὶν μελεϊστὶ ταμὼν προὔθηκεν Ἀχιλλεύς;

'Come now, tell me all the truth: is my son still beside the ships, or has Achilles cut him in pieces and put him out for his dogs?'

Hdt. vi. 69.

λόγους δὲ ἄλλους περὶ γενέσιος τῆς σεωυτοῦ μὴ δέκεο· τὰ γὰρ ἀληθέστατα πάντα ἀκήκοας....

'So don't accept any other stories about your birth; the utmost truth is what you've heard (from me).'

Pl. Apol. 17 a.

καίτοι ἀληθές γε ὡς ἔπος εἰπεῖν οὐδὲν εἰρήκασιν. μάλιστα δὲ αὐτῶν ἓν ἐθαύμασα τῶν πολλῶν ὧν ἐψεύσαντο....

'But one may say, really, that nothing they have said is true. There is however one thing in the lies they have told that specially surprised me....'

Thuc. iv. 120.

εἴ τε θήσεται κατὰ νοῦν τὰ πράγματα, πιστοτάτους τε τῇ ἀληθείᾳ ἡγήσεσθαι αὐτοὺς Λακεδαιμονίων φίλους καὶ τἆλλα τιμήσειν.

'If he should get things done as he wanted, he would consider them in truth to be most faithful friends of the Lacedaemonians and also would honour them in every other way.'

Jos. BJ iv. 154.

ἦν δὲ πρόσχημα μὲν τῆς ἐπιβολῆς ἔθος ἀρχαῖον, ἐπειδὴ καὶ πάλαι κληρωτὴν ἔφασαν εἶναι τὴν ἀρχιερωσύνην, τὸ δ' ἀληθὲς τοῦ βεβαιοτέρου κατάλυσις καὶ τέχνη πρὸς δυναστείαν....

'The pretext for this attempt was ancient custom, since they said that the high priesthood had been determined by lot in ancient times; but in truth it was the abrogation of the better-established practice and a device towards their own supremacy....'

Jud. 9: 15.

καὶ εἶπεν ἡ ῥάμνος πρὸς τὰ ξύλα — εἰ ἐν ἀληθείᾳ ὑμεῖς χρίετέ
με εἰς βασιλέα ἐφ' ὑμῶν, δεῦτε πεποίθατε ἐν τῇ σκέπῃ μου.

'And the thorn bush said to the trees, "If you are really anointing
me as king over you, come and find safety in my shelter".'

Lk. 22: 59.

ἐπ' ἀληθείας καὶ οὗτος μετ' αὐτοῦ ἦν.
'Truly this one was with him too.'

Surely it is beyond dispute that in such a series there is a basic
semantic contrast between what is 'true' and what is falsehood,
pretence, insincerity, outward appearance, and half-truth; and that
neither do the Greek examples refer to 'abstract and metaphysical
truth' nor do the Jewish-Christian ones refer to 'the reality of God
in covenant-relationship, God's being true to himself, truth as
grounded upon God's faithfulness' or anything of the sort. It is
because the basic semantics of the Greek word was not its relation
to abstract and metaphysical thinking but the contrast pattern
between 'true' and 'false' or 'unreal', a contrast pattern which was
normal and living in the actual speech encountered, that the
Seventy were able to use the word quite naturally in their translation. It is true that the Greek philosophers use the word commonly
in a metaphysical sense, and that in the Greek Bible its theological
use with reference to God and his actions greatly outnumbers the
non-theological uses; but this does not mean that the word in
Greek, or the word in Jewish biblical Greek, is predominantly
semantically determined by such philosophy or theology. It should
be noticed that I am not trying to argue that the Greeks and the
Hebrews did not differ in their conceptions of truth, but only (for
the present) that neither Greek metaphysics nor Hebrew conceptions of the reality of God are built into the intrinsic semantic
function of the word ἀλήθεια.

(b) The statement in the first half of the paragraph is not so
much a statement about a Greek word as a delineation of the
contrasts between two theologies, or a philosophy and a theology.
The latter is a biblically-based theology, based among other things

on many sentences in which the word 'truth' occurs. It is characteristic of the school of thought which we are studying to take it that
this whole theology becomes the characteristic semantic marker-
function of the word 'truth'. Hence the unnatural air of many of
the individual interpretations, the impression given of the NT
being a closely-meshed web of relations between terms which are
nearly all mutually interrelated already anyway,[1] and the impossibility of fitting what is said about truth ('the reality of God in
covenant-relationship') to particular cases of the word such as
Jud. 9: 15 or Lk. 22: 59 quoted above. It is as if highly pregnant
and allusive and theological sayings such as 'I am the way, the
truth and the life' (John 14: 6) were taken as the one practical
guide to the semantics of the words 'way', 'truth' and 'life' wherever
they are found in the Bible. This suggestion is by no means meant
as a joke; I am not sure if some theologians would not take it
seriously.

(c) 'Thus the Hebrew ${}^{\jmath e}$met is translated not only by ἀλήθεια but
by πίστις and δικαιοσύνη.' That the word is so translated in
certain cases is not in dispute. What may be questioned is the
'thus', which suggests that this variety of translation for ${}^{\jmath e}$met is the
effect of the theological considerations just mentioned. That there
is a certain kind of situation in which what is related to ${}^{\jmath e}$met in
Hebrew may be reasonably related to πίστις or to δικαιοσύνη in
Greek in certain cases is true. What is not true is that this provides
a linguistic support for Torrance's full exposé of what 'truth' in the
biblical-theological sense is.

The following is a brief review of the translations mentioned:

(a) πίστις = ${}^{\jmath e}$met. This line of connection is a very thin one,
consisting of three or four cases in Proverbs[2] and three in the latter

---

[1] For example there is a certain air of suggestion that Rom. 1: 17 should be
taken as: 'The righteousness (δικαιοσύνη, a term associated with ${}^{\jmath e}$met) of God
(whose self-consistency is the basis and primary sense of all ${}^{\jmath e}$met) is revealed
from πίστις (i.e. ${}^{\jmath e}$munah, from the same root as ${}^{\jmath e}$met and extensively overlapping with it) to πίστις (again ${}^{\jmath e}$munah or ${}^{\jmath e}$met)' — a kind of intricate
spiritual tautology.

[2] There are four if we include two at 14: 22. This verse really has three
renderings of ḥesed we-${}^{\jmath e}$met, giving for ${}^{\jmath e}$met first ἀλήθεια, then πίστις sing.,
then πίστεις plur. Hatch and Redpath are not quite accurate in marking the
second as without Hebrew equivalent.

chapters of Jeremiah. Except for one of the cases at Prov. 14: 22 all the cases in this book have not πίστις but the plural πίστεις, and all are coupled with ἐλεημοσύναι (ἔλεος in 14: 22 c). It is not easy to say precisely what the Proverbs translator meant by πίστεις, but perhaps 'honesty' would represent his meaning adequately; cf. 12: 22, where the opposition is explicitly to 'false lips'; though Hebr. there is ʾᵉmunah, the Gk. πίστεις will probably mean the same throughout. Whether this may fit in with the Hellenistic ethical thinking of the Prov. translator, and in particular with the Stoic connections which have been suggested for him,[1] I find myself unable to judge. There is also one case of πιστός translating ʾᵉmet at 14: 25, with reference to a reliable witness.

The specialization of the cases in Proverbs and in particular their plural form makes it rather unlikely that they are of importance for the semantics of πίστις taken over the biblical literature as a whole, and especially for the use of the same word by NT writers.

Apart from this we have only three cases in the latter chapters of Jeremiah. Of these the first two at any rate (both are in the phrase ἐν πίστει) seem by the context close to the sense 'in truth, really': thus in 35 (28): 9, God has really sent this prophet; 39 (32): 41, I will truly plant them in this land. It is hard to say that πίστις is used here because the context so brought out the aspect of 'faithfulness' that the translator felt he must give up his (the more usual) translation ἀλήθεια. The third case, 40 (33): 6, is not much more persuasive. It is perhaps more likely that we have here simply a translation of etymologizing type, and that the translation reasons that if heʾᵉmin = πιστεύω (occurs twice: 12: 6 and 47 (40): 14) and if ʾᵉmunah = πίστις (four times in Jer. 1–10, plus one of neʾᵉman = ἔχων πίστιν), then ʾᵉmet (=ἀλήθεια five times up to Jer. 33) should now be πίστις too. This way of determining the Greek equivalents is sometimes followed in parts of the LXX and is of course best known from Aquila; who however in this case took πίστις = ʾᵉmunah and ἀλήθεια = ʾᵉmet as the LXX usually do. It is well known of course that there is a change of

[1] Cf. G. Gerleman, *Studies in the Septuagint*: iii. *Proverbs*. Cf. also Bultmann in *TWNT* vi. 181–2.

translation style in the course of Jeremiah; Thackeray fixed the point of change at about 29: 1, but suggestions have more recently been made that the changes did not all uniformly begin at this point. The latter part of Jeremiah was in any case classified by Thackeray among 'literal or unintelligent versions'.[1] In any case the uses of πίστις in Jeremiah must be reckoned within the special translation style of this book and are therefore hardly evidence for the 'conception of truth' in general.

The cases of ᵓᵉmet translated by πίστις are therefore so special and particular, so associated with particular books and their translation techniques, that they can certainly not be used as evidence for a general realization of a relation of πίστις to 'truth'; and still less can they demonstrate that in the exegesis of the New Testament 'again and again' the presence of the Hebrew ᵓᵉmet is to be detected behind πίστις.

(b) δικαιοσύνη = ᵓᵉmet. The evidence here is not much stronger, consisting in fact of 6 cases of the noun δικαιοσύνη and 4 of the adjective δίκαιος. In some cases however we have to reckon with the probable effect of a legal context in suggesting the rendering: so in Zech. 7: 9, Ezek. 18: 8, both 'righteous judgement', and Jer. 49 (42): 5, a 'just witness'. In Is. 61: 8 the Hebrew is badly translated anyway, and the δικαίοις is probably partly induced by the δικαιοσύνη occurring earlier in the sentence. These are all the four adjective cases. The other cases are quite sporadic, one in Gen., one in Jos., two suddenly together in Is. 38–9 (the Isaiah translator, in many ways one of the most irregular, keeps δικαιοσύνη for the ṣdq group of words with only two exceptions apart from these two) and two in Daniel. Though δικαιοσύνη as equivalent for ᵓᵉmet is thus perhaps a little more strongly represented than πίστις for ᵓᵉmet, it is very doubtful if any *rationale* can be given for these scattered variations other than an occasional imprecision or the giving of attention to the general sense of a sentence without special care for each word. At any rate the very sporadic use of δικαιοσύνη does not prove or even suggest that the total theology of 'truth' which Torrance presents was in these cases or indeed ever a conscious concern of the Seventy or an unconscious

[1] H. St. J. Thackeray, *A Grammar of the Old Testament in Greek*, p. 13.

association which affected their work. And it must be very doubtful if the LXX evidence gives any better ground for relating to ᵓ*emet* or to ᵓ*emunah* the δικαιοσύνη than the πίστις of the New Testament. Torrance's statement that 'all of these terms (i.e. πίστις, δικαιοσύνη, and ἀλήθεια) in the LXX may render the same Hebrew conception' thus gives an entirely misleading impression when offered as it is as a guide to the exegesis of Paul.

Later on Torrance discusses the phrase πίστει ἀληθείας of 2 Thess. 2: 13, and thinks that for Paul 'neither πίστις nor ἀλήθεια will express fully what he is after, and so he puts both words together to convey what the Old Testament means by *emet* and/or ᵓ*emunah*'. The Old Testament concept, that is to say, cannot be rendered fully by one term but only by a conjunction of the two which will indicate its total lexical overlap. If the LXX had really been motivated by the theological picture of truth which Torrance presents, they would surely have done just what he supposes Paul to have done here, i.e. given us a conjunction of the two or three words which taken together would represent the lexical overlap of the Hebrew. What they did was quite different; they *occasionally* gave one of the other words *in place of* the customary rendering. It is a mountainous exaggeration to regard the extremely sporadic *replacement* of the word 'truth' by πίστις or δικαιοσύνη as a proof of 'the biblical inclusion of πίστις and δικαιοσύνη in the concept of truth'.

Here we must remark again the confusion of theological and linguistic argumentation. There may be good reason for a biblically-based theology to insist that its biblically-based concepts of faith or righteousness should be comprised within its concept of truth. But the evidence produced here from the LXX goes simply nowhere towards substantiating such an insistence. Not only does it not succeed in fact; but also if there were any clarity in method and theory it would be evident that it could not succeed. The attempt to interweave theological and linguistic argument only produces an ignoring or a wrong assessment of linguistic facts.

At the risk of interrupting the argument excessively I would like to say something more about 'truth' here, since it has already been introduced in the discussion of 'faith'. I may begin by quoting a passage from one of the honoured earlier exponents of the 'biblical theology' movement:[1]

'Before it is possible to use the word "true" without explicitly relating its subject to something else, a standard of truth has to be established in the minds of men, relationship to which will henceforth be implied. Now the Greek ἀλήθεια in the spoken Greek of the first century A.D. did mean very much what the English adjective *true* means to the ordinary Englishman to-day. It meant something genuine and not counterfeit, without emphasis on any particular standard by which a statement or a thing may be judged true or false. When, however, the Greek noun ἀλήθεια and the Greek adjective ἀληθινός were used to reproduce the Hebrew root ᵓ-m-n, the whole emphasis was changed. The standard of truth not only took complete and manifest control of the noun *truth*, of the adjective *true*, and of the verb *to be true*, but also dominated the whole conception of knowledge. The Hebrew mind, in its certainty of a transcendent God, fixed upon him as the standard of truth. How this came about is not certain. It may be that the idea of steadfastness, "truth to one's self", came naturally to be applied to him who was thought of, in no philosophical manner, as everlasting. . . . At all events, the truth of Jehovah was regarded as an integral part of his character.'

This argument displays the same characteristics as those about 'faith' which we have examined. It is simply not true that the use of ἀλήθεια as translation of or with the background of the Hebrew ᵓemet removed its character as semantic marker indicating the contrast true-false. Examples have already been given from LXX, Josephus and the NT where the sense is precisely this. But it is perhaps more important to point out that this is a very frequent (and one might say, the normal) sense in the Hebrew of the OT also. When the Queen of Sheba had seen Solomon she remarked (1 Kings 10: 6): *ᵓemet hayah had-dabar ᵓašer šamaᶜti beᵓarṣi ᶜal-deᵓbareka weᶜal-ḥokmateka*, 'What I heard in my country about your words and wisdom was truth'. It is quite unfounded to suggest that anything about Yahweh as being truth

---

[1] Hoskyns and Davey, *The Riddle of the New Testament*, p. 26 ff.

or as being the standard of truth is to be found here. Numerous examples of the same kind could be cited. What the Queen of Sheba means is in fact 'very much what the English adjective *true* means to the ordinary Englishman to-day'; just like the Greek speaker of the first century A.D., her interest is that the stories she has heard are not fictions or exaggerations but founded on fact. It is not true that 'the standard of truth took complete and manifest control of the noun *truth*' — not at any rate in the sense that the authors appear to intend, viz., that wherever the word 'truth' appears a reference to God as the standard of truth is necessarily included. Likewise it is not true that a change of emphasis of this kind between the usual Greek use of ἀλήθεια and its use in the Greek of the Bible is to be traced to the influence of Hebrew ʾ-*m-n*.

After what I have already said, however, it is hardly necessary to point out how the authors have allowed philosophical-theological and linguistic judgements to mingle confusedly. The first sentence, about the need of standards of truth, is a philosophical judgement. Next we have linguistic description of the Greek of the first century and its supposed change under the influence of a Hebrew word-group. Then we have a mixture of both, for the 'standard of truth' is supposed to have taken 'complete and manifest control' of the words — 'manifest' here presumably is intended to mean 'able to be proved conclusively by linguistic evidence' — but not only this, for it also took control of the conception of knowledge, clearly a philosophical-theological judgement. What follows are pure theological judgements traced back to the Hebrew mind, or historical statements about the Hebrew mind based on theological judgements made by Israelites.

It would have been different if Hoskyns and Davey had been speaking about certain particular linguistic combinations, viz. sentences in which the words 'God' and 'truth' are related to one another. They could then have said that the thought structure indicated by the relation between these two elements in the given unit was a characteristically different one from the thought process indicated by any relation between 'God' and 'truth' or between 'reality' and 'truth' in a typical Greek sentence; or they could have pointed to the greater frequency in which such combinations are formed by the Israelites. What they fail to see is that statements true of sentences in which 'truth' is combined with certain other words are not necessarily, and are not in fact in this case, true of other combinations in which it occurs and therefore true of the word itself.

It is plain that their thinking starts from quite special cases of sentences using the word 'truth', such as 'as truth is in Jesus', 'to do the truth', 'thou art true'. Concentration on the problems of these particularly pregnant and theological usages has made them quite neglect the existence of any other usage. Only thus could they suggest that the reference to the 'standard of truth', namely God, takes complete and manifest control of all usages in the word-group.

We may compare the rather similar treatment of Blackman.[1] Failing to notice that the sense he gives for the Greek ἀλήθεια, 'the actual state of affairs as contrasted with rumour or false report or mythology', is also normal and frequent in Hebrew, he exaggerates the difference between the Greek and the Hebrew uses, but then has to describe their 'fusion' in certain cases in the NT.

Blackman also uses the term 'intellectualist', saying that Pilate's famous question implies 'no more than the intellectualist view of truth made familiar to that age by the Greek philosophers'. Similarly Hoskyns and Davey tell us that the NT usage embraces far more than 'the purely intellectual quality of modern thought' (p. 29). What is really offered by this school in contrast to the 'intellectualist' view of truth is in essence a 'personalist' one, exemplified by the 'true friend' or 'true man', the 'inner self-consistency of God' and the like. But on the list of cases of ἀλήθεια cited above it would be as absurd to find an 'intellectualist' view of truth in the Greek examples as to find a 'personalist' one in the Jewish examples. In other words, the use of the word 'truth' cannot be simply related to these contrasts in understandings of what truth is. It is typical of this school of thought to suppose that because the Greek philosophers conceived of truth in an intellectual manner therefore the Greek word ἀλήθεια itself suggests this meaning, and the opposite for the Hebrew words. In the special

[1] In Richardson's *Theological Word Book* (London, 1950), p. 270.

pregnant cases like 'I am the truth' it is not so much the Hebrew
background that forbids or makes difficult an intellectualist conception of truth as the interpretation of the sentence; it is rather
the juxtaposition of the words 'I' and 'the truth' in this context,
along with the knowledge that the 'I' is Jesus and not a personified
abstraction. Those who suggest that the 'Hebrew background' is
the key to ἀλήθεια here speak as if a sentence like 'I am the truth'
were quite normal in Hebrew speech. Even 'God is truth' is
nowhere found in the OT, although there are a good many
references to 'thy truth' and the like.[1]

The discussion of this matter like others has been obscured also
by etymologizing interpretations of words. Thus the suggestion
of Senft[2] that the Greek word for truth expresses 'the fact that
something stands disclosed, that instead of being concealed it
becomes explicit and freed from the appearances which falsify it'
is clearly intended as a conclusion from the etymology of ἀλήθεια.
I have already said enough to show that such material is not a guide
at all to the semantics of the word in actual usage.

For the Hebrew words the etymologizing approach has a further
effect which is in my opinion dubious, namely that of making the
terms ᵓᵉmunah and ᵓᵉmet nearly synonymous; and in much of the
literature of biblical theology they are in fact treated as almost
indistinguishable. Thus Dodd interprets the words identically and
obscures the evidence of the LXX seriously by giving translation
statistics for them as a block and not separately.[3] Torrance says
that little difference can be seen between them[4] and elsewhere[5] sets
down as an obvious identity the equation 'ᵓᵉmunah = πίστις =
ᵓᵉmet.'

I give here a more particular breakdown of the statistics, in
which however some small variation should be allowed for because
of textual questions:

---

[1] Bultmann in *TWNT* i. 250 perceived with reference to ἀληθινός used as an
attribute of God that 'the Semitic usage comes here very near to the Greek usage
of ἀληθινός'. The treatment of this article as a whole suffers, however, from the
common fault of *TWNT* in devoting most of its investigation of Greek usage to
philosophical-religious usage.
[2] In Allmen, *Vocabulary of the Bible* (London, 1958), p. 431.
[3] Op. cit., pp. 68, 70, and 65–75 generally.
[4] *ET* lxviii (1956–7) 112.   [5] *Royal Priesthood*, p. 2.

(a) *ᵉmunah* is translated by

i. πίστις	× 20	ii. ἀλήθεια		× 22
plus πιστός	× 1	plus ἀληθινός		× 2

(b) *ᵉmet* is translated by

i. πίστις and πιστός	× 7	ii. ἀλήθεια and	
		related words	× 107

Now I do not wish to deny that there may be many cases where the senses of the two Hebrew words were not easy to distinguish. I do suggest, however, that there is also an important area in which they were recognizably different in usage.

First of all, *ᵉmet* is widely and frequently used for 'truth' as opposed to falsity. This is not recognized by the constant attempt to dwell on the etymology. For example the phrase *be-ᵉmunah* means 'in fidelity' but *be-ᵉmet* can always be interpreted from 'in truth', 'really'. We have already seen how Driver rightly gives 'truth' as the sense for the first occurrence in Palestinian-Syrian literature, back in the second millennium B.C. The numerous occurrences of *ᵉmet* in 1QS are, in my opinion rightly, translated 'truth' by many scholarly studies.[1] The difficulties which have been felt by Dodd and others in the LXX translation of *ᵉmet* by ἀλήθεια are therefore exaggerated, and depend unduly on the etymology. I have already shown how special and how out of the way is the rendering of this word by πίστις, on which Torrance has laid so much weight. We may, I think, reasonably suggest that the LXX knew what they were doing when they translated *ᵉmet* by the ἀλήθεια group. And it is unlikely that they were yielding to Hellenistic thought and its divisive splitting up of unitary Hebrew concepts in doing so; for the Targum, which was not likely to be influenced deeply by Hellenism, uses *qšoṭ* or *qušṭa* 'truth' extremely frequently to translate *ᵉmet*. The whole treatment of *ᵉmet* and its relation to ἀλήθεια in biblical theology is damaged by two things, the etymologizing method and the way in which the results achieved by it appear to fit into the thought contrast of Greek philosophy and Hebrew theology.

[1] E.g. P. Wernberg-Møller, *The Manual of Discipline* (Leiden, 1957).

Concerning the rendering of *ᵉmunah* less need be said here, but one main point must be made. The statistics of its translation by ἀλήθεια seem imposing, 24 cases in all, until we notice that 20 of these are from the Psalter, a book in which ἀλήθεια is very frequent (mostly of course for *ᵉmet*) but πίστις occurs only once. This rendering should therefore probably be regarded as an idiosyncrasy of the translator of the Psalms. Perhaps we cannot tell certainly the reason for it. In his text the use of *ᵉmunah* is of course predominantly of qualities of God, and it may be that he understood πίστις normally to mean 'trust, faith', and therefore not to be usually suitable for a divine attribute; or, perhaps more likely, he simply accommodated the translation of *ᵉmunah* to the still more frequent translation of *ᵉmet*. There is something of a parallel in the treatment of *hod* 'glory' in a number of cases as ἐξομολόγησις 'acknowledgement' because *hodah* 'give thanks' was usually ἐξομολογεῖσθαι; cf. ἐξομολόγησις for *todah* 'thanks, thank-offering' sometimes; as Flashar points out, it was not that the translator did not know the meaning of *hod*, which is rendered more exactly in certain places.[1] Very likely we may see two influences at work: firstly an etymologizing procedure, as in the case of *hod*, and secondly a feeling that in the many cases concerning qualities of God, or his words or promises, 'thy truth' was very close to the sense of the Hebrew ('thy faithfulness'), and reasonably enough so. At any rate we may be sure that the translation of *ᵉmunah* by ἀλήθεια cannot be used to obscure the much greater appropriateness of ἀλήθεια for *ᵉmet*.[2]

We may now bring to a close the study of the arguments of

[1] On this see Flashar, *ZATW* xxxii (1912) 175–80.

[2] It is interesting that Jerome in the Gallican Psalter translated these 20 cases naturally and uniformly with *veritas*; in the *Psalterium iuxta Hebraeos*, however, translated from the Hebrew, he changed in seven of the cases to *fides*. This may reasonably be regarded as an effect of greater attention to Hebrew usage, and the fact that he did not carry out the change uniformly may be attributed to the influence of the older version. Of the four cases outside of the Psalter, Jerome used *fides* and cognates in three (Is. 11: 5, 25: 1; 2 Chr. 19: 9).

It is also worth remarking that Aquila, who often tried to mark words of common Hebrew etymology by Greek formations of common origin, used πίστις for *ᵉmunah* and ἀλήθεια for *ᵉmet*, with much consistency (I would take πίστις to be the Aquila reading at Ps. 142 (143): 1, cf. Symmachus Ps. 35: 6). The other Greek translators also prefer πίστις for *ᵉmunah*, but less consistently than Aquila.

Hebert and Torrance by asking how far they have proved the main points which they set out to establish. Their exegesis of NT passages will not be examined in general, nor shall I comment on the theological value of their conclusions.

Hebert set out to show that the word 'faith' as Paul uses it 'carries a Hebrew rather than a Greek meaning'. The general line of thought (though there are some inconsistencies) is that 'faith, believing' as an act of man is the Greek (or European) meaning and 'faithfulness' the Hebrew meaning. I have already shown how this supposed 'Hebrew meaning' was sustained only through great and tendentious selectiveness within the linguistic evidence, through the use of theological argument in lieu of linguistic argument, and in particular through neglect of the verb *he²emin* 'trust, believe', which is by any account the most important Hebrew word for anyone wanting to discuss the meaning of 'faith'.[1]

We must now emphasize the most important fact in this whole question, and one which is almost entirely ignored by both Hebert and Torrance: Hebrew usage, as far as the Old Testament evidence shows (with some possible qualification for Hab. 2: 4), had developed no substantive meaning 'believing, faith' to correspond with its well known verb *he²emin* 'trust, believe' — but Greek had such a word in πίστις. That Hebrew had no such noun is not to be explained from a total theological structure; it is a simple linguistic fact, the kind of fact that has been too much overlooked in this discussion. That the Greek word when used in relation to ultimate and religious matters was the linguistic sign for a much paler and more intellectual attitude than the 'believing' of the Jewish tradition did not matter; it enriched the lexical stock by providing a semantic marker for this Jewish tradition of 'believing' which in the Old Testament was available in verbal but not in nominal form. The LXX did not use it as such because it was translating a Hebrew text in which the nominal form did not exist. But it appears in books with no Semitic original, e.g. 4 Macc.

---

[1] In view of Hebert's intention to prove that the word did not have the supposed Greek or European sense as an act or activity of man, it is specially engaging to find (op. cit., p. 378) that 'it does not fall within our subject to deal at length with his (i.e. Paul's) use of πίστις as an act or activity of man, and of the verb πιστεύειν'.

15: 24, 16: 22, 'faith towards God' and in Philo. There is no reason to doubt that it was a normal part of the Greek of Alexandrian Jews.

Another element however has to be added here, namely the development of the semantic value of 'trust, faith' in certain nouns on the Semitic side also. For Hebrew itself this sense, which became well established in late Hebrew, may well have developed for ʾᵉmunah during the late Judaistic period. From Qumran the most important text is at 1QPHab 8: 2–3; the sense of 'faith' is supported by some scholars here, although it is not certain, since the passage might be translated 'because of their toil and their faith in the teacher' or 'because of their toil and their faithfulness to the teacher'. To me the presence of the preposition bᵉ, which is used with the verb heʾᵉmin 'believe', rather suggests the former.[1]

A similar development is likely for the Aramaic hemanuta. This is found with the sense 'faithfulness' in the Words of Aḥiqar,[2] a sense also found in later Jewish literature. But it is usually taken to have been the word used by Jesus in the passages in the Gospels where the Greek has πίστις, and the meaning here in many cases is clearly 'trust, faith'.[3] In the ability to develop in the two directions of 'faithfulness' and 'trust, faith' the Hebrew ʾᵉmunah and the Aramaic hemanuta show the same characteristic as the Greek πίστις, although the latter seems to have been developed in this way earlier than they were.

Hebert is therefore quite wrong in correlating the question between 'faith' and 'faithfulness' with the question between Greek and Hebrew meanings. The Greek word was able to be used as a semantic marker for both, and that it was in fact used for both in the NT is not really disputed. Hebrew also had semantic markers for both, but for the former only in a verb form until a late period. The former aspect however, i.e. that of 'trust, believing', though it

---

[1] The translation 'faith' will be found in M. Burrows, *The Dead Sea Scrolls*, p. 368; T. H. Gaster, *The Scriptures of the Dead Sea Sect*, p. 238.

[2] A. Cowley, *Aramaic Papyri of the Fifth Century B.C.* (Oxford, 1923), p. 217.

[3] *TWNT* πίστις (Bultmann), p. 199 n. barely mentions this fact, and makes very little of it; this article generally pays little attention to the Gospels and to the Aramaic background in particular.

was important in the Old Testament, received a great increase of importance and centrality in the New Testament, a fact which I think no one will deny. This fact explains the great rise in the representation of the sense 'trust, faith' for πίστις in the NT and its preponderance over the sense 'faithfulness' which is the normal LXX sense. If such a judgement will be permitted, it would seem to the writer most fortunate that a writer like St Paul had at his disposal a word for trust and believing in the syntactically con-venient noun form. The sense 'trust, faith' for πίστις, which most people will hold to be numerically greatly preponderant in the NT, is just as 'Hebraic' as the sense 'faithfulness', and none of the arguments from linguistic evidence advanced by Hebert or Torrance to support the sense 'faithfulness' as pre-eminently 'Hebraic' have any validity.

Torrance both goes less far and farther than Hebert; less far in that he is less anxious to avoid the sense 'faith, trust, believing', and farther in that he wants to have both 'faith' and 'faithfulness' at the same time, as 'a polarized expression denoting the faithful-ness of Christ as its main ingredient but also involving or at least suggesting the answering faithfulness of man, and so his belief in Christ'. Enough evidence has by now been presented to enable the reader to judge for himself whether there is any truth in this idea of a 'polarized expression' in the New Testament. I need only reiterate how extremely misleading the presentation of linguistic evidence in favour of this understanding has been and how completely wrong it is to suppose that the description of 'polarized expression' can be justified by the argument from Hebrew usage which has been made. At the point of identification of the 'polarized expression', which is in a way the summit of the article, as at so many other points linguistic discussion is simply abandoned and replaced by theological discussion. The paragraph following the identification of the 'polarized expression' is a purely theo-logical exposition; tacitly it presupposes that since the relationship of God and man in Christ is a reciprocal one in fact, with the faithfulness of God being answered by the faith and therefore the faithfulness of man, and the faithfulness and faith of Christ stand-ing between and involving both, therefore the usage of πίστις Ἰησοῦ

Χριστοῦ as a linguistic unit by St Paul must itself be an ambivalent or polarized expression.

Here two questions may be put. The first is whether it is not more likely that the phrase is ambivalent in having two *alternative* meanings, and that Torrance's theology, having assimilated the sentences in which each of these occurs, and having integrated them in a theological reciprocity system, is now simply trying to force upon each particular case the entirety of that system. The second is the simple appeal to Pauline usage. This is made quite correctly by Moule in his criticisms. Torrance interprets criticisms such as Moule makes as an attempt 'to interpret Paul's language merely out of the rules of Greek grammar, without careful and exact reference to his Hebraic background and thought'. Of this two things may be said: (a) no one nowadays interprets language 'out of the rules', and it is a sign of a fundamental misunderstanding of modern linguistic methods, and particularly of what an appeal to usage means, when it is interpreted as an appeal to 'the rules' (b) once again the thought contrast of Greek and Hebrew mentality, which has determined so much of the argument already, appears, and the idea seems to be that Paul is not to be read as Greek because his thinking was Hebraic.

Moule makes not only linguistic criticisms of Torrance's linguistic arguments but theological criticisms of his theological ones. This I do not propose to do. I am at present interested only in the method of argument from linguistic evidence. The arguments we have examined seem to me clearly to reveal a philosophy of the relation of language to thought, and of particular languages to the thought of the peoples who used them, which needs to be brought to light and studied critically. In brief it seems to me to be a philosophy of idealist type in which the linguistic structure is an expression of, and reflects the inner relations of, the relevant thought-structure, Greek-metaphysical or Hebrew-theological. The idealist aspect is indicated also by the following :

(a) the inability to keep to linguistic method strictly and the tendency to replace it by theological and philosophical argument;

(b) the blindness to any idea of the socially conditioned nature of language as an arbitrary system of semantic markers;

(c) the inability to see and present linguistic evidence except where it appears to follow the lines of a thought-structure of metaphysical-theological type. In honesty it must be said that the linguistic portions of the essays by Hebert and Torrance contain practically no facts which are not used or presented in extremely misleading ways.

Chapter Eight

Some Principles of Kittel's Theological Dictionary

GENERAL

No single work is perhaps more influential in the study of the New Testament to-day than Kittel's *Theological Dictionary* (*TWNT*). It is therefore of the utmost importance to discover what were the principles on which it was designed. We may say straight away that the small amount Kittel himself wrote about the problems of a venture calling itself a 'Theological Dictionary' does not suggest that he was aware how difficult these problems were.

In the introduction to the first volume[1] the following points are made by Kittel: (*a*) The new work is seen as a continuation of the earlier lexicographical labours of Hermann Cremer and his successor Kögel. Of this I shall say something later. (*b*) The new dictionary intends to treat 'all vocables of the NT to which there clings any religious and theological determination (*Bestimmung*)'. Certain numerals, a number of personal names, and 'all those prepositions which are theologically more important' are included, a large proportion therefore of the total vocabulary. (*c*) The dictionary proposes not to provide what it calls 'external lexicography' but to presuppose it, or at the most to give it a brief treatment; for the material of 'external lexicography' one is directed to the dictionary of Bauer[2] and the concordance of Schmoller. The new work is to take up where 'external lexicography' leaves off, that is, at the 'inner lexicography'. A little later

---

[1] *TWNT* i. v–vii; cf. Friedrich, Kittel's successor as editor, *TWNT* v. iii–iv, and his 'Problematik'.

[2] Cited here from the English edition, W. F. Arndt and F. W. Gingrich, *A Greek-English Lexicon of the New Testament* (Cambridge, 1957).

we hear of 'the task of New Testament concept history' (*Begriffs-geschichte*), and though Kittel does not say so expressly we are probably entitled to understand 'concept history' and 'inner lexicography' as the same thing in his opinion. This very brief guidance is all that is given in the preface to the first volume.

Now certain difficulties are at once apparent. The work of the dictionary is to be in the realm of 'concept history'; but the dictionary itself is a dictionary of Greek *words*. The construction of the work thus brings right to the fore the difficult problem of the relation of word and concept. This is not necessarily insoluble, but one would at least expect some mention of its existence. With a great work of reference professing to study 'concept history' but organized under the scheme of specific Greek words, one is not unlikely to get the impression that the lexical stock of NT Greek can be closely correlated with the concept-stock of the early Christians; and this further, perhaps, with the actual layout of the objects of the theological world, the being, plans, purposes and acts of God. We would thus have a correlation of the lexical stock of the NT with the mind of the early Church, just as in the previous correlation between the morphological-syntactic structure of Hebrew and the Hebrew mind, which we have already studied. And it is clear that the leaving out of the non-theological words, plus the leaving to another work of the 'external lexicography' of those words which are included, might increase this impression. That such an impression has been created among some users of *TWNT* seems probable to me; it also seems probable to me that the writers of some of the articles in *TWNT* held this impression; as for Kittel himself, his preface is so vague about this sort of thing that one feels he never thought about linguistic problems with sufficient precision to formulate the problem.

Kittel also gave some lectures on his lexicographical work, and a quotation from these may help us forward:[1]

'In the New Testament there are a large number of words used for the utterance of speech and the deliverance of a message, not only λόγος, λέγω, λαλέω, but also κηρύσσω, μαρτυρέω,

---

[1] G. Kittel, *Lexicographia Sacra* (*Theology* Occasional Papers, no. 7, London, 1938); German version in *Deutsche Theologie* v (1938) 91-109.

ἀγγέλλω, and their numerous compounds. Now I would suggest that with all of these the emphasis does not lie on what we may term the formal side. These words are not used merely to describe a new doctrine or a new apprehension of God. Much less do they serve a purely literary purpose. On the contrary — and here we discover their essential significance — they are bound up inextricably with a definite historical fact to which they bear witness. The point is, therefore, not the message as such, nor the λέγειν or κηρύσσειν etc., in itself, but the event, the happening, the fact of which the message tells. There would never be any κηρύσσειν if there were not the fact of Christ Incarnate, Crucified and Risen. I would ask you to notice the vital differences between this sort of speaking and, shall we say, the poetical use of language. For a poet, the beauty of the words is itself sufficient. And similarly the philosopher lays all his emphasis upon the depth of the thoughts which his words are expressing. The language of the New Testament has quite definitely but one single purpose, that of expressing that which has taken place, that which God has done in Christ. New Testament words are thus essentially like a mirror; they reflect the fact of Christ, and this they do not in any broken or indirect way, but in actual reality and in genuine truth. That which has taken place in Christ, itself and through its own δύναμις, creates and shapes its own message, the very message which henceforth bears witness to it throughout the whole world. For the words and sentences in which the message is framed are formed by men who are imbued with the fact of Christ. They never speak in order to communicate their own wisdom or any theological or philosophical ideas.'

About this we should first note, without at present discussing fully, the strong Christocentric emphasis, and with it the emphasis characteristic of modern biblical theology on the *Heilsgeschichte* or history of salvation. The important thing is not any system of ideas, any new doctrine or new apprehension of God, but a series of events in history. Now our interest for the present is not in the theology here, but in the use of linguistic evidence; but it is worth while here suggesting that the emphasis on events and the abhorrence of ideas was an obstacle to Kittel's making precise for himself or for others what was a 'concept' in his opinion, and how it was related to the organization of his dictionary under a series of *words*. The idea of the dictionary being a 'history of concepts' (and not only the 'external' history of the words) presupposes some series of mental realities related to the words. Then the question would at once have to be put: is there one 'concept' for each word, or not? Does the lexical stock correspond to the 'concept' stock? Does a particular occurrence of a word imply the signification of the whole of the corresponding 'concept' or only of part of it? Is the concept made up from the totality of the occurrences of the related word, or is the 'concept' fully present each time the word appears? All these questions are fully relevant, but not even a preliminary adumbration of an answer seems to have been thought out. One reason for this is probably the desire of Kittel, like some other biblical theologians, to think of 'events' as what lay behind the words, as in the passage just quoted. He felt therefore that he could eschew the examination of 'ideas' and get on to the events. This was not a favourable climate for a careful examination of the sense of 'concept'.

It is also worth while to remember that the theological movement with which Kittel was associated was strongly opposed to subjective psychological understandings of religion. It would seem however obvious that the use of language is related to processes usually called mental or psychological, even if the events referred to in such speech cannot rightly be interpreted on that plane. But the feeling against the psychological and against anything that suggested 'ideas' (a Hellenic-sounding term!) was so strong that these attempts are made to relate the words directly to the external events or realities.

This still produces contradictions in biblical theology, where people on the one hand extol 'the biblical concept of time' or 'the forms of the Hebrew mind' and on the other deny that the biblical message has any 'ideas' in it at all. Note again how Kittel maintains that the men of the NT 'never speak to communicate any theological ideas'. 'Idea' here has simply become a bad word, just as 'revelation' is a good one.

It is not accidental that under such influences we have a crop of interpretations the weakness of which is their failure to discover *what was meant* and their correspondingly heavy dependence on etymologies and remote associations of words.

The difficulty here is made much greater by what is one of the most irritating things about *TWNT*, the habit of the writers of saying 'concept' (*Begriff*) for the linguistic entity usually called a word. The same is true of a modern dogmatician like Karl Barth; and it was extremely frequent in Cremer and Kögel. Thus (to take one example out of thousands), when Kögel gives a simple list of words the articles on which he has revised, he calls it a 'list of concepts' (Cremer-Kögel, 10th ed., p. 1227).

So in *TWNT* we hear of not 'the Greek word μάταιος' but 'the Greek concept μάταιος' (see above, p. 38); we often read not that 'Paul chooses the word so and so' but that he 'chooses the concept so and so'. This usage may well be a sign of the background of *TWNT*, which lies so often in philosophical and theological rather than linguistic method. Hundreds of examples will be found, but this usage is itself inconsistent. Among other usages I may mention the following:

(*a*) Sometimes we find 'concept' used for one general notion which may be partially or approximately represented by each of several words. Thus according to *TWNT* ii. 81 there is a 'concept of "serving" ' which finds expression in each of no less than five Greek verbs. Each of these is fitted to bring out or emphasize a certain aspect of the concept. Yet each of these words is also a 'concept' — for instance one of them, διακονεῖν, is called a 'concept' on the same page.

(*b*) 'Concept' is also used in phrases like 'the Johannine concept of the Logos' or 'the concept of justification by faith'; in these cases the 'concept' is roughly a phrase or term which can be taken as a brief formulation of the main content of a passage.

(*c*) We also meet cases such as 'the anthropomorphic concept of God' (*TWNT* v. 494). Here the 'concept' is no longer something that could also be called a 'word' or a 'key phrase', but is a tendency of thought easily recognizable, but one which can hardly be identified with any one specific linguistic expression at all.

We thus have at least three senses in which 'concept' is used, in addition to that in which 'word' would be perfectly adequate and would be the normal name of the entity referred to.

This inconsistency is cut across by another inconsistency, in that 'concept' is sometimes used in this tradition with a rather favourable air and sometimes with a pejorative one. Thus when Kittel says that *TWNT* is to work on 'concept history' he quite clearly means that it will investigate something more than mere words, that it will enter into all the inner riches of thought, meaning and allusion, unlike the supposed 'external lexicography'. The fact that 'concept' is a favourite word of the writers agrees with this. The pejorative sense on the other hand appears when Kögel suggests that the task is 'not to let the matter rest with the mere concept'. For him the 'concept world' is a different thing from the 'whole world of thought', and the task of a special lexicon is to restore the connection between them (see below, pp. 242–6). It is not quite clear what is meant by 'concept' in this case. It seems to me probable, however, that what is meant is the giving of a simple word-substitution or general translation equivalence such as, for example, the bare information that Hebr. *bayit* means 'house' or that Greek ἀγάπη means 'love'.

The obvious cure for these many confusions is to avoid saying 'concept' unless we mean something other than 'word'.

At times then Kittel speaks as if there was a word and its corresponding concept; at other times as if there was a word and its corresponding event (or other external reality, but in Kittel's mind all important realities were known in events). But it would seem obvious that these are two different relations. The uncertainty between them produces one of the chief faults in Kittel's work, namely that you are never sure when you are dealing with New Testament words and when you are dealing with the realities signified by them.

Now the oscillation between talking about linguistic phenomena, in this case words, and talking about theological realities like God and his works, is evident in the passage we have quoted from Kittel. Take the sentence:

'The language of the New Testament has quite definitely but

one single purpose, that of expressing that which has taken place, that which God has done in Christ.'

How does Kittel know that 'the language of the New Testament' has this purpose? If he means that the users of this language had this purpose, then there is no difficulty. But that is not what he says, and it is characteristic of Kittel that he does not; although it would make much better sense, because it is rather unnatural to speak of a language having a purpose other than the purpose which its users had in using it. Kittel is after all speaking about a great and comprehensive work purporting to be a study of *language*; and it is a study of language arranged in dictionary form. When he says this about the 'purpose' of the language therefore the reader naturally (and I think rightly) takes him to mean that this purpose, i.e. of expressing what God has done in Christ, will become evident from the kind of study he is talking about, that is, from a lexicographical study on his lines of a word like λέγω in the NT. The objection to this is a simple one: it won't work, and the article on λέγω does not make it work.

It is clear in fact that Kittel has got his idea of a 'purpose' here from the theological purpose of the NT message, but is confusedly associating it with a paragraph beginning with NT *words*, because he sees no reason to doubt that what applies to the message will apply to the words used in it. The same confusion appears throughout. When he says that the point lies not in the message, the λέγειν, the κηρύσσειν, but in the event told of, the contrast is one between the act of proclamation and the event proclaimed; but he is using it as if it were a contrast between the verb 'to proclaim' and the event proclaimed. And hence he will argue shortly that:

'The words and sentences of New Testament language cease to exist for themselves and become, as it were, vessels of transparent crystal which have one sole purpose, that of making their contents visible.'

The crystal vessels are linguistic phenomena, words and sentences, and the contents are the act of God in Christ. A valid contrast between a message and the matter of which it tells is invalidly extended to be a contrast between the linguistic phenomena occurring in the message and the matter of the message. If Kittel had only said 'sentences' it would not have been quite so bad; but a dictionary is a book of words and not a book of sentences, and it is just at the point of the words that Kittel will have most trouble in making his theory fit. And let us notice how dangerously Kittel has (involuntarily, I think) minimized in this part of his treatment the linguistic consciousness, the social convention of the significance of words, which is or should be the middle term between the linguistic material (the lexical units of which form the sections of the dictionary) and the proclaiming of the message; for however unimportant the proclaiming was in comparison with the events proclaimed, the mind of the proclaimers was (unlike the events proclaimed) the thing in direct contact with the linguistic phenomena used.

As soon, however, as the social acceptation of words is neglected and some kind of direct relation between the words and the external events or realities hinted at, an opening is given to those interpretations which, like 'hinterground' for *dabar*,[1] are remote from the actual semantic indication but can be made to fit attractively into the pattern of the events or external realities; and which by an etymologizing or other argument are able to impose themselves with an air of authority as the 'proper' or 'fundamental' meaning. It is by no means true of course that Kittel always drew a direct line from the words to the external events and neglected the social linguistic consciousness — if he *had* done this consistently, we should have known better where we are — but he was willing to talk this way some of the time at any rate.[2]

It is perhaps worth considering whether the method which Kittel toys with here is in part a way of dealing with the other lexicographical tradition which has its chief representative in Deissmann, the strong critic of Kittel's forerunner Cremer.[3] Speaking very generally, Deissmann thought that the language of the NT was the ordinary language of the time and that it was nonsense to speak of Christianity as having exercised a moulding

[1] See above, p. 130 ff.
[2] In *Lexicographia Sacra* other examples will be found in the cases of ἐν and διά (p. 11), κῆρυξ and κήρυγμα (p. 17 f.), καινός and εἰρήνη (p. 29).
[3] On Deissmann and Cremer, see below, pp. 238–44.

or shaping effect on it. Kittel of course pays tribute to Deissmann and acknowledges that many of his arguments have now been accepted without question in the world of New Testament scholarship. None the less, though it is nowhere stated explicitly, one has the impression that Deissmann's interests and points of view, like the Bauer dictionary which belongs to the same tradition, are part of the 'external lexicography' which is to be taken for granted in Kittel's method. But Deissmann, it seems to me, would hardly have accepted the suggestion that his work was only on the externals. He would have claimed that the kind of lexicography on which he worked was a good and adequate guide to what was in the mind of the early Christians. He would certainly however have repudiated any idea that in investigating the lexical stock of the NT he was uncovering the pattern of a series of real divine acts. The line pursued by Kittel, that there is some correspondence between the words and the divine acts, and that there is something special about NT language in this, is perhaps partly a way round the idea of a correspondence between the words and the Christian ideas or the Christian religion, ground that was difficult because it had already been traversed in the controversies of Deissmann and Cremer. It is clear that in *Lexicographia Sacra* Kittel is striving to make some correlation of the NT words with some pattern of Christian truth; and I am suggesting that one reason why he makes the correlation with the external divine events, in spite of its difficulties and inconsistencies, is that the way to certain other kinds of correlation was blocked by the shadow of Deissmann. There were however other influences on Kittel which also worked in this direction, such as the emphasis of the theological movement of his time. He seems to take the assessment which that theology made of the Church as the bearer of the Word of God and simply transfer it bodily into the lexicographical realm.[1]

---

[1] For an·example of the way in which Kittel made apparently linguistic statements which were really no more than a sort of linguistic allegory of theological truth, cf. *Lexicographia Sacra*, p. 29, where, speaking of the 'New' that has come with the Gospel, he says: 'This "new", however, is real, incarnate, personal. And at this point we reach the ultimate stage of all lexicography and of all history of religions. The history of the word εἰρήνη comes to an end in Eph. 2:14: "HE is our peace", αὐτὸς γάρ ἐστιν ἡ εἰρήνη ἡμῶν. He does not bring a new

The usual procedure of a dictionary is to offer not 'concepts' but word-substitutions. For example, Liddell and Scott's *Greek-English Lexicon* in listing a Greek word will give an English word as a provisional substitute. In translating the Greek sentence into English the semantic contribution made by the Greek word will be approximately reproduced by the semantic contribution of the English word. It is well known that in a large number of cases a single word cannot be provided as a fully adequate substitute, and therefore two or three words or expressions are given. Often the usage of a Greek word will divide itself naturally into three or four groups, each of which fairly naturally fits with a different English word or expression; and then the article is sub-divided under these several heads. Since the way in which word-substitutions can be made depends on the syntactical context, special substitutions will be suggested under each head for special cases. No one supposes that the provision of substitutions is in itself an adequate guide to the thought of the people using the words. For that you have to read the context passages as widely as possible. The substitution does try to be an adequate guide to the semantic contribution of the word to the sentences in which it is used. For this purpose it is essential that all basic semantic possibilities should be listed, i.e. that none which is widely different from the others and therefore not covered by them should be omitted. It is not essential that all the uses made of the corresponding or related concepts or ideas in the history of thought should be listed.

Thus for Greek ἔρως Liddell and Scott clearly thought that it was necessary to list the senses 'object of love or desire' or 'pr.n., the god of love', because they differ characteristically from the first sense given, i.e. 'love, mostly of the sexual passion'. But they also clearly thought that they could omit listing the special development of ἔρως in Plato's *Symposium*, because, however original the conception of love there developed might be, the substitution of the English word 'love' is still an adequate provisional guide to the semantic value of ἔρως in the sentences of that work. We have already mentioned the provisional nature of the word-substitution

conception of the term "peace", he *is* it.' The ultimate Kittel is talking of here is purely theological, and not lexicographical or historical.

given. It is an obvious and perpetual problem of all lexicography that substitutions can never be completely adequate in many cases. But it is also true that substitutions should not be totally inadequate or misleading; and it is a presupposition of lexicography that a good proportion of valid and intelligible (though always provisional) substitutions can be made.

I should perhaps make clear that I am not trying here to make any comparison of value between the Liddell and Scott type and the Kittel type. I do have in mind criticisms of other types of dictionaries which are sometimes made by enthusiasts for *TWNT* in order to set off the supposed advantages of the latter. What I have said here about dictionaries in general may seem very obvious. I have said it however partly to help elucidate the problems of *TWNT* and partly because there seems to be so much confusion in modern biblical theology about what dictionaries are trying to do and not trying to do. A typical experience is to be solemnly assured that 'if you look up Liddell and Scott, what you get is a *concept*'. This judgement represents, as far as it means anything, either the idea mentioned above that a simple word-substitution is a 'concept', or else a feeling that if Greek thought (unlike Hebrew thought, of course) was fond of abstract concepts, the lexicographers of the Greek language must have filled their dictionaries with 'concepts' too.

We may now pass on to make some comparison with the method of *TWNT*. In it naturally word-substitutions are found, and translations of passages from the relevant documents are given. But in general this sort of thing is seen as belonging rather to the 'external lexicography' which Kittel wishes to take for granted. The main work of his dictionary is a thorough discussion of what we may call the field of thought with which the words are related. This field of thought is divided in many articles into several sections: a typical division would be into (*a*) Hellenic usage (*b*) Old Testament words and usage (*c*) later Judaism and Septuagint (*d*) New Testament. In all of these it is common to lay special emphasis on the philosophical, religious and theological uses. Thus the article on ἀγαπάω has a section entitled 'The words for "to love" in pre-biblical Greek', and this includes 1½ pages on the philosophical-mystical idea of Eros among the Greeks, even though the article is not on ἔρως at all but on ἀγαπάω. We are in fact coming closer to idea-histories than to word-histories in this method.

Now the principle that the history of an idea is of the utmost relevance for the history of the semantics of words fairly close to it seems to me entirely right.[1] Nevertheless it is important that some possibility of distinction between the two should be kept in view. It is in fact one of the chief difficulties in using *TWNT* that one is sometimes not sure whether the dictionary is talking about what is generally true or was generally believed or whether it is talking about the significative value of a word in certain particular contexts. It is true of course that a word may be used in such a way as to suggest some wide area of recognized thought which can be somehow connected with the word but which goes beyond its normal signification. It is however a central lexical problem to determine to what degree this has happened, and this determination can be done only on the basis of the context at given occurrences. It is misleading in other words to suppose that it can be taken for granted that this is always happening. Thus the articles in *TWNT*, while apparently organized under a Greek word (like ἀγαπάω or ἁμαρτία), have a tendency to be an essay on the biblical conception of Love or of Sin; and in difficult cases to leave it somewhat uncertain whether that whole conception can be taken to be indicated in a particular passage by the word which is the subject of the article.

The problem here is to some extent what is meant by 'meaning' or 'significance'. Two brief examples may be given (not in fact from *TWNT*).

An object or event may be signified by word *a* or by word *b*. This does not mean that *a* means *b*. We have already seen that *dabar* 'matter, thing' may be used of a matter or thing which is in fact a historical event, but that it is not justified therefore to say that *dabar* means 'event' or 'history' or the like.[2] The identity of

---

[1] I would refer for example to the excellent remarks of L. Spitzer in the preface to his *Essays in Historical Semantics*. He rightly holds the entirety of cultural history (and not for example only the usage and literature of one language) to be relevant for the understanding of semantic change.

[2] See above, p. 131 f.

the object to which different designations are given does not imply that these designations have the same semantic value. The mistake of supposing that it does we may for convenience call 'illegitimate identity transfer'.

A term may be used in a number of places. Let us take the example of ἐκκλησία 'church' in the NT. If we ask 'What is the meaning of ἐκκλησία in the NT?', the answer given may be an adding or a compounding of different statements about the ἐκκλησία made in various passages. Thus we might say (a) 'the Church is the Body of Christ' (b) 'the Church is the first instalment of the Kingdom of God' (c) 'the Church is the Bride of Christ', and other such statements. The 'meaning of ἐκκλησία in the NT' could then be legitimately stated to be the totality of these relations. This is one sense of 'meaning'. But when we take an individual sentence, such as 'The Church is the Body of Christ', and ask what is 'the meaning' of 'the Church' in this sentence, we are asking something different. The semantic indication given by 'the Church' is now something much less than 'the NT conception of the Church'. The realization of this is of primary importance in dealing with isolated or unusual cases; the obvious example is 'my ἐκκλησία' in Matt. 16: 18 (cf. 18: 17). In this case the *TWNT* article (K. L. Schmidt) gives separate treatment to the particular passages. The error that arises, when the 'meaning' of a word (understood as the total series of relations in which it is used in the literature) is read into a particular case as its sense and implication there, may be called 'illegitimate totality transfer'.

We may briefly remark that this procedure has to be specially guarded against in the climate of present-day biblical theology, for this climate is very favourable to 'seeing the Bible as a whole' and rather hostile to the suggestion that something is meant in one place which is really unreconcilable with what is said in another (the sort of suggestion which under literary criticism led to a fragmentation of the understanding of the Bible). There may be also some feeling that since Hebrew man or biblical man thought in totalities we should do the same as interpreters. But a moment's thought should indicate that the habit of thinking about God or man or sin as totalities is a different thing from obscuring the value of a word in a context by imposing upon it the totality of its uses. We may add that the small compass of the NT, both in literary bulk and in the duration of the period which produced it, adds a plausibility to the endeavour to take it as one piece, which could hardly be considered so likely for any literature of greater bulk and spread over a longer time.

PARTICULAR EXAMPLES

Thus while *TWNT* clearly surveys a wide range of material relevant to the history of words in the Bible, there are aspects of its method which can lead to misuses very easily; and this danger is increased by two things:

(*a*) Because the giving of word-substitutes, such as most dictionaries offer, is neglected, or is regarded as 'external lexicography', or is not carried out methodically, the problem of the exact semantic indication in each context is often passed over. The same fact may allow the admission of explanations which are etymologizing or which apply to a general 'concept' for which the word is sometimes used, but which would not fit certain contexts.

(*b*) Because of the concentration on the terminology in its religious, philosophical and theological usages, there arises a tendency to overlook those uses which do not fall within this type, and so to exaggerate the decisiveness of philosophical or theological relations for the semantics of the words and therefore the degree to which the use of the words reflects these relations simply.

An example of some of these problems may be taken from the article ἀγαθός (Grundmann). The NT section of this article is excessively dominated by two passages, Matt. 19: 17 εἷς ἐστιν ὁ ἀγαθός (cf. Mk. and Lk. οὐδεὶς ἀγαθὸς εἰ μὴ εἷς ὁ θεός) and Heb. 9: 11, 10: 1, where the phrase τὰ μέλλοντα ἀγαθά 'the future good things' is used. These show the basic meaning, and 'good' therefore applies only either to God himself or to eschatological realities lying in the future. 'There is nothing in this world that strictly speaking deserves the predicate ἀγαθόν and no one who has the predicate ἀγαθός. This insight is completed by the pronouncement of Paul, a deadly stroke against every other conception of life, religious or humanistic, οἶδα γὰρ ὅτι οὐκ οἰκεῖ ἐν ἐμοί, τοῦτ' ἔστιν ἐν τῇ σαρκί μου, ἀγαθόν . . . οὐ γὰρ ὃ θέλω ποιῶ ἀγαθόν, ἀλλὰ ὃ οὐ θέλω κακὸν τοῦτο πράσσω. The natural existence of man is excluded from the good, and cannot realize it for all its longing.'

Now whether this is a good statement or not of the general NT outlook about what is good, its inadequacy appears when we look at a text like Mt. 5: 45, where God sends his sunshine 'upon evil and good people', ἐπὶ πονηροὺς καὶ ἀγαθούς. The understanding of 'good' which Grundmann has worked out will not fit here, for there is nothing about God only being good or about eschatological good things. All he can say is that, in view of the facts which he has allowed to dominate the picture of ἀγαθός and its usage, these earthly distinctions of good and evil are relativized. What has really happened is that the writer, by choosing the passages which seem to him to come nearest to the ultimate understanding of NT theology as a whole, has given a sense to the word which will not fit a particular case like Mt. 5: 45. The departure from actual semantic investigation is marked by the 'strictly speaking' of Grundmann. Perhaps 'strictly speaking' nothing in this world deserves the title 'good', but the writers were not always speaking 'strictly', and in Mt. 5: 45 were in fact not doing so. The appeal to 'strict' speech is an appeal away from the things actually said, an appeal away from usage to what seems theologically more fundamental, or in another case to what from etymology seems more 'proper'.[1]

One effect of such a procedure can be the setting up of inaccurate oppositions. An essential part of lexicography is the observation of the oppositions between words, the points where they become contrasted.[2] An example of a faulty opposition, and one which is characteristic of much theological interpretation of words, may be found in the word-pair λόγος-μῦθος, and the re-

[1] For somewhat similar criticisms of this article see Dodd in *JTS* xxxiv (1933) 283. He also argues against the theological assessment of 'goodness' in the article. I shall not discuss except incidentally the question of theological bias, since my concern is with linguistic method; but in general it is clear that faulty linguistic method makes it easier for theological bias to operate.

[2] For the conception of language generally as a functional system of oppositions, see F. de Saussure, *Cours de linguistique générale*, p. 167 and *passim*.

marks of the *TWNT* article μῦθος (Stählin).[1] According to Stählin μῦθοι are rejected by the NT. He goes on:

'The Gospel deals with τὰ μεγαλεῖα τοῦ θεοῦ, the mighty acts of God. It is therefore λόγος, historical report of facts (*Tatsachenbericht*), or προφητικὸς λόγος, prophetic report of facts (cf. 2 Pet. 1: 19). The μῦθοι of erroneous doctrine on the other hand are *invented stories, devoid of truth, fables*.'[2] Later he argues that the contrast of ἀλήθεια and μῦθος, already made by the Greeks, is given new depth in the NT, because ἀλήθεια has been filled with 'the reality of salvation, the incarnate fullness of God in Christ' — it is now no abstract idea of truth but a divine *factum*.[3] Then he adds that 'To the deepening of the contrast of ἀλήθεια and μῦθος in the NT there corresponds a similar deepening of the contrast between λόγος and μῦθος'. This is supported from passages like 1 Tim. 4: 6–7, where a contrast is made between οἱ λόγοι τῆς πίστεως and οἱ βέβηλοι καὶ γραώδεις μῦθοι. 'Λόγος is the absolutely valid word of God become person; on it everything rests — the faith of the individual and the building of the Church. If the Logos is replaced by Myth, then everything is lost; the Word is betrayed.'

Now the mistake here is to suppose that the lexical opposition of λόγος and μῦθος is identical with the opposition in the passage between the phrase οἱ λόγοι τῆς πίστεως and the phrase οἱ βέβηλοι καὶ γραώδεις μῦθοι. But the true lexical opposition of λόγος and μῦθος in the NT is something like λόγος 'saying, word' and μῦθος 'fable, story'. The semantics of the latter in the NT contain the definite element of falsity or unreliability. It is not true to suppose however that therefore an element of 'true, historical' belongs to λόγος. That it does not is clear from passages like 2 Tim. 2: 17, where the λόγος of the ungodly is precisely the same kind of talk as the μῦθοι of which we hear elsewhere, and it is described explicitly here as κενοφωνία 'empty noise'. In the article λόγος (Kittel) the cases where λόγος is used with adjectives like σαπρός 'rotten' or κενός 'empty' (e.g. Eph. 4: 29; 5: 6) are duly registered. It is thus misleading to

---

[1] This particular article was judged 'brilliant' by R. Hoffmann, generally one of the more discerning early reviewers of *TWNT*, in *WZKM* xlviii (1941) 312 f.

[2] *TWNT* iv. 788.   [3] Ibid., p. 793.

suggest that because the Gospel deals with real events it is 'therefore' λόγος and that λόγος is then to be understood as *Tatsachenbericht*, historical report of facts. This is in other words a case of what I have called 'illegitimate identity transfer'. The Gospel may in fact be a historical report of facts, but this does not mean that 'historical report of facts' is the semantic contribution of the word λόγος in the kind of sentence under consideration. It may to some extent also be a case of 'illegitimate totality transfer', since I think it hard to doubt that part of Stählin's treatment of the λόγος-μῦθος contrast arises from his taking the Johannine Logos as the normative sense and a guide to the usage of the NT as a whole. This is indeed clear in the passage we have already quoted, where he makes a contrast between 'the Logos' and 'Myth' (*der Mythos*), although in the passages where μῦθος occurs in the NT it hardly means the greatly generalized modern sense of 'der Mythos' or 'Myth', nor does λόγος in the passages where its contrast with μῦθος appears mean 'the Logos'.

A great deal of the difficulty here arises from a neglect, which we have noticed before, of syntactical relations, and of groupings of words, factors just as important for the bearing of significance as the more purely lexicographical aspect of the single word. Thus in 1 Tim. 4: 6–7 already quoted the contrast of the μῦθοι is not with λόγος as such but with οἱ λόγοι τῆς πίστεως, 'the words of faith'; it is artificial here to isolate λόγος and thus suggest that it is the bearer of a greater opposition-value to μῦθος than is in fact the case. The same thing is done when you take the ὁ λόγος (with the definite article but no other qualification) of John and try to associate it with a case like οἱ λόγοι τῆς πίστεως. The use of ὁ λόγος with the article in the very special case of John 1 is really a special meaning which cannot be mingled indiscriminately with other cases simply because they also contain the word λόγος. In other words a simple syntactic relation like the adding of the definite article and the absence of other qualification can establish a different semantic field just as well as the transition to another word can.

The excessive concentration of *TWNT* on the theological and philosophical differences and their linguistic expression may not only introduce wrong oppositions between different words in the New Testament; it may also produce quite distorted oppositions between pagan Greek and Jewish Greek usage. A good example of this will be found in the article ἀναγκάζω, ἀναγκαῖος, ἀνάγκη (Grundmann).

The first part of this article is on the stem ἀναγκ- outside of the NT. What it investigates however is not the general spread of the usage of this group in Greek. It is rather the nature of the metaphysical power which the Greeks called ἀνάγκη, but which is by no means the only object of which this word is used. Thus the article begins with a definition by Aristotle, from which it is concluded that τὸ ἀναγκαῖον is the *conditio sine qua non* of being and life. From this we gain two aspects for the understanding of the Hellenistic ἀνάγκη: (a) its divine character as unknowable and omnipresent power (b) its appearance in the cosmological dualism of spirit and matter.

The contrast of Jewish usage is now brought. Here the situation of distress has nothing to do with a dualism of spirit and matter, but appears in persecutions, hostilities, sickness and the like. Then two passages are quoted. The first is supposed to show what ἀνάγκαι mean for the Israelite; it is the καὶ ἔκραξαν πρὸς κύριον ἐν τῷ θλίβεσθαι αὐτούς, καὶ ἐκ τῶν ἀναγκῶν αὐτῶν ἔσωσεν αὐτούς of Ps. 106: 13. The other is the 'day of tribulation and ἀνάγκη' of Zeph. 1: 15. What has not been pointed out in the whole treatment is that this 'Jewish' use of ἀνάγκη for 'trial, distress, tribulation' is a perfectly normal and frequent Greek usage. The senses of 'violence, punishment; duress; bodily pain, anguish' are given in LS and amply illustratable from classical times on. This common Greek use is not however referable to the abstract. Thus when Aeschylus mentions a lion cub which fawns γαστρὸς ἀνάγκαις 'for the needs of its belly',[1] the linguistic usage of ἀνάγκη here has nothing to do with the Greek concept of Necessity or τὸ ἀναγκαῖον. By its silence about Greek usage except in the metaphysical sense the article has wholly misrepresented the originality and distinctiveness of the Jewish Greek use. The reason why such an error was made can be quite simply stated:

[1] Aesch. *Ag.* 726.

it is the influence of the accepted thought contrast of Greek and
Hebrew thought, an influence which predisposes towards emphasizing any abstract and metaphysical use in Greek and towards
emphasizing the opposite 'concrete' or 'personal' use in Jewish
language. Thus two quite different questions are confused; these
are (a) whether the Hebrew religious consciousness had any structure similar to that of Necessity in its Greek metaphysical usage,
and whether it had any structure which was dissimilar but could
at any rate be reasonably contrasted with it; (b) how far the use of
the word ἀνάγκη in Jewish texts shows a semantic variation from
its use in non-Jewish Greek texts. It is clear in fact that roughly
speaking the Jewish Greek usage is close to non-Jewish usage.
The Jewish use does not display a semantic change corresponding
to the difference in the theological structures. The modern thought
contrast of Hebrew and Greek, coupled with the imprecision of
linguistic method, creates a strong prejudice towards the recognition of such a semantic change. The usage of ἀνάγκη, after receiving this distorting treatment, gives an air of being actual evidence
for the relation between the thought distinction and a difference of
linguistic usage, the relation in fact presupposed to begin with.

It is worth remarking in passing that, in spite of the common
devotion of biblical theology to the Hebraic semantic background
and its aversion from Greek classical or pagan usage, it is not
unwilling at times to take an emphasis from such usage where that
emphasis appears likely to support a characteristic interest of such
theology. Thus the *TWNT* article on the common word κτίζω
'create'[1] has a section on LXX usage, in which much play is made
from a contrast between the κτίζω group and the word δημιουργός,
which is not used of divine creation by the LXX. Although he
notices the existence of the poetical use of κτίζω as straightforwardly 'to make', 'to create', the author, Foerster, insists on the
sense 'to found' (a city) as the background to LXX usage. From
this he is able to produce an emphasis on a fundamental spiritual
creative decision of the founder, through which the thing founded
comes to be from nothing and to which it absolutely owes its
existence. 'The city owes its existence as πόλις completely to the

---

[1] *TWNT* iii. 1022–5. Cf. also the use of λειτουργία by Torrance, above, p. 149 ff.

κτίστης.' The verb κτίζω thus suggests 'the ruler, whose command causes a city to arise from nothing, because a ruler's power stands at the disposal of a ruler's word'. Hence the words indicate 'a spiritual and volitional process'.

It must be regarded as very doubtful whether these considerations about the κτίζω group were of importance in the use of these words either by the LXX or by the NT. The characteristics of the founding of cities and colonies which Foerster adduces are too obviously pleasant illustrations of what is generally believed in the Jewish-Christian tradition about the creation of the world. This does not prove that these associations were of importance in the choice of this word; and since the word κτίζω was already well established in the sense of 'make, create', there is every reason to suppose that its Jewish-Christian use followed straight from that sense. The contrast with δημιουργός which Foerster brings is of no demonstrative value; first of all, it is an argument from silence, and the absence of this word does not prove all that Foerster says about another word, namely κτίζω; secondly, other and quite adequate reasons might be adduced why δημιουργός was not used of God as creator in the LXX, most obviously the slightly depreciatory suggestion of the 'workman' — a metaphor which was excellent for a creative artist like Plato, but hardly solemn enough for the synagogue lectionary; thirdly, it is only by deliberately contrasting κτίζω with this word that Foerster is able to emphasize as he does the sovereign and autocratic character of the creative process indicated by κτίζω; but this is surely over-emphasizing the extent to which κτίζω had to signify in itself not only creating but creating from nothing through the absolute spiritual will of a ruler. One of the main reasons for the need to use this word in the LXX was of course the need for more than one Greek word to translate the several Hebrew verbs meaning 'make, create' — although of course some translation techniques in the LXX do not concern themselves to observe this differentiation.

A somewhat similar case is καιρός. Though the sense of 'exact or critical time, season, opportunity' (LS) is well established in classical times and later, it is well known that more general senses such as 'period' or 'time' became increasingly prominent in later

Greek and are well established in the LXX. The *TWNT* article (Delling) registers this use but confines it almost entirely to the subsidiary sections in small print, and lays the whole emphasis on the sense of 'decisive moment', to which alone full treatment is given. In LXX usage the development of καιρός into 'a regular concept of the *Heilsgeschichte*, which even alone and without further determination designates the time of judgement and the end' is given prominence, while the 'purely temporal' sense is admitted to be numerically preponderant but said to be of little theological interest. Moreover, certain cases are rather unnaturally pressed into the meaning of 'decisive moment' and the like; e.g. Lk. 4: 13, where the devil departed from Jesus ἄχρι καιροῦ, which surely means 'for a (short) time' but is interpreted as 'until the moment to be determined by God' (*TWNT* iii. 463); cf. Barth's exegesis as 'until the decisive moment', *KD* iv/1. 290; E.T., p. 264; Acts 13: 11. It is surely clear that the attractiveness to modern biblical theology of the *idea* of a time of decision, or of time as the area of God's work and decisive intervention, has led to a maximizing of the sense 'critical, decisive time' for καιρός, although the predominance of this sense belongs to the classical period and although it cannot be linked exactly with Hebrew linguistic usage either, however much the Hebrews may have thought of time as decisive or critical.[1]

One case where the method of *TWNT* was described as 'strikingly successful' by Dodd, no uncritical admirer of this work, was the study of αἵρεσις by Schlier. After registering the late Greek and Jewish usage of this word as 'party', 'school of opinion', he declares that the Christian development of this word does not arise through an excluding of non-orthodox parties. On the contrary, 'the concept αἵρεσις is inherently (*von vornherein*) suspect in Christianity'. Its existence is due not to the development of an orthodoxy but to 'the new situation which was created by the emergence of the Christian ἐκκλησία'. Thus 'ἐκκλησία and αἵρεσις are contraries *in re* (*sachliche Gegensätze*). The former will not

---

[1] I hope to justify this last statement, and treat the subject at more length in general, in a later article. See in particular G. B. Caird, *The Apostolic Age* (London, 1955), p. 184 n.

tolerate the latter, and the latter excludes the former.' There follow some passages from the New Testament in which αἵρεσις is mentioned. Then the section concludes with the following:

'Αἱρέσεις endanger the foundation of the church, the teaching, (2 Pet. 2: 1), and this in so fundamental a way as to produce a new community alongside the ἐκκλησία. The church cannot tolerate this, for as public and legal assembly of the whole people of God it embraces the latter fully and in one unit. But αἵρεσις is by its nature a private quantity with restricted validity, a school or party. If the ἐκκλησία tolerates αἵρεσις, it makes itself into a αἵρεσις and denies its own comprehensive "political" character....'

It is clear that this confuses throughout at least two questions:

1. How far was there a different attitude to 'parties' within the Church from that prevailing in Hellenism or Judaism?

2. How far is there a semantic change in the use of the word αἵρεσις by the NT?

Schlier's further development of the theme may be criticized thus:

1. No one would doubt that a semantic change in αἵρεσις took place once it developed into the technical sense which is familiar to us in our 'heresy'. But Schlier is quite clear that in the New Testament generally the word does not yet have a technical sense. But this does not stop him trying to trace the origin of 'the Christian concept αἵρεσις' and believing that the concept αἵρεσις was inherently suspect in Christianity. He does not use his evidence to show that by αἵρεσις the Christians meant something different from 'party', which was a widespread Hellenistic and Jewish-Greek usage. What he does try to show is that the disapproval of 'parties' arose in a different way in Christianity from the way in which it had arisen elsewhere. This is a different matter from a semantic change in the word. Thus we may use 'High Church Party' for a group in the church, and we may both disapprove more vehemently of parties in the church than in the state, and believe that the mode of origin of such parties is different from that of parties in the state, but the semantics of 'party' are not essentially different.

2. Thus Schlier obscures rather than clarifies the semantics of αἵρεσις. Real decisions in life of opposition to parties are treated

as a reaction against the inherently suspect *concept* αἵρεσις. This is necessary in Schlier's argument to produce the necessary inherent contradiction with ἐκκλησία. The use of ἐκκλησία seems to assume the kind of interpretation of that word which I have already criticized in this book; it takes it to be not 'church' or 'community' but 'all-embracing church' or 'community-as-comprehensive'. The argument is not that the mind of the church was against the formation of parties but that the term 'party' was contrary to and exclusive of the concept implied in the word ἐκκλησία. The 'new situation' is treated not as the rise of a community which thought differently about parties but as the rise of a community which had a name inherently contradictory to the recognition of party. No evidence is produced that these supposed implications of the word ἐκκλησία were actually in the mind of any of the writers of passages where αἵρεσις occurs in the NT. But only through the quite unjustified emphasis on the implications of the word ἐκκλησία here is it possible for Schlier to work out his picture of a Christian idea of αἵρεσις which was quite different from Hellenistic usage.

3. That the semantics of words in actual contexts have in fact been abandoned in order to trace this Christian concept of αἵρεσις is clear from Schlier's final sentence about how the ἐκκλησία, if it tolerates αἵρεσις, makes itself into a αἵρεσις. There is not the slightest evidence that such a thought was formulated in the New Testament period; it is merely a thought about the Church which is popular in modern times and is dressed up in words from the Greek New Testament.

Thus if Schlier is successful in disclosing some ways in which Christianity is inherently opposed to the formation of parties (and I am not sure that he is), he does it at the expense of obscuring the actual semantics of αἵρεσις in contexts through the emphasis laid on the new Christian 'αἵρεσις concept'; and the identification of the newness of this supposed new concept depends on juggling with a supposed opposition of ἐκκλησία and αἵρεσις as inherently contradictory quantities, an opposition which is nowhere formulated in the NT, which very likely was not intended, and which depends on an understanding of ἐκκλησία which is itself doubtful.

I have already suggested that the method of *TWNT* at places comes nearer to offering idea-histories than word-histories. That this is indeed so may be substantiated with some examples. We have just seen one in Stählin's article μῦθος, which, while it does investigate the actual occurrences of the word in the NT, goes on to try to grapple with the whole series of problems of what we would now call 'Gospel and Myth'. Thus the article has an introductory section called 'The Problematic of the Word "Myth" '; this concludes with a statement that the Christian Church, in as far as it really is Church, follows the judgement that Myth is untrue and therefore religiously valueless.[1] Farther on another section of several pages is devoted to the general discussion of 'Myth'.[2] All this may be interesting and intelligent material, and I have no intention of criticizing it here; but it goes far beyond the elucidation of μῦθος in its actual use in the NT. Indeed there is a certain etymologizing trait here, inasmuch as it is felt that if the modern problem of 'Myth and the Bible' is to be discussed, it should naturally be done in the article on μῦθος, since it is the word from which the modern 'Myth' is derived. But it is hardly to be doubted that the NT cases of μῦθος do not in fact form a broad enough basis for the problem here in mind.[3] The danger is not in the addition of extra material in itself, but in the probability that the semantics of actual usage may be distorted by the intention of the writer to relate these wider problems to this word.

Another example of this weakness may be found in the article on ἁμαρτάνω, ἁμαρτία etc., of which Dodd in an early review[4] complained that it was too much an essay on the doctrine of sin and too little a guide to the detailed usage of the words ἁμαρτάνω and ἁμαρτία. Now this weakness is invited by the organization of this article, for in it we find the section D entitled 'Linguistic Usage and History of ἁμαρτάνω, ἁμάρτημα and ἁμαρτία before and in the NT' (four pages in all), while quite another section (F)

[1] *TWNT* iv. 771–2.
[2] Ibid., pp. 798–803.
[3] Just as, for example, we can do very little to clarify our use of 'dogma' by investigating the use of δόγμα in the NT; as Diem realizes, but only after solemnly trying such a clarification first of all. See his *Dogmatics*, p. 282 f., a passage of remarkable linguistic confusion.
[4] *JTS* xxxiv (1933) 280 ff.

is called 'Sin in the NT', and this has 15 pages.[1] There is indeed a quite considerable number of articles in which different sections are headed 'linguistic' and 'theological';[2] the dangers of such a practice are obvious and serious.

A very bad example of this tendency is the article ἀποκαλύπτω (Oepke). It is only to a very limited extent that this article takes as its starting-point the Greek word ἀποκαλύπτω and the chief corresponding Hebrew word. The real logical starting-point is the conception of 'Revelation' (*Offenbarung*) which is of course a central notion in much theology and was particularly a centre of discussion in the German theology of the thirties and forties. Oepke is aware that there is some difficulty here, and says:

'The words reflect no fully unambiguous concept. In spite of this there is a wide inner unity. The word "revelation" gives some true indication in what direction this unity is to be sought.'

Thus Oepke decides he can start from 'revelation', although he hopes to narrow down his scope a little later on. As a starting definition he works with 'Revelation is manifestation of the divine'. This assimilates the subject to that use of 'revelation' which has become normal through long use in theology, i.e., its use as the normal general term for divine communication to man. The degree to which Oepke fails to take actual linguistic usage as his starting-point can be seen in the two sections C and E, entitled 'Revelation in the OT' and 'Revelation in the NT', where the survey of the linguistic usage comes not at the beginning but as the 4th and 6th sub-sections respectively. The result is that the article is assimilated to modern theological usage to a degree that the actual linguistic material will not bear. On the one hand the commonplace of biblical theology that 'God revealed himself' in or through history, especially in his 'mighty acts' and the events like the Exodus, is echoed, although there is not a place in the OT where these 'mighty acts' are referred to with *g-l-h* 'reveal'. On the other hand the word· ἀποκάλυψις is used in the NT in certain quite special particular usages, e.g. for the 'revelation' which comes to an

---

[1] *TWNT* i. 295–8 and 305–20 respectively. In this case the difficulty may have been enhanced by changes in the authorship, see p. 267 n.
[2] Examples include καινός, νέος, μετανοέω.

individual at a particular time (as in 1 Cor. 14), and this well-documented usage is practically neglected by Oepke.[1] I mention all this not in order to depreciate Oepke's own opinions but to show how far the method of *TWNT* often is from precision about how to deal with linguistic evidence.

The concentration on the theological uses of words produces its most peculiar results with words of very general application, adverbs, prepositions and the like; for example, the articles ἐγώ, εἰς, ἐν, νῦν. Thus on ἐγώ Stauffer has three sections on 'the Theological ἐγώ', 'the Christological ἐγώ', and 'the Anthropological ἐγώ'. One cannot but agree with the judgement of a generally favourable reviewer, G. Lindeskog, writing about the articles εἰς (Oepke) and εἰς (Stauffer), that 'it is a Bible-mysticism, at times sublime, which however has nothing to do with sound scholarship'.[2] I have the impression that some of the more recent articles on words of this kind have avoided these faults, and that this is because they have in fact attempted more of the 'external lexicography' type and have made less attempt to see a profound theological significance in a preposition like 'in' or 'to'. In this way an article like πρός (Reicke) compares very favourably with one like ἐν (Oepke).[3]

We may then sum up these criticisms of *TWNT* by saying that the great weakness is a failure to get to grips with the semantic value of words in their contexts, and a strong tendency to assume that this value will on its own agree with and illuminate the contours of a theological structure which is felt to be characteristic of the NT and distinctively contrasting with its environment. The belief that the distribution of the lexical stock of the NT may be directly correlated with the theological realities of God and his acts is both assumed in the method and fostered in the product. One illustration may be given which illustrates this fault at its full development:

---

[1] On this see my short article 'Revelation' in J. Hastings, *Dictionary of the Bible* (revised one-volume edition).

[2] *SEA* i (1936) 134.

[3] For remarks on prepositions also see Kittel, *Lexicographia Sacra*, pp. 10–11. He holds the prepositions ἐν and διά to have acquired an extraordinary new significance in their use with the name Χριστός.

The Greek verb παραμυθέομαι is found in two senses, (*a*) 'to exhort'; (*b*) 'to comfort'; or to say it another way, these two English words (or similar German words) form adequate substitutions for the Greek in translating the sentence. The *TWNT* article (Stählin) regards each of these as a 'main meaning'. Much the same is true of the verb παρακαλέω, also treated by Stählin. Now, Stählin continues, there is a relation between the action of exhorting and the action of comforting. 'Theoretically' (!) exhorting and comforting are distinguished; but in practice the kind of speech which contains one usually contains the other. But they are so related that in ancient Greek and Roman practice exhortation intends no more than the bringing of lamentation to an end, without any true comfort of the heart (*TWNT* v. 777–8. I cannot fully understand Stählin here, for he seems to deny any real element of comforting in the Hellenistic usage to which he refers, and thus to damage his own distinction, which is between two different ways of relating exhortation and comfort). In the NT however exhorting and comforting are again related, but quite differently and on quite a new basis. 'The unity of exhorting and comforting has its roots in the Gospel itself, which is at the same time gift and task (*Gabe und Aufgabe*); it is one of the forms of use of the dialectic interrelation of Imperative and Indicative in the NT.'

Now there may be a sense in which it can meaningfully be said that in Hellenistic life there was some relation of exhorting to comforting. It is more clearly true that the two were connected in practice in the NT. What is not true is that the relation between these sets of acts in either case has any essential relationship with the fact that both are expressed by the same Greek word. The relation between them would be just the same if different words were used as in English or German, and the connection with the 'double character' of παραμυθέομαι is thus entirely adventitious. Yet Stählin's whole exposition starts from it and depends on it. No more telling example could be given of the fascination found by the school of biblical theology in the semantic and etymological curiosities of language. The whole idea of a correspondence between biblical language and theological reality could hardly be better expressed than in Stählin's sentence about παραμυθέομαι:

'In this substantial (*wesenhaft*) vocable and its sense-picture there is reflected the double character of the "Word", in which from the indicative of the Kerygma there always grows forth the imperative of the Paraenesis'.[1]

It is perhaps worth noticing in passing that a similar argument could be produced from Hebr. *n-ḥ-m*, which is 'comfort' in the *piᶜel* and 'repent' in the *niphᶜal*. The relation between these two senses can be fitted into the theological structure of Christianity just as well as that between the senses of παραμυθέομαι. Such an argument is just as totally valueless as the one from the Greek word.

One or two more general things may now be said in assessment of the kind of linguistic interpretation found in *TWNT* and widely influential through it.

It is clear that Kittel himself, and *TWNT* in general, had the purpose of integrating, or demonstrating the integration of, the detailed linguistic usage of the NT and the deep and living theological thought of the NT. It never seems to have occurred to them that a lexicon, as a book organized under *words*, is not a good instrument for this purpose. Theological thought of the type found in the NT has its characteristic linguistic expression not in the word individually but in the word-combination or sentence. The degree to which the individual word can be related directly to the theological thought depends considerably on the degree to which the word becomes a technical term. The degree to which this has taken place in the NT may well be debatable. But it was Kittel's own opinion, and one with which many would agree, that many important elements in the NT vocabulary were not technical in the sense of many terms of later theology.[2] But under these conditions the attempt to relate the individual word directly to the theological thought leads to the distortion of the semantic contribution made by words in contexts; the value of the context comes to be seen as something contributed by the word, and then it is read into the word as its contribution where the context is in fact different.

[1] See *TWNT* v. 777-8 (including n. 30), 797-8, 816, 819.
[2] So *Lexicographia Sacra, passim*.

Thus the word becomes overloaded with interpretative suggestion; and since a combination of words will be a combination of words each of which has some relation to the general theological structure of the NT, sentences acquire in interpretation that tautological air of which we have seen some examples.

There is indeed in *TWNT* some understanding of this difficulty. Thus for example παῖς θεοῦ is taken as the subject of a separate article from those on παῖς and θεός. The success of this well-known article[1] is due considerably to the fact that it has a subject different in kind from most of the other articles in *TWNT*. But once you accept one word-combination like παῖς θεοῦ there is no very good reason for excluding other significant word-combinations such as καινὸς ἄνθρωπος and treating them only under separate articles for each word. A treatment of such combinations might come nearer to fulfilling the general purpose of *TWNT*; but it would be less like what could be called a dictionary.

To take another example, the article on λαός shows an awareness that an important sense has to depend not on λαός itself but on λαὸς θεοῦ.[2] To make an admission of this kind is at once to lift much of the strain which attends the effort to display the lexical relations of individual words as something reflecting theological reality. But it is clear that to move from the single word to the phrase like παῖς θεοῦ or λαὸς θεοῦ is only a change in degree. Phrases of this kind, like words themselves, are elements in the larger type of linguistic structure such as the sentence, and it is in sentences that the real theological thinking is done. But inasmuch as sentences are normally not recurrent forms like words, it is plain that we now pass beyond the realm which can be handled lexicographically at all. But at least it should be possible to frame a lexicographic plan which would give the user the greatest possible help with the sentences and larger literary units. *TWNT* does not do this because it hankers after the idea that the theological concept structure is directly related to the words.

One example may show the distortion in the understanding of λαός where the dependence on certain contexts like λαὸς θεοῦ is

---

[1] By W. Zimmerli and J. Jeremias; E.T., *The Servant of God* (London, 1957).
[2] *TWNT* iv. 35 (Strathmann).

neglected. Contrasting *laos* and *ethnos*, Torrance[1] tells us how Israel 'became *laos*, God's people', but had a will or aspiration 'to be *ethnos*, a nation like the other nations'; this aspiration meant a 'refusal of Israel to be *laos*'. This is an 'illegitimate identity transfer' and overloads the semantic values of the Greek words. The way this is effected is that the LXX-NT words are used but their semantic value is quietly altered by using them in syntactical contexts in English ('to be *laos*') which are not biblical (for 'to be *laos*' gives quite a different impression from 'to be *a laos*' or 'to be *my laos*', 'to be *a* people' or 'to be *my* people'); this device makes *laos* look like 'people-of-God' and *ethnos* look like 'nation-like-other-nations'.

It might be possible to suggest a better procedure for a dictionary intended to lead in the best possible way from the linguistic detail to the theological thought. This procedure would be to group the words in groups each representing a related semantic field, e.g. the 'holy' group with its chief representatives in ἅγιος, ἁγνός, and ἱερός. Within a general field thus loosely defined an attempt would be made to mark off the semantic oppositions between one word and another as precisely as possible; and from this to proceed to special contexts and word-combinations in which each word occurred — bringing in, of course, the words from outside the loosely defined field freely. This method might overcome something of the over-concentration on the single word which I have just been criticizing.

This principle is in fact adopted occasionally by Kittel; for in the article νοῦς (Behm) it is explicitly planned to treat only the linguistic and semantic presuppositions for the understanding of the word; the NT theological concept is left to be discussed in the article ψυχή, along with the related main anthropological terms ('concepts' as Behm calls them), i.e. καρδία, ψυχή, πνεῦμα, etc.[2]

---

[1] 'Israel and the Incarnation'; see *Judaica* xiii (1957) 6, 9; *Conflict and Agreement* i. 290 f., 293. I keep the words in transliteration, because the argument depends on the way in which they are integrated into the syntax of the English sentences.

[2] Other examples of this procedure will be found, e.g. the taking together in one article of a number of words related to arms and armour (s.v. ὅπλον) and in another of a number of words for eye, vision, to see, etc. (s.v. ὁράω).

Such an organization would avoid one of the misfortunes of the present form of Kittel, namely the separation of words which are very close to each other in meaning: e.g. there are separate articles for μεταμέλομαι and μετανοέω,[1] and for παρακαλέω and παραμυθέομαι, and for ἅγιος, ἁγνός, and ἱερός. Under the organization I suggest it would be much easier to compare the semantics of such words with one another. Much space would also be saved, because the OT background is often common to several words of such groups, and the LXX material, which is the link with the Hebrew, often cannot be divided up on the same lines of division as the NT words show. This saving of space would compensate for the great deal of extra cross-reference which might be needed in such a plan.

We may add that such a dictionary would avoid the organization of words under groups of cognates which is so obvious a feature of *TWNT*. The grouping under cognates is an invitation to etymologizing interpretation. In a work which is mainly interested in the semantics of theological language it is quite wrong to have μετανοέω separated from μεταμέλομαι and associated with other words like ἔννοια and εὔνοια because the latter are also 'related' to νοῦς.

Fortunately the temptation to an etymologizing interpretation is not accepted too often. One or two serious cases can however be quoted. Thus in the article λόγος Kleinknecht[2] writes:

'The decisive elements of the concept . . . can be known from the etymology itself; as substantive to λέγω, λόγος according to its basic meaning is "gathering, collecting (*Lesen*)", this of course in a se-lective (*auslesend*), one might almost say a critical, sense.'

He then goes on to quote Hom. *Od.* xxiv. 107–8, which in fact uses the verb λέγω and not the noun λόγος at all — typically of the etymologizing interpreter, to whom word-formation and syntax do not change the 'basic meaning', and who does not notice the fact that the sense 'gathering' for λόγος appears to be unknown (see LS s.v.). All this procedure is done in order to establish a

---

[1] Michel, who writes the article μεταμέλομαι, thinks its sense to be distinct from that of μετανοέω in the NT. But on any account the two words are close enough together to merit treatment in the same article.

[2] *TWNT* iv. 76.

picture of something like 'selective and critical reason' to fit with the Hellenic understanding of λόγος.[1]

Similarly the article μεταμέλομαι (Michel) seems to make a play on the etymology of μετανοέω (from νοῦς, νοέω, and thus taken to suggest a change of mind or intention) and of μεταμέλομαι (from phrases like μέλει μοι 'I care about', and thus taken to suggest an emotional reaction); but the article μετανοέω itself (Behm, Würthwein) does not follow an etymologizing interpretation of the νοέω element.[2]

A case where an etymologizing interpretation is of particular theological importance is that of ἀνακεφαλαιόομαι in *TWNT* iii. 681–2 (Schlier). Here Schlier admits that the verb is not from κεφαλή 'head' but from κεφάλαιον; indeed it is a denominative from the latter and semantically related to it; in his survey of Greek usage in some detail he does not cite any evidence for a semantic reference to 'head'. Knowing and admitting this, however, he expounds the important occurrence at Eph. 1: 10 entirely from the idea of Christ as the Head of the Church (Eph. 1: 22), on the grounds that the situation of Christ as head of the church has probably led the writer to choose the verb ἀνακεφαλαιόομαι. Hence 'the summing up of all things takes place in the subjecting of them to the Head'; 'as the church receives her Head, all things receive their κεφάλαιον, their sum which concludes, comprehends and (in the Head!) repeats'.

One must say that, although it is possible that the thought of the Head may have crossed the writer's mind, it is rather unlikely that it was so determinative; if it had been, he would scarcely have refrained from bringing in the word κεφαλή precisely at this point, to show the presence of the connection just here. It is rather more likely that Schlier, seeing a connection in fact to exist between the

---

[1] Boman, op. cit., p. 53 f.; E.T., p. 67 f., has much the same argument. The 'basic meaning' is 'put together in order', 'arrange'.

[2] Cf. also the procedure of an article like that on the ἀλλάσσω group (Büchsel). This likes to begin with a 'basic meaning'. Thus for ἀλλάσσω we have 'make otherwise (from ἄλλος)'; for ἀπαλλάσσω 'make otherwise through removal, get rid of'. But for διαλλάσσω and καταλλάσσω it has to be admitted that usage is too complex for it to be possible to get at a 'basic meaning'. This obvious fact does not however lead to a realization that these 'basic meanings' are artificial even where they can be made approximately to fit the sense actually found.

Headship of Christ and the summing up of all things, has been unable to resist the urge so fashionable in the same theological circle to point out an etymological 'relation' between the Greek words and base his exposition on it, although he knows it to be an incorrect etymology and although he knows the verb to be connected semantically in actual usage to the true etymology (from κεφάλαιον). On this cf. Dodd, *JTS* xxxix (1938) 293.

THE LEXICOGRAPHICAL TRADITION BEHIND *TWNT*

We have not yet however traced the fundamental thoughts about the relation of language and Christian theological thought which are active in the conception and planning of *TWNT* and which are probably widely active also independently of any direct influence from *TWNT*. For this we must go back to Cremer, whose lexicographical tradition Kittel as editor of *TWNT* was explicitly carrying on.[1] For Cremer's attitude to the problems we cannot do better than quote from the beginning of his preface to the first edition of his dictionary:[2]

'Lexical works upon New Testament Greek have hitherto lacked a thorough appreciation of what Schleiermacher calls "the language-moulding power of Christianity". A language so highly elaborated and widely used as was Greek having been chosen as the organ of the Spirit of Christ, it necessarily followed that as Christianity fulfilled the aspirations of truth, the expressions of that language received a new meaning, and terms hackneyed and worn out by the current misuse of daily talk received a new impress and a fresh power. But as Christianity stands in express and obvious antithesis to the *natural* man (using this phrase in a spiritual sense), Greek, as the embodiment and reflection of man's *natural* life in its richness and fullness, presents this contrast in the service of the sanctuary. . . .

[1] Kittel, *Lexicographia Sacra*, pp. 4–6, 8–9; *TWNT* i. v.
[2] H. Cremer, *Biblico-theological Lexicon of New Testament Greek* (3rd English ed., Edinburgh, 1886), p. iv. For information about Cremer, and for an assessment of his work warmly sympathetic to the Cremer-Kittel tradition, I am greatly indebted to the doctoral thesis of R. C. Duncan, *The Contribution of Hermann Cremer (1834–1903) to Theological Hermeneutics* (Edinburgh University, 1958; unpublished); I much regret having to differ in many ways from his evaluation of this tradition.

As Rothe says, "We may appropriately speak of a language of the Holy Ghost. For in the Bible it is evident that the Holy Spirit has been at work, moulding for itself a distinctively religious mode of expression out of the language of the country which it has chosen as its sphere, and transforming the linguistic elements which it found ready to hand, and even conceptions already existing, into a shape and form appropriate to itself and all its own." We have a very clear and striking proof of this in New Testament Greek.'

It is well known that the severest critic of Cremer was Adolf Deissmann, and it is not necessary to describe here the full details of their disagreement. Deissmann attacked in particular the idea of 'Biblical Greek', and insisted that the NT was written in the normal *koine*. From the controversy the following points are of some importance for our subject:

(*a*) Cremer went to some pains to point out cases where a word was found only in 'Biblical Greek' or was used with a sense known only in 'Biblical Greek'. It is clear that his interest in this was because such cases seemed to him to exemplify the 'language-moulding power of Christianity'. In this however he was soon to find himself on the defensive. When he first published his dictionary (1867),[1] papyrological research had as yet had little effect, and the Greek of the NT was contrasted more with classical usage and the usage of classicizing Hellenistic literature than with contemporary spoken Greek. From the papyri and inscriptions however Deissmann and others were able to show numerous cases where biblical usage was not at all unique, but reflected normal popular usage. That certain new words were formed in Jewish and Christian Greek was not denied by Deissmann; and the extent of such formations was discussed again by Kittel.[2] The importance of the whole matter for us is that it became impossible to exemplify the 'language-moulding power of Christianity' from a stock of new words within the NT itself.

(*b*) It was even more impossible, however, to trace this

---

[1] Kittel, *Lexicographia Sacra*, p. 4, *TWNT* i. v., makes a curious error in giving 1883 as the date of publication.

[2] *Lexicographia Sacra*, pp. 8–11.

'language-moulding power' in the other great area where language is moulded, namely that of morphology, word-formation and syntax, as Deissmann was quick to point out.[1] Cremer in due course answered that he had never supposed a special accidence or syntax of this sort to exist.[2] There is something a little comic perhaps in retrospect in this part of the controversy. But Deissmann was quite right in seeing its importance. It pushed the notion of a 'language-moulding power' into the purely lexical department, which was in any case Cremer's main interest; and it made the whole idea of a 'language-moulding power' more difficult to believe in general, because such a power might be expected to have some effect on grammar. Now the importance of this argument remains today, because of those opinions which we have surveyed which both see a relation between the structures of the Hebrew mind and the grammatical structures of the Hebrew language, and which also believe the structures of the Hebrew mind to be basic to the thought of the NT. Such opinions have to pay due attention to the use by NT writers of grammatical and syntactical mechanisms which do not correspond to anything in Hebrew.[3]

Though the expression about 'the language-moulding power of Christianity' remained in the editions of Cremer, there were other ways of expressing Cremer's intentions which, especially after

---

[1] A. Deissmann, *Bible Studies* (2nd ed., Edinburgh, 1909), p. 176 f.

[2] Cremer, preface to the 9th German ed. of his *Biblisch-theologisches Wörterbuch der neutestamentlichen Gräzität* (Gotha, 1902).

[3] I think for example of the frequent use of the verb εἰμί 'be' where Hebrew would use the nominal sentence; or of the genitive absolute. Also, if we suppose any of the uses of the perfect in verbs to have a force other than that of the aorist, this is a distinction in NT Greek which cannot be expressed in Hebrew except with much circumlocution. Thus if there is a contrast intended in the use of the tenses between ὁ γεγεννημένος and ὁ γεννηθείς at 1 John 5: 18, this would be hard to express in Hebrew or Aramaic, and was in fact not expressed by the Semitic translations (Peshitto, Ethiopic). Dodd (op. cit., p. 94) says that the Johannine letters are not much influenced by the LXX and show few signs of Semitism; on the other hand Moule (*Idiom Book*, p. 182) registers πᾶς . . . οὐ for οὐδείς as a probable Semitism and frequent in 1 John. The difficulty of rendering many parts of the Pauline letters into Hebrew without awkwardness also illustrates the point. This point is of course separate from the question of how much Semitism there is in NT diction. Even Deissmann admitted the existence of Semitisms in the NT, though he tended to minimize them, and in this the trend of modern scholarship is contrary to his judgement.

Deissmann's criticisms and the surrender of a large part of the lexical stock formerly supposed to have been peculiar to Biblical Greek, became more usable and acceptable. The first of these is the distinction between the 'old' and the 'new'. This appears in Cremer's preface where he talks of the language receiving 'new meaning', 'new impress' and 'new power'; but the phrase which was taken up especially by Kittel[1] and has become most popular is 'new content'. When it became impossible to lay much stress on the exclusive possession of vocabulary by the NT, it was still possible to follow up Cremer's own suggestions about the taking on of 'new content' by the old vocabulary; Kittel indeed takes this as the 'real purpose' (*eigentlicher Zweck*) of *TWNT*.

Now the understanding of this new content in the tradition of Cremer and *TWNT* does not mean in most cases at all the sudden creation of the new content by the impact of Christianity. The new content is just as much or even more the result of the expression in Greek of an ancient heritage of Hebrew thought, in particular through the LXX. Thus the 'old' is the Hellenic-Hellenistic thinking associated with the words, the 'new' is the Hebraic-Christian stream of thought, which itself is ancient but when expressed in Greek creates a 'new content' for the words of that language. The crucial moment here is the LXX, on which Cremer did much work; and his work in this field earned more approval from Deissmann than his other labours.[2] This is important for us, firstly because *TWNT* continued in this tradition, and its attention to OT and LXX usage (though uneven in parts) is one of the great things to its credit; and secondly because we come back again to the problems about the relation of Hebrew thought to Hebrew language which occupied some of the earlier chapters of this study.

Here, then, we find that joint interest in the Hebraic and the Christological which is so prominent in modern biblical theology, and which can be maintained alongside of considerable criticism of Cremer's own methods. Thus Friedrich, Kittel's successor as

[1] *TWNT* i. v.
[2] Deissmann, *ThLZ* xxxvii (1912) col. 521. Nowadays one would have to regard Deissmann's own opinions about the LXX as very one-sided and inadequate.

editor of *TWNT*, describes how Cremer intended to show the special nature of NT Greek, the power of Christianity to mould language. This tendency, however, Friedrich asserts, is false. Jesus was not a new teacher, what he had to say was found in the Old Testament.[1] Thus for Friedrich the essential lexical task is the investigation of the way in which Greek words are vessels for a content of Semitic thought. But clearly it is intended that by such an investigation the special impression of Christ in the Semitic thought and Greek words of the NT will become clearer.

Certain further stages in thought, which were important for the carrying on of the Cremer tradition in lexicography, were formulated by Kögel, who was Cremer's pupil and succeeded him in the editorship of the dictionary.[2] By this time the Deissmann type of philological research was widely received, and Kögel had to add material from the new discoveries and at the same time restate a justification of Cremer's method in general. Kögel was not afraid of placing the NT in the setting of its time, and regretted any tendency to isolate its language; but he still thought that basically, apart from certain wrong directions in detail, Cremer's method had been right, and he believed that attention to the linguistic environment would only help the uniqueness of the New Testament to appear.

Most important in Kögel's theory is the distinction between 'outer' and 'inner'.

'The word is only the outward expression of the inner possession, and this inner possession always remains the first thing. It will always remain the chief question of linguistic research how far to denetrate into this inner possession and how far it is comprehended by starting from the individual concept. The expression has to be judged from within, just as it on the other side leads to the inward. In lexicography the method which gives adequate attention to this moment and this great setting, the mutual involvement of detail

---

[1] Friedrich, 'Problematik', p. 482. This passage shows the use of Christological ideas typical of *TWNT*. What Jesus said was not new teaching; but all that he said about righteousness or holiness was new through him, because he *was* these things in person.

[2] Kögel's edition (the 10th) was completed in 1915, and has not been translated into English. Kögel's preface, from which the following material is taken, is on pp. v–xiv.

and whole that is noticeable in language, is the one and only method which is scientific and is penetrating.'[1]

Thus for Kögel the significance of Cremer's dictionary was that it seriously tried 'to connect the detail rightly with the entirety and not to let the matter rest with the mere concept'. Thus Cremer 'puts the concept in the right light'. Putting it in another way, 'it is only the real (*eigentlich*), the inner, sense of the words that matters'. Cremer had therefore been unnecessarily anxious about finding words which were externally distinctively 'biblical'; for his basic thesis it would not have mattered if there were no such words.

Secondly, Kögel understands and defends his work as the production of a *special* lexicon. Special lexica for particular groups of writings had already appeared. These had partly failed however to understand their task. The special task of such lexica is 'to restore the connection between the concept world on one side and the whole world of thought on the other'; this can be done only within the framework of the spiritual world of one writer or group of writers. It is not quite clear to me how Kögel conceived of the organization of what he calls a 'general lexicon'; but the idea appears to be that it would outline the general framework of a language which would be common necessarily to all users of that language, but that the special lexicon (and Kögel believed that any special lexicon, for example to Plato or Aristotle, should follow the pattern of his work on the New Testament[2]) would show how the individual writer or group had used this framework and made it possible through it to enter into his own inner world of thought.

Thirdly, Kögel has some remarks about a 'statistical method of lexicography' which, he hopes, is soon to be left behind. He does not name any lexica of this type; but he says they strive only 'to quote as many passages as possible, to show in what authors the words are found and in what connections, in order to obtain the meaning for each occasion in all brevity'. Thus they 'communicate only a mechanical, external knowledge'. From other things he says

[1] Kögel, op. cit., p. x. R. C. Duncan, op. cit., p. 75, very justifiably describes this formulation by Kögel as 'in language that betrays the influence of Schleiermacher'.

[2] Cf. Kögel, op. cit., Epilogue, p. 1228 f.

it is clear that Kögel is here criticizing that unthinking submission to the dictionary which supposes that 'what's in the dictionary must be the meaning'. Works that encourage this are needed for the laity (!) and schoolboys, and may be generally indispensable, but are not scientific. In this Deissmann would agree, and is in fact quoted. The trouble however is that Kögel farther on suggests that any dictionary not working on his own plan, not tracing the mutual involvement of 'inner' and 'outer', of 'detail' and 'entirety', is just 'mechanical and formal', something to be used as a schoolboy uses his vocabulary book. This suggestion is a fateful one and seems to have remained in the minds of the admirers of the Cremer-Kögel-Kittel tradition.

Fourthly, in the New Testament the relation of thought and speech, of spirit and word, which is the main object of Kögel's lexical method, is connected with the question of revelation. The men of the NT were filled with new experiences and a new spirit, which could not be perfectly expressed; they could only stammer with such words and 'concepts' as were available. They were the old words — and yet completely new words. Thus the relations with the environment which spoke the same language are to a considerable extent merely external, formal and mechanical.

With Kögel we have in essence the theory of lexicography which is taken over in *TWNT*. Kittel and Friedrich both make some criticisms of Cremer which are now widely accepted, but do not seem to depart in any essential point from Kögel. The expression 'inner lexicography' used by Kittel is clearly the same idea as Kögel had. With Kittel there is explicit what seems to be suggested by Kögel, the recognition of two types of dictionary, the 'external' (for the NT, the type of Bauer) which registers the words and their occurrences and combinations, and gives semantic indications by word-substitutions in another language; and the 'inner', which intends to penetrate to the inner world of thought. Here also there appears the connection with the Hebraic thought-structure, for though a word may be 'externally' Greek its 'inner meaning' may be Hebraic-Christian.

The whole Kögel-Kittel theory of lexicography must be judged an erroneous one. The basic reason for this is that the type of lexicography which is called 'external' is already dealing with semantics, i.e. with the signifying function of words. There is no extra department of words therefore for the 'inner' lexicography to deal with, for words have no more than their semantic function ('semantics' here of course includes emotional suggestion, reference to traditional patterns and ideas, references and values usual only in certain groups and speakers, and so on). An 'external' type of lexicography can be separated off only if it is confined to lists of words in various combinations and forms in the original language, with no attempt being made to indicate the sense. And while the idea of a 'special lexicon' is undoubtedly a justified one, the difference cannot be carried out in the way which Kögel suggests. A general lexicon of a language has to deal with semantics just as a special lexicon of one writer or group must; it has to record usage of special groups if known; and it is extremely precarious to suggest that one must penetrate to 'the inner world of thought' in a way that the other does not.

In expanding this, two main points may be made. The first is more negative and less important. Many more recent biblical theologians seem to be convinced, as Kögel perhaps thought, that the results achieved by certain normal linguistic procedures are 'external' or 'surface' or 'mechanical' or 'formal', and that they hemselves understand methods which lead to an 'inner' or 'depth' understanding of language. This conviction is the chief ingredient in the *hubris* which has produced such enormous departures from well-known and registered linguistic fact as some of the interpretations quoted in this book.

Secondly and more important, the fault lies in the attempt to do far too much by lexicographic method. The reason for this attempt is a confusion about the units of thought. To the word 'truth' there may presumably correspond a mental or psychological reality or 'concept' of 'truth'. To the sentence 'God is truth' there also corresponds a mental or psychological reality. But these are different kinds of thing. The 'inner thought-world' of the early Christians would be formed in the main by notions of the 'God is truth' type. But notions like 'God is truth' cannot be lexicographically handled, in the way in which words like 'truth' can be listed and handled. They are not linguistic functional units but formulations; they are not interchangeable like words, and do not fit freely into contexts as words do. It is a presupposition of doing any lexicography at all that words differ in this way from formulations such as 'God is truth' or 'Christ is risen'.

The error therefore is to try to use a lexical method for this aim of passing from the detailed linguistic material to the 'inner world of thought'. Modern biblical theology in its fear and dislike of the 'proposition' as the basis of religious truth has often simply adopted in its place the smaller linguistic unit of the word, and has then been forced to overload the word with meaning in order to relate it to the 'inner world of thought'. Likewise in its reserved attitude to any psychological treatment of religious thought it has paid insufficient attention to that frontier of linguistics and psychology which is seen in the relation between any word and the mental reality or concept corresponding to it; and from this neglect is forced either into the attempt to relate the words directly to the divinely or theologically existing realities, or else into a normative interpretation of words, for example by etymologizing. No one perhaps would question that the examination of a body of texts should lead to what Kögel calls the 'inner world of thought'; in contrast with Cremer's earlier outlook, Kögel did much more to insist that the dictionary was the place where this should be done. But if the dictionary is to trace how the words as the outward expression lead into the inner thought-world, then the dictionary is to be a full interpretation of the New Testament; for what else has the task of interpretation to do? The result of this logic is a dictionary like *TWNT* which is as much an interpretation of the New Testament as a guide to the semantics of words used in it.

CHRISTIANITY AND LANGUAGE

We are now in a position to turn to the phrase about the 'language-moulding power of Christianity', and we may say at once that Deissmann was right in believing that, placed as it was by Cremer at the beginning of his preface and taken as something which a dictionary should hope to demonstrate, it was both wrong

in itself and an obstacle to scientific investigation.[1] That the belief
in such a 'language-moulding power' commonly depends on a
simple and thoughtless transference into the linguistic realm of
what is theologically true may be illustrated with the following
quotation:

'With the advent of Christianity there was let loose in the
world a transforming energy which made itself felt in all
domains, including that of language. Old, worn-out expressions
were rejuvenated and given new lustre. In a few cases, when
nothing adequate seemed to be available, new words and phrases
were coined. Words expressing servility, ignominy and sin were
washed clean, elevated, and baptized with new meaning. Others,
standing in the bright light of the gospel, were revealed to be
even more sombre and wicked in their significance than had
been previously realized. This mighty, transfiguring, creative
force within Christianity is pervasive throughout the language of
the entire New Testament and cannot be successfully set forth
in isolated particulars.'[2]

With respect to the scholarship of the author, I cannot regard
this paragraph as other than a romanticization which comes from a
simple transfer to the sphere of linguistic change of the soterio-
logical effects which Christianity claims to have made in life in
general. Its contrast with the careful scientific method of the rest of
Metzger's article is very noticeable. Its character as a sort of
linguistic allegory is clear from the impossibility of clarity within
linguistic method of such terms as the 'cleansing' or 'rejuvenation'
of words. Especially striking is the picture of words the full
wickedness of whose meaning had not been known to anyone
before the gospel came to reveal it.

To say this, however, is not to suggest that Christianity had no
effect on language. Deissmann himself would perhaps have been
willing to go farther towards recognizing such an effect, had not
the prevailing assertion of the 'language-moulding power of
Christianity' seemed to him (rightly) to have a primarily dogmatic

[1] Deissmann, *Bible Studies*, p. 176–7.
[2] B. M. Metzger, 'The Language of the New Testament', *The Interpreter's Bible* vii. 56.

origin and purpose. Metzger like other modern scholars pays a tribute to Deissmann but points out his neglect of two important factors: 'the influence of the language of the Old Testament, and the creative vitality of the Christian faith'.[1] Now, he says, the pendulum has swung the other way and 'it is now perceived also that the most distinctive and the really important words in the New Testament are either borrowed from the Old Testament or are common, everyday words which the Spirit of God filled with new significance'.

Either as a theologian or as a linguist, however, one must in all seriousness and reverence question whether the activity of the Holy Spirit can legitimately be listed among the causes of semantic change. And the term 'creative vitality' depends on how it is taken. That the Christians were vital people in some sense and that their life formed a new social body with special traditions and practices, and with certain special linguistic usages, need not be doubted. It may well be true that Deissmann underestimated this fact and failed to appreciate the growth of technical usages within the Jewish-Christian tradition and the way in which normal semantic values and oppositions were used in the special material of that tradition. None of this justifies us in taking the phrase 'creative vitality', which would be commonly and characteristically understood in a theological sense as a characteristic of the faith in its effect on men and their life, and assuming that it can also be applied univocally to semantic change in language.[2]

We can thus speak of an effect of Christianity in language, but on two conditions which make the phrase appear rather different: (a) the effect is produced not by the divine or revelatory character of the new religion, but by its existence as a social group with a certain technically (in this case, sacrally) recognized pre-existent tradition; (b) the effect is like other linguistic changes logically (or theologically) haphazard and by its nature cannot be related

---

[1] Op. cit., p. 53-4.
[2] Cf. the continuing discussion in the study of Christian Latin: C. Mohrmann, 'Le Latin commun et le latin des chrétiens', *VChr* i (1947) 1-12; 'Quelques traits caractéristiques du latin des chrétiens', *Studi e Testi* cxxi (1946) 437-66; E. Löfstedt, *Syntactica* (Lund, 1933, 2 vols.) ii. 458-73; *Late Latin* (Oslo, 1959), pp. 68-92; C. Mohrmann, 'Linguistic Problems in the Early Christian Church', *VChr* xi (1957) 11-36.

directly to or correlated with the patterns of the theologically known divine acts and realities.

The following considerations must be added:

This means that the formula 'new content', as an expression of the characteristic position of important words in their NT usage, is quite unsatisfactory and should be abandoned. I have already shown in the case of ἀλήθεια how one of the words which in the school of biblical theology is especially supposed to have received a new content was used in fact in important NT contexts without such change of content. The extent to which words received 'new content' is to a large extent related to the degree in which words became technical. But many of the most important words of the NT were not technical unambiguously, but only in certain syntactical combinations; e.g. I would say that ἀπόστολος or βάπτισμα are pretty nearly technical, but ἀλήθεια is not. Ὁ λόγος with verbs of 'being' in John 1 is not exactly technical but is deeply allusive to technically known and regulative thoughts and phrases; but in οἱ λόγοι τῆς πίστεως it is not technical. Some words, such as the words for 'God' or 'holy', are likely to be 'technical' in a sense in any language. They are technical to religious life, but not necessarily technical to the cult of a particular deity; their use of the Jewish-Christian God is not necessarily, and in the case of NT Greek is, I think, in fact not, a case of semantic change, but only of the use of the word with the same semantic value for a new person; linguistically no more than its extension, say, to Dionysus when his cult came into Greece. In many other words which are essential for the expression of God's acts towards men, such as ἄνθρωπος or ἔργον, we have no semantic change.

I must repeat one of the main points of my argument, namely that the new content of the Jewish-Christian tradition and of the Christian gospel was expressed linguistically *in sentence form* (actually of course in complexes larger than sentences, but in any case not smaller); that the content of these sentences was something largely foreign to the Hellenistic ethos (precisely *how* largely foreign, it is beyond my purpose to discuss); but that for the formation of these sentences Greek words could often be employed in the same semantic function as they normally had in the usage of Hellenistic speakers.

This is of supreme importance for one of the difficult questions which has become noticeable as a result of the modern trend in exegesis towards an emphasis on the Hebrew background, and especially in the lexicography of the *TWNT* type with its insistence on the 'new content' of words, a content deeply associated with their OT background. It could be argued that this emphasis upon the Hebraic background of ideas may indeed have been present in the minds of instructed Jews like St. Paul, but that the words which had this series of associations for him would for the most part be *understood* by Gentile Christian hearers, and especially by the less instructed among them, in the normal Hellenistic sense of the words. Thus Bauer warns us to reckon with:

'The possibility that what, for instance, Paul said, conditioned as he was by his Jewish past, was not always understood in the same terms by his Gentile Christian hearers, who were also unable to dissociate themselves entirely from their previous ways of thought.'[1]

This problem is, so far as I can see, insoluble as long as we think of a 'new content', (i.e. a Hebraized content), which the Pauline words individually had and which was therefore accessible to lexicographical treatment. But I suggest that the impress of the Jewish tradition in the Pauline letters and speeches was borne mainly by the things that he said, his sentences, his complex word-combinations, his themes and subject-matter; and that this impress remained even where the individual semantic value of many words was not changed from the average Hellenistic, and was not greatly deepened where words were technically overprinted with a Jewish reference. This is surely the most natural way with the problem of understanding. The problem has arisen in fact through an exaggeration of the importance of lexical method. One may add that if misunderstanding arose through words with a Hebraic background being used by Paul and understood by others in a Hellenistic sense one would have expected Paul to have realized this and pointed it out somewhere — and no doubt some people suppose that this is

[1] Arndt and Gingrich, op. cit., p. xxi.

what the Pauline arguments really were. Might a short lexical
note on the lines of an article in *TWNT* have cleared up the
troubles in Corinth more quickly?[1]

Another point about the idea of 'new content' has already been
brought out in the study of ἀλήθεια and need only be recapitulated
here: namely, that many Greek words which are used in the great
philosophic systems are still not so technical to such usage as to
become semantically bound to it. Thus ἀλήθεια is used in Greek
without any reference to typical Greek metaphysical usage, just as
it is used in Jewish-Christian Greek without any reference to God
alone being the truth, although there are in fact statements that
God (or Christ) is indeed the truth. It is one of the illusions of
much modern biblical theology that any Greek word normally
carries as its semantic value its reference in the most abstract
philosophic system in which it is used; and, on the principles of
such theology, very much needs an infusion of 'new content' before
it can be used in Christianity. There is here a strong intellectualism
in the approach to words, which sees them first and most naturally
in their philosophical and theological usages. This is encouraged
by the procedure of *TWNT*, which for many words gives first of
all any religious and philosophical connections in which it is used
in the Hellenistic world, with less attention to everyday or common
usage, and then for the Jewish-Christian use emphasizes the most
pregnant theological usage, thus producing a strong contrast.
But often it is probable that a Greek word came into the Jewish-
Christian tradition in a non-theological and non-metaphysical use.
I would understand ἀλήθεια for example in this way. As the
Egyptian Jew in quite secular connections ceased to say his ᵓᵉmet

---

[1] A roughly similar argument to the above may be used to correct Deissmann's
exaggerated (as it seems to me) impression of the Hellenization of the OT
through its translation by the Egyptian Jews; op. cit., p. 77, etc. No amount of
'modern' Egyptian Greek could make the Bible look like a product of Egyptian-
Hellenistic culture rather than a (perhaps somewhat garbled) account of the
doings of the ancestors of the Jews in Palestine and their God. This is less so of
course in books like Proverbs and Job, where the Greek translators or para-
phrasers made more assimilation of the material to Greek ethical ideals; on this
see Gerleman, *Studies in the Septuagint*. It must be remembered that in these
books the specifically Israelite content was much less from the beginning, so
that the treatment in the LXX can hardly be thought of as a violent distortion of
the material.

or his *quẙta* he began to say ἀλήθεια or ἀληθῶς, and later when
the Bible was translated into Greek ἀλήθεια was normally put for
ᵊᵉmet. Similar circumstances would probably surround the πίστις-
πιστεύω group, and much that is said in the attempt to show a
contrast with pagan Greek religious usage (e.g. the very limited use
of πίστις in connection with the gods in pagan usage) may not be
specially relevant.

I should add here that in the discussion and assessment of the
Septuagint, which is of course extremely important here, the
modern school of biblical theology seems to me to go much too far
at times in the degree to which it asserts the Old Testament in
Greek took on Hellenized characteristics of 'static' thought,
anthropocentricism and so on. It is the judgement of Bertram for
example that the LXX is anthropocentric, and determined by the
Hellenic idea of humanity; that in it the theological statements of
the OT were used and valued psychologically and paedagogically;
that development and education took the place of law and command; that *Gottesoffenbarung* became *Gottesvorstellung*.[1] To discuss
this adequately would be a work in itself; here I want only to point
out that even a good number of details in which a change of emphasis of this kind is made does not mean a corresponding change of
emphasis in the impression made by the Greek OT as a whole.
Knight seems to me greatly to exaggerate the baleful effects on the
Church of its using the OT in Greek and not in Hebrew during the
early Christian centuries.[2]

Thus for example Knight maintains that the words of Gen. 6: 6
'and God repented that he had made man' (Hebr. *way-yinnaḥem*)
did not exist in the Bible of the early Church. This was because
the LXX 'under the influence of the Greeks' replaced the biblical
idea of the living and acting God by a static unchanging conception
of God. There are two good reasons against this interpretation.
(*a*) The LXX translation καὶ ἐνεθυμήθη ὁ θεός 'God was angry'
may not be exact, but can only to a very slight extent be said to
obscure the changing of God's mind, since the whole context in the

---

[1] G. Bertram in *BZATW* lxvi (1936) 103. Bertram is the main adviser on
Septuagint to *TWNT*.
[2] Knight, op. cit., pp. 7–8, cf. 1–5, 30.

LXX as in the Hebrew makes it quite plain that God did regret his previous action; and there is not the slightest ground for finding a static unchanging conception in this angry deity of the LXX. (b) The LXX elsewhere in a number of places translate the phrase about God's 'repenting' literally: thus μετανοεῖν is used of God at Am. 7: 3, 6; Joel 2: 13 f. (twice); Jonah 3: 9 f. (twice), 4: 2; Jer. 18: 8, 10, a large proportion in fact of the cases where the Hebrew phrase occurs of God.[1]

Knight also believes the rendering of the famous 'I am that I am' passage at Exod. 3: 14 by ἐγώ εἰμι ὁ ὤν to have been inspired by a presupposition in favour of a static and unchanging Hellenic conception of God. This is surely most unlikely. The motive is more likely to have been the need to make some intelligible Greek for one of the most important (and obscure) sayings in the Bible. At Exod. 3: 14, as at Gen. 6: 6, the context in both Greek and Hebrew surely makes it impossible to understand ἐγώ εἰμι ὁ ὤν as intended to suggest pure Being or some other remote and unchanging deity.

I may here point out that the LXX give many examples of (a) words which are pretty consistently adopted within certain books, while in others a different word is used; and this difference must be traced mainly to different translation methods (b) certain words and locutions being preferred because they fit more naturally into the ductus of what has to be translated. In both of these cases the phenomena have to be explained from contingent linguistic facts, and an attempt to evaluate them on a basis of special theological content here or there will often be false. Examples of this have already been seen in connection with the words for 'faith' and 'truth'.

For (a) we may compare such statistics as:

qahal translated by	Tetrateuch	Deut.	Jos. to Kings	Chron. to Neh.	Prophets	Psalms
συναγωγή	19	2	—	—	13	1
ἐκκλησία	—	5	10	40	4	10

[1] Even if it were true (as it clearly is not) that the LXX had a policy of excluding or disguising references to change or change of mind in God, this would not necessarily indicate Greek influence; they might simply be following out the logic of the explicit statement in good Hebrew in 1 Sam. 15: 29 that God, unlike man, does not change his mind.

Another example is the translation of ʿebed 'slave, servant'. For the facts see Zimmerli in *TWNT* v. 672 ff.; E.T., *The Servant of God*, pp. 35–40. Some of his interpretations are in my opinion doubtful. He maintains that the use of θεράπων, an absolutely normal word for 'servant', is 'daring' and 'far removed from the Hebrew attitude'. The support for this evaluation is the statement that the noun θεραπεία 'does not of itself fit into the language of the OT religion of revelation, but into that of heathendom'. This argument displays the usual disregard of word-formation, as if the use of a word meaning 'service, cult' in paganism makes very daring or un-Hebraic the use of another word meaning 'servant' merely because they are cognate words; and with it the usual tendency of *TWNT* to see theological preferences in what may be largely matters of literary and translation style.[1]

For (*b*) we have such an example as the use of words 'to know'. In the LXX as a whole γινώσκω along with ἐπιγινώσκω is some three times commoner than οἶδα. In Ezekiel the difference is suddenly much greater, the former appearing over 80 times and. the latter not once. This is not to be explained by a sudden dislike by the Ezekiel translator for what *TWNT* would call 'the οἶδα concept', but by the fact that the Ezekiel contexts require almost entirely futures and passives which could not be provided by οἶδα. The future εἴσομαι is not found in LXX Greek.

Something should also be said here about the methods of the Bauer dictionary. I have already pointed out that it is impossible to regard this kind of work as 'external lexicography', although *TWNT* rather suggests that it should be so regarded, because it does make real semantics its business and runs to a fair extent parallel with *TWNT*; and I have suggested that by its methodical procedure of suggesting word-substitutions it approaches the problem of the semantic values of words in their particular contexts often better than *TWNT*. There is however a serious criticism of its semantic method, namely that it is too content to give semantic indications which presuppose, and are intelligible only in terms of, a more modern intellectual and cultural *Weltanschauung* than that

---

[1] Concerning the words meaning 'servant', I can make no sense of the argument of Torrance in *Royal Priesthood*, p. 11 f.

of the NT. It does not sufficiently realize how often the terms and distinctions which seem clear and adequate to the modern culti- vated person talking about religion cut across the terms and distinctions meant in the NT. In particular there is a tendency at the more theologically specialized words to use those terms taken from a fairly traditional Christian theology which have, in a rather fossilized form and rather isolated from the total systems in which they were once used and had their meaning, remained in the speech of educated people about religion. 'Supernatural' is the best example of this, and is much too frequently used by Bauer.

Thus the article on ζωή divides the usage of this word into two great sections: 1. 'life in the physical sense', and 2. 'the supernatural life belonging to God and Christ, which the believers will receive in the future, but which they also enjoy here and now'. The artificiality, of this dichotomy is clear when we observe that 'the indestructible life of those clothed in the heavenly body' (2 Cor. 5: 4) appears in the former category.

The word 'religion' is similarly too willingly accepted by Bauer. He tells us that μετάνοια is 'mostly of the positive side of repentance, as the beginning of a new religious and moral life'. Modern biblical theology would surely more rightly say 'as the beginning of a new relation with God'. When not accompanied by a genitive or other complement, πίστις is held to be used 'as true piety, genuine religion', in other cases 'as a Christian virtue'.[1] That 'true piety, genuine religion' is a good guide to the meaning of πίστις in many of the passages here cited, e.g. Rom. 3: 27 f., seems to me little short of fantastic. That there may be many modern people of religious sympathies, for whom 'true piety, genuine religion' occupies roughly the same place in their scheme of things as πίστις did in Paul's, only shows how different these people are from Paul, and therefore how likely they are to be misled by the semantic guidance given here by Bauer. Anyone trying to interpret πίστις has to say not only that it roughly corresponds to what some people may call 'true religion', but also why Paul uses πίστις in fact in these passages and not (say) θεοσέβεια or θρησκεία, and why it makes a completely different

[1] Bauer, op. cit., p. 669.

argument out of the Pauline theology if you substitute θεοσέβεια or θρησκεία for πίστις; yet these words beyond doubt are reasonably represented by 'piety' or 'religion'.

This kind of semantic guidance is dangerous, not because it uses substitutions not taken in themselves from NT language but because the substitutions and distinction here offered are ones which have already been used in a long theological tradition, and one which has at points recognizably departed from adequate agreement with the NT. Their use is therefore in danger of guiding the understanding into categories established and hardened by long usage, categories which because of their long usage are specially liable to be an obstacle to new discovery of the original meaning. The Bauer dictionary gives a certain impression of a cheerful acceptance of and confidence in these formulations, an impression which is just as disconcerting as the more involved and tortured arguments of *TWNT* in its attempts at an intra-biblical system of understanding.

I make these criticisms of the Bauer dictionary to show that I do not think it has used methods which are infallible either; in particular it has failed to be sufficiently self-critical in the semantic indications it has given. I must add however that *TWNT* shares this fault with the Bauer dictionary, and differs rather in that it has a different group of words which it thinks it can use cheerfully and definitely without fearing any risk of misrepresenting biblical thinking. Thus it would hardly use 'supernatural' as Bauer does, but it repeatedly uses the catchwords of biblical theology such as 'Heilsgeschichte' or 'revelation'. In favour of *TWNT* it may be said that such words were used at any rate with the *intention* of finding terms which are really appropriate in reference to biblical thinking, which is more than the impression one has from some words used in the Bauer dictionary. But against *TWNT* must be said:

(a) These words are not so unambiguously 'biblical' as the *TWNT* writers think. They are rather key words of bible interpretation than key words of the Bible, and are in fact heavily charged with the values set upon them in certain schools of modern theology.[1]

---

[1] I have already mentioned that the use of 'revelation' as a general term for divine communication, and of 'revelation in history', is not in agreement with

(b) Detailed linguistic uses being described are often related to these terms like *Heilsgeschichte* or Revelation or Eschatology by mere association; that is, for example, if a word is used in a context which has something to say of the historical acts of God or of his purposes, the word is thus deemed to be filled with eschatological content or orientated to the history of salvation.

(c) Because of the kind of remote control which these terms in *TWNT* exercise over the atmosphere of the interpretation, rather than appearing in detailed semantic indications, it becomes much more difficult for their inadequacy to be revealed by the immediate context as is the case in the rather less adequate indications of the Bauer dictionary. This is a consequence of the failure to attend to semantic values in contexts which I have mentioned above.

CONCLUSION

I have already used the word 'idealist' to characterize certain aspects of the kind of interpretation of linguistic evidence which we have been examining. It is not surprising in fact to find this kind of interpretation appealing in its own support to the great idealist philosopher-theologian Schleiermacher, and in particular to his work *Hermeneutik und Kritik*.[1] From him comes the phrase about 'the language-moulding power of Christianity', the sentence that says 'An assembly of all the various elements in which the language-forming power of Christianity manifests itself would be a sciagraphy to a dogmatic and ethic of the New Testament', and the conception of the interpretative task as a double one, 'outer' and 'inner', or 'grammatical' and 'psychological', to use his own terms.[2] Schleiermacher also, like the modern school of biblical theology, paid attention to the Hebrew background of NT diction; and like it also, he wanted to use the Bible without accepting as guiding principle its perfection and infallibility. Several other characteristics of the outlook of biblical theology on language are found in his work.

biblical use, see above, p. 230; the criticisms there made of *TWNT* ἀποκαλύπτω apply to numerous other articles which also use 'revelation'.

[1] F. Schleiermacher, *Hermeneutik und Kritik mit besonderer Beziehung auf das neue Testament* (herausg. F. Lücke, Berlin, 1838).

[2] See ibid., pp. 68–9, 13, 19, etc.

Obviously what is needed here is a criticism in full of Schleiermacher's ideas of language and principles of interpretation; but this cannot be provided here. A few points may however be made. To anyone who knows modern biblical theology it must be obvious that there is something *prima facie* contradictory about its making even a partial alliance with Schleiermacher, to whose points of view it is commonly rather hostile, just at this particularly important point of biblical interpretation.

Some insight into Schleiermacher's hermeneutic ideas may be got by considering the judgement of his follower and critic Dilthey. To find the roots of individuality in a work of art, according to Schleiermacher, (I quote H. A. Hodges)[1] 'We must go behind the outer form of the work, and behind the "inner form" or idea of it in its developed form, to the primary synthetic act, or "germinal determination" (*Keimentschluss*) in the author's mind, in which the character of the developed work was implicitly contained.'

Now, according to Hodges, 'Schleiermacher's hermeneutic attracted Dilthey from his early years, and his influence over him grew continually as time went by. Yet as early as 1860 . . . he had put his finger on its weak point, which was the doctrine of the germinal synthesis. If every stage in the development of an individual is predetermined, and all he can do is to show more fully what he really was from the beginning, then all change is merely formal, and time brings no real novelty. The philosopher will therefore be able to forget about the details of the process, and find the clue to the understanding of a man not in his social and historical situation, but in some timeless principle which he embodies. Schleiermacher actually did so. He believed that the personalities of individual men flow from the Absolute by a timeless dialectic, and in his historical studies he leaned more on his notion of the Idea embodied in a person than on the historical evidence as to what that person was and did.'

If this is a true picture of Schleiermacher's views, it is clear that it is in many ways just the point of view which modern biblical theology has professed to repudiate. How then is it possible that some representatives of that theological direction are so willing to

[1] H. A. Hodges, *The Philosophy of Wilhelm Dilthey* (London, 1952), p. 13 f.

welcome as a guide to biblical interpretation a lexical tradition (in both Cremer and Kittel) which so explicitly accepted guidance at crucial points from Schleiermacher?[1] I do not pretend to provide the whole answer to this. But I have already pointed out certain aspects in which interpretation has distorted linguistic facts in a way that can be intelligibly accounted for only by an underlying idealism, through which the language must somehow reflect certain paramount relations existing in the theological realities. The picture of the work of interpretation as a circular one, working from the part up to the whole and yet needing the knowledge of the whole to interpret the part, as Schleiermacher saw it, is only too well fulfilled in that type of interpretation which works to a statement of the centre of Scripture, i.e. the lineaments of Christ and the salvation history of which he is the chief point, and then goes back to the details to impose on them the pattern of this whole. All the polemic in modern biblical theology against 'ideas' and 'systems' does not disguise that the patterns and lineaments of biblical events and institutions as discerned by such theology play the same part towards the linguistic material as the 'idea' does in Schleiermacher. The attempt to relate the various relations and stocks of biblical language to a comprehensive and ultimate series of theological realities is an essentially idealist programme. On an academic level it is equivalent to an attempt of the systematic

---

[1] For the influence of Schleiermacher on Cremer see Duncan, op. cit., pp. 18–22. He maintains that 'while Cremer followed Schleiermacher in his methodology he did not follow him in his theological appraisal of the results'. Later (p. 238 f.) he seems to hold that the heritage of Schleiermacher in another and wholly malignant form is to be found in Bultmann, transmitted through men like Dilthey and Wach. Torrance in *CJT* ii. 129 f. also traces a line from Schleiermacher to Bultmann. He says however that 'Schleiermacher's hermeneutical analysis went to the heart of the matter'. One must wonder how a thinker whose general viewpoints were so wrong and whose heritage was so disastrous in Bultmann can at the same time be deemed to have reached the heart of the matter in hermeneutics and be venerated for his deep influence on the Cremer-Kittel tradition, to which he gave some of its basic formulations. In any case Torrance's description of Schleiermacher's position seems to me inaccurate. It is true that Schleiermacher required psychological interpretation as well as grammatico-historical exposition. This was not however, as Torrance here suggests, because the language of the NT was Greek while its thought was Hebrew. The double exposition, grammatical and psychological, is required by Schleiermacher for all exposition, of any text. What he does arrive at because of this doubleness of the NT is the need for a 'special hermeneutic' for it.

theological consciousness to dominate the biblical exegesis. And
with regard to the linguistic problems in particular, the setting of
the problems by Schleiermacher carries us back to a time when
modern linguistic science was unknown and brings us into a mode
of discussion in which its methods and insights are irrelevant.

It must be remembered however that Schleiermacher's theology
was not a biblicistic one, close as his interest in biblical interpretation was. His recognition of the importance of Hebrew for the
language of the NT was modified by the fact that in his thinking
the OT itself had only a somewhat deuterocanonical status. In the
strongly biblicistic mind of Cremer, however, the use of Schleiermacher's comprehensive phrases about the 'language-moulding
power of Christianity' and about the 'sciagraphy' of NT doctrine
and ethics lexically composed, became all the more dominating
within the thought as a whole. And while Cremer seems to have
taken the phrase about the 'language-moulding' in a rather literal
sense, which led him to notice and emphasize any words and senses
found in 'Biblical Greek' only (and this was surely a right interpretation of Schleiermacher's meaning), the increasing emphasis
on the 'inner meaning' and the 'new content' under Kögel and
Kittel enlarged the area over which the 'language-moulding' could
be supposed to have taken place, at the same time as the unique
area of 'Biblical Greek' was being surrendered. The 'Bible-
mysticism' of which Lindeskog spoke in certain articles of *TWNT*
has a certain romantic-idealist element in common with Schleiermacher and the thought of his time.

Duncan believes that in Cremer's work one can see 'an integrated
theological method'. Linguistic, theological and homiletic work
belong together and must be integrated. Thus he says:[1]

'Through the labours of Cremer and those who followed him,
the lexicography of the biblical languages has been brought into
the realm of biblical theology where it belongs. The lexicographical
task is no longer left in the hands of a philologist who does not
share the faith or the aims of the theologian. The kind of biblical
philology envisaged by Cremer is to be no less scientific because it
is theological and no less theological because it is scientific.'

[1] Duncan, op. cit., p. 235.

No doubt this statement represents the belief of many of those who now support the movement towards biblical theology. The idea of theology and philology belonging together is in general a pleasant and attractive one. But I have quoted enough from recent efforts to make them belong together, and on the lines of Cremer and Kittel, to show how easily it can produce a scientific failure; and many such failures can be traced to the philosophy of language which allows a theological argument to do duty for a linguistic one, or assumes that the linguistic facts will fit the patterns of theological relations. Such a misuse of argument arises, I repeat, not from a deliberate intrusion of theology as such but from a philosophy which believes the language of the Bible somehow to reflect in its structure the pattern of the biblical events themselves. I think nevertheless that this ill-defined philosophy of language has been followed and cultivated because it seemed to serve and support the interests of certain types of theology.

I have not tried here to give an account of *TWNT* in general but only to point out its place in relation to the particular point of interpretation of linguistic evidence from which I started. A full study of *TWNT* would have to point out faults and weaknesses of which I have said nothing here; it would also have to point out riches and values of which I have had nothing to say here. Most important, it would have to point out that the faults which I have mentioned are not always found where they might have been found; in other words, that errors in the conception of the work and in the philosophy of language and of the relation between language and theology, which were fostered in the planning, were not always unchecked in the execution. The dictionary may well be better than the principles on which it was planned; whether because writers of articles have had a different conception of the matter from the original ideas of the editor, or because the linguistic material has proved rather difficult to fit into that original plan. I claim however that those aspects of *TWNT* which I have criticized are not minor accidents or slips but are integral parts of the general conception of the work, or follow from that general conception, or follow from the fact that certain problems were ignored in the forming of that conception.

The fact then that *TWNT* may often be better than those parts of its general conception which I have criticized is therefore no reason why these criticisms should not be made; rather it is good reason why they must be made. Here there are several points to make. Firstly, it may well be that *TWNT* will do more harm through its bad linguistic conceptions than it will do good through the useful material compiled in it, and in particular that those aspects of its linguistic philosophy which I have criticized, and which were foremost in the mind of the editors, may become widespread far beyond the range of the actual readers of *TWNT*. I do not doubt that this has already come to be so. Secondly, some of the harmful ideas of *TWNT* have been held in check by the very fact that it is a dictionary; even where it becomes rather a series of theological essays on the doctrines associated at certain points with certain words, it is still to some extent controlled by the usage of the literature relevant. But when the same conceptions of language and its relation to theological statement go out from the more purely lexicographical task to the task of theological construction, these checks become weaker and the use of arbitrary and theo-logically-dictated pseudo-linguistic arguments becomes easier.

Far from it being the case therefore that *TWNT* is 'in many ways the most valuable achievement in biblical studies of this century',[1] it is rather true that progress can only begin to be made, even with the material assembled by *TWNT*, through an awareness of the great and sweeping linguistic misconceptions which have become more widespread through its influence.

[1] Church of Scotland, *Interim Report* on Baptism, p. 3.

Chapter Nine

Language and the Idea of 'Biblical Theology'

It is now time to say something of a better way to approach biblical language in its relation to theology. It seems to me that the connection between the two must be made in the first place at the level of the larger linguistic complexes such as the sentences. It is the sentence (and of course the still larger literary complex such as the complete speech or poem) which is the linguistic bearer of the usual theological statement, and not the word (the lexical unit) or the morphological and syntactical connection. Neither the Christian preaching nor the religious structure of ancient Israel (nor indeed, I would suppose, any other religious structure) consisted primarily (if at all) in the issuing either of new words or of new word-concepts or of new conceptual 'content' for old words. The newness or uniqueness of the structure consisted rather in new combinations of words, in which it was often possible for the semantic value of the words to be changed only slightly or not at all, and for the new or distinctive concept to be indicated by the word-combination. It is true of course that the use of a word might come in due course to be specially stamped by its frequent recurrence in sentences of a particular kind, and so to undergo a semantic change. But I have already suggested that such semantic change is not at all to be related in its extent proportionately to the degree of newness or originality of the statements in which it occurs. And it has to be related to other factors, such as the degree of specialization of the word in earlier usage, and the degree to which it becomes completely technical in its use in the new statements. The degree of semantic change has thus no proportional relation to the importance of the word, and of the statements which use it, in the new religious structure. It follows that the attempt to read off a theological structure or pattern from a survey of the lexical stock in general, or (as Schleiermacher conceived it in his 'sciagraphy' idea) from that part of the lexical stock which showed clearly the 'language-moulding power' of the religion, is a misguided one, and one which if carried out only leads to a distortion of the linguistic material in the interests of the theological pattern.

The point we have here made, namely that the real communication of religious and theological patterns is by the larger word-combinations and not by the lexical units or words, is of real importance for one of the problems which I mentioned in the beginning, namely the problem of the translation of the Bible — something that is, naturally, of the greatest practical importance for the Church. Those who have thought to discern in the morphological-syntactical mechanisms of the Hebrew language or in the distribution of its lexical stock something reflecting the theological realities are brought rather near the position that Hebrew is untranslatable. The depreciation of the first really important work of translation, the Septuagint,[1] is a natural accompaniment of this. The great Hebraist and humanist Reuchlin appears to have thought that translation from Hebrew was destructive to the real value of the text; and such translations as he gave were not an attempt to provide an alternative, a rendering of the same substance in another tongue, but simply a guide for the learner to assist him in understanding the Hebrew.[2] The veneration

---

[1] Perhaps 'depreciation' suggests a more systematic approach to the LXX than has really existed; for the judgements of their work tend to be made *ad hoc* and to depict them at one moment as gross Hellenizers splitting up the unity of Hebrew language and thought, at another as careful and cunning expositors of the Hebraic mind. Thus Torrance in *SJT* i (1948) shows how the LXX allowed the essential unity of certain Hebrew conceptions to be split up and impoverished (p. 63 ff.); but only a few pages back (p. 57) these same men are 'the shrewd translators of the LXX' carefully avoiding their usual translation χάρις in certain cases so as 'to avoid the possibility of χάρις corrupting the Old Testament thought of the grace of God into something semi-physical and aesthetically pleasing'. Numerous similar cases occur in *TWNT*.

[2] For this information I am indebted to W. Schwarz, *Principles and Problems of Biblical Translation* (Cambridge, 1955), p. 84 ff. Of course the situation was quite different in Reuchlin's time. There was the widespread belief that Hebrew was the first tongue of man; and there was the ecclesiastical insistence on the Vulgate, against which men like Reuchlin wanted to assert the authority of the original text.

for the Hebrew structure as a reflection of the theological realities and as the one authoritative guide to the meaning of the NT must mean a similar uncertainty about the value that translations can have.[1]

But the problem arises because of the false emphasis on the morphological-syntactical mechanisms of Hebrew and on the distribution of its lexical stock. If the Hebrew 'construct state' connection betokens a way in which the 'biblical mind' sees the relation between realities, how can this be reflected when we translate into a language which has to content itself with the genitive case or the preposition 'of'? If the Hebrew sense of totality manifests itself in the use of the nominal sentence, how seriously we shall lose that sense of totality, and with it an essential part of the biblical message, when in English we have to use the so-called copula 'is', except in the few cases where we can change the order of words and use the nominal sentence even in English! If Hebrew *n-ḥ-m* means 'comfort' in one theme and 'repent' in another, how disastrous it is that in English we have no word which will span the same area for us in its various forms! We have already seen that the conception of the relation between linguistic and theological structures out of which such questions arise is a false one. The real bearer of the theological statement is the large complex like the sentence, in which are used words having a certain semantic function and various morphological and syntactic mechanisms (such as case, construct state, verb tense, word order). The theological statement can be restated in another language, even though the mechanisms are not the same in the new language and even though the words used in the new language may have certain other significances elsewhere which the original words did

[1] Important problems about the theory of translation in general are discussed by J. R. Firth, 'Linguistic Analysis and Translation', *For Roman Jakobson* (The Hague, 1956), pp. 133–9. For an approach to translation typical of biblical theology, see C. Tresmontant, *Études de métaphysique biblique* (Paris, 1955), p. 253 ff. Because the thought structure of the Hebrews and that of the Greeks are entirely heterogeneous, it would seem quite impossible to translate Hebrew into 'a language informed by Greco-Latin civilization'. Tresmontant escapes from this difficulty under a smoke-screen of theological metaphors. We hear of how 'incarnation' takes place in language; language is 'renewed' and 'sanctified'. This theological account of translation only screens the failure to see the linguistic basis of translation.

not have (that is, a certain degree of lexical overlap or non-coincidence exists); provided that the semantic value of the words within the new (i.e. the translated) sentence when taken as a whole does not misrepresent the semantic value of the original sentence taken as a whole. There is likely to be some loss in translation, because it is seldom possible to reproduce all the nuances of another language. But the extent of this loss is limited in principle. I say 'in principle' because a bad translation may lose a great deal more than a good one. A good translation is able to represent in a new language the effective content of a passage in spite of the unavoidable losses, because it will give a sufficient representation of the sense of the whole for that sense in its turn to give some guidance for the closer understanding of the particular semantic value of each word in this context. And the losses which occur in translation from Hebrew to Greek or to English are losses simply because the Hebrew is the original linguistically and not because its structure reflects the theological reality of the biblical message.[1]

The other great presupposition of the Bible translations, of the older ones at any rate, is that the book is being translated because it is already the sacred book of a community which not only reveres this book but wishes to identify itself with or involve itself in the story of the book and of the people of Israel and the NT church who first lived out this story. This implies first of all a certain familiarity with the matter of the Bible and a certain accept-ance of it as a kind of special sphere or special context of its own to some degree. This is of importance in such cases as the use of ὁ θεός 'God' in the LXX. The semantic contribution of this word in the LXX is 'the god, God' as in any Greek text, and to quote it as a case of being 'filled with new content' would, I think, be wrong. But the LXX is designed for a community who were already quite familiar with who 'God' was — he was the God of

---

[1] Perhaps I might dare the quite personal (and quite unimportant, even if rather shocking) opinion that there is rather less lost on the whole in translating Hebrew poetry into English than in translating classical Greek or Latin poetry. For this there are a number of reasons. I might mention the difficulty of representing in English the free Latin word order, and on the other hand our uncertainty about the metres of ancient Hebrew verse; on this latter however some real progress is being made; cf. especially the work of S. Segert of Prague, *AO* xxi (1953) 481–542, xxv (1957) 190–200; *VT* Suppl. vii (1960).

Israel and the God of the Bible. The fact that such words were also used in heathen cults did not affect the matter seriously, for such usage was not taken to have marked them in such a way as definitely to indicate something foreign to the community's point of view. I do not doubt that there were words avoided because they were felt to be so marked, but from the nature of the case it is difficult to say precisely why words which were not used were not used.[1] The familiarity of the community with the Bible means that the words used in the translation do not need to be unambiguously related in their individual semantics to the biblical faith and correspondingly demarcated in themselves from their use outside that faith.

It is also because the Bible represents a sacred text to the community and its story a past story in a somewhat different, or greatly different, environment, that the translation of the Bible is likely to differ to some extent from the usual speech of the members of the community. That the Semitisms of the LXX arose from the translation techniques and therefore were not necessarily evidence for the Greek spoken by the Egyptian Jews in general was seen and emphasized by Deissmann.[2] But while, as Deissmann also saw, the translation meant that the Bible was to some extent 'Egyptian-ized' and 'modernized', it is equally true that the nature of the document as a whole set limits to the extent to which this could take place. There were of course passages where the translators used a more or less blind system of equivalences and produced a phrase which had no other claim to intelligibility than that it was a substitution of Greek words for the Hebrew words; and taken on the whole the effect is such that clearly the biblical text is under-stood to be a traditional and sacred datum from the past, so that 'modernizations' make little difference to the general impression of it, while obscurities and unintelligibilities may occur here and there such as would not be allowed in ordinary speech.[3] Although

---

[1] On the question of the avoidance of certain words in the LXX and the NT, see the detached note, below, p. 282 ff.

[2] Deissmann, op. cit., p. 69.

[3] See above, p. 251 n. The considerations I advance here are also a necessary corrective to the (highly exaggerated, as it seems to me) impression given by Deissmann of a Greek OT which meant something substantially different in the

a much greater degree of accuracy in translation is possible than the
LXX showed, and is commonly achieved, it probably remains true
that an English translation of the Bible will differ somewhat from
the speech of an English Christian even about the same subjects —
even among biblicistic people who quote scripture a great deal of
the time. All this depends to some extent on the relation of the
community to the Bible as sacred scripture and on the commitment
of the community to see its story as its own and to familiarize itself
with its style and expressions.

The second important consequence of the relation of the Bible
to the community which reveres it and uses it is the existence of
cultural conflict between this community and the wider circle of
those speaking the same language. The centre of this is religious
conflict, but I say 'cultural' because the relevant factors may be
very widespread. The result or outcome of the transcultural
translation of biblical language depends not only on purely
linguistic questions but on the relations in fact achieved between
the Christian community and the surrounding culture. Numerous
possibilities lie open here. Sometimes there will be customs or
institutions for which no designation in the new language can be
found, and which are taken over bodily, such as 'ephod' into
English or πάσχα into Greek. Sometimes even more central terms
must be created, as for example in the no small number of
languages in which the English 'God' or the pseudo-Hebrew
'Jehovah' have been inserted as more or less foreign bodies,
presumably because it was felt that no word existed in the
languages which did not have a place in the cultural consciousness
which would be misleading if used in reference to the God of the
Bible.[1] On the other hand, when words are taken from the new

imperial period from what it meant in the Ptolemaic period; or which meant
something substantially different to a gentile Christian in Rome from its meaning
to Paul; ibid., p. 79.

[1] *The Gospel in many Tongues* (British and Foreign Bible Society, London,
1948) lists on p. 180 ff. a number of American Indian, Asian and Pacific languages
in which some form of 'Jehovah' or some variation of the English 'God' is used
as the word for 'God' in standard Bible translations. I leave aside of course the
question whether the translators of such versions were right in believing that the
importation of this name was the best course to adopt. Much interesting material
on these problems will be found in the periodical *The Bible Translator* (United
Bible Societies, London).

language and used in the Bible, the success of their use and the future of their semantics depends to a great extent on the way in which Christianity in due course relates itself to the culture. In the Germanic sphere, where Christianity became dominant and the old religion died out, many words became so related to Christian usage that the pre-Christian sense ceased entirely to be effective. In cases where the pre-Christian culture and religion do not succumb, so that Christianity remains a minority, the use of vocabulary remains uncertain and may need to be revised.[1]

Let us now return to the main point here being made, namely that the linguistic bearer of the theological statement is usually the sentence and the still larger literary complex[2] and not the word or the morphological and syntactical mechanisms.

The most important consequence of this arises because the sentence unlike the word is unique and non-recurrent. A language has a vocabulary, i.e. a stock of words which are constantly available and may be used again and again; but it does not have a stock of sentences. This has a manifold importance for the interpretation of the Bible.

First of all, the question of distinctiveness of biblical thinking has to be settled at this level and not at the lexical level. The attempt in much recent biblical theology to demonstrate the existence of a biblical lexical stock of words or 'concepts' (in this case what we may call 'word-concepts' and not 'sentence-concepts') which are semantically distinctive, that is to say, which have a semantic distinctiveness which can be set in close correlation with the distinctiveness of the faith and theology of the Bible, is in principle a failure. That it appears to work at certain points is because some words become specialized, although others which are equally important theologically do not, or because some words become specialized, but only in certain syntactical contexts; the case for a semantic distinctiveness of the words as made by biblical

---

[1] Cf. the famous example of the words for 'God' used in the Jesuit mission in China; for general orientation see K. S. Latourette, *History of the Expansion of Christianity* (London, 1939), iii. 340–52, and literature cited there.

[2] I use the word 'literary', of course, in a sense which will include oral statement and oral tradition, and not in that sense in which it is used only of written literature.

theology depends on a haphazard method which exploits these occasional specializations. But as a whole the distinctiveness of biblical thought and language has to be settled at sentence level, that is, by the things the writers say, and not by the words they say them with. And this after all is the ground on which the distinctiveness of a writer or a class of literature is usually decided; and one would suppose that a good case could be made for a distinctiveness of a large area of biblical thought on this basis.

One may well ask therefore why the biblical theology movement has not been content with this kind of distinctiveness and the kind of approach which would lead to it. The first answer is probably because the acceptance of a distinctiveness of this kind for the Bible will also mean the acceptance of the same kind of distinctiveness within the Bible and thus lead to the fragmentation of the Bible. The essentially synthetic method of biblical theology is in fact something created in its modern form very much in reaction to the combined effects of literary criticism and of an evolutionary history of religions, which made the message of Jesus something different from that of Paul, and it in its turn different from that of John, and so on. The reaction to this danger is the laying of the emphasis on the common fund of words or 'concepts' used by all of them, a common fund which is used in different and thus original ways by each but which itself is common to the Bible and distinctive of it. It is not necessary to discuss the further ramifications of this problem here. I want only to point out that it is not only by the synthetic biblical theology that some of the obvious faults of the older approach can be overcome. In fact a great deal of bad literary criticism has been overcome by better literary criticism and by greater use of the categories of oral tradition; and in the history of religions also much of the naiver evolutionistic schematism has been replaced, or is being replaced, by an appreciation of the totality of a religious consciousness. Biblical theology is tempted to suppose itself to be the only cure for certain ills and not to perceive that other directions of study have also been able to overcome these ills.

The second reason is probably an unwillingness to be content with this kind of distinctiveness, which is too much like a distinctiveness on a literary level like the distinctiveness of Greek tragedy or of Norse epic. There is a certain drive for a distinctiveness on a higher level than this. This is connected with the unwillingness to deal with 'ideas' in the Bible. An 'idea' is a bad thing but a 'concept' is a good one. From the words of the Bible, or the 'concepts' which more or less coincide with them, there is a hankering to go right on not to the thoughts or 'ideas' of those using the words but to the events themselves or to Christ himself. The things John or Paul say might be construed as thoughts or ideas of these men, but 'behind' what they say is a framework visible at points in the lexical structure, a framework which points to or patterns forth the shape of Christ. This is something like the 'ultimate element' which Kittel was interested in detecting.[1] The weaknesses and fallacies in these arguments should now be evident.

- The question of the distinctiveness of biblical thinking, then, must be discussed not at the lexical level but at the level of the things that were said. But it must be said that theologians may have to think again about pressing the question of distinctiveness in any dogmatic relation to the thought and language of the Bible. One might at any rate suggest the possibility that distinctive or unique events would be known through quite non-distinctive linguistic expression. The question is also connected with the doctrine of the authority or inspiration of Scripture in the Church. Modern circles of biblical theology rather scorn the old orthodox Protestant doctrine of Scripture, on the ground that it offered statements or propositions which were taken to be divinely inspired, and these are disliked as being something like 'static ideas'. But if we are to have proof-words instead of proof-texts I doubt if we are making progress. A 'text' might at least be a sentence with a proper significance-content of its own. The question of the relation of the doctrine of the authority of Scripture to the lexicographical methods used by theologians is a complicated one into which I shall not go.[2]

---

[1] Kittel, *Lexicographia Sacra*, p. 25 f.

[2] Deissmann thought that the isolating of 'Biblical Greek' was in part an after-effect of a mechanical doctrine of inspiration; *Light from the Ancient East*, p. 67. I am not sure of the position of Cremer himself; see R. C. Duncan, op. cit., pp. 212–18. In general it seems true that with the loss of stress on the

Linguistically, the main result of the suggestions I have made about biblical language would seem to be that investigation should proceed to a much greater degree in the realm roughly of stylistics, and that too much has been attempted by lexicographical methods. The considerations advanced earlier in this chapter about the relation of the Bible to the community as its sacred tradition, and about the importance of the cultural conflict or symbiosis of the worshipping community and the larger surrounding area which uses the same language, are to a considerable degree of a stylistic nature, although conflicts over particular words in the lexical realm are more obvious and easier to illustrate when they occur. It seems to me that there is a recognizable biblical style, or series of biblical styles, and that research into them is a rewarding field. Many aspects of biblical style are already shaped by an early date in the Israelite monarchy.. The perpetuation of the material as sacred tradition gives it a classical status in the eyes of later traditionists. The relation between the meaning of sentences and larger units on the one hand and the mode of their expression on the other is a stylistic matter and cannot be fully handled by the lexical methods discussed above. And the other important point is that, unlike the lexical distribution and the syntactic mechanisms of Hebrew, the biblical style is to a fairly large degree preservable in translation, and thus preserves important elements of the relation of the linguistic expression to the thinking of the men of the Bible. In addition it is in stylistics in particular, as Sandmann seems to intend,[1] that the questions of ethno-psychology, implied in so much that we have discussed, can perhaps best be handled.

historical accuracy and doctrinal perfection of Scriptural statements in modern. times, there has gone an effort to emphasize the inner coherence of the Bible in some way, and that the importance placed on this inner coherence by some theologians, in respect both of lexicography and of synthetic biblical theology, is perhaps a compensation for the apparent thinning down of biblical inspiration.

[1] Op. cit., p. 42 f. I would not however accept Sandmann's conceptions here without reserve. I find difficulty for instance with his suggestion that stylistics, working together with grammar, can show for example that the perfective aspect of the French future is typical of a certain logical mentality, while the durative aspect of the German form 'reflects the indefinite German dynamism, which is to its Latin neighbours such a disquieting trait in the Teutonic character', and the 'modal' English future reflects 'the politeness and diplomacy based on morality which are so characteristic of the English'. This I find wholly unconvincing.

Theologically, we must ask how these considerations affect the idea of 'biblical theology'. Here we may start from two possible understandings of what 'biblical theology' is. These two may be distinguished for clarity, but with the understanding that very few people confine themselves strictly to one or the other. The first is the understanding of 'biblical theology' as a descriptive discipline, belonging definitely within the biblical sciences along with language, history, literary criticism and so on, and distinctly not belonging to dogmatics or systematic theology. This is for example the understanding of Old Testament theology followed by Eichrodt in what is one of the most important treatments the subject has had.[1] In his opinion the task of Old Testament theology is 'to gain a comprehensive picture of the world of faith of the Old Testament'. It does not belong to the normative discipline of dogmatics at all; it differs from a task like literary criticism or history of religions only in having the *cross-section* of the Old Testament as its material. The characteristic of this kind of 'biblical theology' then is primarily its synthetic method in contrast with certain analytic procedures.

The second sense in which we hear about a 'biblical theology' is rather a kind of dogmatics; it is roughly that type of dogmatic which lays a heavy emphasis on the Bible and takes it as the basic or the only source of authority.

Both of these senses are quite clear, and the work done on their principles fairly easily controllable. But a great deal of work that is done and that would be roughly classified as 'biblical theology' lies rather between the two senses. It is not dogmatics in the usual sense, since its main concern is not with doctrinal formulations; but it shares the interest of dogmatics in that it sees itself to have a kind of normative function. It is 'expounding the Bible as the Word of God'. In this respect it certainly abandons the principles which Eichrodt set for his kind of Old Testament theology, for it is not purely descriptive. It rather tries to be descriptive-authoritative at the same time. But in order to be this it adopts another central

---

[1] W. Eichrodt, *Theologie des alten Testaments* (5th ed., Stuttgart, 1957), i. 1–8. Cf. my 'The Problem of Old Testament Theology and the History of Religion', *CJT* iii (1957) 141–9.

principle of Eichrodt's method, namely the synthetic procedure. It is emphatically 'seeing the Bible as a unity' — and this of course includes the OT and the NT together (for Eichrodt himself of course the place of the NT was marginal). It is in this third or intermediate kind of 'biblical theology' that most of the linguistic arguments which I have criticized lie.

It is no part of the purpose of this study to discuss the values and relations of these conceptions of 'biblical theology' in general. The question is how far they are affected by the discussion of the use of linguistic evidence which has been the subject of this study. Here there are two main points to be made.

Firstly, it seems to me clear that the insistence on a synthetic approach, on 'seeing the Bible as a unity', on overcoming the divisions which literary criticism and religious history caused to appear throughout the Bible, has been much to blame for the exaggerations and misuses of the interpretation of words, especially from their Hebrew background, which have been illustrated in this study. I have already suggested elsewhere[1] that the synthetic method of survey of the Bible is a necessary part of an approach to the Bible, but that it is mistaken to think that it has any finality or that it forms the highest and deepest stage in biblical study, and that it should be understood as a guide or tool for our assistance as we go back to the detailed texts and attempt an exegesis of the particular passages. I now would wish to reaffirm this much more forcibly, with especially the insistence that lexicographic research should be directed towards the semantics of words in their particular occurrences and not towards the assembly of a stock of pervasive and distinctive terms which could be regarded as a linguistic reflection of the theological realities. It is worth noticing that Old Testament theology at any rate, where it has followed a synthetic method, has had to accept that this is also a selective method.[2] What is pervasive and permanent forms the material. It is obvious that a synthetic method worked out in this way may be helpless before the aberrant or abnormal passage; and also that

[1] *CJT* iii (1957) 148 f.
[2] See *CJT* iii (1957) 147, and references there to Eichrodt, Rowley, Dentan and Koehler; also my review of Rowley, *The Faith of Israel*, in *JSS* ii (1957) 397-9.

it is very difficult to avoid in this method the imposition upon the semantic investigation of words of a pattern which is held to be theologically regulative.[1] Likewise the drive to demonstrate a system of intra-biblical connections is a main cause for the interpretation of words by etymologizing and other illegitimate methods which lead away from the actual semantic value. And this really means that in that type of exposition of 'the Bible as a unity' which formed our third or mixed sense of 'biblical theology' the interests of dogmatics have been allowed to dominate over responsible exegesis.[2]

I do not wish however to suggest that the linguistic considerations I have advanced demonstrate in themselves that the synthetic approach to the Bible is a wrong one. My concern at present is simply that if this approach is continued it must be adequately guarded against the misinterpretations of language which, I suggest, have been encouraged by it.

Secondly, something should be said about the position of that kind of study which has been called 'hermeneutics', and on which the more important literature in recent times has been in German. The main thing I have to say about it is that it seems to have paid little systematic attention to the problems which I have discussed in this book.[3] Though frequent mention will be found of 'the problem of language' or 'the phenomenon of human language', the questions which have been discussed in this kind of hermeneutics have not been linguistic questions, although occasional reference

---

[1] Any reader of *TWNT*, for example, will feel the very strong influence of the categories of Christology, eschatology and *Heilsgeschichte*, and the effort that is made in some articles to make those uses of the word which can be connected with these categories the regulative ones. Cf. the remarks of Dodd on *TWNT* προάγω, *JTS* xxxiv (1933) 284; on εἰρήνη, *JTS* xxxix (1938) 289 f.

[2] I am anxious not to add to the animus of biblical scholars against dogmatics, of which I think there is too much already. But of much work in biblical theology I feel that it is paradoxically moved by a certain animus against dogmatics as a separate discipline and at the same time excessively influenced by dogmatic categories and considerations.

[3] I would mention particularly R. Bultmann, 'The Problem of Hermeneutics'; E. Fuchs, *Hermeneutik* (Bad Canstatt, 1954); Barth, *KD* i/2. 513 ff.; E.T., pp. 465 ff.; K. H. Miskotte, *Zur biblischen Hermeneutik* (Zollikon, 1959); J. Wach in *JBL* lv (1936) 59–63; Ebeling in *RGG*[3], where more general orientation and full bibliography will be found. For a valuable recent study in English, see J. L. Mays, 'Exegesis as a Theological Discipline' (Union Theological Seminary, Richmond, 1960).

may be made to linguistic facts, but philosophical-theological
questions. The chief questions are such as 'How can human speech
be used as the vehicle of divine communication?' or 'How can the
Bible, which is a body of literature or tradition composed entirely
in human language, be expounded or interpreted as the Word of
God?' The essays contributed to a recent conference of German
theologians and devoted to 'The Problem of Language' make little
or no contact with linguistics (in spite of the clear competence of
some of the writers as biblical scholars) and are really interested in
philosophical-theological questions of the kind mentioned.[1]

If this kind of theological hermeneutics has been concerned with
a quite different series of questions than those discussed in this
book, it is by no means my intention to suggest that these questions
are not proper ones or that the ones I have discussed are more
important. I *am* concerned to point out the danger that answers
suggested for these questions may be taken to be also an answer to
the properly linguistic questions, or (as I think seems to have
happened) that the preoccupation with these questions should
mean that the linguistic questions should not be known to exist
at all. Thus when Barth regards as illegitimate 'a kind of hearing,
which attends to the biblical words but not to that to which these
words point' or 'an understanding of the biblical words *from* their
immanent linguistic and actual context instead of an understanding of them *in* this context but *from* what they say and what is to
be heard as said by them',[2] this, whether right or wrong, can make
sense only as a statement about the Bible, about a given body of
literature or communication by language. As a statement about a
morphological structure like the Hebrew 'tense' system, or a
syntactic mechanism like the construct state, or the semantic
function of a Greek or Hebrew word, it does not make sense.
There is no evidence that Barth intended it to include this latter
case; but also there is no evidence that the problems of this latter
case had sufficiently occurred to him for him to exclude it. It is
clear enough however that the kind of hermeneutical statement

---

[1] *Das Problem der Sprache in Theologie und Kirche* (ed. Schneemelcher,
Berlin, 1959).
[2] *KD* i/2. 516; E.T., p. 466.

which I have exemplified from Barth has been widely taken to apply to the latter case; for most of the interpretations of linguistic phenomena which I have criticized are attempts to make such phenomena be not 'merely' words or linguistic mechanisms but make them 'point to' something beyond their linguistic function. The language Barth uses about 'pointing to' and about 'immanent linguistic context' and so on is purely philosophical-theological and entirely distorting when referred to units of a language system; what for example would 'immanent' mean in the latter case? All such units have a 'pointing' or semantic function; they have no further function beyond this; but what Barth means by 'pointing to' *is* something beyond the normal semantic function of linguistic units; he is therefore certainly referring to something other than such units, or making nonsense of them.[1]

This kind of theological hermeneutics seems to me also to have done harm by the perpetuation, as a result of its neglect of linguistics as a science, of very old-fashioned views about language. Thus to Bultmann (op. cit., p. 236) '*Philology* is the science which has for its object the interpretation of literary texts, and which for this purpose makes use of hermeneutics.' Such a statement is completely out of contact with modern linguistics. Equally out of date is the interest in 'the old hermeneutical rules', or the idea that we are saying something up to date by pointing out their in-adequacy. Writers like Bultmann and Barth, alike primarily interested in philosophical-theological problems, seem (in their writings on hermeneutics at any rate, whatever their practice elsewhere) not to see semantics as a part of linguistics and semantic functioning as an immediate effect of any dealing with language; thus they have some idea of a rather mechanical grammatical or philological procedure, to which is added the procedure which is really interesting to them, the 'psychological' understanding (Schleiermacher), the existential or de-mythologizing interpreta-

---

[1] Cf. the complaint of Torrance, quoted above, p. 188, against the treatment of NT ἀλήθεια 'merely as a Greek word'. Linguistically, a Greek word is a Greek word, in this case a unit in the Greek language system of the NT, and cannot be treated 'as' anything else. The understanding of the 'background', on which he insists, is a normal part of our treating a Greek word 'merely as' a Greek word.

tion (Bultmann) or the exposition of the (theological) reality to which the words 'point' (Barth).[1]

In some such ways, then, caution is needed to prevent the study of theological hermeneutics, so much of which lies outside linguistic matters and in such realms as the exposition of the Bible as the Word of God or the communication of the Gospel to the modern man, from having unfortunate and often unintentional effects on the assessment of linguistic evidence specifically.

I may conclude by drawing together various aspects of that kind of interpretation of language which we have studied and relating them to the biblical theology movement.

I began from the contrast between Greek and Hebrew thought, which is common currency in theology of many kinds to-day. The existence and use of this contrast is not itself dependent on its extension into a linguistic contrast in realms of grammar and lexicography. It is evident however that such an extension has been widely made within biblical theology; it is equally evident that the validity of making such an extension has been boldly assumed, without the bringing of any justification related to general linguistics (unless those of over a hundred years ago) and without the bringing of detailed linguistic evidence within the biblical area itself. Now the validity of the thought contrast within its own sphere is of great importance for the present type of theology, with its sharp opposition of biblical thought to extra-biblical. The transference of the contrast into the linguistic sphere, however innocently intended, has been used as an instrument in the imperialism of dogmatic method towards biblical exegesis. The theological consciousness, sure of the validity of the thought contrast, strives to guide linguistic description into the same patterns and feels confident in rejecting as clearly inadequate interpretations of linguistic evidence which do not present the patterns expected from the thought contrast. Thus an appeal to the usage of NT Greek can be discredited on the ground that it neglects the Hebrew background, and a description of a Hebrew linguistic

---

[1] A lack of critical sense towards the conceptions held of language seems to me to be a grave defect of the long work of J. Wach, *Das Verstehen* (Tübingen, 1926-33, 3 vols.).

phenomenon which does not produce the patterns expected from the thought contrast can be discredited as obviously assuming a European point of view.[1] Boman, though not himself entirely typical of biblical theology, begins also with the thought contrast, which forms the title of his book; but has tried harder than any other writer to give a systematic correlation of that contrast with linguistic characteristics. Whether his account of the thought contrast is an accurate one or not, it is clear that his linguistic discussion is full of impossible constructions of phenomena, often claims as a Hebrew peculiarity something that is not at all unique but appears to fit into the peculiarities of Hebrew thought, and often fails to make any examination of Greek or any other language and compares Hebrew language direct with what is supposed to be Greek thought or European thought. This failure is fundamentally because his programme does not arise from linguistic description at all, but is extended or extrapolated from the thought contrast; and the same failure appears in work of the same kind done from the more explicit biblical theology side.

The importance of the extension of the contrast to linguistic material in this way is for biblical theology the support that it seems to give to the synthetic approach to the Bible and the encouragement it appears to afford to the explanation of biblical language through this method. In the more extreme formulations of the matter,[2] the adoption of this approach is thought to exclude automatically our own preconceived ideas and to guarantee that the Bible is speaking its own word to us; there is philological accuracy because the Bible is being interpreted within its own special milieu, and theological validity because we are letting the Word of God control us. From the studies in this book it must be clear that such a belief is a gross and complacent illusion. Some of the interpretations of linguistic data which we have studied here have involved the imposition in a high degree of patterns popular in present-day biblical theology; in some cases only the pre-existence of these patterns in the mind of the interpreter can

---

[1] Torrance against Moule, above, p. 204; Boman against Bergsträsser, above, pp. 21–22.
[2] E.g. in the Church of Scotland report on Baptism, above, p. 5 f.

explain the way in which so erratic a linguistic interpretation came
to be adopted. My criticism is not that these patterns are themselves non-biblical, although sometimes they may be so in spite
of their appearance; it is rather that they represent those certain
themes and patterns within the Bible which are basic to biblical
theology and attractive to its consciousness, and which it therefore
tries to find reflected in the other themes and patterns. Some of
these favourite patterns have been cited in the discussion of
TWNT.[1] The supposed pervasiveness of these theological patterns
makes more plausible the attempt to display a reflection of them in
the biblical linguistic structure, and since this structure is itself
apparent throughout the Bible, thus to display a reflection of them
in the other themes and patterns.

It need hardly be pointed out that these tendencies are dangerous not only because of the harm done by them to the linguistics
of the Bible, but also because of the harm done to theology itself,
for example by the over-easy solution of the problem of biblical
authority in theology, or by the set-back to the investigation of
other methods of relating Bible and theology.[2] And in some of the
more extreme cases where particular problems have been investigated by the methods I have criticized it will be a major task to
discover whether any real and lasting theological construction
remains after the mass of pseudo-linguistic argument is removed.

An important question may also be asked about the relation
between biblical theology and communication. The complaints
which are often heard against the obscurity of diction in the
'biblical theology' school are often countered with the injunction to
'think biblically'. We have seen however that a number of inter-

---

[1] See above, p. 275 n.
[2] Cf. the interesting remarks of W. Nicholls from the dogmatic side, *SJT* xiii
(1960) 72. He suggests that what has been called 'biblical theology' is often an
evasion of exact study on both the exegetical and the dogmatic sides and does
harm to both. 'Biblical theology' can thus be a kind of concealed dogmatics
while claiming to be highly scientific biblical research. This is certainly true in
the linguistic matters, which Mr Nicholls does not have principally in mind;
and here we find the dogmatic theological mind trying even to lay down what is
scientific in method for the approach to biblical linguistic material; an attempt
which is absurd when coming as it sometimes does from writers who not only
boldly transgress modern linguistic methods but do not even know what they are.

pretations of language by this school are notable for their neglect of the social consciousness of the meaning of words, and of the exact contribution made by a word in its context and communicated between the speaker and the hearer, or the writer and the reader. They are notable, in other words, for an emphasis not on descriptive semantics but on etymology and other associations which are supposed to 'lie behind' the words used. It seems to me not unfair to suggest that, apart from biblical investigation, the diction of biblical theology develops a kind of rhetoric of its own, in which certain favourite words recur interminably (such as *'Heilsgeschichte'*, 'covenant' and 'eschatology') but with a peculiar sliding back and forward of sense which makes them rather 'good words' or signs of an accepted point of view than useful symbols of communication; there are also 'bad words' used always with a depreciatory purpose. Etymologies may also be used to a considerable extent, but often in senses which were not those with which the derivation occurred. The impression given by such diction is one of exasperation at the neglect of the social acceptation of language. It is a hard thing to say, but not I think unfair, that a criticism of this turgid diction in relation to the social linguistic consciousness is avoided in part because such a criticism would be disastrous to the treatment of biblical language also in the same school. If it is true that modern philosophy (of which I have only an amateur knowledge) lays much emphasis on the examination of everyday language, it may be that we have here a point at which the isolation of biblical theology from such philosophy within the intra-biblical area is a source of much harm.

No doubt there will always be a use of biblical language in theology, and I would not suggest it should be otherwise. But surely the most sound and reliable use will be that in which ample and unambiguous evidence from usage leads us to suppose that we use a word in a way that adequately conveys a deliberate and conscious purpose of communication performed in the sentences spoken or written by the men of the Bible. Thus we shall use the word 'creation' in theology because there are whole passages clearly and evidently devoted to the statement of events adequately represented by this English word. We shall be on much less certain ground if we lay the same kind of emphasis on the etymology of the Hebrew or Greek words for 'create', or on the fact that the Hebrew word is found with only God as subject, or on other associations which may be beside the main point of what the traditionists wished to convey. When Jesus said that he would build his ἐκκλησία upon a certain rock, one agrees that it is hard to know exactly what body was envisaged by the use of this word, but still the purpose of the sentence must be seen in the relation between the ἐκκλησία, whatever it was, and the rock; he did not say that he would build his ἐκκλησία upon the etymology of the word, or upon the associations here and there in the Bible of the corresponding Hebrew word.

Detached note on the non-use of certain words in the Greek Bible

Kittel, *Lexicographia Sacra*, p. 20 and *passim*, and many passages in *TWNT*, are very misleading in the interpretation placed on the absence, or the very infrequent use, of certain Greek words either in the LXX or the NT or both. I refer especially to interpretations which suggest that such words were avoided because they were central or characteristic 'concepts' of Greek religion. I shall illustrate this firstly from ἱερός and associated words. Of this word, which is used in the NT only once except in the phrase τὸ ἱερόν 'the temple', Schrenk says (*TWNT* iii. 229):

'This basic concept was avoided because it is anchored in Greek mythology and reflects the entire world of religion which is connected with the ancient conception of God and of nature, and because it particularly and with painful accuracy brought to mind all that which the Christian had to reject as the service of false gods.' The case of 2 Tim. 3: 15 is then described as the only slight concession made to this Greek way of speaking. A similar account of the non-use of ἱερός is given by Procksch in the article ἅγιος (*TWNT* i. 87–116) and by Kittel himself.

We may begin from LXX usage, for it is here that the avoidance of a term of Greek religion is supposed to have been decisive. The facts themselves are greatly exaggerated by Kittel (loc. cit.) when he says that ἱερός appears only twice in the whole LXX. Presumably he means the books of the Hebrew canon (though even then his statement is not true), for ἱερός is very frequent in the other books, especially in 1 Esdras and Maccabees. We may first look at the fact that τὸ ἱερόν is seldom used for the Jerusalem temple in the LXX. All the writers mentioned follow the suggestion of Flashar in *ZATW* xxxii (1912) 245 (date given wrongly by Procksch *TWNT* i. 95); Flashar interprets this as 'the conscious striving to avoid the customary word for the heathen sanctuaries, i.e. ἱερός'. For the word ἅγιος, however, the word very frequently accepted in the LXX, the same note of Flashar points out the use of τὸ ἅγιον for 'the holy place' in the Ptolemaic inscription Ditt. *Or.* 56: 59; this information, which rather weakens the *TWNT* interpretation, is noted but discounted without reason by Procksch, loc. cit.

It is much more likely that the LXX did not use τὸ ἱερόν in translating Hebrew words for the temple because the words they had were naturally translated otherwise. The common word is *bayit* 'house', which the LXX normally and naturally translated by οἶκος. *Hekal* was a part of the building, or the building generally, and was usually rendered by ναός. The use of this word in the LXX, a word normally associated with heathen sanctuaries also, argues against the assessment of ἱερός by Kittel and his group. Schrenk's argument that ναός could be safely used, unlike τὸ ἱερόν, because 'basically only ἱερόν involves a religious assertion' is very lame (*TWNT* iii. 232). The word *miqdaš* 'sanctuary' was translated by words of the ἅγιος group to fit in with the usual rendering of q-d-š 'holy' by this group. That the LXX was not embarrassed by invincibly pagan associations in ἱερός is shown by its appearance occasionally with reference to the Jerusalem temple or its furniture or other holy objects: Jos. 6: 8; 1 Chr. 9: 27, 29: 4; 2 Chr. 6: 13; Ezek. 45: 19; Dan. 1: 2 LXX, 9: 27 both Theod. and LXX. When we go outside the books of the Hebrew canon we find the use for the temple of τὸ ἱερόν much more frequent, either because they were not translating from Hebrew or because a different technique of translation in this respect was used. More will be said in a moment about the usage in these books. In the NT also the use of τὸ ἱερόν (and ναός) is frequent and unembarrassed. Schrenk's argument that for the NT writers (unlike the LXX translators) the tie to the temple cult had been overcome, so that they had no interest in finding an appropriate word to emphasize the moment of revelation in the cult, and that they therefore found it logical to use the general Greek word (τὸ ἱερόν) for the former cultic centre and to do nothing to lift it out of the heathen religious environment (*TWNT* iii. 234), is a midrashic romance typical of *TWNT*; but some such explanation was perhaps forced upon him by the line he had already taken in explaining the LXX usage.

For the adoption of ἅγιος in general as the usual word for 'holy' it is hard to speak with complete certainty, but the following points would seem relevant. (*a*) "Αγιος in the sense of roughly 'holy' is perfectly well established in classical and Hellenistic times, as Procksch himself shows (*TWNT* i. 87–8) and there is no good reason for the constant play on its 'scarcity' (ib., p. 95; Kittel, loc. cit.; both with the idea that a 'scarce' word was less compromised by connection with Hellenistic religion). In Hellenistic times we should note in particular the use as an epithet of Egyptian and Syrian deities, as shown by Procksch himself (*TWNT* i. 88). (*b*) The translators from Hebrew needed a word which could be used naturally as a divine attribute or epithet, and we have just seen that ἅγιος was frequently so used in the period of the translation, while ἱερός is not much used if at all in this way, as biblical theologians as early as H. Cremer were pointing out — see his *Lexicon*, p. 292, cf. p. 34 ff.; cf. also Schrenk *TWNT* iii. 223. (*c*) Ἱερός had a very wide range of meaning like 'associated with the gods' or 'associated with religion', and as early as classical times we find the more special meaning of 'holy' being given by ἅγιος; for instance, ἱερόν commonly means pretty well the same as our 'temple', and to say 'holy temple' you say ἱερὸν ἅγιον as in Hdt. ii. 41, 44, and cf. Isocr. *Areop.* 29 and Hellenistic inscriptions mentioned by Procksch, loc. cit. Schrenk himself (op. cit., p. 222) points out that ἅγιος suggests an element of consecration and dedication which makes it more suitable for rendering *q-d-š*. In other words, the non-use of ἱερός was because of its semantic non-coincidence with *qadoš*. The rejection of pagan associations is not necessarily, and I think not in fact, important for this linguistic choice; but Schrenk goes on to lay great emphasis on it (e.g. op. cit., p. 226). The difference is surely not between a word with pagan associations and a word only slightly so associated, but between two words with pagan associations, one of which had much greater semantic coincidence with Hebr. *qadoš*. The much greater frequency of ἱερός in comparison with ἅγιος in pagan Greek usage is partly explained by its much wider and more general application in certain respects.

We now return to those books of the LXX in which ἱερός was much more frequently used than in the main body of the Hebrew canon. Here Schrenk says (*TWNT* iii. 226): 'Quite on one side ἱερός found abundant entry into one quite limited circle of Jewish writings which laid itself open without reserve to the Hellenistic spirit. These are 1, 2 and 3 Ezra and 1, 2 and 4 Macc.' He also mentions Josephus and Philo, whom I leave aside for the present.

Now while it is true that ἱερός is notably frequent in these books, many of the cases especially in 1 Esdras and 1 and 2 Macc. are of τὸ ἱερόν 'the temple', a sense which, as I have already argued, was quite neutral, which involved no real concessions to Greek piety, and which was avoided in the other books mainly because there were other words which adequately fitted the Hebrew originals. Further we must notice that these books have by no means abandoned the normal LXX word for 'holy', i.e. ἅγιος, in order to introduce the 'Hellenistic' term ἱερός. The former word in fact appears in 1 Esdras 10 or 11 times; in 1 and 3 Macc. it is more frequent than ἱερός, and in 2 Macc. we have over 20 cases against some thirty-odd of ἱερός. 2 and 3 Esdras, also named by Schrenk, may be neglected, since they have in fact only one case of ἱερός apiece. It is quite clear in fact that when these books had a definite sense of 'holy' in mind they mostly used ἅγιος, e.g. for a holy day (1 Esdr. 9: 50), for the people 'holy to the Lord' (8: 57), for the holy land and the holy place (2 Macc. 1: 7, 12, 29). That they used τὸ ἱερόν in the straightforward sense of 'temple' is clear because like other Greek speakers they said ἱερὸν ἅγιον or the like for 'holy temple'. The only change we have to register is rather more use for such objects as 'sacred garments' (1 Esdr. 8: 70) with ἱερός, but this is already occasionally found in the other books, e.g. Jos. 6: 8 of trumpets. The usage of these books is not materially different from the LXX generally. Only in 4 Macc., where ἅγιος is not used at all, and where the Hellenic atmosphere is notoriously powerful, would I admit Schrenk's picture of the situation to have any validity.

To sum up, then, it must be regarded as most improbable that ἱερός was avoided in the LXX out of hostility to a most characteristic term of Greek piety, and the choice of ἅγιος came about by purely semantic considerations, i.e. through trying to find a Greek word with a suitable spread of meaning to fit the Hebrew words. The treatment of the whole matter has arisen not through some fairly minor miscalculation by the *TWNT* writers, but by a general bias towards finding the Greek-Hebrew theological contrast reflected in any linguistic choice or, conversely, by a prejudgement of how word usage must have been affected by the meeting of Greek and Jewish culture and religion.

Of other cases mentioned by Kittel (ibid.), that 'neither τὸ ἱερόν nor ναός are used for the meeting-place of the Christians' is true but is a different matter, as is his argument about the absence of persons called ἱερεύς in NT Christianity. It is quite incorrect for Kittel (ibid.) to say that 'τέμενος is quite unknown to biblical vocabulary', for there are several cases in the LXX; but no doubt he means that it is not used except of sanctuaries generally (3 Macc. 1: 13) or of heathen sanctuaries in particular. This is true, but it must be thought doubtful if this is because τέμενος is more marked with the stain of pagan worship than (say) ναός, which is repeatedly used for the Jerusalem temple or part of it. I would suppose that certain Greek words came not to be used by the Greek-speaking Jews for their own religious institutions, and any such words were in due course snapped up to meet the need for terms for heathen institutions, especially in abusive contexts. Also τέμενος was unsuitable because it means a sacred area rather than a building, and was something for which the LXX either did not need a word because they did not have the thing so named, or had another word already. The Jerusalem temple court was indeed holy and inviolable, but the LXX were

content to describe it by the neutral term αὐλή 'court', corresponding exactly to the Hebrew. They felt no need for τέμενος as a
name for the court (Philo, however, with his fuller use of Greek
vocabulary, and hardly because he was influenced by Greek
philosophy, used it of the tabernacle court quite naturally, *de vita
Mos.* ii. 89); and they could not use it of the building of the
temple.

I would also regard as very unlikely the suggestions made by
Kittel (op. cit., p. 17 f.) that κῆρυξ is used sparingly in the NT,
while κηρύσσω and κήρυγμα are frequent, because the Greek
herald was a sacrosanct person, while in Christianity no such
sacrosanct persons existed although the κήρυγμα might be said to
be sacrosanct. Few people will suppose that three occurrences of
κῆρυξ in the NT entitle us to talk of reluctance to use the word,
and the midrashic character of the whole discussion of it is obvious.
Concerning this word I must say in passing that I find difficulty
with the arguments of J. J. Vincent (*SJT* x (1957) 267 n.), who
wants to suggest that the *karoz* of Dan. 3:4 is not derived from
Greek κῆρυξ as a loan-word but 'from the Hebrew and Aramaic
verb *k-r-z*'; I can interpret this only as motivated by an anxiety not
to have a Greek origin for a term of importance in the OT. It is
the non-existence of this 'Hebrew and Aramaic verb', or its clear
nature as a denominative from the loan-word *karoz* when it does
appear, that has been the reason for the derivation from Gk.
κῆρυξ. In fact the word is now usually interpreted from the Old
Persian *xrausa 'caller'.

One last example. For Kittel (op. cit., p. 18) 'it is remarkable
that ἄθεος occurs only once in the NT. The most probable
explanation of this is that in the NT we find scarcely any trace at
all of polemic against the pagan gods. The Gospel is not primarily
negative in character . . .' But is it likely that this word would in
any case be used frequently in polemic against those who did not
worship no gods but rather the wrong ones? (After writing the
above, I was pleased to find that Flashar's assessment of the non-
use of τὸ ἱερόν 'the temple' in the LXX had already been rejected
as improbable, on grounds similar to those which I have argued,
by E. Williger in his careful study *Hagios*, pp. 105 n., 107 n.).

Chapter Ten

Languages and the Study of Theology

This study has been devoted to what I believe to be an unsound method of using linguistic evidence in theological thinking. I do not wish to exaggerate the extent to which theologians in general are influenced by this unsound method. What is important is that even where a good use has been made of language and of linguistic evidence the methodological considerations for the use of such evidence have not been made sufficiently clear to prevent misuses arising. It is worth while to inquire how far this can be attributed to the way in which languages are taught and used in the study of theology.

In a Presidential Address to the American Oriental Society in 1935[1] the well-known Orientalist and Indo-Europeanist Roland G. Kent asserted that much of what was written about Semitic linguistics fell far behind Indo-European scholarship in the degree of its scientific accuracy and validity; and he named certain points in particular, such as failure to distinguish between speech and writing, failure to use a strict and consistent terminology, failure to take adequate account of the regularity of sound-changes under given conditions, and haphazard use of comparisons where the phenomena of the languages concerned were not strictly comparable. Later in his address he offered an explanation for this backwardness of Semitic scholarship; it was, he suggested, because most of those who worked on Semitic studies had been trained in the first instance as theologians and had only later and secondarily turned to linguistic scholarship.[2]

I should have thought that Kent was wrong here if he supposed that it was the subject-matter of a previous training in theology that later formed an obstacle to advance in linguistic scholarship. More probably the fault lies in the kind of language study which is commonly included in a theological education. This language study is, if it does not seem too paradoxical, commonly not of a linguistic but of a literary nature. Its design is directed towards the modest but entirely praiseworthy purpose of reading the OT and NT texts in their original language. As in other literary studies, it is quite reasonably thought that the texts can be very much better understood and appreciated when read in the original. The learning of the languages is a necessary stage of preparation towards this end. Such language study is for most people poorly integrated with general linguistics, and takes relatively little systematic account of the matters which Kent has in mind, such as the difference between speech and writing or the regularity of sound-changes. A systematic description of a language is not aimed at, and quite reasonably so, since an excellent reading or speaking knowledge can be, and commonly is, combined with considerable ignorance of a linguistic structure.

Now as long as the purpose is the reading of the Bible in the original languages and the much greater access to the meaning of the text which the knowledge of the original language affords, this kind of language study may be quite adequate. As soon, however, as we meet arguments from the nature of a linguistic structure as such — and to say this is to include all those arguments about the verbal structure of Hebrew thought, the correspondence of linguistic and mental structures in Israel or in Greece, the possibility or impossibility of expressing Hebrew thought in Greek or in any other language, and so on — then the inadequacy of this kind of linguistic study becomes a glaring one. It not only does not furnish answers to such problems, it does not even provide procedures by which they can be systematically approached.

A few points may be added briefly here. Firstly, the argument sometimes made in favour of study of the biblical languages in theology, on the grounds primarily of the understanding of the linguistic (and therefore perhaps the mental) structure thus afforded, ignores the fact that the language study as usually practised, in isolation from systematic and general linguistics, is not in fact designed and adapted for such an end. Secondly, it is of course true that important elements of linguistic structure are brought to notice even in the prevailing 'literary' method of study; but they are noticed really because they are peculiarities which have to be explained in the process of learning, and not because structure is being examined as such. Such procedures naturally set the curiosities and peculiarities of a language like Hebrew in high relief. Thirdly, in the other main biblical language, Greek, there may be fewer elements of structure which are thought to present actual difficulties in the actual acquisition of the language; hence the tendency which we have noted in some arguments to reveal an ignorance or neglect of the actual structure of Greek.

We must conclude emphatically that if the type of thinking about language and theology which has formed the subject of this book is to continue as a centre of attention, it will receive a proper assessment only where the study of the biblical languages is integrated with general linguistics. In other words, it is wrong to suppose that 'knowing Hebrew' or 'knowing more Hebrew' will be the solution for these problems. One or two illustrations may be given:

I have already pointed out how the teaching of Hebrew as it has widely been practised is neither consistently historical nor consistently descriptive. Great inconsistency is commonly used in the handling of the so-called 'root' in that in many cases no 'root' form is extant (strictly the 'root' is quite theoretical) and (sometimes even when the simple forms like the *qal* of the verb exist) the 'basic meaning' of the 'root' is only historically or etymologically related to the semantics of the extant forms; and in that this 'root meaning' is often allowed to be taken as an obvious guide to the semantics of the words, taken synchronously or descriptively. The result of this is often to give to students an impression of the possession by Hebrew of a stock of semantically-charged roots of extraordinary flexibility, spreading the tentacles of an underlying meaning through a whole series of words and concepts. The harm this does is greatly increased by two circumstances: (*a*) that only very sporadic excursions are made into the historical grammar of Hebrew, so that such historical information as is given is quite isolated and wrongly focused, and (b) the impression of something quite extraordinary about Hebrew here is increased by the fact that the student has probably not been given the same amount of etymological information about the 'roots' of English or Greek or any other language he has learned. He has not for example heard it suggested that the roots *men-* 'think, remember' and *men-* 'remain', as found in Latin and Greek *maneo, memini, μιμνῄσκω, μένω* etc., are ultimately identical.[1] Thus the isolation of Hebrew from general linguistics tends to heighten the impression of Hebrew (or at any rate of the Semitic family as a whole) being quite extraordinarily unique in its structure. This defect is made fatally serious in some of the contrasts between Greeks and Israelites in their linguistic and thought structures, as we have already seen, in that most of these comparisons have not made a real investigation of the Greek structure, but have rather assumed it to be some kind of linguistic reflection of Aristotelian logic and of the general European point of view.

The problem, however, goes deeper than this sort of thing, and involves all sorts of questions about the relation of thought and language at the level where philosophy, psychology and linguistics meet. I have already suggested that behind some of the opinions I have reviewed there lies an uncriticized philosophy of language in which thought structures are somehow reflected in linguistic structures, 'dynamic' thinking in a 'dynamic' language and so on — a philosophy which is the heir to age-old superstitions about language but which in its present form is inherited from the idealism of the period just before modern linguistic science took its rise. I have not ventured to suggest an alternative philosophy of language here. My purpose has been to show how the linguistic evidence clashes with certain approaches which have been made.

The further examination of this series of problems requires an approach through general linguistics. The approach which is perhaps more familiar in the theological world, i.e. that through philosophy and logic, takes only incidentally if at all account of differences of languages, of linguistic history, and of the variety of linguistic devices in fact available; and for the linguistic problems

[1] I quote this case from Kronasser, op. cit., p. 189.

it can thus be dangerous. We have seen tendencies to remark as something wonderful the fact that the Hebrew linguistic structure does not coincide with the structure of Aristotelian logic, when in fact the linguistic structure of Greek or of English does not do so either. And we have seen how a central preoccupation with problems of theology and philosophy can misuse linguistic structures by trying to trace out its own problems in them.

And it is mistaken to suppose that the problem can be studied on a basis of the semantics of religious terms alone. The involvement in general semasiology and therefore in the whole realm of general linguistics means that full space has to be given to such matters as phonology, and to a full survey of morphological realities as well as of their functions.[1] A haste to get to grips with the religious or theological problems, even when disguised as a desire to investigate the 'inner meaning' while the rest can be left as 'external', can be fatal here.

On the other hand the difficulties here must not be attributed to the influence of the theological interests too simply, whether in the rather neutral sense intended by Kent or in any other. It cannot be said that semantic problems as such have been in the foreground of non-theological Semitic scholarship; and within the biblical field a great deal of the most valuable work is going into the elucidation of rare words and difficult passages, mostly with the help of material from the cognate languages. Important as it is that the meaning of every word should be known precisely and that the most obscure corners of the biblical tradition should be cleared up, it is idle to suppose that this is the way to answer the kind of problems which have been discussed in this study. In a way the extent of the work that has to be done in primary research into unusual words and the like is a function of the relative youth of modern Semitic philology in comparison with Indo-European philology.

On the other hand, since the mind of the ancient Semitic peoples is a very strongly religious mind, there can be no hope of making progress with these problems through a philology which with-

[1] For a valuable outline of the relations of the various subdivisions of linguistic study, see Ullmann, *The Principles of Semantics*, pp. 31–42, and especially the diagram on p. 39.

draws from making statements about religion on the ground that theology is not its province. The valid and correct analysis and description of religious structures is an essential correlate of linguistic progress in much of the semantic field. It seems to me that here the modern movement towards biblical theology has made it rather harder for the non-theological linguist to make this correlation. It is for theologians here, it seems to me, to make it clear that, whatever their own ideas about biblical theology may be, what they ask from the non-theological linguist is not what the latter would understand as 'theology', but rather a description of religious phenomena. This should be all the easier inasmuch as a very large area of biblical theology is in fact religious description, however much it differentiates itself in theory. It is reasonable for the theologian on the other hand to ask that the non-theological biblical scholar should be prepared to give an account of what a Jeremiah or an Ezra was saying and what, as he sees it, was in his mind. The thought of such men, and this means their religious and theological thought, is a foremost part of the facts of the culture, the linguistic aspect of which it is the task of the linguist to understand.

On the general relations between theology and linguistic study some interesting things have been said by Birkeland,[1] even if not all will agree entirely with his opinions:

(For the danger that Hebrew linguistic material may be misused) 'not only students of theology must be held responsible; the fault is quite as much that of the linguists themselves. They have too often neglected to inform students of theology in an appropriate way of linguistics as a specific science. . . . It cannot be denied that a certain amount of contempt of theology and a tendency towards linguistic self-satisfaction have contributed to the regrettable situation. . . . A successful popularization of linguistic methods specially addressed to theologians will no doubt cause a greater respect among the latter for linguistics as a science distinct from philology, and at least make them cautious in questions of a purely linguistic character.'

[1] 'Semitic and Structural Linguistics', *For Roman Jakobson* (The Hague, 1956), p. 49 ff.

One or two final remarks may now be made. Firstly, about the understanding of linguistics among theologians. I have tried in this book not to do the work of linguists for them, and so have neither tried to give a description of modern linguistic methods nor to argue a case between different schools of linguistics; but I am aware that I have implicitly taken sides in a number of matters where I might more discreetly have avoided a commitment. I have tried to begin as far as possible from linguistic data and linguistic methods which might be expected to be known to theological scholars, and I believe I have shown by examples of the misuse of such data that false assumptions about language are widely current in certain theological circles. I shall not be sorry if the criticism of linguists forces me to modify some of the things I have said; and it is because it is the criticism *of linguists* that I shall value it, because it will mean a bringing to bear of more valid linguistic method in the theological realm.[1]

In particular I have criticized what seems to me to be a distorted and erroneous view of the relation between thought and language. I am aware however that the Humboldtian heritage of belief that a language contains an implicit metaphysics is still alive today, and that a significant school of linguists is maintaining that 'language is the intermediary world (*Zwischenwelt*) between subject and object'.[2]

I shall not argue these matters here, though I do not conceal my sympathy for the position of a linguist like Greenberg in his approach to the matter as a whole and in particular in his statement[3] that 'to make the proposition true that a language contains

[1] It has, for example, in my opinion been a great misfortune that a work like *TWNT* has, as far as I have been able to discover, been very little reviewed by general linguists other than theological scholars.

[2] H. Basilius, 'Neo-Humboldtian Ethnolinguistics', *Word* viii (1952) 99; this article will offer a good introduction to the movement to which I refer. Also B. L. Whorf, *Language, Thought and Reality*, and the valuable discussion from the philosophical side by Max Black, *PR* lxviii (1959) 228–38; also the interesting symposium in *Language and Culture*, ed. H. Hoijer. For an earlier stage cf. L. Weisgerber, *Muttersprache und Geistesbildung*. I sometimes wonder whether there is any kinship between Weisgerber's understanding of language, and especially his division of the 'word' into two elements, the 'name' and the 'concept', and the use of 'concept' in a work like *TWNT*. For Weisgerber's early statement of this view, see *GRM* xv (1927) 161–83.

[3] In Hoijer, op. cit., p. 134, and more generally pp. 1–19, 127–47, and *passim*.

an implicit metaphysics, one would have to use either the word "language" or the word "metaphysics" in an unusual sense'. I wish only to point out that, even should there be some sense in which it is linguistically true that there is some kind of 'metaphysics' implicit in a language as the 'Sapir-Whorf Hypothesis' supposes, there will still be good reason for theologians to hesitate before assuming that the 'implicit metaphysics' of the Hebrew language, and of the Greek New Testament as influenced by it, are symmorphous with the structure of Jewish-Christian theology.

Similarly, even if it should come to be agreed that linguistic study has been weakened by formalism, or that the use of structural methods has been accompanied by lack of attention to 'meaning',[1] it must be remembered that in theological study the concept of structural linguistics and of language systems has hardly yet come to be known, and their values have hardly been recognized, much less exhausted; so that too ready an acceptance of 'neo-Humboldtian' conceptions would mean in theology not a recovery from structuralist formalism but an increase of the present undisciplined confusion, which I have illustrated for certain theological circles. Too many theological minds are moulded in their appreciation of language by the three following elements: the simple and semi-scientific way of 'learning Hebrew' (or Greek), designed for the limited aim of reading the biblical texts, and perhaps achieving this aim reasonably well, but giving no understanding of the quite different methods required for an approach to many questions; the interest in etymology, coupled with a neglect of other aspects of historical linguistics and hence a failure to realize the strictly historical nature of etymological study; and the notion of the reflection of Hebrew thought in Hebrew language. The interpretative procedures which I have criticized are the nemesis of such an approach to language.

Nevertheless it is true beyond doubt that there is a solid body of careful biblical scholarship in theology which has never been deceived by the kind of argument from linguistic evidence which we have studied. The rather traditional kind of biblical philology has not, however, generally been able to show good reasons why

---

[1] Cf. the opinions of S. Ullmann, op. cit., pp. 317-21.

such interpretations must be wrong. Nor has it been able to give a good and sufficient answer to the arguments advanced from the nature of the Hebrew mind; and when in the New Testament sphere it has appealed to contemporary Greek usage it has appeared to the enthusiast for the Hebrew background to be 'Hellenizing' in tendency; the appeal to Greek usage has been thought to exclude an understanding of the Hebrew background, and the absence of this latter understanding has been thought a fatal objection to an interpretation offered. Nor has the more traditional biblical philology been able to provide arguments which were an adequate compensating force against the theological attraction, for certain schools of theology at any rate, of the methods and 'results' which we have studied.

The reason for this lies largely in the rather traditional and old-fashioned 'philology', designed for the interpretation of ancient written texts and performing great and accurate services here, but working somewhat atomistically and in particular neglecting the study of a language system or structure in general, and most important for us, neglecting to approach the problems of semantics in general and in integration with the work of general linguistics. Only by a direct and systematic approach to the significative function of language in general can false theological methods of interpretation be adequately resisted. This book has developed a few examples where such methods are criticized. It is probable that a greater awareness of general semantics, of general linguistic method in all its aspects, and an application of such awareness in biblical interpretation, would have valuable and important results for theology.

Abbreviations

AO	*Archiv Orientálni.*
BAss	*Beiträge zur Assyriologie.*
BDB	F. Brown, S. R. Driver and C. A. Briggs, *Hebrew and English Lexicon of the Old Testament* (Oxford, 1907).
BKW	*Bible Key Words* (English translations of articles from *TWNT*, quoted with the English title of the article).
BL	H. Bauer and P. Leander, *Historische Grammatik der hebräischen Sprache des alten Testaments* (Halle, 1922).
BWANT	*Beiträge zur Wissenschaft vom alten und neuen Testament.*
BZATW	*Beihefte zur Zeitschrift für die alttestamentliche Wissenschaft.*
CJT	*Canadian Journal of Theology.*
ET	*Expository Times.*
GB	Gesenius, *Hebräisches und aramäisches Handwörterbuch über das alte Testament* (17th ed. by F. Buhl, Leipzig, 1921).
GK	*Gesenius' Hebrew Grammar* (ed. E. Kautzsch, 2nd English ed. by A. E. Cowley, Oxford, 1910).
GRM	*Germanische-romanische Monatschrift.*
GThT	*Gereformeerde Theologische Tijdschrift.*
IJAL	*International Journal of American Linguistics.*
IZAS	*Internationale Zeitschrift für allgemeine Sprachwissenschaft.*
JAOS	*Journal of the American Oriental Society.*
JBL	*Journal of Biblical Literature.*
JBR	*Journal of Bible and Religion.*
JJS	*Journal of Jewish Studies.*
JTS	*Journal of Theological Studies.*
KB	L. Koehler and W. Baumgartner, *Lexicon in veteris testamenti libros* (Leiden, 1953).
KD	Karl Barth, *Kirchliche Dogmatik* (Zollikon, from 1932); E.T., *Church Dogmatics* (Edinburgh, from 1936).
KZ	*Zeitschrift für vergleichende Sprachforschung.*
LS	H. G. Liddell and R. Scott, *Greek-English Lexicon* (revised ed. by H. S. Jones and R. McKenzie, Oxford, 1940).
MSL	*Mémoires de la société de linguistique de Paris.*

NTT	*Norsk Teologisk Tidskrift.*
OED	*Shorter Oxford English Dictionary.*
PBB	*Beiträge zur Geschichte der deutschen Sprache und Literatur.*
PR	*Philosophical Review.*
PW	Pauly-Wissowa, *Realencyklopädie der classischen Altertumswissenschaft.*
*RGG*³	*Religion in Geschichte und Gegenwart* (3rd ed., Tübingen, from 1957).
SEA	*Svensk Exegetisk Årsbok.*
SJT	*Scottish Journal of Theology.*
ThLZ	*Theologische Literaturzeitung.*
ThZ	*Theologische Zeitschrift.*
TWNT	G. Kittel (ed.), *Theologisches Wörterbuch zum neuen Testament* (Stuttgart, from 1933). References are either by volume and page or by the name of the article.
VChr	*Vigiliae Christianae.*
VT	*Vetus Testamentum.*
WZKM	*Wiener Zeitschrift für die Kunde des Morgenlandes.*
ZATW	*Zeitschrift für die alttestamentliche Wissenschaft.*
ZDMG	*Zeitschrift der deutschen morgenländischen Gesellschaft.*
ZfDA	*Zeitschrift für deutsches Altertum.*
ZfPh	*Zeitschrift für Phonetik.*

Bibliography

This bibliography does not include all works mentioned in the text or footnotes, but only those of more direct importance for the principal line of argument.

W. F. Arndt and F. W. Gingrich, *A Greek-English Lexicon of the New Testament and other early Christian Literature* (translated and adapted from the German of W. Bauer, Cambridge, 1957).

H. Basilius, 'Neo-Humboldtian Ethnolinguistics', *Word* viii (1952) 95–105.

A. H. Basson and D. J. O'Connor, 'Language and Philosophy — some suggestions for an empirical approach', *Philosophy* xxii (1947) 49–65.

H. Bauer, 'Die Tempora im Semitischen', *BAss* viii (1910) 1–53.

G. Bergsträsser, *Hebräische Grammatik* (Leipzig, 1918–29, 2 vols.).
    Einführung in die semitischen Sprachen (Munich, 1928).

G. Bertram, 'Das Problem der Umschrift und die religionsgeschichtliche Erforschung der Septuaginta', *BZATW* lxvi (1936), *Werden und Wesen des alten Testaments*, pp. 97–109.

H. Birkeland, 'Semitic and Structural Linguistics', *For Roman Jakobson* (The Hague, 1956), pp. 44–51.

Max Black, 'Linguistic Relativity: the Views of Benjamin Lee Whorf', *PR* lxviii (1959) 228–38.

F. Blass, *Grammatik des neutestamentlichen Griechisch* (10th ed., revised by A. Debrunner, Göttingen, 1959).

L. Bloomfield, *Language* (London, 1935).

T. Boman, 'Den semitiske tenknings egenart', *NTT* xxxiv (1933) 1–34.
    Das hebräische Denken im Vergleich mit dem griechischen (2nd ed., Göttingen, 1954); E.T., *Hebrew Thought compared with Greek* (London, 1960).

W. Brandenstein, 'Ueber die Annahme einer Parallelität zwischen Denken und Sprechen', *GRM* xii (1924) 321–7.

G. Brockelmann, *Grundriss der vergleichenden Grammatik der semitischen Sprachen* (Berlin, 1908–13, 2 vols.).
    Lexicon Syriacum (2nd ed., Halle, 1928).
    Hebräische Syntax (Neukirchen, 1956).

K. Brugmann, 'Das Nominalgeschlecht in den indogermanischen Sprachen', *IZAS* iv (1889) 100–9.

K. Brugmann and B. Delbrück, *Grundriss der vergleichenden Grammatik der indogermanischen Sprachen* (2nd ed., Strassburg, from 1897).

R. Bultmann, 'The Problem of Hermeneutics', in *Essays* (London, 1955), pp. 234–61.

Church of Scotland, Special Commission on Baptism, *Interim Report* (Edinburgh, 1955).

H. Cremer, *Biblisch-theologisches Wörterbuch der neutestamentlichen Gräzität* (9th ed., Gotha, 1902; 10th ed., revised by J. Kögel, Gotha, 1911–15); E.T., *Biblico-theological Lexicon of New Testament Greek* (3rd ed., Edinburgh, 1886).

K. J. Cremer, 'Oudtestamentische Semasiologie', *GThT* xlviii (1948) 193–209; xlix (1949) 1–15, 79–99.
'Semasiologie en haar betekenis voor de oudtestamentische Exegese', *Vox Theologica* xx (1949–50) 100–10.

M. Cohen, *Le Système verbal sémitique et l'expression du temps* (Paris, 1924).
Essai comparatif sur le vocabulaire et la phonétique du chamito-sémitique (Paris, 1947).

A. B. Davidson, *Hebrew Syntax* (2nd ed., Edinburgh, 1896).
An Introductory Hebrew Grammar (24th ed., revised by J. E. McFadyen, Edinburgh, 1932).

A. Deimel, *Šumerisches Lexikon* (Rome, 1925–50).

A. Deissmann, *Bible Studies* (2nd ed., Edinburgh, 1909).
Light from the Ancient East (2nd ed., London, 1927).

A. Dillmann, *Lexicon Linguae Aethiopicae* (Leipzig, 1865).

C. H. Dodd, *The Bible and the Greeks* (London, 1935).

J. C. C. van Dorssen, *De Derivata van de Stam ʾ-m-n in het Hebreeuwsch van het oude Testament* (Amsterdam, 1951).

G. R. Driver, *Problems of the Hebrew Verbal System* (Edinburgh, 1936).
'Gender in Hebrew Numerals', *JJS* i (1948–9) 90–104.

R. C. Duncan, *The Contribution of Hermann Cremer (1834-1903) to Theological Hermeneutics* (Edinburgh University, 1958; unpublished).

G. Ebeling, 'The Meaning of "Biblical Theology" ', *JTS NS* vi (1955) 210–25.
'Hermeneutik', *RGG³*.

W. Eichrodt, *Theologie des alten Testaments* (5th ed., Stuttgart, 1957).

A. Erman and H. Grapow, *Wörterbuch der ägyptischen Sprache* (Leipzig, 1926–31, 5 vols.).

F. Field, *Origenis hexaplorum quae supersunt* (Oxford, 1875, 2 vols.).

J. R. Firth, 'Linguistic Analysis and Translation', *For Roman Jakobson* (The Hague, 1956), pp. 133–9.

M. Flashar, 'Exegetische Studien zum Septuagintapsalter', *ZATW* xxxii (1912) 81–116, 161–89, 241–68.

G. Friedrich, 'Die Problematik eines theologischen Wörterbuchs zum neuen Testament', *Studia Evangelica* (ed. Aland, Berlin, 1959).

G. Gerleman, *Studies in the Septuagint*: i. *Job* (Lund, 1946); iii. *Proverbs* (Lund, 1956).

   'Struktur und Eigenart der hebräischen Sprache', *SEA* xxii–xxiii (1957–8) 252–64.

I. Guidi, *Vocabolario Amarico-Italiano* (Rome, 1953).

G. Guillaume, *Temps et verbe* (Paris, 1929).

L. Gulkowitsch, *Die Bildung von Abstraktbegriffen in der hebräischen Sprachgeschichte* (Leipzig, 1931).

E. Hatch and H. A. Redpath, *A Concordance to the Septuagint* (Oxford, 1897).

A. G. Hebert, '"Faithfulness" and "Faith" ', *Theology* lviii (1955) 373–9.

J. G. Herder, *The Spirit of Hebrew Poetry* (translated by James Marsh, Burlington, 1833, 2 vols.).

H. Hoijer (ed.), *Language in Culture* (*The American Anthropologist* lvi, no. 6, part 2, Memoir no. 79, Chicago, 1954).

E. Hoskyns and F. N. Davey, *The Riddle of the New Testament* (3rd ed., London, 1947).

W. von Humboldt, *Sprachphilosophische Werke* (ed. Steinthal, Berlin, 1884).

E. Jacob, *Theology of the Old Testament* (London, 1958).

M. Jastrow, *A Dictionary of the Targumim, the Talmud Babli and Yerushalmi, and the Midrashic literature* (London, 1903).

O. Jespersen, *Language. Its Nature, Development and Origin* (London, 1922).

   The Philosophy of Grammar (London, 1924).

G. Kittel, *Lexicographia Sacra* (*Theology* Occasional Papers, no. 7, London, 1938); German version in *Deutsche Theologie* v (1938) 91–109.

G. A. F. Knight, *A Biblical Approach to the Doctrine of the Trinity* (Edinburgh, 1953).

G. Koschmieder, *Zeitbezug und Sprache* (*Wissenschaftliche Grundfragen* xi, Leipzig, 1929).

J. D. W. Kritzinger, *Qᵉhal Jahwe: wat dit is en wie daaraan mag behoort* (Kampen, 1957).

H. Kronasser, *Handbuch der Semasiologie* (Heidelberg, 1952).

E. W. Lane, *Arabic-English Lexicon* (London, 1863–77, 8 vols.).

W. Leslau, *Lexique Soqoṭri* (Paris, 1938).

G. Lindeskog, 'Ett teologisk standardverk', *SEA* i (1936) 126–34.

E. Löfstedt, *Late Latin* (Oslo, 1959).

J. Macmurray, *The Clue to History* (London, 1938).

J. D. A. Macnicol, 'Word and Deed in the New Testament', *SJT* v (1952) 240.

B. M. Metzger, 'The Language of the New Testament', in *The Inter-preter's Bible* (Nashville and New York, 1952–7, 12 vols.) vii. 43–59.

C. Mohrmann, 'Le latin commun et le latin des chrétiens', *VChr* i (1947) 1–12.

    'Quelques Traits caractéristiques du latin des chrétiens', *Studi e Testi* cxxi (1946) 437–66.

    'Linguistic Problems in the Early Christian Church', *VChr* xi (1957) 11–36.

C. F. D. Moule, *An Idiom Book of New Testament Greek* (Cambridge, 1953).

W. Munzinger, *Vocabulaire de la langue Tigré* (1863; published as an appendix to Dillmann's *Lexicon*).

W. Muss-Arnolt, *Concise Dictionary of the Assyrian Language* (Berlin, 1905, 2 vols.).

C. von Orelli, *Die hebräischen Synonyma der Zeit und Ewigkeit* (Leipzig, 1871).

J. L. Palache, 'Over Beteekenisverandering der Woorden in het hebreeuwsch (semietisch) en andere Talen', in *Sinai en Paran* (Leiden, 1959), pp. 101–32.

J. Pedersen, *Israel. Its Life and Culture* (London, 1926, 2 vols.).

    Hebraeisk Grammatik (Copenhagen, 1926).

E. Pfeiffer, 'Glaube im alten Testament', *ZATW* lxxi (1959) 151–64.

J. Pokorny, *Indogermanisches Etymologisches Wörterbuch* (Bern, 1948–1959).

C. H. Ratschow, *Werden und Wirken. Eine Untersuchung des Wortes hajah als Beitrag zur Wirklichkeitserfassung des alten Testaments* (*BZATW* lxx (1941)).

J. A. T. Robinson, *The Body. A Study in Pauline Theology* (London, 1952).

H. B. Rosen, 'Aspektim u-zmanim ba-ivrit ha-mikrait', *Sefer Biram* (Jerusalem, 1956), pp. 205–18.

K. C. Rossini, *Chrestomathia arabica meridionalis epigraphica* (Rome, 1931).

L. Rost, *Die Vorstufen von Kirche und Synagoge im alten Testament: eine wortgeschichtliche Untersuchung* (*BWANT*, 4te Folge, Heft 24, Stuttgart, 1938).

F. Rundgren, *Ueber Bildungen mit Š- und n-t- Demonstrativen im Semitischen* (Uppsala, 1955).

M. Sandmann, *Subject and Predicate* (Edinburgh, 1954).

F. de Saussure, *Cours de linguistique générale* (Paris, 1955).

F. Schleiermacher, *Hermeneutik und Kritik mit besonderer Beziehung auf das neue Testament* (ed. F. Lücke, Berlin, 1838).

W. Schneemelcher (ed.), *Das Problem der Sprache in Theologie und Kirche* (Berlin, 1959).

F. Schulthess, *Lexicon Syropalaestinum* (Berlin, 1903).

C. Serrus, *Le Parallélisme logico-grammatical* (Paris, 1933).

N. H. Snaith, *The Distinctive Ideas of the Old Testament* (London, 1944).

'The Language of the Old Testament', in *The Interpreter's Bible* (Nashville and New York, 1952–7, 12 vols.) i. 220–32.

L. Spitzer, *Essays in Historical Semantics* (New York, 1948).

J. Stenzel, 'Ueber den Einfluss der griechischen Sprache auf die philosophische Begriffsbildung', in *Neue Jahrbücher für das klassische Altertum* xlvii (1921) 152–64; also in his *Kleine Schriften* (Darmstadt, 1957), pp. 72–84.

E. Struck, *Bedeutungslehre. Grundzüge einer lateinischen und griechischen Semasiologie* (Stuttgart, 1954).

H. St J. Thackeray and R. Marcus, *A Lexicon to Josephus* (Paris, from 1930).

T. F. Torrance, *Royal Priesthood* (Edinburgh, 1955).

'Israel and the Incarnation', *Judaica* xiii (1957) 1–18, also in *Interpretation* x (1956) 305–20.

'One Aspect of the Biblical Conception of Faith', *ET* lxviii (1956–7) 111–14.

Conflict and Agreement in the Church (London, 1959–60, 2 vols.; includes the last two items).

C. Tresmontant, *Études de métaphysique biblique* (Paris, 1955).

E. Ullendorff, 'What is a Semitic Language?' *Orientalia* xxvii (1958) 66–75.

S. Ullmann, *The Principles of Semantics* (2nd ed., Oxford, 1957).

W. C. van Unnik, 'Reisepläne und Amen-sagen', in *Studia Paulina* (de Zwaan Festschrift) (Haarlem, 1953), pp. 215–34.

L. Weisgerber, 'Die Bedeutungslehre — ein Irrweg der Sprachwissenschaft?', *GRM* xv (1927) 161–83.

Muttersprache und Geistesbildung (Göttingen, 1929).

Vom Weltbild der deutschen Sprache (Düsseldorf, 1950).

B. L. Whorf, *Four Articles on Metalinguistics* (Washington, 1952).

Language, Thought and Reality (ed. J. B. Carroll, New York, 1956).

E. Williger, *Hagios* (*Religionsgeschichtliche Versuche und Vorarbeiten*, vol. 19, Giessen, 1922).

Index of Hebrew Words

ʾadam, 105, 144 ff.
ʾᵃdamah, 144 n.
ʾaheb, 84 n.
ʾahar, ʾahᵃrit, ʾehar, 76 f.
ʾayin, ʾen, 56–63.
ʾᵉlohim, 23 n.
ʾamen, 168, 179.
ʾimmen, 167.
ʾᵉmunah, 103, 130, 162–6, 169, 181, 188–200.
ʾᵉmet, 103, 130, 187–200, 251 f.
ʾᵉnoš, 144 ff.
ʾap, 118, 147 n., 148.
ʾašre, 116.

bataḥ, 180 f.
baśar, 35, 37 n., 159 n.
bᵉśorah, 159 n.
bᵉrakah, 94.

geber, 144 ff.
galah, 230.

dabar, 129–40, 217 f.
dᵉbir, 130, 136 f., 139.

heʾᵉmin, 103, 163–5, 173, 175–87.
hod, 200.
hodah, todah, 200.
hayah, 59, 64, 68–72.
hay-yaśar, 32.
hekal, 283.
hipgiaᶜ, 183 f.
hiṣdiq, 178, 182.
haškem, 77.

zebaḥ, 155.
zaqen, 54 ff.

hataʾ, 118.
hemah, 148.

ṭob, 105.

yad, 39.

yeš, 59–63.
yašab, 51, 53.

kihen, 15.
kol, 99.
ken, 170.
kᵉneset, 129.

leḥem, 102.

moʾab, 105.
mahaneh, 95.
milhamah, 102.
melek, 93, 105.
min, 76, 97, 104 f.
minhah, 155.
miqdaš, 283.
mᵉrubbaᶜ, 99.

neʾᵉman, 173 f., 179.
niham, 116 f., 233, 252, 265

ᶜebed, 103, 254.
ᶜᵃbodah, 103.
ᶜedah, 119–29.
ᶜolah, 151.
ᶜamad, 53.

qedem, 77.
qadoš, 283 ff.
qahal, 119–29, 138 ff., 253
qaṭal (perfect), 82.
qaṭon, 54, 56, 97.
qol, 119–22, 126 f.

rab, 97.
rabuaᶜ, 99 f.
ruaḥ, 39, 118.
rekeb, 105 f.

šᵉnayim, 97.
šum dabar, 138.

tabnit, 152–5.

Index of Greek Words

'Αγαθός, 32, 219 f.
ἀγαπάω, ἀγάπη, 211, 216 f.
ἅγιος, ἡγιασμένος, 111, 235 f., 282–6.
ἁγνός, 235 f.
ἄθεος, 287.
αἵρεσις, 226 ff.
ἀλήθεια, ἀληθινός, ἀληθῶς, 130, 187–200,
  221, 249, 251 f., 277 n.
ἀλλάσσω (δι-, ἀπ-, κατ-), 237 n.
ἁμαρτάνω, ἁμαρτία, 118, 217, 229.
ἀμήν, 168.
ἀνάγκη, ἀναγκάζω, 223 f.
ἀνακεφαλαιόομαι, 237.
ἀποκαλύπτω, -ψις, 230, 256.
ἀπόστολος, 249.
αὐλή, 287.

βάπτισμα, -μός, 140–4, 249.
βέβαιος, -ότης, -οῦν, -ωσις, 166–70.

γένοιτο, 168.
γινώσκω, 254.

δημιουργός, 224 f.
διά, 213 n., 231 n.
διακονεῖν, 210.
δικαιοσύνη, 188, 191, 193 f.
δόγμα, 229 n.

ἐγώ, 231.
ἔθνος, 124 n., 235.
εἶδος, 152 f., 156.
εἴδωλον, 156.
εἰμί, 59 n., 68, 240 n.
εἰρήνη, 213 n., 214 n., 275 n.
εἰς, 231.
εἷς, 231.
ἐκκλησία, 119–29, 218, 226 ff., 253, 282.
ἐν, 213 n., 231.
ἐντυγχάνω, 184.
ἐξομολόγησις, 200.
ἔρως, 215, 217.
ἔτυμον, 114.
εὐαγγέλιον, 159 n.

ζωή, 255.

θεός, 151, 266.
θεοσέβεια, 255 f.
θεράπων, 254.
θρησκεία, 255 f.
θυσία, 152 n., 155 f.

ἱερεύς, 286.
ἱερός, 111, 235, 282–7.

καινός, 213 n., 230 n., 234.
καιρός, 225 f.
κεφάλαιον, 237.
κήρυγμα, 84, 140, 143 f., 213 n., 287.
κῆρυξ, 213 n., 287.
κηρύσσω, 207 f., 212, 287.
κρύπτω, 38.
κτίζω, 224 f.

λαός, 124 n., 126 n., 149, 234 f.
λατρεία, -εύω, 103.
λέγω, 207 f., 212, 236.
λειτουργία, 149 ff.
λόγος, 49 n., 130, 134, 138 n., 207,
  220 ff., 236 f., 249.

μάταιος, 38, 210.
μένω, 291.
μεταμέλομαι, 236 f.
μετανοέω, -νοια, 230 n., 236 f., 253, 255.
μιμνήσκω, 291.
μῦθος, 220 ff., 229.

ναί, 170.
ναός, 283, 286.
νέος, 230 n.
νοῦς, 235.
νῦν, 231.

οἶδα, 24, 254.
οἰκοδεσπότης, 92.
οἶκος, 283.
ὅπλον, 235 n.
ὁράω, 235 n.
ὀργή, 147.
ὅσιος, 111

παῖς θεοῦ, 234.
παράδειγμα, 152 ff.
παρακαλέω, 232, 236.
παραμυθέομαι, 232, 236.
πιστεύειν, 172–5, 201 n.
πίστις, 130, 166, 169, 172–5, 188, 191–4, 198–203, 221 f., 252, 255 f.
πιστός, 166, 172–4.
πνεῦμα, 39.
προάγω, 275 n.
πρός, 231.

ῥῆμα, 130, 137–8.
ῥητός, 137–8.

σάρξ, 35, 37, 159 n.

σπλαγχνίζομαι, 156 f.
στηρίζω, 166–70.
συναγωγή, 119, 121, 127 ff., 253.
σῶμα, 35, 37.

τέμενος, 286 f.
τύπος, 154 f.

ὑγιής, -αίνειν, 111.
ὑπόδειγμα, 152–4.

χάρις, 264 n.
χρηματιστήριον, 136.

ὤν, ὁ, 253.

Index of Persons and Subjects

Abstract nouns, 15 f., 28 ff., 44 f., 84 n., 90 n., 96 f., 183.

Abstract thought, 11 f., 15 f., 27–33, 44 f., 72, 84 n., 96, 105, 164, 180, 187 f., 190, 198, 216, 224, 251.

Accadian, 31, 43, 58, 60, 82, 118, 158, 186.

Action, linguistic representation of, 46–88; by nouns, 82 ff., 104.

Activity, 'Inner', 55, 71, 87.

Adjective, Hebrew, 16, 28 f., 56, 89.

Aeschylus, 110, 223.

Ahiqar, Words of, 202.

Aktionsart, 52.

Amharic, see Ethiopic.

Anger, 147 ff.

Aquila, 110 n., 136, 152, 168 f., 192, 200 n.

Arabic, 34, 75, 91, 116, 126, 133, 158, 185.

Aramaic and Syriac, 82, 126, 128, 133, 152, 167 f., 170, 186, 202, 240 n., 287.

Aristotle, 32, 36, 37 n., 65 f., 67 n., 72, 86, 149 f., 223, 243, 291 f.

Armenian, 98.

Arndt, W. F., and Gingrich, F. W., 206, 250 n.

Ascension of Christ, 151 f.

Aspect, see Tense.

Association, Argument by, 103, 148, 155, 257, 281 f.

Baetke, W., 112 n.

Baptism, 140–4.

Baptism, Church of Scotland Report on, 6 n., 141, 262 n., 279 n.

Barth, K., 57, 156 f., 210, 226, 275 n., 276 ff.

Basilius, H., 50 n., 294 n.

Basson, A. H., and O'Connor, D. J., 26 f., 31, 33, 58 ff., 99.

Bauer, H. (including Leander, P.), 21, 40 ff., 49 n., 60 n., 67, 82, 91 n., 95, 97 n., 126, 178, 183 n.

Bauer, W., 206, 214, 244, 250, 254–257.

Bauernfeind, O., 38.

'Be', The Verb, 13, 16, 26 f., 46, 58–72, 240 n.

Behm, J., 235, 237.

Bergsträsser, G., 21 f., 49 n., 60 n., 67, 91 n., 178, 183, 279 n.

Bertram, G., 252.

Bible, Distinctiveness of, 269 ff., 274, 278; as sacred canon, 266 ff.; inspiration and authority of, 260, 271, 280.

Bible-mysticism, 231, 260.

'Biblical Greek', 239 ff., 260.

Biblical theology, in general, 5 f., 209, 263–82, 293; various senses of, 273 ff.; emphasis on Greek-Hebrew thought contrast in, 5 f., 8 f., 35, 46 f., 137, 139 f., 199, 216, 224, 251 f., 278 f.; aversion from Greek thought and usage, 9 f., 35, 106, 117, 216, 224, 251 f., 278 f., 282–7; linguistic methods and assumptions of, 20, 24, 26 f., 33, 35, 37 f., 46 f., 49, 58, 61, 67, 106, 117, 137 n., 147 f., 155, 178, 184, 195, 198 f., 209, 216, 218, 226, 232, 251 f., 255, 260 f., 263–72, 274 f., 278–87; etymology and, 117, 159, 198 f., 232, 275; lexical procedures in, 5, 260 f., 263 f., 270 f., 278; Boman and, 22 n., 46 f., 106, 279; Schleiermacher and, 258 ff.; religious description and, 292; synthetic methods of, 149, 155, 184, 218, 270, 273 ff., 279 f.; and biblical translation, 264–9; and communication, 280 f.; and LXX, 252 f., 264, 266 ff., 282–7.

Birkeland, H., 83 n., 293.

Black, M., 294 n.

Blackman, E. C., 197.

Blass, F., and Debrunner, A., 141 n., 142 n.

Bloomfield, L., 29, 30, 101, 112 n.

'Blue', the colour, 148 n.
Boman, T., 17, 21 f. 26 n., 33, 39, 46–79, 83 n., 87 f., 96–100, 104 ff., 148 n., 178, 184, 237 n., 279.
Bonfante, G., 32.
Botterweck, G. J., 127 n.
Brandenstein, W., 43 n.
Brockelmann, C., 21, 40 n., 49 n., 56 n., 58 n., 60 n., 82 n., 91 n., 97 n., 126 n., 186 n.
Brown, F., Driver, S. R., and Briggs, C. A., dictionary of, 60, 62, 120 n., 138, 172.
Brugmann, K., and Delbrück, B., 40 n., 97 n.
Bühler, K., 33 n., 49 n.
Bultmann, R., 46 n., 192 n., 198 n., 202 n., 259 n., 275 n., 277 f.
Burrow, T., 40 n.
Burrows, M., 202 n.

Caird, G. B., 226 n.
Campbell, J. Y., 129 n.
Casares, J., 108.
Cassirer, E., 49 n., 97, 99.
Causative, see Hiph'il.
China, Jesuit mission in, 269.
Christianity, 'Language-moulding power' of, 213 f., 238 ff., 242, 246 ff., 257, 260, 264; 'creative vitality' of, 247 f.
Christology, 150, 208, 241, 242 n., 259, 275 n.
'Church', 114, 119–29, 218, 226 ff.
Cleasby, R., and Vigfusson, G., 112 n.
Cohen, M., 58 n., 70 n., 127, 136 n.
Collective nouns, 96 f., 105 f.
'Comfort', 232 f., 265.
Compound words in Indo-European, 92.
'Concept', Use of for words, 38, 71, 168, 226 ff., 230, 242 ff., 254; different senses of in TWNT, 210 f.; pejorative sense of, 211, 216, 242 f.; 'formal concept', 179 ff.; 'concept-history', 207, 209, 211.
Concreteness in vocabulary, 30 f.
'Consecutive' tenses in Hebrew, 83 n.
Construct state, 29, 39, 76, 89–96, 148, 265, 276.
Copula, 55 f., 58, 60, 63 f., 82, 85, 265.
Corinth, 251.

Covenant, 119 f., 123, 125, 128, 148 f., 173 f., 182, 187 f., 190 f., 281.
Cowley, A., 202 n.
Creation, 57, 224 f., 281 f.
Cremer, H., 44, 206, 210, 213 f., 238–244, 259 ff., 271 n., 284.
Cremer, K. J., 114 f.
Culture, cultural conflict, 4, 8, 268 f., 272.
Cushitic, 127, 136.

Davey, F. N., 125, 195 ff.
Davidson, A. B., 66, 92 ff., 101 n.
Dead Sea Scrolls, see Qumran.
Definite article, 26 f., 31 ff., 90 f., 122–125.
Deimel, A., 186 n.
Deissmann, A., 213 f., 239–42, 244, 246 ff., 252 n., 267, 271 n.
Delling, G., 226.
Denominative verbs, 15, 76, 120, 179, 237.
Dentan, R. C., 274 n.
Diem, H., 84 n., 229 n.
Dillmann, A., 185.
Dilthey, W., 258, 259 n.
Dodd, C. H., 161 n., 165 n., 170 n., 173 n., 198, 220 n., 226, 229, 238, 240 n., 275 n.
'Dogma', 229 n.
Dogmatics, 147, 210, 247, 257, 259 f., 271, 273, 275, 278, 280 n.
Dorssen, J. C. C. van, 173 n., 185 n., 187 n.
Driver, G. R., 82, 97, 158 n., 187 n., 199.
Duncan, R. C., 238 n., 259 n., 260, 271 n.
Dynamic thought, 10 f., 14 f., 21, 27, 46 f., 50–57, 60 f., 63, 69 ff., 82–88, 97–99, 130 ff., 188, 272 n., 291.

Ebeling, G., 6 n., 275 n.
Egyptian, 53, 186.
Eichrodt, W., 273 f.
Erman, A., and Grapow, H., 53 n., 186 n.
Eschatology, 120, 123, 128, 219 f., 257, 275 n., 281.
Esdras, Greek books of, 283, 285.
Ethiopic (and other South Semitic, except Arabic), 118, 185 f., 240 n.

Ethno-psychology, 22, 24, 42, 96 n., 133, 272.
Etymology, nature and values of in general, 107–110, 158 ff., 290 f., 295; popular, 109 f., 121, 136 f., 144 n., 150, 152, 170; etymologizing interpretation, cases of, 73, 76, 98, 100, 103, 110 n., 111–57, 163, 165, 168, 179, 187, 198 ff., 210, 213, 219 f., 229, 232, 236 ff., 275, 281 f., 290 f., 295.
Evolutionism, 270.
Exhortation, 232.
Existence, mere, 58 ff., 61 ff.
Existentialism, 277.
'External' approach to language, 'external lexicography', 22, 117, 206 f., 209, 211, 214, 216, 219, 231, 242–5, 254, 292.
Ezekiel, Greek version of, 254.

Faith, faithfulness, 17, 130, 159 n., 161–205, 255 f.
Fichte, J. G., 86.
Fichtner, J., 147.
Firth, J. R., 265 n.
Flashar, M., 200, 283, 287.
Foerster, W., 224 f.
Form and matter, 36 f., 63 f.
Forms, liturgical, 156.
Forms, Platonic, 78 n., 105 ff., 152, 154.
Freedman, D. N., 18 n.
Friedrich, G., 10 n., 84, 206 n., 241 f., 244.
Fuchs, E., 275 n.

Galling, K., 78.
Gaster, T. H., 202 n.
Gender, grammatical, 39 f., 45 n., 96 f.
General linguistics, 2, 21–45, 289 f., 293, 296; distinct from 'philology', 277, 293, 295 f.
Genitive absolute, 240 n.
Gerleman, G., 33 f , 192 n., 251 n.
German, 'dynamic' character of, 87 f., 272 n.
Germanic vocabulary, effect of Christianity on, 269.
Gesenius, W., and Buhl, F., dictionary of, 120 n.
Gesenius, W., and Kautzsch, E., grammar of, 49 n., 64 n., 65 ff., 78 f., 177, 179 n., 183.

'God', translation of, 266, 268, 269 n.
Goethe, J. W. von, 86.
'Good', 32, 86, 219 f.
Gothic, 92, and see Ulfilas.
Grammars, effects of elementary, 92–96.
'Grammatical interpretation', 257, 259 n., 277.
Greek Bible, supposed avoidance of certain words by the, 282–7.
Greek language, general character of, 21, 44, 74, 86 f., 238, 289 ff.
Greek philosophy, 9–15, 20, 27, 72, 86 f., 164, 190, 197, 204, 251.
Greenberg, J. H., 294.
Grether, O., 147.
Grønbech, V., 184 n.
Grundmann, W., 219 f., 223.
Guidi, I., 186.
Guillaume, G., 79 n.
Gulkowitsch, L., 28.

Hebert, A. G., 17, 161–6, 175–7, 184, 201–5.
Hebrew language, supposed extreme peculiarity of, 44, 48 f., 81, 166, 290 f.; regarded as reflecting ultimate truth, 43 f., 127, 146, 261; contrasted with thought rather than language of other peoples, 51 f., 54, 63 f., 72–75, 77, 79, 106, 279.
Hebrew thought, contrast with Greek thought, 5 f., 8–20, 27, 46 ff., 50, 101, 117 n., 204, 278 ff.; correlation of this contrast with linguistic contrast, 14–45, 50–85, 101 f., 117 f., 224, 278 ff.; as basis for New Testament, 5 f., 8 ff., 19, 83, 204, 240 ff., 250, 278, 296; complementary to Greek thought, 46 f.
Hebrews, Letter to the, 151–5.
Heidegger, M., 160 n.
Heilsgeschichte, 208, 226, 256 f., 259, 275 n., 281.
Hempel, J., 46 n., 78.
Hendry, G. S., 156 n., 157 n.
Herder, J. G., 14 n., 85.
Hermeneutics, 257–60, 275–8.
Herodotus, 153, 189, 234.
Hessen, J., 14 n.
Hexapla, 136.
Hill, A. A., 30.

Hiphᶜil theme, function of, 102, 176–187.
'Historicism', 139.
History, 11, 14, 21, 34, 42, 47, 74, 78 f., 130 ff., 208, 217, 221 f., 230, 258.
Hittite, 40, 45.
Hodges, H. A., 258.
Hoffmann, R., 221 n.
Hoijer, H., 77 n., 294 n.
'Holy', 28 f., 98, 101 f., 111–14, 165, 282–7.
Holy Spirit, 113, 239, 248.
Homer, 36, 189, 236.
Homonyms, 158.
Honeyman, A. M., 106 n.
Hort, F. J. A., 125 f.
Hoskyns, E., 125, 195 ff.
Humboldt, W. von, 26 n., 48 ff., 86 ff., 294 ff.
Hypostatization, 38, 71, 130.

'I-Thou Relationship', 98.
Idea, 208 f., 271; for Platonic Idea, see Forms.
Idea histories, 217, 229.
Idealism, 48 f., 88 n., 106, 204, 257–60, 291.
Identity Transfer, 218, 222, 235.
'Immanent' of language, 276 f.
Incarnation, 83, 159 n.
Indo-European languages, 17 f., 24, 31 f., 40 n., 42, 67 f., 73 ff., 77, 83 n., 92, 98, 101, 106, 118, 288.
Infinitive, 34.
'Inner lexicography', 206 f., 209, 211, 216, 242–5.
'Inner' sense of language, 118, 168, 211, 242, 244 f., 257, 260, 292.
'Inner world of thought', 243–6, 257.
Intellectualization, 12, 197 f., 251.
Isaiah, Greek version of, 193.
Isocrates, 284.

Jacob, E., 108, 144–7.
Jastrow, M., 167.
Jensen, H., 98 n.
Jeremiah, Greek version of, 136, 192 f.
Jeremias, J., 234 n.
Jerome, 109, 136, 170, 200 n.
Jespersen, O., 28, 30 n., 40 n., 43 n., 60 n., 65 n., 68, 107 n.
Job, Greek version of, 251 f.

Johannesson, A., 112 n.
Josephus, 126, 189, 195, 285.

Kainz, F., 49 n.
Kent, R. G., 288 f., 292.
Kerygma, 84, 233.
Kierkegaard, S., 78, 106 n.
Kittel, G., 206–9, 221, 233, 238 f., 241, 244, 259 ff., 271, 282 ff., 286 f.
Kittel dictionary (*TWNT*), study of, 206–62; antecedents and general conception of, 206–19, 238–52, 256–62; cited in general, 129 n., 150, 172, 192 n., 198 n.; examples of methods of 38, 141, 147, 151, 168, 170, 179 ff., 198 n., 202 n., 210, 216 f., 218–38, 264 n., 282–7; basic faults of, 231, 244 ff., 249, 256 f., 261 f.; over-emphasis on philosophical uses in Greek, 198 n., 216, 222 ff., 251 f.; use of etymology, 114 n., 147 f., 168, 170, 236 ff.; favourite themes of, 242 n., 257, 275, 280; possible alternative organization, 234 ff.; avoidance of certain Greek words, 282–7; separate linguistic and theological sections, 229 f.; tries to be an interpretation of NT, 246.
Kleinknecht, H., 236.
Knight, G. A. F., 10 n., 16 n., 19 n., 23 n., 28 f., 39, 89 n., 252 f.
Knothe, L., 46 n.
Koehler, L. (including Baumgartner, W.), 118 n., 120 n., 136, 172, 186 n., 274 n.
Kögel, J., 206, 210, 242–6, 260.
Koine Greek, 9, 239.
Koschmieder, G., 79 n.
Kritzinger, J. D. W., 124 n., 126 n.
Kronasser, H., 4 n., 24, 30 n., 31 n., 81, 118 n., 135 n., 291 n.

Lane, E. W., 185.
Language, Supposed correspondence of thought and, 19 f., 24–49, 72–84, 95, 127, 146, 184, 204, 214, 231 ff., 240, 261, 289, 291.
Languages, Teaching of in theology, 288–96.
Latin, 31, 41–45, 68, 77, 90 f., 98, 107 f., 118, 133.
Latin, Christian, 248 n.

Latourette, K. S., 269 n.
Leisegang, J., 126 n.
Leslau, W., 136, 186.
Levison, N., 183.
Lexical methods, limitations of, 233, 245 f., 250, 269–72.
Lexical stocks, 5, 16 f., 26, 31 n., 33–38, 106 n., 146, 207, 209, 214, 231, 264 f.,269, 271 f.
Lexicography, lexicology, 2 n., 14, 104, 107, 206–62, 282–7.
Lexicography, 'Statistical', 243.
Lexicon, special, 211, 243, 245.
Lightfoot, J. B., 143 n.
Lindeskog, G., 231, 260.
Linguistics in general, see General Linguistics.
Linguistic structure, relation to patterns of thought, 1, 3, 5, 14–49, 85–88.
Linguistic argument, confusion of theological argument with, 162 ff., 166, 194–7, 201, 203 f., 210, 247 f., 261.
Literary criticism of the Bible, 9, 218, 270, 273 f.
Löfstedt, E., 248 n.
Logic, 1, 40, 43 f., 64–67, 82, 85, 93, 180, 291 f.
Logicism, 93–96, 100, 102, 182 f.
Logico-grammatical parallelism, 43, and see Logicism.
Logos, 210, 221 f.
Longacre, R. E., 37 n.
Love, 4, 44, 84 n., 159 n., 215 ff.

McAllaster, A. R., 45 n.
Maccabees, Books of, 201 f., 283, 285 f.
McLeod, G. F., 110 n.
Macnicol, J. D. A., 137 n.
Macquarrie, J., 160.
Man, 12 f., 16, 29, 34 ff., 144–7.
Mandel, H., 24.
Mays, J. L., 275 n.
'Meaning', 217.
Meillet, A. (with Vendryes, J.), 67, 68 n.
Meissner, R., 112 n.
Metaphysics, 187 f., 190, 204 f., 223 f., 251, 294 f.
Metre, 266 n.
Metzger, B. M., 247 f.
Michel, O., 236 n., 237.

Middle voice in Greek, 87.
Miracle, 147.
Miskotte, K. H., 275 n.
Mohrmann, C., 248 n.
Morphology, 29 n., 34, 38–46, 89–106, 207, 240, 263 ff., 269, 276, 292.
Moule, C. F. D., 52 n., 102 n., 161 n., 204, 240 n.
Müller, M., 24 n.
Munzinger, W., 186.
Muss-Arnolt, W., 186 n.
Myth, 221 f., 229.

Names, personal, 109 f.
Names, place, 109.
Nationality and language, 47 ff., 86 f.
Natural theology, 10.
Necessity, 223 f.
'New content', 241, 244, 249 ff., 260, 263, 266.
New Testament, Language of, in general, 3–6, 9, 18 n., 34, 68, 206–14, 238–41, 246–52.
Nicholls, W., 103, 280 n.
Niphᶜal theme, function of, 57.
Nominal sentence, 58, 63–68, 90 n., 265.
Normative approach to language, 107 f., 110, 113, 158 f., 219 f., 246.
Noth, M., 109 n.
Nouns, as contrasted with verbs, 14, 82–86.
Numerals, Hebrew, 23 n., 89, 90 n., 96–100.

Oepke, A., 38, 141 f., 230 f.
Oertel, H., 24.
Old Testament, distinctiveness of, 10, 18 ff.; effect of Greek translation on, 251 n., 252 ff., 264, 267; theology of, 273 f.
Oppositions, linguistic, 220, 223.
Orelli, C. von, 75, 77 n.
Origen, 109.

Palache, J. L., 118 n., 126 n.
Paraenesis, 233.
Parker, P., 45 n.
Parts of speech, 29, 101, 105.
Paul, 35, 37, 151, 154 f., 161, 170, 173 n., 194, 201, 203 f., 210, 219, 250 f., 255 f., 270.
Pauly-Wissowa, 150.

Pedersen, J., 30 f., 33, 41 f., 44, 47, 72, 83 n., 89 ff., 96 n., 101 n., 104 f., 134 f., 181–4.
Perfect tense in Hebrew, 56.
Perry, E., 173 n.
Personalism, 98, 197, 224.
Pfeiffer, E., 176 n., 177 ff., 181.
Philo, 109, 126, 202, 285, 287.
'Philology', 277, 295 f.
Philosophy, in general, 3, 26, 35 ff., 46, 178, 180, 188 ff., 208, 251, 275 ff., 281; of language, 1 f., 25 ff., 46–49, 86 ff., 171, 204, 261 f., 275 ff., 291; modern 'linguistic', 2, 281; use of language in, 3, 216, 222, 251; comparison of philosophical-theological systems, 27 f., 196, 222, 224. See also Metaphysics, Logic, Greek philosophy.
Phonology, 2 n., 288 f., 292.
Plato, 14, 37 n., 46, 78 n., 105 f., 152–155, 189, 215, 225, 243. See also Forms, Platonic.
Poetry, 85, 208, 266 n.
Pokorny, J., 97 n., 118 n.
Polysemy, 147.
Predicate, Predication, 63–67, 85.
Priesthood, 152 ff.
'Primitive' of language, 30 f.
Procksch, O., 282 ff.
Pronoun, 2nd person, 98.
Prophecy, 221.
Proposition, 246, 271.
Proverbs, Greek version of, 191 ff., 251 n.
Psalter, Greek version of the, 68, 200.
Psychology, 12, 21 f., 24 f., 33, 42, 47, 49, 51, 83 n., 91 ff., 99, 133 ff., 182, 184, 209, 245 f., 252, 272, 291.
'Psychological interpretation', 257, 259 n., 277.

Qumran documents, 19 n., 122, 128, 199, 202.

Rabin, C., 122 n.
Ramsey, I. T., 1 n.
Ratschow, C. H., 69 n.
Reason, 236 f.
Reicke, B., 231.
'Religion' as used by Bauer, 255.
Religious language in general, 1 ff., 292.

Repentance, 117, 230 n., 236 f., 253, 255.
Resurrection, 83.
Reuchlin, J., 264.
Revelation, 10, 230, 244, 252, 254, 256.
Robinson, J. A. T., 35 ff.
Roots, root fallacy, 76, 78 n., 86, 100–106, 111, 114–16, 159 f., 290 f.
Rosen, H. B., 79 n.
Rossini, K. C., 126 n., 186.
Rost, L., 124 n., 126 n.
Rostovtzeff, M., 150.
Rothe, R., 239.
Rowley, H. H., 274 n.
Rundgren, F., 60 n., 138.

Sacrifice, 151 f., 155.
Sandmann, M., 43 n., 65 n., 68 n., 272 n.
Sapir, E., 14 n., 295.
Saussure, F. de, 220 n.
Schleiermacher, F., 238, 243, 257–60, 264, 277.
Schlier, H., 168, 170, 226 ff., 237.
Schmidt, K. L., 114 n., 121, 129 n., 218.
Schmoller, A., 206.
Schneemelcher, W., 276 n.
Schrenk, G., 282–6.
Schulthess, F., 126 n.
Schwarz, W., 264 n.
Schwyzer, E., 32 n.
Sciagraphy, 257, 260, 264.
Segert, S., 266 n.
Seidler, H., 33 n.
Semitic philology in general, 288, 292.
Semitic thought other than Hebrew, 17–20, 33, 41.
Semitisms in LXX, 267.
Semitisms in NT, 240 n.
Senft, C., 198.
Sentence as expression of theological thought, 196 f., 233 f., 249, 263–6, 269 ff.
Septuagint, 3, 37 f., 44, 59 n., 68, 110 n., 119 ff., 124 ff., 128 ff., 134, 136 ff., 150–6, 167–70, 172–5, 178, 187–95, 198–203, 216, 223–6, 236, 241, 251–4, 264, 266 ff., 282–7.
Serrus, C., 43 n., 65 n., 93.
Shires, H. H., 45 n.
Simultaneity, 78 f., 106 n.
Sin, 4, 114 n., 217, 229.

Snaith, N. H., 20, 84 n., 115 ff.
Social character of language, 113, 159, 188, 204, 213, 281.
Socrates, 86.
Sophocles, 68.
Space, 73–77, 79, 97 ff.
Specialization in language, 3, 263, 269 f.
Spitzer, L., 217 n.
Stählin, G., 221 f., 229.
States, Hebrew verbs denoting immobile, 50–54.
Stative verbs in Hebrew, 54–57, 82, 87.
Stauffer, E., 231.
Stenzel, J., 86 ff.
Stoicism, 115, 192.
Strathmann, H., 150 f.
Struck, E., 118 n.
Structural linguistics, 289 f., 295 f.
Stylistics, 33 f., 54, 83 n., 254, 272.
Suffering Servant, 103.
Sumerian, 43, 186.
'Supernatural', 255 f.
Symmachus, 136, 169 f., 200 n.
Syntax, 29, 33 f., 38–46, 89–106, 114 f., 138, 157, 207, 215, 222, 235 n., 236, 240, 263 ff., 269, 272, 276.
Syriac, see Aramaic.

Targum, 199.
Tautology, 63, 191, 234.
'Technical' terms, 124, 151, 227, 233, 248 f., 263.
Temple, 113, 130, 282 ff.
Tense in verbs, 22, 26 f., 39, 41 f., 46, 52, 72–75, 82 f., 86 f., 265, 276.
Tense in Greek verbs, 52, 87, 240 n.
Thacker, T. W., 82 n.
Thackeray, H. St J., 126, 193.
Thomas, D. Winton, 158 n.
Thucydides, 141, 189.
Time, 11, 13, 16, 21 f., 39, 41 f., 47, 72–80, 83 n., 86 f., 209, 225 f.

Torrance, T. F., 44, 106 n., 120 n., 124, 129 n., 133, 134 n., 136, 141 n., 149 ff., 152–6, 161–7, 171–7, 184, 187, 191, 193 f., 198 f., 201–5, 235, 254 n., 259 n., 264 n., 277 n., 279 n.
Totality, 13, 16, 52 n., 53, 63–67, 89 f., 92, 96, 99, 104 ff., 160, 179 f., 184, 199, 218 f., 265.
Totality transfer, 218, 222.
Transitive, 57, 178, 183.
Translation, 4, 81, 211, 216, 253, 264–268.
Tresmontant, C., 265 n.

Ugaritic, 187, 199.
Ulfilas, 111.
Ullendorff, E., 101 n.
Ullmann, S., 1 n., 26 n., 43 n., 147, 292, 295 n.
Unity of the Bible, 5 f., 9, 218, 271 n., 274 f.
Unnik, W. C. van, 102 n., 160 f., 170.

Verbs in general, 14 f., 21, 34, 47, 50–88, 97–100, 104.
Verbs, nominal origin of some Hebrew forms, 56, 82.
Vincent, J. J., 287.
Vulgate, 264 n.

Wach, J., 259 n., 278 n.
Weiser, A., 171, 172 n., 179 ff.
Weisgerber, L., 87 f., 294 n.
Wernberg-Møller, P., 82 n., 199 n.
Whorf, B. L., 38, 77, 294 n., 295.
Williger, E., 287.
Word-combinations, 222, 233–6, 263; -formation, 102, 111, 140–4, 150, 165, 236, 239 f.; -substitutions, 215 f., 219, 254, 256.
Wundt, W., 49 n.
Würthwein, E., 237.

Zimmerli, W., 234 n., 254.